P9-DFW-718

THE BEST AMERICAN

NONREQUIRED
READING

2010

THE BEST AMERICAN

NONREQUIRED
READING™

2010

■

EDITED BY

DAVE EGGERS

INTRODUCTION BY

DAVID SEDARIS

MANAGING EDITOR

JESSE NATHAN

A MARINER ORIGINAL
HOUGHTON MIFFLIN HARCOURT
BOSTON ▪ NEW YORK
2010

Copyright © 2010 by Houghton Mifflin Harcourt Publishing Company
Introduction copyright © 2010 by David Sedaris

ALL RIGHTS RESERVED

The Best American Series is a registered trademark of Houghton Mifflin Harcourt Publishing Company. *The Best American Nonrequired Reading* is a trademark of Houghton Mifflin Harcourt Publishing Company.

For information about permission to reproduce selections from this book, write to Permissions, Houghton Mifflin Harcourt Publishing Company, 215 Park Avenue South, New York, New York 10003.

www.hmhbooks.com

ISSN: 1539-316x
ISBN: 978-0-547-24163-0

Printed in the United States of America
DOC 10 9 8 7 6 5 4 3 2 1

"This Is Just to Say" (excerpt of 4 lines) by William Carlos Williams, from *The Collected Poems: Volume I, 1909-1939.* Copyright ©1938 by New Directions Publishing. Reprinted by permission of New Directions Publishing.
"Those Winter Sundays." Copyright © 1996 by Robert Hayden, from *Collected Poems of Robert Hayden* by Robert Hayden, edited by Frederick Glaysher. Used by permission of Liveright Publishing Corporation.
"I Am Sorry that I Didn't Write a Comedy Piece" by Wendy Molyneux. First published at www.therumpus.net as part of the "Funny Women" series. Copyright © 2009 by Wendy Molyneux. Reprinted by permission of the author.
"A Note from Stephen Colbert" by Stephen Colbert. First published in *Newsweek* on June 15, 2009. Copyright © 2009 by Newsweek, Inc. Reprinted by permission of *Newsweek*.
Six-Word memoirs copyright © 2009 by the authors. Reprinted by permission of *Smith Magazine.*
"Best American Letter to the Editor" by Nazlee Radboy. First published in *Bidoun.* Copyright © 2009 by Nazlee Radboy. Reprinted by permission of the author.
"Overqualified Cover Letters" by Joey Comeau. First published in *Overqualified.* Copyright © 2009 by Joey Comeau. Reprinted by permission of the author.
"The Trail" by Barry Lopez. First published in *Orion.* Copyright © 2009 by Barry Lopez. Reprinted by permission of the author.
"Best American Illustrated Missed Connections" by Sophie Blackall. First published at www.missedconnectionsny.blogspot.com. Copyright © 2009 by Sophie Blackall. Reprinted by permission of the artist.
"Best American Poems Written in the Last Decade by Soldiers and Citizens in Iraq and Afghanistan" by Salam Dawai, Soheil Najm, Khadijah Queen, Brian Turner, Haider Al-Kabi, Sadek Mohammed, Abdul-Zahra Zeki, and Sabah Khattab. Certain of these poems first appeared in *Flowers of Flame, Powder: Writing by Women in the Ranks, from Vietnam to Iraq, Phantom Noise,* and the *Northwest Review.* Copyright © 2009, 2010 by the authors. Reprinted by permission of the authors, Kore Press, and/or Alice James Books.

"War Dances" from *War Dances* by Sherman Alexie. First published in *The New Yorker*. Copyright © 2009 by Sherman Alexie. Reprinted by permission of the author and Grove/Atlantic, Inc.

"Like I Was Jesus" by Rachel Aviv. First published in *Harper's Magazine*. Copyright © 2009 by Rachel Aviv. Reprinted by permission of the author.

"Burying Jeremy Green" by Nora Bonner. First published in *Shenandoah*. Copyright © 2009 by Nora Bonner. Reprinted by permission of the author.

"The Carnival" by Lilli Carré. First published in *MOME*. Copyright © 2009 by Lilli Carré. Reprinted by permission of the artist.

"Capital Gains" by Rana Dasgupta. First published in *Granta*. Copyright © 2009 by Rana Dasgupta. Reprinted by permission of the author.

"The Encirclement" by Tamas Dobozy. First published in *Granta*. Copyright © 2009 by Tamas Dobozy. Reprinted by permission of the author.

"Man of Steel" by Bryan Furuness. First published in *Ninth Letter*. Copyright © 2009 by Bryan Furuness. Reprinted by permission of the author.

"Half Beat" by Elizabeth Gonzalez. First published in *The Greensboro Review*. Copyright © 2009 by Elizabeth Gonzalez. Reprinted by permission of the author.

"Gentlemen, Start Your Engines" by Andrew Sean Greer. First published in the *San Francisco Panorama*. Copyright © 2009 by Andrew Sean Greer. Reprinted by permission of the author and *McSweeney's*.

Excerpt from *The Photographer* by Emmanuel Guibert, Didier Lefèvre and Frédéric Lemercier. English language translation by Alexis Siegel. English language translation copyright © 2009 by First Second. Reprinted by arrangement with Henry Holt and Company, LLC.

"What, of This Goldfish, Would You Wish?" by Etgar Keret, translated by Nathan Englander. First published in *Tin House*. Copyright © 2009 by Etgar Keret and Nathan Englander. Reprinted by permission of the author and the translator.

"Fed to the Streets" by Courtney Moreno. First published in *L.A. Weekly* as "Help Is on the Way." Copyright © 2009 by Courtney Moreno. Reprinted by permission of the author.

"The Tiger's Wife" by Téa Obreht. First published in *The New Yorker*. Copyright © 2009 by Téa Obreht. Reprinted by permission of the author.

"Breakdown" by T. Ott. First published in *MOME*. Copyright © 2009 by T. Ott. Reprinted by permission of the artist.

"Ideas" by Patricio Pron, translated by Mara Faye Lethem. First published in *The Paris Review*. Copyright © 2009 by Patricio Pron and Mara Faye Lethem. Reprinted by permission of the author and the translator.

"Vanish" by Evan Ratliff. First published in *Wired*. Copyright © 2009 by Evan Ratliff. Reprinted by permission of the author.

"Seven Months, Ten Days in Captivity" by David Rohde. First published in the *New York Times*. Copyright © 2009 by David Rohde and the *New York Times*. Reprinted by permission of the author and the *New York Times*.

"Tent City, U.S.A." by George Saunders. First published in *GQ*. Copyright © 2009 by George Saunders. Reprinted by permission of the author.

"The Nice Little People" from *Look at the Birdie: Unpublished Short Fiction* by Kurt Vonnegut. Published in *Zoetrope: All-Story*. Copyright © 2009 by Kurt Vonnegut, Jr. Trust. Reprinted by permission of Delacorte Press, an imprint of the Random House Publishing Group, a division of Random House, Inc.

"Freedom" by Amy Waldman. First published in *Boston Review*. Copyright © 2009 by Amy Waldman. Reprinted by permission of the author.

CONTENTS

II

Amy Waldman. FREEDOM • 439

EDITOR'S NOTE

FORGIVE ME IF YOU ALREADY KNOW THIS, but this collection is assembled every year with the assistance of two groups of high school students—one from the San Francisco Bay Area, and one from the Ann Arbor and Ypsilanti areas of mid to lower Michigan.

I run the class that meets in San Francisco, so I'll describe what happens there (I can't speak for Michigan, but I expect they would use more candles and smoke machines). Once a week, we meet in the basement of McSweeney's, a small publishing company in the Mission District of San Francisco. Some of the students take the subway and get off at the 16th and Mission stop. Some take the bus; some get rides from their parents. And a few are lucky enough to have a vehicle of their own. In any case, they travel up to an hour, each way, to sit around and talk about contemporary literature.

In this basement, we have a bunch of couches, chairs, and even a beanbag (which no one uses because beanbags should never have been manufactured, as they are an affront to all that is holy). The students feel good in this basement, in large part because the space is dingy, ill kept, and smells of laundry that needs washing but can't be found. When they arrive, the students first look through the mail. Every week we get about twenty new literary journals, magazines, self-published zines, comics, and various other periodicals. The students read these periodicals, looking for stories that hit them in the gut. They pick up the *Kenyon Review* or *Tin House* looking to be wowed. When the wow happens, the student gives that story or essay or whatever it is to our managing editor, Jesse Nathan—who is, it should be said, a Jewish Mennonite (really!) from Kansas—and he makes copies for the whole class so we can read and discuss.

Sometimes the discussions are spirited, sometimes not so much, sometimes too much so. Sometimes no one can understand what the hell the student first saw in the story. Other times the class splits, literally in two. This year was especially interesting, given that we had two very vocal members, Tenaya Nasser-Frederick and Will Gray, who often ended up on opposite sides of the room and of opinion. They would bark back and forth at each other—respectfully, it should be said—and then, at the end, Will would have the final say. His final say sounded something like, "Well, I'm pretty sure you're wrong and I'm right and I think this discussion is over." This is how he got the nickname "The Hammer." (More about the Hammer, and all of the students from the Bay Area and Michigan, is available in the back of the book, starting on page 463.)

But no matter what the selection process is, it's always astoundingly subjective. We have no scientific method, no spreadsheets or checks and balances. We have only bins that say *Yes* and *No* and *Maybe*. When we get close to having enough Yeses to make a book, we put copies of all the selections on a Ping-Pong table in the basement. This is not a joke. We put all the yeses on one side of the net, and then we look at each story, and when we're absolutely sure that that Yes is a *Yes*, and should be printed in these pages, then we "move it over"—meaning we actually move it over the net—into the *Definite Yes* area. That is the most official and scientific part of the process, that jumping of the net.

Each year we try to strike many balances simultaneously. We try to strike a balance between fiction, nonfiction, comics, and other forms. Most of all, we try to strike a balance between end-of-the-world scenarios and coming-of-age stories. These two topics, it turns out, constitute about eighty percent of what we read in a given year, and we've decided that a few examples of each are enough.

Next we choose a cover artist and an introducer. Every year we start with a long list, which invariably includes Dave Chapelle and

Oprah Winfrey, neither of whom are likely to see a letter we might write them. So we begin to think of people we might be able to get a letter close to, and this year the students overwhelmingly chose Maurice Sendak to provide the cover art. He opened up his sketchbooks, and suggested a page of drawings that formed a narrative about a girl who is almost eaten by her television set. We agreed that this was perfect for the collection, and we thank him heartily for being generous, for being kind, and for having great mischievous eyes and a mouth unable to tell lies.

We'd also like to thank David Sedaris, who is pretty much a saint for all he's done for the organization known as 826. As you might know, the proceeds from this book go toward 826 National, which helps support a network of independently operated writing and tutoring centers around the country. At the 826 centers, the work we do serves kids ages six to eighteen, and runs the gamut from helping English language learners with basic reading and writing skills to advanced publishing projects with high schoolers.

One of the ways we raise money for the programs is by asking well-known authors like Mr. Sedaris to edit books and donate the proceeds to 826. The first such book was edited by Michael Chabon (who, with his spouse, the writer Ayelet Waldman, has supported 826 in a thousand ways from the start). Chabon edited a book called *Thrilling Tales*, which extolled the virtues of so-called genre writing, and encouraged contemporary writers to explore the western, the mystery, the horror story, and sci-fi. The sales of *Thrilling Tales* paid the rent on our San Francisco building for a full year. Talk about the power of the written word!

So, after that, we embarked on a program of publishing at least one of these "benefit books" a year. For the second "benefit book," we thought, Who could follow Michael Chabon? Who has that kind of genius and generosity? And we thought of David Sedaris. And did Sedaris hesitate? We don't know. He was living in France at the time, and we could not see his behavior while he was deciding. But he didn't *seem* to have hesitated. He said yes and picked his favorite short stories for a collection that became *Children Playing Before a Statue of Hercules*. That book paid the rent on the building for another year, and our faith in the power of publishing was again renewed.

So when the *Best American Nonrequired Reading* group chooses an introducer, every year—in addition to Oprah Winfrey and Dave Chapelle—the students invariably suggest David Sedaris. But because he'd done that above-named collection, we've always given him a break. But this time, after five or so years of giving him a break, I allowed the students to go ahead and ask Mr. Sedaris to write the intro, and they did so by sending him this photo:

How could anyone say no to a photo like that? The answer is that no one can. And Sedaris did not say no. He wrote a very edifying intro, different from virtually anything he's written before, and for this we're endlessly thankful. We're also thankful that you picked up this book, and we hope you like the selections. This year, maybe more than ever before, we really went eclectic, and we think we have a fantastically diverse and challenging group of stories that somehow, improbably, cohere around what it's like to be alive right now, in 2010—as opposed to 1822, which would have been far dustier.

—D. E.

INTRODUCTION

Who Ate the Plums?

THE YEAR AFTER MY MOTHER DIED, I was presented with a box. In it were letters I'd sent from summer camp ("I'll pay you to come and get me") and from my first year at college ("I *swear* I'll pay you to come and get me"). There were other things in there as well, and though I thought I would plow right through them, the task proved too depressing. The box went into storage in New York, and when my boyfriend, Hugh, and I moved to France, I had it shipped to Normandy, where it sat on a shelf in the room I use as an office. It was only recently that I reopened it. The letters were there, and, beneath them, a mildewed envelope with my name on it. The handwriting was my mother's, and inside, amongst the report cards and vaccination certificates, I found two poems I had written in the fifth grade.

You, I thought.

Like most children, I wrote a lot in elementary school: articles on whales, essays praising presidents and Thanksgiving, all of them forgotten, and for good reason. These poems, however, had stuck with me, haunted me for over forty years. The first one is titled, "Will We Ever Find Peace?"

If man will ever find peace is a question to behold
Will we ever stop finding soldier's bodies dead and cold?
I think that I would rather die while sleeping in my bed
Than die in Vietnam, a bullet through my head

The men who come out of war I think can surely tell
That General Sherman was right when he said that war is hell.

Because I was only twelve, I think I can forgive myself the sloppy meter. What I can't forgive, regardless of my age, is the self righteous tone, and the demand to be taken seriously. "I think that I would rather die while sleeping in my bed / Than die in Vietnam, a bullet through my head."

Oh, really. How perfectly odd of you. Because the rest of us would love to spend our last few hours in an unforgiving jungle, far from friends and family, being stabbed and shot at by people in pointed sun hats who put peanut butter on chicken.

And quoting General Sherman?

I got an A-minus on my first poem, and a note from the teacher—"Good Work!"—written in the margins of my second, which was titled, simply, "War."

You find some bit of creative writing you did in the fifth grade, and hope it will tell you something about your life: Here is a fight I had with my best friend. This is what it smells like when you lay your mother's pocketbook on the grill. For a while I thought that these poems told me nothing. Then I realized that they did—it just wasn't something I wanted to be reminded of. Behind their clumsiness, they tell me who I wanted to be—not my petty, self-absorbed self, but society's conscience, the justice seeker who opens your eyes to the suffering that's all around you.

I don't know what drove my mother to hang on to those poems. Perhaps she saw them as evidence of a change, seeds of the person I would hopefully grow up to become. When I found them in her dresser drawer the summer after the sixth grade, and tried to throw them away, she grabbed them out of my hands.

"But they're awful," I told her.

"Maybe so, but they're mine," she said.

I figured she'd put them in one of three hiding places, spots my parents thought of as safe, but that my sisters and I had been raiding since we were old enough to walk: the crawl space above the car port, for instance. That was like the hidden tomb in a mummy movie, the sort of place that should have been marked with carvings: the head of a bird, a cane with thorns on it, three laughing skulls turned toward the wind, symbols that, when translated, spelled "Do not enter here unless you wish to be changed forever."

We found unspeakable things in that crawl space. Things that took our childlike innocence, and, in the time it took to focus a flashlight, obliterated it. There were the lesser hiding places as well, lockups for confiscated machetes and homemade battle axes. My mother must have carried the poems upon her person, secured, maybe, in some sort of girdle as I looked everywhere, and I mean *everywhere* for them, with no success.

In time I lost my ability to quote from "Will We Ever Find Peace," but never was it or "War" forgotten. The disdain I felt toward my own poems affected the whole genre, the only exception being limericks, which are basically dirty jokes that rhyme. The other kinds of poetry, the kind written entirely in lower case letters, or the kind where a single sentence is broken into eight different lines, I find confounding. I think I was out sick the day we learned to read them, and it never occurred to me that I could catch up, or, heaven forbid, teach myself.

In William Carlos Williams's "This Is Just To Say," for instance, do you begin with "I have eaten" and then wait a while before moving onto "the plums"?

Should an equal amount of time pass before "that were in" and "the icebox"?

If not, why not just put it all on the same line? *I have eaten the plums that were in the icebox.*

I get the idea that poets are paid, not by the word, but by how much space they take up.

How
else
to
explain
it
?

It's easy to believe when looking at such things that parts of them are missing, that words and commas got erased or were blown away, like one of those church signs after a strong wind. The bits that are left function as clues, the poem itself not a story, but a problem, something to be sweated over and solved. Why not make things easier and just say what you mean? Why be all, well, *poetical* about it?

It's the way a lot of people view contemporary art—as if it's beyond them, as if, without the references and countless inside jokes, they can't possibly get a foothold. I've found, though, that if you relax, you can pretty much tell what, say, a Robert Gober sculpture is about. This is something I learned in art school. A slide would be shown of a crazy looking installation and after feeling stupid and intimidated, I'd actually look at the thing. A few minutes later the teacher would offer an interpretation, and I'd find that I had gotten it after all, that a piece of art, much like a short story, could be read. The key was to not be uptight about it, to enjoy the attempt. To surrender.

I only recently realized that the same approach could be applied to poetry. What enlightened me was a podcast in which the host and a guest listen to a poem, and then proceed to talk about it. Before going further, I need to identify myself as an audiophile. There are those who dismiss the idea of listening to literature, who feel that it doesn't count the way that reading does. And it's true that they're different sensations.

When sitting on the sofa and reading with my eyes, I enter the world of the book. When listening, on the other hand, the book comes into *my* world, the place where I iron clothes, defrost the freezer, and break up firewood with an ax. I started with audio in the early nineties, back when the titles were recorded onto cassettes. Then I moved on to CDs and, eventually, to the MP3 player, which lead me, in turn, to podcasts, and one in particular called *Poetry Off the Shelf.*

I originally downloaded it thinking, not of myself, but of Hugh's mother, who likes serious things. I was going to force her to sit in a chair with my iPod on, but then I ran out of books to listen to. Company was coming, I had a day's worth of house work ahead of me, so I thought, *What the hell.*

The first podcast that I listened to featured the late James Schuyler reading "Korean Mums." I don't know when he recorded it, but his voice was old-sounding, and he read the way one might read an item from the paper. This is to say that he was steady but not overly dramatic. After listening to him twice, I listened to a short analysis offered by the podcast's host, and the week's special guest. A few small references went over my head, but otherwise, I seem to have gotten everything. Equally surprising is that it never felt like work, that it was, in every sense of the word, a pleasure.

In the next podcast, I discovered Robert Hayden, who died in 1980, and who wore glasses with superthick lenses. This might seem beside the point, but I liked the fact that he was not in any way fashionable-looking—was, in fact, quite nerdy. The poem they featured was about his father, who'd busted his ass to get up early and warm the house while everyone else was in bed. The poet never thanked him for it—treated him, from the sounds of it, pretty poorly. Now he looks back, and ends with the following lines:

> Speaking indifferently to him,
> who had driven out the cold
> and polished my good shoes as well.
> What did I know, what did I know
> of love's austere and lonely offices?

The poem says eloquently in five cut-up lines what I have been trying to say my whole life.

Why don't poets just come out with it?

Uh, actually, I think they do.

From Robert Hayden I moved to Philip Larkin, then to Fanny Howe and Robert Lowell. The more I'm exposed to, the more enraptured I become, the world feeling both bigger and smaller at the same time. *Poetry*, I think. *Where has it been all my life!* I said to Hugh, "I feel like I've discovered a whole new variety of meat.

And
it's
free!"

DAVID SEDARIS

BEST AMERICAN FRONT SECTION

THE BEST AMERICAN front section is a carefully engineered container designed to hold and preserve a not entirely scientific cross section of the year's best short things: the ephemera, the poems, the lines, the notable patents filed, the best names of fictional characters, noteworthy names of American farms, letters to the editor, lawsuits, headlines, missed connections, endangered words, and a good many other nonrequired things.

Best American Woman Comedy Piece Written by a Woman

WENDY MOLYNEUX

FROM www.therumpus.net

The other day while sounding out the words on a website called www.therumpus.net, I saw this article asking for women to submit more comedy pieces. So I put down my giant chocolate bar, stopped crying, and thought, yes, that is what I will do. I will write a comedy piece. But just as I sat down in my bay window (filled with pillows that I knitted myself while waiting by the phone for potential husbands to call) and opened my pink Mac laptop, I happened to see a lady walking down the street with a baby of her very own.

So then I started crying again because I don't have a baby. I cried big rolling tears that fell down onto my "Mrs. Stamos" T-shirt that I purchased off of eBay and photographed myself in for my eHarmony profile. I always say, "Dress for the job you want," and the job I want is being Mrs. John Stamos! So, once my shirt was soaked, I had to go change it. I walked into my closet, which is gigantic because women love to wear lots of expensive clothes and shoes all the time, and I thought, "I know what will make me feel better! I will feel better if I try on all my clothes and shoes to the tune of an upbeat Motown song such as 'My Girl.'"

And so I did that. I tried on all my clothes, and I felt better until I tried on one pair of pants that didn't fit me anymore. And then I totally started to cry again, because I am so fat. I cried for a little while on the floor while my cats crawled all over me, purring and being symbols of how lonely I am. My cats love to be symbols of my loneliness. Sometimes, I have to be like, "Stop signifying so loudly guys, I'm watching *Grey's Anatomy*!"

At this point I still had not written my comedy piece written by a woman. So I went back to the window, opened my pink computer again and looked at pictures of cute baby ducks for a while until I felt like writing. But then I remembered that I hadn't made anything for dinner! Every night, I like to make an elaborate dinner. Then, I set it on the table and open all the windows. My fondest hope is that the wafting smells of a home-cooked meal will lure men who are passing by to come inside and eat dinner. And then after they eat dinner, I hope they'll eat something else. If you know what I mean. Get it? Eat something. I mean dessert. I want them to eat dessert. Because the way to a man's heart is through his stomach. Also, they are always leaving the toilet seat up! Am I right?

Anyway, twelve hours later, after I had cooked, baked, cried, sewn a blanket for my hope chest, called a telephone psychic, had all my favorite *Cathy* comic strips laminated, and then stayed up all night trying on all my clothes and shoes again, I finally felt ready to write my comedy piece. I decided to start by asking myself, "What's funny?"

That is a tough one for me because I have no sense of humor. I mean, I assume that I have no sense of humor because all of the funny things that are made especially for women like me, such as

Sex and the City, 27 Dresses, and yogurt commercials, don't even make me laugh. But I guess my humor deficiency is one of those womanly crosses I have to bear, along with PMS, making seventy cents on the dollar, and paying for my own rape kit. You know what they say though, you can't make the willing pay for their own rape kits! I think they say that. Probably somebody said that. God knows I didn't say it myself! I only say things like: "What are numbers?"

Oh, there I go again on one of my tangents. I guess it's time for me to get serious about writing this comedy piece. Emoticon. I mean, I probably shouldn't even try to write a comedy piece since Christopher Hitchens wrote an article in *Vanity Fair* saying that women just aren't funny. He's probably right. And even if he isn't, I think it's great that we live in a country where you can say anything you want, like that women aren't funny or that Christopher Hitchens is a huge douche who runs a successful child pornography business and has an inability to get an erection unless he's reading Nazi literature.

Well, would you look at that? I've totally run out of time, and now instead of writing a comedy piece, I have to go report to my regular day job knitting tampon cozies and being best friends with everybody.

Oh well, I probably would have been terrible at it anyway.

Best American Sentences on Page 50 of Books Published in 2009*

It is turning out to be the most beautiful, most quiet, largest, most generous, sky-vaulted summer I've ever seen or known—inordinately blue, with greener leaves and taller trees than I can remember, and the sound of the lawnmowers all over this valley is a sound I could hum to forever.
Nicholson Baker, *The Anthologist*

---

* Varies slightly based on edition (paperback, hardcover, or galley)

Our leader does not frolic at math parties, partake of our pizza sweating in the cardboard delivery box, sip our tepid beer.
MAUREEN HOWARD, *The Rags of Time*

We are besieged by simple problems.
ATUL GAWANDE, *The Checklist Manifesto*

The fairground's gates open just about the time parents are near to losing their minds with the endlessly blazing midsummer days.
PAT WILLARD, *America Eats!*

Even with that perfectly reasonable explanation, and perfectly realized home page, I still feel the need to defend my idea, by tracing the synaptic misfires that went into creating it.
JESS WALTER, *The Financial Lives of the Poets*

(Although his father disapproved of peeing outdoors, Ketchum had taught young Dan to enjoy it.)
JOHN IRVING, *Last Night in Twisted River*

RR had a brother, a fact that may or may not be pertinent in regard to the problem of the monster.
ELISABETH SHEFFIELD, *Fort Da: A Report*

On certain days, driving into Santa Monica was like having hallucinations without going to all the trouble of acquiring and then taking a particular drug, although some days, for sure, any drug was preferable to driving into Santa Monica.
THOMAS PYNCHON, *Inherent Vice*

As curiosity consumed her, compassion gave way to desperation, and her expression, which a moment ago was saying, Please tell me the truth, now was pleading, Please tell me a lie.
ORHAN PAMUK, *The Museum of Innocence*

No computer has been able to master poker.
JONAH LEHRER, *How We Decide*

While he slimmed down, I porked up, pregnant with our first child.
SARAH PALIN, *Going Rogue: An American Life*

Shit, I think Hillbilly just went in the drink.
STEPHEN COONTS, *The Disciple*

I have killed fish and various domestic animals, but only for our own table, and have had cattle slaughtered for the same reason; since the latter had been given names by my sons, we found ourselves referring with mixed feelings to Mable and Bonnie while admiring the taste and texture of their flesh.
GRAEME GIBSON, *The Bedside Book of Beasts*

Shoes of every conceivable fashion hazardously studded the entire matrix.
BILL COTTER, *Fever Chart*

Under the whispering branches of an African tree she pulls down her trousers with great emotion.
A.B. YEHOSHUA, *Friendly Fire*

There were seventeen bubbles remaining in my nearly stagnant beer.
JEFFREY ROTTER, *The Unknown Knowns*

In one movement the succubus turned and kicked, her long skirts rustling, and Maggie Brown was somersaulting from the table to avoid the blow, landing on the floor in time to meet the succubus as she came head on, using her talons like swords.
A.E. MOORAT, *Queen Victoria: Demon Hunter*

That's where I'm sitting now, between the medicinal sweet and the sour estrangement.
ANGELA JACKSON, *Where I Must Go*

You meet a rational God and you say, Well, okay, that's not my cup of tea right now, Heavenly Father, I'll come back at a better time.
COLUM MCCANN, *Let the Great World Spin*

Best American Magazine Letters Section

STEPHEN COLBERT

FROM *Newsweek*

Stephen Colbert guest-edited the June 15 issue of Newsweek. The letters section began with "A Note from Stephen Colbert." It said this: "Newsweek has bestowed upon me the honor of choosing this week's letters — huge mistake! Because now I'm just going to print all the letters I sent that the magazine didn't run. In your face, Other Letters!"

Ten cents an issue? Why, that's robbery! You should be ashamed of yourself the way FDR should be ashamed of his socialist New Deal and these newfangled Drive-In movie theaters should be ashamed of promoting premarital gear shifting! I give your rag a year, tops. (Full disclosure: I have not been born yet.)

Stephen Colbert, Heaven's Waiting Room

Feb. 16, 1933

I write in reference to your coverage of the so-called Watergate "scandal." What's the big deal? So they broke into a crummy hotel room. If the President wants to, he can break into my room anytime. And when he does, please ask him not to look in the blue duffel bag in the back of my closet labeled "Not *Playboys*."

Stevie C., Charleston, S.C.

July 29, 1974

Your story on the heroic U.S. invasion of Grenada was a rare job well done. Tiny Caribbean island nations will now think twice before posing a threat to our national security. I'm looking at you, Trinidad. (Tobago, we're still cool.)

Stephen Colbert, Hanover, N.H.

Nov. 1, 1983

Dear *Newsweek*, I never thought this kind of thing would happen to me. I was at the library making last-minute edits to the *Dartmouth Review* when Miss Shimock, the young librarian, walked up to my table wearing nothing but a copy of *Atlas Shrugged*. She made a strong case that it was in my rational self-interest to take off my pants . . . Wait, I think I'm writing this letter to the wrong magazine.

   Stephen Colbert, Hanover, N.H.

   Sept. 18, 1984

Once again, your liberal panty lines are showing. Putting Bill Clinton on the cover, just because he won the election? You completely neglected the big story of the week: Pat Buchanan turned fifty-four!

   Stephen Colbert, Patterson Springs, N.C.

   Nov. 14, 1992

Your coverage of last week's Clinton-Dole debate failed to mention that Ronald Reagan is the greatest president in our nation's history. For the record, you also failed to mention it in your article about rap producer Sean "Puffy" Combs and the review of *That Thing You Do!*

   Stephen Colbert, Patterson Springs, N.C.

   Oct. 10, 1996

Wake up, America! The Y2K bug is coming! Once computers are asked to divide by zero, they'll realize humankind's fallibility, become self-aware and take over the planet. I beg you all, on New Year's Eve, surround your computers with powerful magnets so they can't chase us. And if I don't make it out of my Y2K bunker alive, please see that George Will gets my collection of awkward baseball metaphors.

   Stephen Colbert, New York, N.Y.

   Nov. 21, 1999

Your so-called Ronald Reagan "memorial" issue was a half-hearted disaster. Would it have been so hard to change the name of this week's issue to *Reagansweek* in his memory? Oh, wait, that sounds like he's weak. On second thought, how about *Reaganstrong*?

   Stephen Colbert, New York, N.Y.

   June 15, 2004

Regarding your cover story "Obama on Obama"—I know print media isn't thriving right now, but you guys can't even splurge for a reporter? Making the President interview himself?! For shame!
Stephen Colbert, New York, N.Y.
May 26, 2009

Your June 15 issue was a tour de force! Such breathtakingly fresh views! Such virtuosic guest-editorship!
Sir Dr. Stephen T. Colbert, D.F.A., New York, N.Y.
June 15, 2009

Best American Fast-Food-Related Crimes

Fast food was invented in Kansas, made famous in Los Angeles, and has since become as American, if not as noble, as baseball, jazz, and apple pie. The fast-food joint has of late, however, become the focal point for a slew of crimes. Catalogued here are a few noteworthy examples.

Michael Ackerman of Greenville, South Carolina, was arrested and charged with driving under the influence after doing so on his lawnmower through a Jack in the Box drive-through.
DRAWN FROM www.foxcarolina.com

Jean Fortune of Boynton Beach, Florida, was charged with abuse of 911 communications for calling police about a Burger King being unable to offer him lemonade.
DRAWN FROM Associated Content

Latreasa Goodman of Florida was charged with misusing the 911 system after calling 911 three times about a miscommunication with a McDonald's cashier regarding Chicken McNuggets.
DRAWN FROM www.yahoo.com

Jermaine Askia Cooper of Fort Wayne, Indiana, faced several charges after leading police on a sixteen-minute, two-county car chase that ended at a Taco Bell, where the man, wanted for various drug possessions, said he wanted to get a last burrito before "going to jail for a while."

DRAWN FROM *The Fort Wayne Journal Gazette*

Jacob Skipworth, a Michigan parolee, was charged with a felony adulterated food count after spitting into the Egg McMuffin that a Berrien County sheriff's deputy had ordered at the McDonald's where the felon was employed.

DRAWN FROM www.thesmokinggun.com

Denver Police Officer Derrick Curtis Saunders faced felony menacing and weapons charges for drawing his gun after getting impatient at a McDonald's drive-through window.

DRAWN FROM *The Denver Post*

James Tyler Markle of Diboll, Texas, was charged with making a felony terroristic threat after he convinced a worker at a Lufkin McDonald's to set off the restaurant's fire suppression system, which released a liquid from overhead extinguishers. Markle then told the employee that the liquid contained a toxin and directed the worker to break the windows in order to ventilate the building. He was charged for an identical prank the next day at a Wendy's in Louisiana.

DRAWN FROM *Free Republic* and www.thesmokinggun.com

Best American Gun Magazine Headlines

In 2008 and 2009, forty-seven new laws making it easier than ever to own and carry guns passed throughout the United States. The Oakland Tribune *called 2009 the "year of the gun." Laws in Arizona, Florida, Louisiana, and Utah, for instance, made it illegal for businesses to prohibit their employees from keeping a firearm in their cars on company property.*

A new law in Tennessee permits handguns in bars. Meanwhile, dozens of gun-related publications, in print and online, have flourished. The headlines here represent the most bizarre (and frightening) of 2009.

"Puttin' The Ho-Ho in a Happy Handgunner Christmas,"
  JOHN CONNOR, *American Handgunner*
"Clean that Cannon, Cowboy!" JOHN CONNOR, *American Handgunner*
"One-on-One with Chuck Norris," CHRIS COX, *American Rifleman*
"How Handloading Can Improve Your Love Life: Actually It Can't, but I
  Felt I Had to Get Your Attention. And If It Can, You Are a Pretty
  Strange Person," DAVID E. PETZAL, *Field & Stream*
"Five Recession-Proof Rifles," DAVID E. PETZAL, *Field & Stream*
"Take Squirreling to the Next Level," T. EDWARD NICKENS,
  Field & Stream
"A Cruel Blow: Using a Gun as a Club Doesn't Work—and It Can Hurt
  the Gun!" WALT RAUCH, *Handguns*
"Light Makes Right: Cure Trigger-Control Errors and Other Woes
  with Lasers," GREG RODRIGUEZ, *Handguns*
"And They Call Us Paranoid," JEFF KNOX, *Shotgun News*
"Home Alone . . . with a Gun," CLAYTON E. CRAMER, *Shotgun News*
"Painting Your Piece," DENNY HANSEN, *S.W.A.T. Magazine*
"Real Men Shoot .22s: Why Don't You?," ASHLEY EMERSON,
  S.W.A.T. Magazine
"The PPSH41 Submachine Gun: Rude and Crude, but Way Too
  Effective," MIKE "DUKE" VENTURINO, *Guns Magazine*
"My Wife's Guns: I Thought Some Were Mine, but I Was Wrong,"
  MIKE "DUKE" VENTURINO, *Guns Magazine*
"The Happiest Place on Earth: My Shooting House,"
  MIKE "DUKE" VENTURINO, *Guns Magazine*
"Gunwriterese: Sounds Good on the Surface, but It Sometimes Makes
  All Too Little Sense," JOHN BARSNESS, *Guns Magazine*
"Custer's Last Gun," GARRY JAMES, *Guns & Ammo*
"Social Shotgun," J. GUTHRIE, *Guns & Ammo*
"Kids and Guns: A Great Combination," KEVIN MICHALOWSKI,
  Gun Digest

Best American Six-Word Memoirs on Love and Heartbreak

FROM *Six-Word Memoirs on Love and Heartbreak*

Several years ago, the online magazine Smith asked its readers and hundreds of other people to write their life stories in exactly six words. One collection published last year (edited by Larry Smith and Rachel Fershleiser) was devoted to romance and its consequences. What follows are a few of that book's best offerings.

My least favorite word is platonic.
—NICOLE BOHN

I loved the idea of you.
—AUDREY ADU-APPIAH

Baseball is much better without you.
—NICOLE PHILLIPS

Fake agony over farts in bed.
—JIM GLADSTONE

Former child star seeks love, employment.
—JUSTIN TAYLOR

Leap of faith. Shit, no parachute.
—KATHERINE YUNKER

Wanted a wife. Got a cat.
—ANDERS PORTER

Happily single. No one believes me.
—ELIOT SHERIDAN

Best American New Patents

FROM United States Patent and Trademark Office

In 2009, there were 482,871 applications for patents filed with the United States Patent and Trademark Office; 191,927 of those were granted. Here are a few of the oddest and most creative designs.

SHEEP-SHAPED KEYLIGHT

WEARER-ATTACHABLE FOOD TRAY

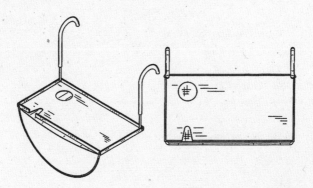

INSERTABLE POPCORN-BUTTERING APPARATUS

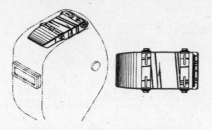

DEFOGGER FAN FOR WELDING HELMET

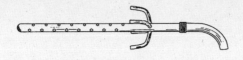

ANIMAL-SHAPED SLEEPING AREA FOR CHILDREN

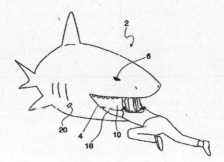

Best American Tweets

FROM www.twitter.com

Twitter, created in 2006, is a microblogging service that allows users to send 140-character messages, called tweets. Users can also sign up to receive other people's tweets. The following are the best tweets in the history of tweeting.

@chewbacca: graaawnnnn wwrrroooooooohhhh

@chewbacca: wruurrrrwww blooarrrrggghhh

@chewbacca: eeeewrrrrhhhnnn nnnrrrrwww

@chewbacca: wwwhhrreeehhh . . . . RRRRRrrrrnnnn

@chewbacca: ahhhrhrhhnnnnn GRRRRHHhhh wwhhreeeh-rhrnnnn

@chewbacca: wwhehrweehhhwhwnnnn

@chewbacca: AAAAAaaaahurrrrrrrrrrrrrrrrrnnnn! WWHheeer-rrrRRRRrrrrn.

@chewbacca: awWWwhhhrrrNNNNnnnn

@hodgman: If those two guys who are skulking on the roof of the building next door are on twitter then YOU SHOULD KNOW I CAN SEE YOU.

@chewbacca: aaaeewwwhhnnwrewhwnn! :: beginning a whheeer-hhnn working day on that flying peperoni pizza named millennium falcon

@chewbacca: mmmwaahhhrrrrwwaaaaaa :: going to mall to buy a very very big can of shampoo

@chewbacca: mwaahhhnnnnn eeeewwrhwwehehw :: looking for awwwhh cheap python hosting serviceeeewwhhhnnn

@hodgman: I prefer to think JD Salinger has just decided to become extra reclusive.

Best American Letter to the Editor

FROM *Bidoun*

Bidoun is an arts-and-culture quarterly that covers the Middle East and its diaspora. The letter that follows was published therein.

Dear Bidoun,

The one thing I hate about parents is they worry about you too much!!! Like one time I was on the phone with Alissa and we didn't know my mom was listening until Aaaaaaaaccchhhhooo! My mother sneezed! I was so mad. They don't even let me walk two blocks away to school. I have seen kindergarteners walk by themselves. I mean seriously. It drives me crazy. I try to do stuff that normal people do. It doesn't work because of PARENTS. If there was no grown ups all the kids would do whatever they want. They would go to stores and get whatever they want. They would go to their friend's house and chill. But the world would probably be crazier. I think it would be so cool to drive and stuff but I think we still need parents and grown ups for some small things.

Nazlee Radboy, age 10
Seattle, Washington

Best American Overqualified Cover Letters

JOEY COMEAU

FROM *Overqualified*

Overqualified is a collection of cover letters written and actually sent by Joey Comeau to various companies in Canada and the U.S. Every letter, however, quickly deviates from the conventions of the form. Formality goes by the wayside and digression invades. The author describes the creative process like so: "You start threatening instead of begging. You tell impolite jokes. You talk about your childhood and your sexual fantasies. You sign your real name and you put yourself honestly into letter after letter and there is no way you are ever going to get this job. Not with a letter like this. And you send it anyway." And now for a quick buffet of Comeau's best.

*   *   *

To: Nintendo
Re: Game Design

Thank you for taking the time to consider my resume. I am writing to apply for the position of game designer. We have a chance here to help children experience games that are more true to life than ever before. Computer graphics have improved and improved and improved, and some day soon we're going to have to ask ourselves where we can go next in our search for realism.

We need virtual pet games where you clean and feed and love your furry little friend, but where that car still comes out of nowhere so smoothly, a god of aerodynamics and passenger safety. Where your mother says, "Good thing we kept this." And she takes a shoebox down from your closet. Where you hear your father's quiet joke that night, when he thinks you are asleep.

We need an airport simulator, where the planes carry your whole family from A to B, job to job, and dad still drinks in the shower when you have to pee. Your older sister still comes home at three in the morning and wakes you up so she can sit on the edge of your bed and cry. Where you try to make friends faster at each new school, so you tell jokes even though you don't know anybody and nobody gets them. Everybody says you're the weird new kid. So at the next school you don't say anything at all and then you're the weird quiet kid. The plane touches down and you all lean forward in your seats because of inertia, and again and again someone says, "I hate to fly."

We need a new Mario game where you rescue the princess in the first ten minutes, and for the rest of the game you try to push down that sick feeling in your stomach telling you she's "damaged goods," a concept detailed again and again in the profoundly sex-negative instruction booklet, and when Luigi makes a crack about her and Bowser, you break his nose and immediately regret it. Peach asks you, in the quiet of her mushroom castle bedroom, "Do you still love me?" and you pretend to be asleep. You press the A button rhythmically, to control your breath, to keep it even.

Yours,
Joey Comeau

* * *

To: Human resources, Hallmark Cards
Re: Only sixteen shopping days left

Thank you for taking the time to review my resume. I haven't got any experience with greeting cards or with graphic design. But this morning it occurred to me that you need a new holiday. Mother's day is fine, but some of us have lost our mothers. Not everyone has someone to share their life with, Hallmark. But we all have one thing in common. We all have strangers on the edges of our lives.

We can all be secret admirers. Look around the next time you're at the mall. Or look online. Social networking sites. The internet is full of people to secretly admire. There's a girl who makes detailed maps of her neighborhood and she knows a boy who hates Allen Ginsberg—except for one line that he thinks is perfect. He has crooked eyes and takes all these pictures of balls bouncing. That is his obsession, bouncing rubber balls. He knows a girl who, in every picture, is pulling her shirt up to show off her belly. She's all like, "What's up? A camera? Yeah yeah. Let me get my belly out." She looks so happy just to be here. She knows a trashy girl in a tank top, wearing a little too much makeup, out drinking with her sorority friends in every picture. She has bleached blonde hair and only one interest. Carnival of Souls (1962).

What ever happened to secret admirers? Are they just stalkers now? If you notice someone, if you pay too much attention, that's weird. All of a sudden you're that guy who sits on the bench in the mall, right in front of the store where she works and stares inside all day. Or, worse, you're the guy who keeps going in. The guy with the Orange Julius who keeps saying, "I'm just browsing."

But I love writing notes to strangers.

"You have the best laugh I have ever heard. The only thing I know about you is that you work with maps and you always take the second straw from the dispenser — I do that too!"

And I don't think I'm alone, Hallmark.

International Stalker Day. I have to go decorate my room.

Joey Comeau

* * *

To: Human Resources, Nova Magnetics
Re: Tech Sales position!

Dear Sirs or Madams!

I am enclosing my resume in the hopes that you will consider me for a position with Nova Magnetics. My resume details my experience with magnet technical sales, but I would like to take some time to explain my other qualifications as well. I have a very special relationship with magnetic sales, and with magnets in particular. When I was a child I accidentally consumed a small fridge magnet in the shape of a kitten. Due to the magnet's odd shape, it has not passed through my system. It is lodged in my intestine somewhere or other, and I hope to god that it stays there. Why? Because it gives me special powers.

These powers aren't related to magnets. I can't make metal hover, or anything that you might find in a comic book. No. But I have always known I was different. I have abilities that set me apart from others. I have powers. Do you know anyone who can see perfectly in the dark? I'll bet you do. What's special about that? Cats can do it. Owls. Heck, my little brother has abnormally high night vision. But do you know anyone who goes completely blind if the sun even goes behind a cloud? I do. Me.

But that's the least of my powers. I have others. For example, I have a form of ESP that allows me to consistently pick losing lottery numbers, and generally make poor life choices. I used to rub these powers in other people's faces. I had a shirt made up that says "I consistently make poor life choices." It was not very popular, but that is how great my powers are. Did I mention my other powers? I can come up with t-shirt slogans on the spot.

"Kiss me, I have no night vision."

"I can't even think correctly!"

"This womb drops babies!"

But I realize that while these powers give my life the sheen of wonder, and they are borne of the magnet lodged in my intestines, they might not convince you that I can be a good technical sales guy. Well, I assure you that I can! If you would like to speak with me about this position, I would ask that we meet in person. I do not own a telephone, because I do not trust them. You can't see the other person! It could be anyone. Did you see Terminator 2, where the robot imitates the mother's voice and HE KILLED HER?

No way, man. If you want to hire me we're going to have to meet up somewhere. I think McDonald's is a good place. There's lots of people, and I feel safe there. Meet me there at three o'clock Thursday morning if you're interested. I feel my qualifications would make me a valuable addition to your team! I look forward to meeting you at McDonald's in order to learn more while not being murdered by a robot from the future.

Yours,
Joey Comeau

Best American Fictional Character Names

The following is a list of the oddest character names from fiction published in 2009. It's in honor of literature's long tradition of exceptionally strangely named characters. Think of them: Huckleberry Finn, Ebenezer Scrooge, Apollo Champagne, Ramona Quimby, Holden Caulfield, Captain Underpants, Eliza Doolittle, William Tell, Hester Prynne, Sancho Panza, Dumbledore, Reb Tevye, Falstaff, Eeyore, Shere Khan. . .

Perkus Tooth (*Chronic City*, JONATHAN LETHEM)
Oona Lazlo (*Chronic City*, JONATHAN LETHEM)
Candace Weld (*Generosity*, RICHARD POWERS)
Gladys Feet (*I Am Not Sidney Poitier*, PERCIVAL EVERETT)
Leander Buttons (*Everything Ravaged, Everything Burned*, WELLS TOWER)
Tecumseh Sparrow Spivet (*The Selected Works of T. S. Spivet*,
    REIF LARSEN)
Phoebus K. Dank (*The Cardboard Universe*, CHRISTOPHER MILLER)
Paul Chowder (*The Anthologist*, NICHOLSON BAKER)
Jig Johnson (*Impossible Princess*, KEVIN KILLIAN)
Ensenada Slim (*Inherent Vice*, THOMAS PYNCHON)
Rudy Blatnoyd (*Inherent Vice*, THOMAS PYNCHON)
Flaco the Bad (*Inherent Vice*, THOMAS PYNCHON)
Buddy Tubeside (*Inherent Vice*, THOMAS PYNCHON)
Petunia Leeway (*Inherent Vice*, THOMAS PYNCHON)
Scott Oof (*Inherent Vice*, THOMAS PYNCHON)
Trillium Fortnight (*Inherent Vice*, THOMAS PYNCHON)
Sauncho Smilax (*Inherent Vice*, THOMAS PYNCHON)
Rhus Frothingham (*Inherent Vice*, THOMAS PYNCHON)
Art Tweedle (*Inherent Vice*, THOMAS PYNCHON)
Horace Bonepenny (*The Sweetness at the Bottom of the Pie*,
    ALAN BRADLEY)
Jacob Tingle (*The Sweetness at the Bottom of the Pie*, ALAN BRADLEY)
Gladdy Fitzgibbon (*Lark and Termite*, JAYNE ANNE PHILLIPS)
Termite Leavitt (*Lark and Termite*, JAYNE ANNE PHILLIPS)
Rufus Lamarck White (*Lowboy*, JOHN WRAY)

Elspeth Noblin (*Her Fearful Symmetry*, AUDREY NIFFENEGGER)
Valentina Poole (*Her Fearful Symmetry*, AUDREY NIFFENEGGER)
Mortal Sword Tulgord Vise (*Crack'd Pot Trail*, STEVEN ERIKSON)
Well Knight Arpo Relent (*Crack'd Pot Trail*, STEVEN ERIKSON)
Hal Little (*American Salvage*, BONNIE JO CAMPBELL)
No-Fingers La Fleur (*Last Night in Twisted River*, JOHN IRVING)
Ehren ex Cursori (*First Lord's Fury*, JIM BUTCHER)
Romeo Burpee (*Under the Dome*, STEPHEN KING)
Ruffles (*Sounds Like Crazy*, SHANA MAHAFFEY)
Treelore (*The Help*, KATHRYN STOCKETT)
Zaphod Beeblebrox (*And Another Thing...*, EOIN COLFER)
Gawn F'zing (*And Another Thing...*, EOIN COLFER)
Constant Mown (*And Another Thing...*, EOIN COLFER)
Orpen Wren (*Love and Summer*, WILLIAM TREVOR)
Rosemarie Ramee (*Fort Da: A Report*, ELISABETH SHEFFIELD)
NP (*Sag Harbor*, COLSON WHITEHEAD)
Z.G. (*Shanghai Girls*, LISA SEE)

Best American 350-Word Story

BARRY LOPEZ

FROM *Orion*

According to www.350.org, 350 parts per million "is what many scientists, climate experts, and progressive national governments are now saying is the safe upper limit for CO_2 in our atmosphere." The CO_2 level in our atmosphere is presently at 390 ppm, and that number's rising. As part of the campaign to reign in CO_2 production, writers around the country wrote 350-Word stories at the encouragement of the aforementioned website. The following is one of the best of these written. It's called "The Trail."

On a winter afternoon, along a trail in the Sierra Madre in the state of Mensajero, beneath an immense rampart of rising cumulonimbus cloud, a deeply imperfect man bent over to collect a small piece of black glass. He recognized its kind: obsidian, a thick sliver of it. When the molten interior of the Earth is thrown into the frigid sky and cools quickly, it becomes a stone like this. People say of its edges that no knife is sharper, and of its color that it is transparent but bottomless, like the sea's, so it cannot be rendered on paper or canvas.

The man turned the spalled flake over in the palm of one hand with the fingers of the other. He tested the edge with his thumb and held it up to the sun. He knew of no volcanoes in these mountains, but the trail was many centuries old, and people had carried red coral, abalone shells, and turquoise up and down it for generations. Someone dropped this, he thought, in the time when his grandfather was alive, or in the year of his own birth, or a pilgrim might have dropped it, only days ago.

It glittered in his palm, like sunlight in ice, and he wondered, as the heaving clouds encroached on the sun and the shard of glass darkened, what his obligations were. Should he give it back to the trail or pocket it for the single daughter he was traveling to see? In another age he would not have hesitated to take it to the girl. Now he felt he must put it back, even if later someone else might take it. He believed he had come upon a time in his life when everything, even the things of God, needed protection. When he met his daughter, he would tell her he had found a black tear in the dust of the narrow path and understood he must leave it be. And she would ask whose tear it was, and he would have to use his imagination, in the way his people had once done.

Best American Farm Names

The agrarian roots of the United States are manifest these days in the hundreds of farming operations scattered around the country. Here's a list (alphabetized by state) of some of the most creatively named American agricultural efforts, yeoman or otherwise.

Charlie Rump (Alabama)
Coosa Hatchery (Alabama)

Gobbler Creek (Alabama)
Humble Heart (Alabama)
Arctic Organics (Alaska)
Basically Basil (Alaska)
Crooked Carrot (Arizona)
Pork On a Fork (Arizona)
Superstition (Arizona)
Creation Groans Gardens (Arkansas)
Falling Sky (Arkansas)
Farmcat Minnow Shed (Arkansas)
Hooligan's Hen House (Arkansas)
Rose Rustlers Flower (Arkansas)
Youngblood Grassfed (Arkansas)
Gas Point Worm (California)
Burt Pumpkin & Popcorn (Georgia)
Double Thorne Alpacas (Iowa)
Genuine Faux (Iowa)
Pride of the Wapsi (Iowa)
The Laughing Cantaloupe (Iowa)
Flying W Beefalo (Kansas)
Laughing Rooster (Kansas)
Merry Dairy (Kansas)
Screamin' Oaks (Kansas)
The Rare Hare Barn (Kansas)
Tornado Alley Poultry (Kansas)
Bear Wallow (Kentucky)
Strange Brothers Turtle (Louisiana)
The Other Red Meat From Maine Family (Maine)
Thyme for Goat (Maine)
Barney's Joy (Massachusetts)
Shy Brothers (Massachusetts)
Big Dan's U-Pick 'em (Michigan)
Super Bee Orchards (Nebraska)
Sleeping Monk (New Hamphire)
Toad Hill Maple (New York)
Tatum Bobby C & Betty Hog (North Carolina)
Hargus Hog (Oklahoma)

Sly Worm (Oklahoma)
The Peppermint Dragon (Oklahoma)
The Toomey's Black 'n Blue Thornless Berry (Oklahoma)
Thundering Prairie Productions (South Dakota)
Itty Bitty Acres Miniature Donkey Farm (Tennessee)
Aardvark Alpacas (Texas)
Moss Gathers (Texas)
Lazy Lady (Vermont)
Sneads Asparagus (Virginia)
Sassy Cow Creamery (Wisconsin)
Sugar Maple Emu (Wisconsin)

Best American First Lines of Poems Published in 2009

First lines, like last lines and first impressions, stick vividly in memory. To wit: "Whose woods these are I think I know" (Robert Frost), "How do I love thee? Let me count the ways" (Elizabeth Barrett Browning), "Hope is the thing with feathers" (Emily Dickinson), and "What happens to a dream deferred?" (Langston Hughes). Forthwith the best first lines published in 2009.

No!
LOREN GOODMAN, "In Character"

Drew down the curse of heaven on her umbrella
JAMES SCHUYLER, "Sweet Romanian Tongue"

plain cloth cast upon the cool banks, the mere warbling frogs
D. A. POWELL, "no picnic"

Bend into my mouth
SAMIYA BASHIR, "Stabilimentum"

You got my letter, said the troll.
MATTHEW ZAPRUDER, "Petrified by Sunlight or Invisible Curses"

Instead of a big inflated theoretical hooey expert
RON PADGETT, "Beavers vs. the Surrealists"

Everywhere, women asleep
OLIVIA CLARE, "Don Giovanni"

I can't see all of any horse at once
CHLOË HONUM, "Come Back"

We were well down the ventral axis
R. A. VILLANUEVA, "Swarm"

Then tomorrow? Then tomorrow.
JOHN ASHBERY, "The Logistics"

This is the shift of the heart's tumbled pin,
JENNIFER HOULE, "Talk of Mermaids"

Don't ask me, I merely thought the tree had a face
MYRON MICHAEL, "Chronicles of Shove: The Cougar and the Calf"

Praise the sonogram's glow: spine's colonnade
CHRISTINE STEWART-NUÑEZ, "Ode at Twenty-One Weeks"

He passed his time unfastening his memory.
VANESA GUITÉRREZ, "Hello"

I wake up somewhere in Ohio. Or, that's how it smells—
KARYNA MCGLYNN, "Ok, but You Haven't Seen the Last of Me"

No one will read to the end of a poem about butterflies.
MIKE WHITE, "Butterflies"

Daybreak on my marshland: a single egret, blotched,
TIMOTHY DONNELLY, "Globus Hystericus"

The light, half crippled from the cold, nevertheless limps into town.
MAX GARLAND, "Grit"

Best American Academic Journal Article Titles Published in 2009

Year after year, hundreds of academic journals—often based at universities—regularly publish fascinating (if not arcane) material. Here's a list of some of the most intriguing titles for articles run in 2009.

"The Owl in Phoenician Mortuary Practice," PHILIP C. SCHMITZ, *Journal of Ancient Near Eastern Religions*
"Eating Cold Food, Changing Old Fire for New, and Celebrating Easter," PANG PU, *Contemporary Chinese Thought*
"The Use of Eschatological Lists within the Targumim of the Megilloth," CHRISTIAN M. M. BRADY, *Journal for the Study of Judaism*
"Female Voice, Male Authority: A Nun's Narrative of the Regularization of a Female Franciscan House in Borgo San Sepolcro in 1500," JAMES R. BANKER and KATE LOWE, *The Sixteenth Century Journal*
"Medicine and Nonsense in French Renaissance Mock Prescriptions," HUGH ROBERTS, *The Sixteenth Century Journal*
"Person, Animal, Thing: The 1796 Dog Tax and the Right to Superfluous Things," LYNN FESTA, *Eighteenth-Century Life*
"Thinking about Feeling, 1789-1799," SOPHIA ROSENFELD, *French Historical Studies*
"What Reasonableness Really Is," JAIME NUBIOLA, *Transactions of the Charles S. Pierce Society*
"Glottalization and Lenition in Nuu-chah-nulth," EUN-SOOK KIM and DOUGLAS PULLEYBLANK, *Linguistic Inquiry*

"Primum Non Nocere: How To Cause Chaos With a Bronchoscope in the ICU," ANDREW BUSH, *Chest*

"Humans: The Party Animal," MICHAEL SAUNDERS GAZZANIGA, *Daedalus*

"Here Be Dragons? No, Big Cats! Predator Symbolism in Rural West Wales," SAMANTHA HURN, *Anthropology Today*

"Accidental Incest," NAOMI CAHN, *Harvard Journal of Law & Gender*

"Why Use an Ox-cleaver to Carve a Chicken?" ERICA BRINDLEY, *Philosophy East and West*

"On Certain Properties of Pied-piping," FABIAN HECK, *Linguistic Inquiry*

"Must Religion Be a Conversation-stopper?" STUART ROSENBAUM, *Harvard Theological Review*

"Nobody Tosses a Dwarf!" CARLO LEGET, PASCAL BORRY, and RAYMOND DE VRIES, *Bioethics*

"Why is Russia so . . . Russian?" ANDREW C. KUCHINS, *Current History*

Best American Illustrated Missed Connections

SOPHIE BLACKALL

FROM www.missedconnectionsny.blogspot.com/

The classifieds website www.craigslist.org, started in 1995 by Craig Newmark, features a popular section called "Missed Connections." These are personal ads posted by people who had a brush with a stranger they were interested in meeting but, for whatever reason, did not. The Missed Connection is a call for the stranger in question to step forward and have congress with the person posting the call. Early in 2009, artist Sophie Blackall undertook to illustrate some of her favorite Missed Connections from the Greater New York City Area.

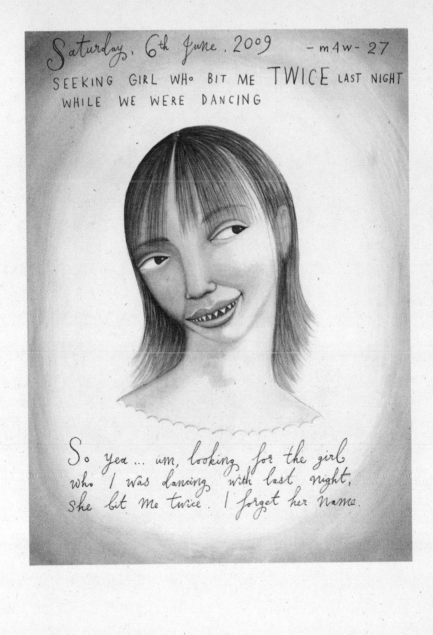

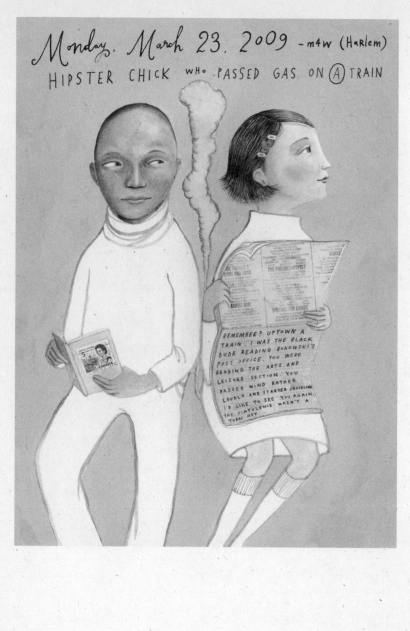

Wednesday, March 11, 2009
— m4w (Ridgewood)

Dear girl with silk screen on the M—

I WASN'T FOLLOWING YOU;

I LIVE DOWN THAT BLOCK.

You LEFT YouR CoAT
HERE LAST WINTER -w4w

... oR RatHeR, you let me weaR it Home.
I found FuN dip iN oNe pocket aNd youR
NYPL caRd iN the otHeR.
It's goiNg to keep me deliciously waRm
this WiNteR as I Rack up mouNtaiNs
of oveRdue fiNes.

Best American New Band Names

The following is a list of bands that to the best of the editors' knowledge were new (newly formed or released their first album) in 2009.

Edward Sharpe & the Magnetic Zeros, Volcano Choir, The xx, The Drums, Sleepy Sun, Fashawn, Dead Man's Bones, Spiral Stairs, We Were Promised Jetpacks, Nuclear Power Pants, Electric Courage Machine, The Phenomenal Handclap Band, The Big Pink, Cymbals Eat Guitars, Fever Ray, The Smith Westerns, Illuminations, The Dead Weather, The Pains of Being Pure at Heart, Sleigh Bells, Ganglians, Memory Tapes, Fleshgod Apocalypse, Neon Indian, Micachu and the Shapes, Japandroids, Joy Orbison, Washed Out, Gold Panda, Hot Panda, Javelin, Major Lazer, Beans on Toast, Broken Records, The Peelies, The Terror Pigeon Dance Revolt!, Whyzdom, The Christopher Walk-Ins, Girls, Mayer Hawthorne, Outrageous Things Said Casually, The Van Gobots, Peter Wolf Crier, Get Busy Committee, We Fell to Earth, Florence and the Machine, Stubby's Crack Co., Shark Pants, Das Racist, Ginsu Wives, Muscle Hawk, Chlamydiot, Handshake, Zola Jesus, Dum Dum Girls, Cold Cave, Surfer Blood, Fanfarlo, La Roux, Hockey, tUnE-yArDs, Rain Machine, Allo Darlin', Akina Adderley & The Vintage Playboys, And So I Watch You From Afar, Best Coast, Crystal Fighters, Diagonals, I Fight Dragons, Magic Wands, Wild Moccasins, Golden Silvers, Mi Ami, Romance on a Rocketship, Sex Worker, So Cow, Floating Action, Freelance Whales, Drive Like Maria, Elizabeth and the Catapult, Band of Skulls, The Rural Alberta Advantage, Young Fathers, Young Prisms, What's Up?, Telepathe, Get Back Guinozzi!, Water Borders, The Second Hand Marching Band, The Temper Trap, Little Boots, Dinosaur Pile-up, Red Light Company, Delphic, Broken Bells, Clues, The Invisible, Dead by Sunrise, Them Crooked Vultures, Tinted Windows, Raygun, Nick Jonas and the Administration, Titus Andronicus, 2NE1, Boyz IV Men, Atoms for Peace, Celine Dion 2013

Best American Lawsuits

It was another banner year for strange lawsuits. A woman sued an Egyptian hotel after her thirteen-year-old daughter returned from vacation pregnant. Magdalena Kwiatkowska claimed that "stray sperm" in the hotel pool, which her daughter had used during her visit, was responsible for the pregnancy. Now for a handful of the most outlandish suits filed in the U.S. in 2009.

A Florida woman who claims the G-forces from a theme park ride relieve her chronic pain sued Walt Disney World for breaching its contract with visitors by limiting her to four rides per visit on its Tower of Terror. In a complaint filed last month in Osceola County, Denise Mooty alleges she needs the Tower of Terror for therapy rather than thrills. Disney denies the charges and says Mooty was made to leave the park "for causing a disturbance within the presence of other guests and using foul language toward a Cast Member."

DRAWN FROM www.cfnews13.com

The North Face is asking for unspecified damages and wants the court to prohibit Jimmy Winkelmann from continuing to offer his alternative clothing line, The South Butt. The South Butt offers fleece jackets, shorts, and other apparel with its name and a logo that is a mirror image of The North Face's famous mountain logo. Winkelmann's attorney, Albert Watkins, argued that the public knows the difference between a face and a butt and that those wanting a North Face product won't accidentally purchase one from South Butt.

DRAWN FROM *The San Francisco Examiner*

A Florida man filed a lawsuit against Hanesbrands, Inc. asking for five thousand dollars in damages. The man says a gap in his underwear that caused him "painful rubbing." Alfred Freed, representing himself, claimed he suffered an abrasion due to the underwear's tendency to "gap" as he walked. But the presiding judge ruled that the suffering Freed had endured was more likely caused by the manner in which Freed dons his underwear, and not by the actual garment; during his hearing, Freed testified that "he dresses by placing his underwear inside the pants he plans to wear that day and then pulls both on together."

DRAWN FROM *The Pensacola News Journal*

Trina Thompson, who says she can't find a job, sued Monroe College, where she earned a bachelor's degree. The twenty-seven-year-old is seeking the seventy thousand dollars she spent on tuition.

DRAWN FROM www.nbcnewyork.com

Comic Sunda Croonquist was sued by her mother-in-law after making said mother-in-law the punchline of too many jokes. The mother-in-law is accusing Croonquist of spreading false, defamatory, and racist lies via the in-law jokes that have become a staple of Croonquist's routine in nightclubs and on television. The comedian maintains that the in-law jokes are a logical, natural result of living through one comical culture-clash moment after another: she is half-black, half-Swedish, grew up Roman Catholic, and married into a Jewish family.

DRAWN FROM *The New York Daily News*

High school senior Justin Gawronski sued Amazon.com for ruining his homework assignment. By wirelessly deleting George Orwell's *1984* from his Kindle, Gawronski claimed, Amazon also erased his copious digital notes and ruined the work he was preparing for a homework assignment. The company settled for $150,000.

DRAWN FROM *The Wall Street Journal*

Janine Sugawara sued PepsiCo., Inc. for "full restitution of all money gained" through misleading advertising on the composition of the "berries" in its Cap'n Crunch breakfast cereal. Sugawara said she'd been led to believe that Crunch Berries really exist. In her suit, she demanded the company be explicit about the "true composition" of the berries. It was dismissed. A similar suit was filed last year against Froot Loops.

DRAWN FROM www.nevadacounty.com

Best American Poems Written in the Last Decade or So by People Living or Fighting in Iraq or Afghanistan

The United States has spent more in the last ten years on war than it has on education in its entire history. The fighting in Iraq and Afghanistan has claimed the lives of thousands of soldiers and civilians, and disrupted the lives of countless others. Some of those soldiers and civilians have been writing poems drawn from their harrowing and varied experiences. The poetry gathered here represents a fraction of that material.

When He Exploded

1.
When he exploded
Nobody fell
Nobody fled
Nobody cared.
So he collected his fragments
And disappeared, ashamed.

2.
The wounds
Grew into enchanted trees.
Whenever the wind shook their branches
Unbelievable fruits fell down.

—*Salam Dawai*
(translated by Soheil Najm)

Stretcher II

An engineman
who will not make it.
Who catches the eye
of the storekeeper next to him
when he takes his last breath.
When he takes his last breath,
a young man laughs:
"You are dead, American!" he shouts
into a bleeding ear, snatches
ring and watch and golden
cross, runs into smoke
and crowd and flight.

— *Khadijah Queen*

* * *

In the Valley of the Souls

O traveler whom we left alone
In the valley of the souls
Ships have taken us far
But my eyes are still waving
To the squeak of your stubbornness:
This city is not for me.

— *Abdul-Zahra Zeki*
(translated by Sadek Mohammed)

* * *

Bombardment

The city sits quietly
The sky, above her, is
A hammer

The city is empty
Whispers disturb her tranquility
Steps glitter
And their echoes
Like bats
Cling to balconies

The city is jammed with vehicles
Vainly
They spin their wheels
On the oil
Of the streets

The city breaks her mirror—
The river
Splitting her
Like a crooked slash

The river rises upward in a blaze
Seagulls stretch out their necks
Amid the shipwrecks—
The river collapses
And drags them to the bottom

The city cannot
Gather in her children.
Sometimes they crawl
Sometimes they fly
They cling to her like sins
They are flung like fruits
Her branches vainly reaching out for them
She tries to break loose from her roots
To gather up her little ones
The city is standing
Her head in her hands

She swirls
Swirls
Swirls
Becomes dizzy
Sinks amid signboards

The city takes a cup
Of water
To swallow her words

Now she is hushed
Silencing her children
Straining her ears
She waits the sudden falling
Of the sky

—*Haider Al-Kabi*
(translated by Sadek Mohammed)

* * *

Stopping the American Infantry Patrol Near the Prophet Yunus Mosque in Mosul, Abu Ali Shows Them the Cloth in His Pocket

Do you see this weathered strip of cloth, the golden threads
of its embroidery—how inconsequential it must appear to you,
only a strip of cloth—but my friends, this silk and cotton dyed black
once draped over the Black Stone; it is from the *Kiswah*,
and it is only with me now because my father made the long journey
to the *Kaaba*, to The House of God, and walked the circles
as the angels once circled God's throne; he kissed
that Black Stone, and ran between the hills, as one must,
before you were even born; his pilgrimage
part of our religion, something I have not yet done,
this war of no help in that, believe me.

When you address me, do not call me *Hajji,*
I have not been so fortunate—and you?
You do not understand the words you speak.

—*Brian Turner*

* * *

More Than One, Less Than Two

Every line I write, I'm afraid,
will erase a line from your memory.

What negligent god has left you derelict?
What charm has made you write poems?
You look like a soldier from 1914.
How charming! How charming!
How can a poem be possible,
with so much shrapnel in your chest?
One splinter would burn up a volume of poems.
How can you extract poems and shrapnel from your chest
at the very same time?
Our fathers lied to us—
They never told us this was possible.

How have you aged and slackened in so little time?
God grant you a cheerful death!
You are the furious storm,
produced by words of peerless calm.

Has my silence worn you out? Has my forgetfulness frightened you?
Have you flung your hand out searching for me?
Have you hunted for something? Has something hunted for you?
Have you trusted that the gravedigger
will not put a cadaver in the grave,
but hay and lint and other trash?
A man is nothing but a nest.

"How the questions vanished,
leaving the answers alone!"
Have you found out who guides all these inhabited wagons,
and in what direction he is leading them?

There is no way, neither forward nor backward.
Who was it, before going to his garden, threw you here all alone
in this trash heap?

I'm afraid you'll say "you."
I'm afraid.

—*Sabah Khattab*
(translated by Haider Al-Kabi)

SHERMAN ALEXIE

■

War Dances

FROM *War Dances*

1. My Kafka Baggage

A few years ago, after I returned from a trip to Los Angeles, I unpacked my bag and found a dead cockroach, shrouded by a dirty sock, in a bottom corner. "Shit," I thought. "We're being invaded." And so I threw the unpacked clothes, books, shoes, and toiletries back into the suitcase, carried it out onto the driveway, and dumped the contents onto the pavement, ready to stomp on any other cockroach stowaways. But there was only the one cockroach, stiff and dead. As he lay on the pavement, I leaned closer to him. His legs were curled under his body. His head was tilted at a sad angle. Sad? Yes, sad. For who is lonelier than the cockroach without his tribe? I laughed at myself. I was feeling empathy for a dead cockroach. I wondered about its story. How had it got into my bag? And where? At the hotel in Los Angeles? In an airport baggage system? It didn't originate in our house. We've kept those tiny bastards away from our place for fifteen years. So what had happened to this little vermin? Did he smell something delicious in my bag—my musky deodorant or some crumb of chocolate Power Bar—and climb inside, only to be crushed by the shifts of fate and garment bags? As he died, did he feel fear? Isolation? Existential dread?

2. Symptoms

Last summer, in reaction to various allergies I was suffering from, defensive mucus flooded my inner right ear and confused, frightened, untied, and unmoored me. Simply stated, I could not fucking hear a thing from that side, so I had to turn my head to understand what my two sons, ages eight and ten, were saying.

"We're hungry," they said. "We keep telling you."

They wanted to be fed. And I had not heard them.

"Mom would have fed us by now," they said.

Their mother had left for Italy with her mother two days ago. My sons and I were going to enjoy a boys' week, filled with unwashed socks, REI rock wall climbing, and ridiculous heaps of pasta.

"What are you going to cook?" my sons asked. "Why haven't you cooked yet?"

I'd been lying on the couch reading a book while they played and I had not realized that I'd gone partially deaf. So I, for just a moment, could only weakly blame the silence—no, the contradictory roar that only I could hear.

Then I recalled the man who went to the emergency room because he'd woken having lost most, if not all, of his hearing. The doctor peered into one ear, saw an obstruction, reached in with small tweezers, and pulled out a cockroach, then reached into the other ear, and extracted a much larger cockroach. Did you know that ear wax is a delicacy for roaches?

I cooked dinner for my sons—overfed them out of guilt—and cleaned the hell out of our home. Then I walked into the bathroom and stood close to my mirror. I turned my head and body at weird angles, and tried to see deeply into my congested ear. I sang hymns and prayed that I'd see a small angel trapped in the canal. I would free the poor thing, and she'd unfurl and pat dry her tiny wings, then fly to my lips and give me a sweet kiss for sheltering her metamorphosis.

3. The Symptoms Worsen

When I woke at three a.m., completely unable to hear out of my clogged right ear, and positive that a damn swarm of locusts was wedged inside, I left a message for my doctor, and told him that I would be sitting outside his office when he reported to work.

This would be the first time I had been inside a health-care facility since my father's last surgery.

4. Blankets

After the surgeon cut off my father's right foot—no, half of my father's right foot—and three toes from the left, I sat with him in the recovery room. It was more like a recovery hallway. There was no privacy, not even a thin curtain. I guessed it made it easier for the nurses to monitor the postsurgical patients, but still, my father was exposed—his decades of poor health and worse decisions were illuminated—on white sheets in a white hallway under white lights.

"Are you okay?" I asked. It was a stupid question. Who could be okay after such a thing? Yesterday, my father had walked into the hospital. Okay, he'd shuffled while balanced on two canes, but that was still called walking. A few hours ago, my father still had both of his feet. Yes, his feet and toes had been black with rot and disease but they'd still been, technically speaking, feet and toes. And, most important, those feet and toes had belonged to my father. But now they were gone, sliced off. Where were they? What did they do with the right foot and the toes from the left foot? Did they throw them in the incinerator? Were their ashes floating over the city?

"Doctor, I'm cold," my father said.

"Dad, it's me," I said.

"I know who are you. You're my son." But considering the blankness in my father's eyes, I assumed he was just guessing at my identity.

"Dad, you're in the hospital. You just had surgery."

"I know where I am. I'm cold."

"Do you want another blanket?" Another stupid question. Of course he wanted another blanket. He probably wanted me to build a fucking campfire or drag in one of those giant propane heaters that NFL football teams used on the sidelines.

I walked down the hallway—the recovery hallway—to the nurses' station. There were three women nurses, two white and one black.

Being Native American-Spokane and Coeur d'Alene Indian, I hoped my darker pigment would give me an edge with the black nurse, so I addressed her directly.

"My father is cold," I said. "Can I get another blanket?"

The black nurse glanced up from her paperwork and regarded me. Her expression was neither compassionate nor callous.

"How can I help you, sir?" she asked.

"I'd like another blanket for my father. He's cold."

"I'll be with you in a moment, sir."

She looked back down at her paperwork. She made a few notes. Not knowing what else to do, I stood there and waited.

"Sir," the black nurse said. "I'll be with you in a moment."

She was irritated. I understood. After all, how many thousands of times had she been asked for an extra blanket? She was a nurse, an educated woman, not a damn housekeeper. And it was never really about an extra blanket, was it? No, when people asked for an extra blanket, they were asking for a time machine. And, yes, she knew she was a health care provider, and she knew she was supposed to be compassionate, but my father, an alcoholic, diabetic Indian with terminally damaged kidneys, had just endured an incredibly expensive surgery for what? So he could ride his motorized wheelchair to the bar and win bets by showing off his disfigured foot? I know she didn't want to be cruel, but she believed there was a point when doctors should stop rescuing people from their own self-destructive impulses. And I couldn't disagree with her but I could ask for the most basic of comforts, couldn't I?

"My father," I said. "An extra blanket, please."

"Fine," she said, then stood and walked back to a linen closet, grabbed a white blanket, and handed it to me. "If you need anything else—"

I didn't wait around for the end of her sentence. With the blanket in hand, I walked back to my father. It was a thin blanket, laundered and sterilized a hundred times. In fact, it was too thin. It wasn't really a blanket. It was more like a large beach towel. Hell, it wasn't even good enough for that. It was more like the world's largest coffee filter. Jesus, had health care finally come to this? Everybody was uninsured and unblanketed.

"Dad, I'm back."

He looked so small and pale lying in that hospital bed. How had that change happened? For the first sixty-seven years of his life, my father had been a large and dark man. And now, he was just another pale and sick drone in a hallway of pale and sick drones. A hive, I thought, this place looks like a beehive with colony collapse disorder.

"Dad, it's me."

"I'm cold."

"I have a blanket."

As I draped it over my father and tucked it around his body, I felt the first sting of grief. I'd read the hospital literature about this moment. There would come a time when roles would reverse and the adult child would become the caretaker of the ill parent. The circle of life. Such poetic bullshit.

"I can't get warm," my father said. "I'm freezing."

"I brought you a blanket, Dad, I put it on you."

"Get me another one. Please. I'm so cold. I need another blanket."

I knew that ten more of these cheap blankets wouldn't be enough. My father needed a real blanket, a good blanket.

I walked out of the recovery hallway and made my way through various doorways and other hallways, peering into the rooms, looking at the patients and their families, looking for a particular kind of patient and family.

I walked through the ER, cancer, heart and vascular, neuroscience, orthopedic, women's health, pediatrics, and surgical services. Nobody stopped me. My expression and posture were that of a man with a sick father and so I belonged.

And then I saw him, another Native man, leaning against a wall near the gift shop. Well, maybe he was Asian; lots of those in Seattle. He was a small man, pale brown, with muscular arms and a soft belly. Maybe he was Mexican, which is really a kind of Indian, too, but not the kind that I needed. It was hard to tell sometimes what people were. Even brown people guessed at the identity of other brown people.

"Hey," I said.

"Hey," the other man said.

"You Indian?" I asked.

"Yeah."

"What tribe?"

"Lummi."

"I'm Spokane."

"My first wife was Spokane. I hated her."

"My first wife was Lummi. She hated me."

We laughed at the new jokes that instantly sounded old.

"Why are you in here?" I asked.

"My sister is having a baby," he said. "But don't worry, it's not mine."

"Ayyyyyy," I said—another Indian idiom—and laughed.

"I don't even want to be here," the other Indian said. "But my dad started, like, this new Indian tradition. He says it's a thousand years old. But that's bullshit. He just made it up to impress himself. And the whole family just goes along, even when we know it's bullshit. He's in the delivery room waving eagle feathers around. Jesus."

"What's the tradition?"

"Oh, he does a naming ceremony right in the hospital. Like, it's supposed to protect the baby from all the technology and shit. Like hospitals are the big problem. You know how many babies died before we had good hospitals?"

"I don't know."

"Most of them. Well, shit, a lot of them, at least."

This guy was talking out of his ass. I liked him immediately.

"I mean," the guy said, "you should see my dad right now. He's pretending to go into this, like, fucking trance and is dancing around my sister's bed, and he says he's trying to, you know, see into her womb, to see who the baby is, to see its true nature, so he can give it a name—a protective name—before it's born."

The guy laughed and threw his head back and banged it on the wall.

"I mean, come on, I'm a loser," he said and rubbed his sore skull. "My whole family is filled with losers."

The Indian world is filled with charlatans, men and women who pretended—hell, who might have come to believe—that they were holy. Last year, I had gone to a lecture at the University of Washing-

ton. An elderly Indian woman, a Sioux writer and scholar and char-
latan, had come to orate on Indian sovereignty and literature. She
kept arguing for some kind of separate indigenous literary identity,
which was ironic considering that she was speaking English to a
room full of white professors. But I wasn't angry with the woman, or
even bored. No, I felt sorry for her. I realized that she was dying of
nostalgia. She had taken nostalgia as her false idol—her thin blanket—and it was murdering her.

"Nostalgia," I said to the other Indian man in the hospital.

"What?"

"Your dad, he sounds like he's got a bad case of nostalgia."

"Yeah, I hear you catch that from fucking old high school girl-
friends," the man said. "What the hell you doing here anyway?"

"My dad just got his feet cut off," I said.

"Diabetes?"

"And vodka."

"Vodka straight up or with a nostalgia chaser?"

"Both."

"Natural causes for an Indian."

"Yep."

There wasn't much to say after that.

"Well, I better get back," the man said. "Otherwise, my dad might
wave an eagle feather and change my name."

"Hey, wait," I said.

"Yeah?"

"Can I ask you a favor?"

"What?"

"My dad, he's in the recovery room," I said. "Well, it's more like a
hallway, and he's freezing, and they've only got these shitty little blankets, and I came looking for Indians in the hospital because I figured—well, I guessed if I found any Indians, they might have some
good blankets."

"So you want to borrow a blanket from us?" the man asked.

"Yeah."

"Because you thought some Indians would just happen to have
some extra blankets lying around?"

"Yeah."

"That's fucking ridiculous."

"I know."

"And it's racist."

"I know."

"You're stereotyping your own damn people."

"I know."

"But damn if we don't have a room full of Pendleton blankets. New ones. Jesus, you'd think my sister was having, like, a dozen babies."

Five minutes later, carrying a Pendleton Star Blanket, the Indian man walked out of his sister's hospital room, accompanied by his father, who wore Levi's, a black T-shirt, and eagle feathers in his gray braids.

"We want to give your father this blanket," the old man said. "It was meant for my grandson, but I think it will be good for your father, too."

"Thank you."

"Let me bless it. I will sing a healing song for the blanket. And for your father."

I flinched. This guy wanted to sing a song? That was dangerous. This song could take two minutes or two hours. It was impossible to know. Hell, considering how desperate this old man was to be seen as holy, he might sing for a week. I couldn't let this guy begin his song without issuing a caveat.

"My dad," I said. "I really need to get back to him. He's really sick."

"Don't worry," the old man said and winked. "I'll sing one of my short ones."

Jesus, who'd ever heard of a self-aware fundamentalist? The son, perhaps not the unbeliever he'd pretended to be, sang backup as his father launched into his radio-friendly honor song, just three-and-a-half minutes, like the length of any Top Forty rock song of the last fifty years. But here's the funny thing: the old man couldn't sing very well. If you were going to have the balls to sing healing songs in hospital hallways, then you should logically have a great voice, right? But, no, this guy couldn't keep the tune. And his voice cracked and wavered. Does a holy song lose its power if its singer is untalented?

"That is your father's song," the old man said when he was finished. "I give it to him. I will never sing it again. It belongs to your father now."

Behind his back, the old man's son rolled his eyes and walked back into his sister's room.

"Okay, thank you," I said. I felt like an ass, accepting the blanket and the old man's good wishes, but silently mocking them at the same time. But maybe the old man did have some power, some real medicine, because he peeked into my brain.

"It doesn't matter if you believe in the healing song," the old man said. "It only matters that the blanket heard."

"Where have you been?" my father asked when I returned. "I'm cold."

"I know, I know," I said. "I found you a blanket. A good one. It will keep you warm."

I draped the Star Blanket over my father. He pulled the thick wool up to his chin. And then he began to sing. It was a healing song, not the same song that I had just heard, but a healing song nonetheless. My father could sing beautifully. I wondered if it was proper for a man to sing a healing song for himself. I wondered if my father needed help with the song. I hadn't sung for many years, not like that, but I joined him. I knew this song would not bring back my father's feet. This song would not repair my father's bladder, kidneys, lungs, and heart. This song would not prevent my father from drinking a bottle of vodka as soon as he could sit up in bed. This song would not defeat death. No, I thought, this song is temporary, but right now, temporary is good enough. And it was a good song. Our voices filled the recovery hallway. The sick and healthy stopped to listen. The nurses, even the remote black one, unconsciously took a few steps toward us. The black nurse sighed and smiled. I smiled back. I knew what she was thinking. Sometimes, even after all of these years, she could still be surprised by her work. She still marveled at the infinite and ridiculous faith of other people.

5. Doctor's Office

I took my kids with me to my doctor, a handsome man—a reservist—who'd served in both Iraq wars. I told him I could not hear. He said his nurse would likely have to clear wax and fluid, but when he scoped inside, he discovered nothing.

"Nope, it's all dry in there," he said.

He led my sons and me to the audiologist in the other half of the building. I was scared, but I wanted my children to remain calm, so I tried to stay measured. More than anything, I wanted my wife to materialize.

During the hearing test, I heard only thirty percent of the clicks, bells, and words—I apparently had nerve and bone-conductive deafness. My inner ear thumped and thumped.

How many cockroaches were in my head?

My doctor said, "We need an MRI of your ear and brain, and maybe we'll find out what's going on."

Maybe? That word terrified me.

What the fuck was wrong with my fucking head? Had my hydrocephalus come back for blood? Had my levees burst? Was I going to flood?

6. Hydrocephalus

Merriam-Webster's dictionary defines hydrocephalus as "an abnormal increase in the amount of cerebrospinal fluid within the cranial cavity that is accompanied by expansion of the cerebral ventricles, enlargement of the skull and especially the forehead, and atrophy of the brain." I define hydrocephalus as "the obese, imperialistic water demon that nearly killed me when I was six months old."

In order to save my life, and stop the water demon, I had brain surgery in 1967 when I was six months old. I was supposed to die. Obviously, I didn't. I was supposed to be severely mentally disabled. I have only minor to moderate brain damage. I was supposed to have epileptic seizures. Those I did have, until I was seven years old. I was on phenobarbital, a major league antiseizure medication, for six years.

Some of the side effects of phenobarbital—all of which I suffered to some degree or another as a child—include sleepwalking, agitation, confusion, depression, nightmares, hallucinations, insomnia, apnea, vomiting, constipation, dermatitis, fever, liver and bladder dysfunction, and psychiatric disturbance.

How do you like them cockroaches?

And now, as an adult, thirty-three years removed from phenobarbital, I still suffer—to one degree or another—from sleepwalking, agitation, confusion, depression, nightmares, hallucinations, insomnia, bladder dysfunction, apnea, and dermatitis.

Is there such a disease as post-phenobarbital traumatic stress syndrome? Most hydrocephalics are shunted. A shunt is essentially brain plumbing that drains away excess cerebrospinal fluid. Those shunts often fuck up and stop working. I know hydrocephalics who've had a hundred or more shunt revisions and repairs. That's over a hundred brain surgeries. There are ten fingers on any surgeon's hand. There are two or three surgeons working on any particular brain. That means certain hydrocephalics have had their brains fondled by three thousand fingers.

I'm lucky. I was only temporarily shunted. And I hadn't suffered any hydrocephalic symptoms since I was seven years old. And then, in July 2008, at the age of forty-one, I went deaf in my right ear.

7. Conversation

Sitting in my car in the hospital parking garage, I called my brother-in-law, who was babysitting my sons.

"Hey, it's me. I just got done with the MRI on my head."

My brother-in-law said something unintelligible. I realized I was holding my cell to my bad ear. And switched it to the good ear.

"The MRI dude didn't look happy," I said.

"That's not good," my brother-in-law said.

"No, it's not. But he's just a tech guy, right? He's not an expert on brains or anything. He's just the photographer, really. And he doesn't know anything about ears or deafness or anything, I don't think. Ah, hell, I don't know what he knows. I just didn't like the look on his face when I was done."

"Maybe he just didn't like you."

"Well, I got worried when I told him I had hydrocephalus when I was a baby and he didn't seem to know what that was."

"Nobody knows what that is."

"That's the truth. Have you fed the boys dinner?"

"Yeah, but I was scrounging. There's not much here."

"I better go shopping."

"Are you sure? I can do it if you need me to. I can shop the shit out of Trader Joe's."

"No, it'll be good for me. I feel good. I fell asleep during the MRI. And I kept twitching. So we had to do it twice. Otherwise, I would've been done earlier."

"That's okay; I'm okay; the boys are okay."

"You know, before you go in that MRI tube, they ask you what kind of music you want to listen to—jazz, classical, rock, or country—and I remembered how my dad spent a lot of time in MRI tubes near the end of his life. So I was wondering what kind of music he always chose. I mean, he couldn't hear shit anyway by that time, but he still must have chosen something. And I wanted to choose the same thing he chose. So I picked country."

"Was it good country?"

"It was fucking Shania Twain and Faith Hill shit. I was hoping for George Jones or Loretta Lynn, or even some George Strait. Hell, I would've cried if they'd played Charley Pride or Freddy Fender."

"You wanted to hear the alcoholic Indian father jukebox."

"Hey, that's my line. You can't quote me to me."

"Why not? You're always quoting you to you."

"Kiss my ass. So, hey, I'm okay, I think. And I'm going to the store. But I think I already said that. Anyway, I'll see you in a bit. You want anything?"

"Ah, man, I love Trader Joe's. But you know what's bad about them? You fall in love with something they have—they stock it for a year—and then it just disappears. They had those wontons I loved and now they don't. I was willing to shop for you and the boys, but I don't want anything for me. I'm on a one-man hunger strike against them."

8. World Phone Conversation, Three a.m.

After I got home with yogurt and turkey dogs and Cinnamon Toast Crunch and my brother-in-law had left, I watched George Romero's *Diary of the Dead*, and laughed at myself for choosing a movie that featured dozens of zombies getting shot in the head.

When the movie was over, I called my wife, nine hours ahead in Italy.

"I should come home," she said.

"No, I'm okay," I said. "Come on, you're in Rome. What are you seeing today?"

"The Vatican."

"You can't leave now. You have to go and steal something. It will be revenge for every Indian. Or maybe you can plant an eagle feather and claim that you just discovered Catholicism."

"I'm worried."

"Yeah, Catholicism has always worried me."

"Stop being funny. I should see if I can get Mom and me on a flight tonight."

"No, no, listen, your mom is old. This might be her last adventure. It might be your last adventure with her. Stay there. Say hi to the Pope for me. Tell him I like his shoes."

That night, my sons climbed into bed with me. We all slept curled around one another like sled dogs in a snowstorm. I woke, hour by hour, and touched my head and neck to check if they had changed shape—to·feel if antennae were growing. Some insects "hear" with their antennae. Maybe that's what was happening to me.

9. Valediction

My father, a part-time blue-collar construction worker, died in March 2003, from full-time alcoholism. On his deathbed, he asked me to "Turn down that light, please."

"Which light?" I asked.

"The light on the ceiling."

"Dad, there's no light."

"It burns my skin, son. It's too bright. It hurts my eyes."

"Dad, I promise you there's no light."

"Don't lie to me, son, it's God passing judgment on Earth."

"Dad, you've been an atheist since '79. Come on, you're just remembering your birth. On your last day, you're going back to your first."

"No, son, it's God telling me I'm doomed. He's using the brightest lights in the universe to show me the way to my flame-filled tomb."

"No, Dad, those lights were in your delivery room."

"If that's true, son, then turn down my mother's womb."

We buried my father in the tiny Catholic cemetery on our reservation. Since I am named after him, I had to stare at a tombstone with my name on it.

10. Battle Fatigue

Two months after my father's death, I began research on a book about our family's history with war. I had a cousin who had served as a cook in the first Iraq war in 1991; I had another cousin who served in the Vietnam War in 1964–65, also as a cook; and my father's father, Adolph, served in World War II and was killed in action on Okinawa Island, on April 5, 1946.

During my research, I interviewed thirteen men who'd served with my cousin in Vietnam but could find only one surviving man who'd served with my grandfather. This is a partial transcript of that taped interview, recorded with a microphone and an iPod on January 14, 2008:

Me: Ah, yes, hello, I'm here in Livonia, Michigan, to interview—well, perhaps you should introduce yourself, please?

Leonard Elmore: What?

Me: Um, oh, I'm sorry, I was asking if you could perhaps introduce yourself.

LE: You're going to have to speak up. I think my hearing aid is going low on power or something.

Me: That is a fancy thing in your ear.

LE: Yeah, let me mess with it a bit. I got a remote control for it. I can listen to the TV, the stereo, and the telephone with this thing.

It's fancy. It's one of them Bluetooth hearing aids. My grandson bought it for me. Wait, okay, there we go. I can hear now. So what were you asking?

Me: I was hoping you could introduce yourself into my recorder here.

LE: Sure, my name is Leonard Elmore.

Me: How old are you?

LE: I'm eighty-five-and-a-half years old (laughter). My great-grand-kids are always saying they're seven-and-a-half or nine-and-a-half or whatever. It just cracks me up to say the same thing at my age.

Me: So, that's funny, um, but I'm here to ask you some questions about my grandfather—

LE: Adolph. It's hard to forget a name like that. An Indian named Adolph and there was that Nazi bastard named Adolph. Your grandfather caught plenty of grief over that. But we mostly called him "Chief," did you know that?

Me: I could have guessed.

LE: Yeah, nowadays, I suppose it isn't a good thing to call an Indian "Chief," but back then, it was what we did. I served with a few Indians. They didn't segregate them Indians, you know, not like the black boys. I know you aren't supposed to call them boys anymore, but they were boys. All of us were boys, I guess. But the thing is, those Indian boys lived and slept and ate with us white boys. They were right there with us. But, anyway, we called all them Indians "Chief." I bet you've been called "Chief" a few times yourself.

Me: Just once.

LE: Were you all right with it?

Me: I threw a basketball in the guy's face.

LE: (laughter)

Me: We live in different times.

LE: Yes, we do. Yes, we do.

Me: So, perhaps you could, uh, tell me something about my grand-father.

LE: I can tell you how he died.

Me: Really?

LE: Yeah, it was on Okinawa, and we hit the beach, and, well, it's hard to talk about it—it was the worst thing—it was Hell—no, that's not even a good way to describe it. I'm not a writer like you—I'm not a poet—so I don't have the words—but just think of it this way—that beach, that island—was filled with sons and fathers—men who loved and were loved—American and Japanese and Okinawan—and all of us were dying—were being killed by other sons and fathers who also loved and were loved.

Me: That sounds like poetry—tragic poetry—to me.

LE: Well, anyway, it was like that. Fire everywhere. And two of our boys—Jonesy and O'Neal—went down—were wounded in the open on the sand. And your grandfather—who was just this little man—barely five feet tall and maybe one hundred thirty pounds—he just ran out there and picked up those two guys—one on each shoulder—and carried them to cover. Hey, are you okay, son?

Me: Yes, I'm sorry. But, well, the thing is, I knew my grandfather was a war hero—he won twelve medals—but I could never find out what he did to win the medals.

LE: I didn't know about any medals. I just know what I saw. Your grandfather saved those two boys, but he got shot in the back doing it. And he laid there in the sand—I was lying right beside him—and he died.

Me: Did he say anything before he died?

LE: Hold on. I need to—

Me: Are you okay?

LE: It's just—I can't—

Me: I'm sorry. Is there something wrong?

LE: No, it's just—with your book and everything—I know you want something big here. I know you want something big from your grandfather. I knew you hoped he'd said something huge and poetic, like maybe something you could have written, and, honestly, I was thinking about lying to you. I was thinking about making up something as beautiful as I could. Something about love and forgiveness and courage and all that. But I couldn't think of anything good enough. And I didn't want to lie to you. So I have to be honest and say that your grandfather didn't say anything. He just died there in the sand. In silence.

11. Orphans

I was worried that I had a brain tumor. Or that my hydrocephalus had returned. I was scared that I was going to die and orphan my sons. But, no, their mother was coming home from Italy. No matter what happened to me, their mother would rescue them.

"I'll be home in sixteen hours," my wife said over the phone.

"I'll be here," I said. "I'm just waiting on news from my doctor."

12. Coffee Shop News

While I waited, I asked my brother-in-law to watch the boys again because I didn't want to get bad news with them in the room.

Alone and haunted, I wandered the mall, tried on new clothes, and waited for my cell phone to ring.

Two hours later, I was uncomposed and wanted to murder everything, so I drove south to a coffee joint, a spotless place called Dirty Joe's.

Yes, I was silly enough to think that I'd be calmer with a caffeinated drink.

As I sat outside on a wooden chair and sipped my coffee, I cursed the vague, rumbling, ringing noise in my ear. And yet, when my cell phone rang, I held it to my deaf ear.

"Hello, hello," I said and wondered if it was a prank call, then remembered and switched the phone to my left ear.

"Hello," my doctor said. "Are you there?"

"Yes," I said. "So, what's going on?"

"There are irregularities in your head."

"My head's always been wrong,"

"It's good to have a sense of humor," my doctor said. "You have a small tumor that is called a meningioma. They grow in the meninges membranes that lie between your brain and your skull."

"Shit," I said. "I have cancer."

"Well," my doctor said, "these kinds of tumors are usually noncancerous. And they grow very slowly, so in six months or so, we'll do another MRI. Don't worry. You're going to be okay."

"What about my hearing?" I asked.

"We don't know what might be causing the hearing loss, but you should start a course of Prednisone, the steroid, just to go with the odds. Your deafness might lessen if left alone, but we've had success with the steroids in bringing back hearing. There are side effects, like insomnia, weight gain, night sweats, and depression."

"Oh, boy," I said. "Those side effects might make up most of my personality already. Will the 'roids also make me quick to pass judgment? And I've always wished I had a dozen more skin tags and moles."

The doctor chuckled. "You're a funny man."

I wanted to throw my phone into a wall but I said good-bye instead and glared at the tumorless people and their pretty tumorless heads.

13. Meningioma

Mayoclinic.com defines "meningioma" as "a tumor that arises from the meninges — the membranes that surround your brain and spinal cord. The majority of meningioma cases are noncancerous (benign), though rarely a meningioma can be cancerous (malignant)."

Okay, that was a scary and yet strangely positive definition. No one ever wants to read the word "malignant" unless one is reading a Charles Dickens novel about an evil landlord, but "benign" and "majority" are two things that go great together.

From the University of Washington Medical School Web site I learned that meningioma tumors "are usually benign, slow growing, and do not spread into normal brain tissue. Typically, a meningioma grows inward, causing pressure on the brain or spinal cord. It may grow outward toward the skull, causing it to thicken."

So, wait, what the fuck? A meningioma can cause pressure on the brain and spinal fluid? Oh, you mean, just like fucking hydrocephalus? Just like the water demon that once tried to crush my brain and kill me? Armed with this new information — with these new questions — I called my doctor.

"Hey, you're okay," he said. "We're going to closely monitor you. And your meningioma is very small."

"Okay, but I just read—"

"Did you go on the Internet?"

dren's hearts, collectively and individually, 612 times and you did this without ever striking any human being in anger. Does this absence of physical violence make you a better man than you might otherwise have been?

• Without using the words "man" or "good," can you please define what it means to be a good man?

• Do you think you will see angels before you die? Do you think angels will come to escort you to heaven? As the angels are carrying you to heaven, how many times will you ask, "Are we there yet?"

• Your son distinctly remembers stopping once or twice a month at that grocery store in Freeman, Washington, where you would buy him a red-white-and-blue rocket popsicle and purchase for yourself a pickled pig foot. Your son distinctly remembers the feet still had their toenails and little tufts of pig fur. Could this be true? Did you actually eat such horrendous food?

• Your son has often made the joke that you were the only Indian of your generation who went to Catholic school on purpose. This is, of course, a tasteless joke that makes light of the forced incarceration and subsequent physical, spiritual, cultural, and sexual abuse of tens of thousands of Native American children in Catholic and Protestant boarding schools. In consideration of your son's questionable judgment in telling jokes, do you think there should be any moral limits placed on comedy?

• Your oldest son and your two daughters, all over thirty-six years of age, still live in your house. Do you think this is a lovely expression of tribal culture? Or is it a symptom of extreme familial codependence? Or is it both things at the same time?

• F. Scott Fitzgerald wrote that the sign of a superior mind "is the ability to hold two opposing ideas at the same time." Do you believe this is true? And is it also true that you once said, "The only time white people tell the truth is when they keep their mouths shut"?

• A poet once wrote, "Pain is never added to pain. It multiplies." Can you tell us, in twenty-five words or less, exactly how much we all hate mathematical blackmail?

• Your son, in defining you, wrote this poem to explain one of the most significant nights in his life:

"Yes."

"Which sites?"

"Mayo Clinic and the University of Washington."

"Okay, so those are pretty good sites. Let me look at them."

I listened to my doctor type.

"Okay, those are accurate," he said.

"What do you mean by accurate?" I asked. "I mean, the whole pressure on the brain thing, that sounds like hydrocephalus."

"Well, there were some irregularities in your MRI that were the burr holes from your surgery and there seems to be some scarring and perhaps you had an old concussion, but other than that, it all looks fine."

"But what about me going deaf? Can't these tumors make you lose hearing?"

"Yes, but only if they're located near an auditory nerve. And your tumor is not."

"Can this tumor cause pressure on my brain?"

"It could, but yours is too small for that."

"So, I'm supposed to trust you on the tumor thing when you can't figure out the hearing thing?"

"The MRI revealed the meningioma, but that's just an image. There is no physical correlation between your deafness and the tumor. Do the twenty-day treatment of Prednisone and the audiologist and I will examine your ear, and your hearing. Then, if there's no improvement, we'll figure out other ways of treating you."

"But you won't be treating the tumor?"

"Like I said, we'll scan you again in six to nine months   "

"You said six before."

"Okay, in six months we'll take another MRI, and if it has grown significantly—or has changed shape or location or anything dramatic—then we'll talk about treatment options. But if you look on the Internet, and I know you're going to spend a lot of time obsessing on this—as you should—I'll tell you what you'll find. About five percent of the population has these things and they live their whole lives with these undetected meningiomas. And they can become quite large—without any side effects—and are only found at autopsies conducted for other causes of death. And even when these kinds of tumors become invasive or dangerous they are still rarely fatal. And your tumor, even if it grows fairly quickly, will not likely become an issue for many years, decades. So that's what I can tell you right now. How are you feeling?"

"Freaked and fucked."

I wanted to feel reassured, but I had a brain tumor. How does one feel any optimism about being diagnosed with a brain tumor? Even if that brain tumor is neither cancerous nor interested in crushing one's brain?

14. Drugstore Indian

In Bartell's Drugs, I gave the pharmacist my prescription for Prednisone.

"Is this your first fill with us?" she asked.

"No," I said. "And it won't be the last."

I felt like an ass, but she looked bored.

"It'll take thirty minutes," she said, "more or less. We'll page you over the speakers."

I don't think I'd ever felt weaker, or more vulnerable, or more absurd. I was the weak antelope in the herd—yeah, the mangy fucker with the big limp and a sign that read, "Eat me! I'm a gimp!"

So, for thirty minutes, I walked through the store and found myself shoving more and more useful shit into my shopping basket, as if I were filling my casket with the things I'd need in the afterlife. I grabbed toothpaste, a Swiss Army knife, moisturizer, mouthwash, nonstick Band-Aids, antacid, protein bars, and extra razor blades. I grabbed pen and paper. And I also grabbed an ice scraper and sunscreen. Who can predict what weather awaits us in heaven?

This random shopping made me feel better for a few minutes but then I stopped and walked to the toy aisle. My boys needed gifts: Lego cars or something, for a lift, a shot of capitalistic joy. But the selection of proper toys is art and science. I have been wrong as often as right and heard the sad song of a disappointed son.

Shit, if I died, I knew my sons would survive, even thrive, because of their graceful mother.

I thought of my father's life: he was just six when his father killed in World War II. Then his mother, ill with tuberculosis, die few months later. Six years old, my father was cratered. In most wa he never stopped being six. There was no religion, no magic trick and no song or dance that helped my father.

Jesus, I needed a drink of water, so I found the fountain and dran and drank until the pharmacist called my name.

"Have you taken these before?" she asked.

"No," I said, "but they're going to kick my ass, aren't they?"

That made the pharmacist smile, so I felt sadly and briefly worthwhile. But another customer, some nosy hag, said, "You've got a lot of sleepless nights ahead of you."

I was shocked. I stammered, glared at her, and said, "Miss, how is this any of your business? Please, just fuck all the way off, okay?"

She had no idea what to say, so she just turned and walked away and I pulled out my credit card and paid far too much for my goddamn steroids, and forgot to bring the toys home to my boys.

15. Exit Interview for My Father

• True or False?: when a reservation-raised Native American dies of alcoholism it should be considered death by natural causes.

• Do you understand the term "wanderlust," and if you do, can you please tell us, in twenty-five words or less, what place made you wanderlust the most?

• Did you, when drunk, ever get behind the tattered wheel of a '76 Ford three-speed van and somehow drive your family one thousand miles on an empty tank of gas?

• Is it true that the only literary term that has any real meaning in the Native American world is "road movie"?

• During the last road movie you saw, how many times did th characters ask, "Are we there yet?"

• How many times, during any of your road trips, did your ch dren ask, "Are we there yet?"

• In twenty-five words or less, please define "there."

• Sir, in your thirty-nine years as a parent, you broke your c

Mutually Assured Destruction

When I was nine, my father sliced his knee
With a chain saw. But he let himself bleed
And finished cutting down one more tree
Before his boss drove him to EMERGENCY.

Late that night, stoned on morphine and beer,
My father needed my help to steer
His pickup into the woods. "Watch for deer,"
My father said. "Those things just appear

Like magic." It was an Indian summer
And we drove through warm rain and thunder,
Until we found that chain saw, lying under
The fallen pine. Then I watched, with wonder,

As my father, shotgun-rich and impulse-poor,
Blasted that chain saw dead. "What was that for?"
I asked. "Son," my father said, "here's the score.
Once a thing tastes blood, it will come for more."

• Well, first of all, as you know, you did cut your knee with a chain saw, but in direct contradiction to your son's poem:

A) You immediately went to the emergency room after injuring yourself.

B) Your boss called your wife, who drove you to the emergency room.

C) You were given morphine but even you were not alcoholically stupid enough to drink alcohol while on serious narcotics.

D) You and your son did not get into the pickup that night.

E) And even if you had driven the pickup, you were not injured seriously enough to need your son's help with the pedals and/or steering wheel.

F) You never in your life used the word "appear" and certainly never used the phrase "like magic."

G) You also agree that Indian summer is a fairly questionable seasonal reference for an Indian poet to use.

H) What the fuck is "warm rain and thunder"? Well, everybody knows what warm rain is, but what the fuck is warm thunder?

I) You never went looking for that chain saw because it belonged to the Spokane tribe of Indians and what kind of freak would want to reclaim the chain saw that had just cut the shit out of his knee?

J) You also agree that the entire third stanza of this poem sounds like a Bruce Springsteen song and not necessarily one of the great ones.

K) And yet, "shotgun-rich and impulse-poor" is one of the greatest descriptions your son has ever written and probably redeems the entire poem.

L) You never owned a shotgun. You did own a few rifles during your lifetime, but did not own even so much as a pellet gun during the last thirty years of your life.

M) You never said, in any context, "Once a thing tastes blood, it will come for more."

N) But you, as you read it, know that it is absolutely true and does indeed sound suspiciously like your entire life philosophy.

O) Other summations of your life philosophy include: "I'll be there before the next teardrop falls."

P) And: "If God really loved Indians, he would have made us white people."

Q) And: "Oscar Robertson should be the man on the NBA logo. They only put Jerry West on there because he's a white guy."

R) And: "A peanut butter sandwich with onions. Damn, that's the way to go."

S) And: "Why eat a pomegranate when you can eat a plain old apple. Or peach. Or orange. When it comes to fruit and vegetables, only eat the stuff you know how to grow."

T) And: "If you really want a woman to love you, then you have to dance. And if you don't want to dance, then you're going to have to work extrahard to make a woman love you forever, and you will always run the risk that she will leave you at any second for a man who knows how to tango."

U) And: "I really miss those cafeterias they used to have in Kmart. I don't know why they stopped having those. If there is a heaven then I firmly believe it's a Kmart cafeteria."

V) And: "A father always knows what his sons are doing. For instance, boys, I knew you were sneaking that *Hustler* magazine out of my bedroom. You remember that one? Where actors who looked like Captain Kirk and Lieutenant Uhura were screwing on the bridge of the *Enterprise*. Yeah, that one. I know you kept borrowing it. I let you borrow it. Remember this: men and pornography are like plants and sunshine. To me, porn is photosynthesis."

W) And: "Your mother is a better man than me. Mothers are almost always better men than men are."

16. Reunion

After she returned from Italy, my wife climbed into bed with me. I felt like I had not slept comfortably in years.

I said, "There was a rumor that I'd grown a tumor but I killed it with humor."

"How long have you been waiting to tell me that one?" she asked.

"Oh, probably since the first time some doctor put his fingers in my brain."

We made love. We fell asleep. But I, agitated by the steroids, woke at two, three, four, and five a.m. The bed was killing my back so I lay flat on the floor. I wasn't going to die anytime soon, at least not because of my little friend, Mr. Tumor, but that didn't make me feel any more comfortable or comforted. I felt distant from the world—from my wife and sons, from my mother and siblings—from all of my friends. I felt closer to those who've always had fingers in their brains.

And I didn't feel any closer to the world six months later when another MRI revealed that my meningioma had not grown in size or changed its shape.

"You're looking good," my doctor said. "How's your hearing?"

"I think I've got about ninety percent of it back."

"Well, then, the steroids worked. Good."

And I didn't feel any more intimate with God nine months later when one more MRI made my doctor hypothesize that my meningioma might only be more scar tissue from the hydrocephalus.

"Frankly," my doctor said. "Your brain is beautiful."

"Thank you," I said, though it was the oddest compliment I'd ever received.

I wanted to call up my father and tell him that a white man thought my brain was beautiful. But I couldn't tell him anything. He was dead. I told my wife and sons that I was okay. I told my mother and siblings. I told my friends. But none of them laughed as hard about my beautiful brain as I knew my father would have. I miss him, the drunk bastard. I would always feel closest to the man who had most disappointed me.

"Yes."

"Which sites?"

"Mayo Clinic and the University of Washington."

"Okay, so those are pretty good sites. Let me look at them."

I listened to my doctor type.

"Okay, those are accurate," he said.

"What do you mean by accurate?" I asked. "I mean, the whole pressure on the brain thing, that sounds like hydrocephalus."

"Well, there were some irregularities in your MRI that were the burr holes from your surgery and there seems to be some scarring and perhaps you had an old concussion, but other than that, it all looks fine."

"But what about me going deaf? Can't these tumors make you lose hearing?"

"Yes, but only if they're located near an auditory nerve. And your tumor is not."

"Can this tumor cause pressure on my brain?"

"It could, but yours is too small for that."

"So, I'm supposed to trust you on the tumor thing when you can't figure out the hearing thing?"

"The MRI revealed the meningioma, but that's just an image. There is no physical correlation between your deafness and the tumor. Do the twenty-day treatment of Prednisone and the audiologist and I will examine your ear, and your hearing. Then, if there's no improvement, we'll figure out other ways of treating you."

"But you won't be treating the tumor?"

"Like I said, we'll scan you again in six to nine months—"

"You said six before."

"Okay, in six months we'll take another MRI, and if it has grown significantly—or has changed shape or location or anything dramatic—then we'll talk about treatment options. But if you look on the Internet, and I know you're going to spend a lot of time obsessing on this—as you should—I'll tell you what you'll find. About five percent of the population has these things and they live their whole lives with these undetected meningiomas. And they can become quite large—without any side effects—and are only found at autopsies conducted for other causes of death. And even when these kinds of tumors become invasive or dangerous they are still rarely fatal. And your tumor, even if it grows fairly quickly, will not likely become an issue for many years, decades. So that's what I can tell you right now. How are you feeling?"

"Freaked and fucked."

I wanted to feel reassured, but I had a brain tumor. How does one feel any optimism about being diagnosed with a brain tumor? Even if that brain tumor is neither cancerous nor interested in crushing one's brain?

14. Drugstore Indian

In Bartell's Drugs, I gave the pharmacist my prescription for Prednisone.

"Is this your first fill with us?" she asked.

"No," I said. "And it won't be the last."

I felt like an ass, but she looked bored.

"It'll take thirty minutes," she said, "more or less. We'll page you over the speakers."

I don't think I'd ever felt weaker, or more vulnerable, or more absurd. I was the weak antelope in the herd—yeah, the mangy fucker with the big limp and a sign that read, "Eat me! I'm a gimp!"

So, for thirty minutes, I walked through the store and found myself shoving more and more useful shit into my shopping basket, as if I were filling my casket with the things I'd need in the afterlife. I grabbed toothpaste, a Swiss Army knife, moisturizer, mouthwash, nonstick Band-Aids, antacid, protein bars, and extra razor blades. I grabbed pen and paper. And I also grabbed an ice scraper and sunscreen. Who can predict what weather awaits us in heaven?

This random shopping made me feel better for a few minutes but then I stopped and walked to the toy aisle. My boys needed gifts: Lego cars or something, for a lift, a shot of capitalistic joy. But the selection of proper toys is art and science. I have been wrong as often as right and heard the sad song of a disappointed son.

Shit, if I died, I knew my sons would survive, even thrive, because of their graceful mother.

I thought of my father's life: he was just six when his father was killed in World War II. Then his mother, ill with tuberculosis, died a few months later. Six years old, my father was cratered. In most ways, he never stopped being six. There was no religion, no magic tricks, and no song or dance that helped my father.

Jesus, I needed a drink of water, so I found the fountain and drank and drank until the pharmacist called my name.

"Have you taken these before?" she asked.

"No," I said, "but they're going to kick my ass, aren't they?"

That made the pharmacist smile, so I felt sadly and briefly worthwhile. But another customer, some nosy hag, said, "You've got a lot of sleepless nights ahead of you."

I was shocked. I stammered, glared at her, and said, "Miss, how is this any of your business? Please, just fuck all the way off, okay?"

She had no idea what to say, so she just turned and walked away and I pulled out my credit card and paid far too much for my goddamn steroids, and forgot to bring the toys home to my boys.

15. Exit Interview for My Father

• True or False?: when a reservation-raised Native American dies of alcoholism it should be considered death by natural causes.

• Do you understand the term "wanderlust," and if you do, can you please tell us, in twenty-five words or less, what place made you wanderlust the most?

• Did you, when drunk, ever get behind the tattered wheel of a '76 Ford three-speed van and somehow drive your family one thousand miles on an empty tank of gas?

• Is it true that the only literary term that has any real meaning in the Native American world is "road movie"?

• During the last road movie you saw, how many times did the characters ask, "Are we there yet?"

• How many times, during any of your road trips, did your children ask, "Are we there yet?"

• In twenty-five words or less, please define "there."

• Sir, in your thirty-nine years as a parent, you broke your children's hearts, collectively and individually, 612 times and you did this without ever striking any human being in anger. Does this absence of physical violence make you a better man than you might otherwise have been?

• Without using the words "man" or "good," can you please define what it means to be a good man?

• Do you think you will see angels before you die? Do you think angels will come to escort you to heaven? As the angels are carrying you to heaven, how many times will you ask, "Are we there yet?"

• Your son distinctly remembers stopping once or twice a month at that grocery store in Freeman, Washington, where you would buy him a red-white-and-blue rocket popsicle and purchase for yourself a pickled pig foot. Your son distinctly remembers the feet still had their toenails and little tufts of pig fur. Could this be true? Did you actually eat such horrendous food?

• Your son has often made the joke that you were the only Indian of your generation who went to Catholic school on purpose. This is, of course, a tasteless joke that makes light of the forced incarceration and subsequent physical, spiritual, cultural, and sexual abuse of tens of thousands of Native American children in Catholic and Protestant boarding schools. In consideration of your son's questionable judgment in telling jokes, do you think there should be any moral limits placed on comedy?

• Your oldest son and your two daughters, all over thirty-six years of age, still live in your house. Do you think this is a lovely expression of tribal culture? Or is it a symptom of extreme familial codependence? Or is it both things at the same time?

• F. Scott Fitzgerald wrote that the sign of a superior mind "is the ability to hold two opposing ideas at the same time." Do you believe this is true? And is it also true that you once said, "The only time white people tell the truth is when they keep their mouths shut"?

• A poet once wrote, "Pain is never added to pain. It multiplies." Can you tell us, in twenty-five words or less, exactly how much we all hate mathematical blackmail?

• Your son, in defining you, wrote this poem to explain one of the most significant nights in his life:

Mutually Assured Destruction

When I was nine, my father sliced his knee
With a chain saw. But he let himself bleed
And finished cutting down one more tree
Before his boss drove him to EMERGENCY.

Late that night, stoned on morphine and beer,
My father needed my help to steer
His pickup into the woods. "Watch for deer,"
My father said. "Those things just appear

Like magic." It was an Indian summer
And we drove through warm rain and thunder,
Until we found that chain saw, lying under
The fallen pine. Then I watched, with wonder,

As my father, shotgun-rich and impulse-poor,
Blasted that chain saw dead. "What was that for?"
I asked. "Son," my father said, "here's the score.
Once a thing tastes blood, it will come for more."

• Well, first of all, as you know, you did cut your knee with a chain saw, but in direct contradiction to your son's poem:

A) You immediately went to the emergency room after injuring yourself.

B) Your boss called your wife, who drove you to the emergency room.

C) You were given morphine but even you were not alcoholically stupid enough to drink alcohol while on serious narcotics.

D) You and your son did not get into the pickup that night.

E) And even if you had driven the pickup, you were not injured seriously enough to need your son's help with the pedals and/or steering wheel.

F) You never in your life used the word "appear" and certainly never used the phrase "like magic."

G) You also agree that Indian summer is a fairly questionable seasonal reference for an Indian poet to use.

H) What the fuck is "warm rain and thunder"? Well, everybody knows what warm rain is, but what the fuck is warm thunder?

I) You never went looking for that chain saw because it belonged to the Spokane tribe of Indians and what kind of freak would want to reclaim the chain saw that had just cut the shit out of his knee?

J) You also agree that the entire third stanza of this poem sounds like a Bruce Springsteen song and not necessarily one of the great ones.

K) And yet, "shotgun-rich and impulse-poor" is one of the greatest descriptions your son has ever written and probably redeems the entire poem.

L) You never owned a shotgun. You did own a few rifles during your lifetime, but did not own even so much as a pellet gun during the last thirty years of your life.

M) You never said, in any context, "Once a thing tastes blood, it will come for more."

N) But you, as you read it, know that it is absolutely true and does indeed sound suspiciously like your entire life philosophy.

O) Other summations of your life philosophy include: "I'll be there before the next teardrop falls."

P) And: "If God really loved Indians, he would have made us white people."

Q) And: "Oscar Robertson should be the man on the NBA logo. They only put Jerry West on there because he's a white guy."

R) And: "A peanut butter sandwich with onions. Damn, that's the way to go."

S) And: "Why eat a pomegranate when you can eat a plain old apple. Or peach. Or orange. When it comes to fruit and vegetables, only eat the stuff you know how to grow."

T) And: "If you really want a woman to love you, then you have to dance. And if you don't want to dance, then you're going to have to work extrahard to make a woman love you forever, and you will always run the risk that she will leave you at any second for a man who knows how to tango."

U) And: "I really miss those cafeterias they used to have in Kmart. I don't know why they stopped having those. If there is a heaven then I firmly believe it's a Kmart cafeteria."

V) And: "A father always knows what his sons are doing. For instance, boys, I knew you were sneaking that *Hustler* magazine out of my bedroom. You remember that one? Where actors who looked like Captain Kirk and Lieutenant Uhura were screwing on the bridge of the *Enterprise*. Yeah, that one. I know you kept borrowing it. I let you borrow it. Remember this: men and pornography are like plants and sunshine. To me, porn is photosynthesis."

W) And: "Your mother is a better man than me. Mothers are almost always better men than men are."

16. Reunion

After she returned from Italy, my wife climbed into bed with me. I felt like I had not slept comfortably in years.

I said, "There was a rumor that I'd grown a tumor but I killed it with humor."

"How long have you been waiting to tell me that one?" she asked.

"Oh, probably since the first time some doctor put his fingers in my brain."

We made love. We fell asleep. But I, agitated by the steroids, woke at two, three, four, and five a.m. The bed was killing my back so I lay flat on the floor. I wasn't going to die anytime soon, at least not because of my little friend, Mr. Tumor, but that didn't make me feel any more comfortable or comforted. I felt distant from the world—from my wife and sons, from my mother and siblings—from all of my friends. I felt closer to those who've always had fingers in their brains.

And I didn't feel any closer to the world six months later when another MRI revealed that my meningioma had not grown in size or changed its shape.

"You're looking good," my doctor said. "How's your hearing?"

"I think I've got about ninety percent of it back."

"Well, then, the steroids worked. Good."

And I didn't feel any more intimate with God nine months later when one more MRI made my doctor hypothesize that my meningioma might only be more scar tissue from the hydrocephalus.

"Frankly," my doctor said. "Your brain is beautiful."

"Thank you," I said, though it was the oddest compliment I'd ever received.

I wanted to call up my father and tell him that a white man thought my brain was beautiful. But I couldn't tell him anything. He was dead. I told my wife and sons that I was okay. I told my mother and siblings. I told my friends. But none of them laughed as hard about my beautiful brain as I knew my father would have. I miss him, the drunk bastard. I would always feel closest to the man who had most disappointed me.

RACHEL AVIV

■

Like I Was Jesus

FROM *Harper's Magazine*

LAST SUMMER, FORTY CHRISTIAN missionaries, members of the
Child Evangelism Fellowship, roamed the housing projects of Connecticut telling children the condensed and colorful story of Jesus's
life. The goal was salvation, but the missionaries rarely used that
long word. They employed monosyllabic language and avoided abstract concepts and homonyms. "Holy" was a problem, the missionaries said, as children thought it meant "full of holes." "Christ rose
from the dead" was also tricky because children mistook the verb for
a flower.

One afternoon in July, on a basketball court in Waterbury, Scott
Harris, a black nine-year-old in an oversized sleeveless jersey, was
inspecting a wound on his knee. The wound was sloppily stitched
and looked grotesque, like a pair of lips. "I'm mad at Adam and Eve,"
Scott said to a missionary named Isaac Weaver. "If they hadn't eaten
that apple, there would be no more bushes, prickers, and bugs. I
wouldn't have busted my knee open."

"But do you ever think," Isaac asked, "'What if I were the first
one?' I think I'd probably make the same mistake as Eve."

"No, I wouldn't have tasted that fruit," said Scott, his voice high
and hoarse. "I'm trying not to get in trouble all the time. People say,
'Sit down,' and I'm already sitting down. They say, 'Be quiet,' and I'm
not even saying anything."

Isaac, twenty-six years old, blue-eyed, tan, and willowy, picked up
his EvangeCube, a plastic toy of eight interlocking blocks that tell the
Gospel in pictures. (The cube comes in a box that bears the slogan

UNFOLDING THE ANSWER TO LIFE'S GREATEST QUESTIONS.) He pointed to the image of heaven: a pastel hole in the clouds emanating milky rays of light. "You were right about Adam and Eve," Isaac said. "Where they lived, everything was perfect." He asked Scott if he knew his ABCs, and when the boy nodded, Isaac explained that "accepting Jesus is as easy as A B C. A stands for Admit you are a sinner. B is for Believe that Jesus went on the cross and died for your sins. And C is for Choose to accept Him as the boss of your life and go to heaven forever."

"But what if you sin when you're in heaven?" Scott took the Evange-Cube from Isaac and jiggled it in the air. The blocks flipped, moving from the picture of Jesus's crucifixion to heaven and back again.

"You don't."

"But what if you do?"

"You can't. You're in heaven."

"Oh, it's like an ability."

Isaac nodded vigorously. "Now, Scott, it's time to tell Jesus you believe what He did for you. And one day when Jesus comes back, He will make everything right."

"What?"

"Tell Him you believe He died to take your sins away," Isaac gently prodded.

"What does that mean?"

"It means you really do believe He came and took away your sins. Do you believe that?"

"Yeah, I do." Scott's nostrils flared. "You died for me — from taking my sins away."

Three young boys approached the basketball court, and Scott turned to watch them. When they called his name, he slowly stood up and dusted off the back of his nylon shorts. "I've got to play now," he told Isaac bashfully.

Isaac obliged, gathering together his props — the cube and a worn Bible, bristling with sticky notes. Although he and Scott had only gotten to "B: Believe," he said he was pleased with the conversation. It was the first time he had performed what the Fellowship calls "open-air evangelism," approaching strangers with no introduction besides "Do you want to hear a great story?" Before introducing himself to

Scott on the basketball court, he had been overtaken by anxiety. He sat down on the curb with another missionary, and they bowed their sweaty heads in prayer. "Father, I don't know if I can do this," Isaac said quietly, flicking a fly off his sneaker. "To me it seems like an odd thing to do. But, Lord, if this is what You are calling us to do, then I say no to fear. Please direct us to the right people so that we can show You to them. They need You. We need You."

The world's largest children's ministry, the Fellowship conceives of its mission as overseas proselytizers did at the turn of the twentieth century. Its members swoop down on deprived, often illiterate people and inundate them with foreign notions: "Jesus died on the cross"; "Because He loves me"; "I will meet Him in heaven." The missionaries' textbook, *Teaching Children Effectively: Level I*, instructs them to draft a map of each neighborhood they visit, drawing crosses by the homes where children have atoned for their sins. According to the Fellowship, once children begin to understand the difference between right and wrong—somewhere between the ages of five and twelve—they are cognitively capable of salvation, and, crucially, at risk for eternal damnation. After apologizing for wrongdoing and praying to accept the Lord's grace, children are pronounced "saved." Conversions often take less than ten minutes. Some hear the Gospel while on their bikes or while bathing in inflatable pools in their front yards. Others attend the Fellowship's Bible classes in parks, homes, and public schools. The ministry is based in Warrenton, Missouri, and maintains chapters in 158 countries and in every American state. It keeps careful count of the number of youngsters it has saved: last year, there were more than one million worldwide.

I followed the Connecticut ministry on its summer missions, often crouching beside children while they prayed to be reborn. Every day for a blisteringly hot week last July, Isaac drove a team of six teenage missionaries to Country Village Apartments, a grand name for a cluster of squat brick row houses arrayed in a U around a central road, the pavement cracked. The largely black and Hispanic neighborhood is located at the northern edge of Waterbury, a city of chain stores and abandoned brassware factories. When the missionaries arrived, they canvassed every home in the neighborhood, passing out

Bible club invitations to whoever answered the door: an elderly man in boxers in the midst of a teary phone call; a teenager on his way to work; a mother wearing a T-shirt that warned MOST LIKELY TO STEAL YOUR BOYFRIEND.

The majority of the missionaries were white—some had heard of the clubs through their local churches; a few had themselves been saved by the Fellowship—and they stuck out as they shuffled from door to door in their crisp khakis or long, loose skirts. They were loath to skip a single house, even when it was clear that nobody was home. Only once did I hear someone express concern about safety, when a fifteen-year-old shrieked that she'd seen a sign that said TRESPASSERS WILL BE PERSECUTED. In fact, it read TRESPASSERS WILL BE PROSECUTED, and she was put at ease when the distinction was made. She lived in a world of biblical proportions: prosecution was an abstraction while persecution felt probable and near.

The Bible clubs were held on a quilt under a drooping oak tree in the neighborhood park, close enough to the basketball court that children coming to play could be recruited for worship. Although parents were invited to observe the clubs, few attended. Some viewed them as free babysitting. The time was filled with songs, prayers, Bible stories, a personal tale about a missionary, and Scripture memorization. The missionaries taught the line, "For I am not ashamed of the Gospel of Christ: for it is the power of God unto salvation to everyone that believeth." They encouraged children to practice the sentence while hopping on one foot, twirling in place, patting their bellies, or tickling themselves. At the end of each session, an instructor asked the students to bow their heads and close their eyes. Those who wanted to "believe on Jesus"—missionaries use the outmoded phrase from the King James translation—were told to follow the instructor away from the quilt where in private they could rid themselves of their sins. They defined sin as "anything we think, say, or do that makes God sad," drawing a tear on their cheeks.

There were roughly nine children in the club, depending on the day, and several said the ABC steps for salvation and apologized for their sins: shouting, teasing, pushing, stealing, disobeying their mothers. (A few who attended did not complete the steps but seemed to enjoy the snacks.) The older children in particular warmed to the message that there was something deeply, irrevocably wrong with them. (The Fellowship heartily reinforces the doctrine of original sin.) Countless times I heard children articulate their guilt, amorphous but ever-present, by describing a fantasy that must have been learned from cartoons: an angel is fluttering over one shoulder, and Satan is hovering over the other; each is barking opposing commands.

Scott Harris, the most serious student in the class, was shaken by the discovery that numerous times a day he was personally distressing the Lord. "Yesterday I took ice cream without asking, and I started to tremble," he told me. He spoke with an embarrassed smile yet seemed eager to share his newfound religious commitment. "I knew I'd get in trouble. Later, I was throwing a ball with my friends, and I threw like a little baby. It only went like five inches. Jesus took away my strength, I think."

The children had a nebulous sense of time, and when they were told after club to return the next day at three o'clock, the reminder was useless. "But I don't have a clock," whimpered a six-year-old named Karizma. "And I don't know what three is." The notion that their lives could be transformed in a mere ten minutes did not seem to many children preposterous. The distinction between minutes, hours, and days does not bear much weight until one realizes that these markers will inevitably come to an end. The world described by the missionaries was far removed from the mundanity of school bells and bedtimes. The Bible offered entry into a fairy-tale realm where time is everlasting: the good creatures really do live happily ever after while the bad endure a dark eternity of pain. By saying their vows and consenting to the truth of the Bible, the children became players in a mythical tale that both preceded them and had called them into being. They could enter the story and choose their own ending.

When I first met Joshua Guido, the twenty-four-year-old director of the Child Evangelism Fellowship of Connecticut, I told him I had been an uncomfortably religious child, vaguely Jewish but mostly superstitious. I had worried that the Lord would punish me for bad behavior by killing my mother. I was constantly apologizing to Him: for stepping on my own shadow; closing the sock drawer too abruptly; turning the lights off before the moment when I felt a sign, a subtle thrumming through my body, that it was right to flick the switch. I thought I could become the words I spoke and would carefully avoid such threats as "death" (made worse because it rhymed with my mother's name, Beth) and "Hell." With the help of a few prayers I learned in Hebrew school, I turned the childhood taunt "Step on a crack, break your mother's back" into a religious worldview. It would have been a relief if someone had given me a rigid and alphabetized set of beliefs like those the Fellowship offers. (Instead, my parents sent me to therapy.)

Before I met Josh, one of the youngest state directors in the country, I had contacted Fellowship ministry directors in New York and New Jersey, but they both refused me access to their ministries when I told them I was writing for a secular publication. The Fellowship has never been forthcoming with the media, but since it won the right, in a controversial 2001 Supreme Court decision, to hold after-school Bible clubs in public schools, the leadership has been particularly skittish. In my initial talks with Josh at his office in Southington, a town twenty miles south of Hartford, we adopted a mode of conversation that I later realized was fundamental to the ministry: confession. I described how my early excess of religious energy, which dimmed by adolescence, had left me curious as to whether children are naturally inclined toward faith. Although Josh had some reservations about my religious background, he was open to outsiders and said he did not want to "interfere" in case I'd been sent by the Lord. It was clear that he hoped my work might lead to something more than an article, and he encouraged me to research not just through books but lived experience. Abstract learning, he warned, would not get me far. "Unless ye turn and become as little children," he quoted from Matthew, "Ye shall not enter the kingdom of heaven."

Josh, who has pale skin, soft, green eyes, and a long Italian nose, grew up in an evangelical Christian family in Waterbury. He has worked for the Fellowship since his teens, and, by his own reckoning, he has led more than a thousand people to Christ. A charismatic and disciplined man, he is well regarded among children and other Fellowship staff. "I'm not someone you look at and say, 'Oh wow, I could never be like him.' I'm pretty average, going by my IQ and SAT scores." For Josh, as for Isaac and many of the missionary leaders, speaking can become an exercise in self-abnegation. He does not choose what he reads, for instance, but lets "the Lord put certain books in my path." A ministry saying is "I cannot, but God can, so I will let Him do it through me." Josh believes children are an ideal receptacle for the Lord's words because they are still willing to believe, without proof, in the invisible. "The Muslims understand the importance of youth," he said. "So did the Communists." He sometimes recites the line, "Give me a child for five years, and I'll have him for the rest of his life." He attributed the quotation once to Adolf Hitler and another time to Fidel Castro. When his father, who is active in the ministry, delivered the same line, he cited Karl Marx.*

In the Book of Matthew, Jesus holds up the young child as the pinnacle of spiritual wisdom: "I praise You, Father, Lord of heaven and Earth, that You have hidden these things from the wise and intelligent and have revealed them to infants." In his radical vision, Jesus presents the child's faith—his undiminished sense of terror and awe—as a model for adults.

The Bible designates no age of accountability, or "age of reason," although the Church has seldom directed missionary activity toward children younger than seven. When Jesse Overholtzer, a self-described "unobtrusive little farmer" who founded the Child Evangelism Fellowship in 1937, first began counseling children, he hid it from his parishioners, unsure himself whether the effort was not in vain. He called it his "knicker and pigtail experiment." But what was once a tentative venture has gained increasing acceptance among evangelical Christians. In the past half-century, the born-again child has been emblazoned as an ideal believer, a mascot for anti-intellectualism. In his 2003 book *Transforming Children into Spiritual Champions*, George Barna, a pioneer in the field of religious marketing, scolds the evangelical community for neglecting youngsters—"the great myth of modern ministry: adults are where the Kingdom action is"—and treating them merely as "people en route to significance." Barna produces his own calculations to show that between the ages

---

* The source is more likely a Jesuit maxim, "Give me the child, I will give you the man," sometimes attributed to St. Ignatius Loyola.

of five and twelve, there is the greatest "probability of someone embracing Jesus as his or her Savior."

In course books and publicity materials, the Fellowship proudly cites Barna's many statistics. *Teaching Children Effectively: Level I* calls children a "harvest field . . . virtually untouched" and blames this oversight on a culture that distorts the importance of intellect: "subtle worldly philosophies have persuaded the majority of Christians that children cannot make a decision for Christ until they can 'reason.'" In the textbook's top-ten list of "Satan's Attacks on the Child," number three, after drugs and sex, is "humanism," man's capacity for fulfillment through the mind.

In the United States, the Fellowship's arena for battling these worldly philosophies has been the legal system. By the 1980s, a series of court decisions had effectively removed religious groups from campus during the school day. In 1996, the Fellowship gained a renewed sense of mission when it sued Milford Central School in upstate New York for preventing it from holding Good News Clubs on school premises. In its request to the school board, the ministry described the clubs, which were held at three p.m., four minutes after the end of the last class of the day, as "a group of boys and girls meeting one hour a week for a fun time of singing songs, hearing a Bible lesson, and memorizing scripture."

Five years later, in a 6–3 decision, the Supreme Court ruled in the Fellowship's favor, accusing the school district of "viewpoint discrimination," because it permitted other after-school clubs, such as the Boy Scouts and 4H, to use its facilities. In his dissent, Justice David Souter wrote that the "majority's statement ignores reality" and stands for the "remarkable proposition that any public school opened for civic meetings must be opened for use as church, synagogue, or mosque." Steven K. Green, the former legal director of Americans United for Separation of Church and State who filed a brief on behalf of Milford, said, "The instruction takes place in the same school, with snacks, to attract the kids. It's a little devious. They know if they held it an hour later, the children wouldn't show up. They are trying to dovetail into the school machinery. For many young children, there won't be any distinction between this and the rest of the school day. It is a seamless web."

Since the ruling, the Fellowship, funded by donations, has en-
gaged in more than twenty follow-up suits against schools that refused to comply with the Milford decision. Hundreds of other cases
not directly involving the Fellowship have cited the ruling, leading to
a level of church-state entanglement that had been prohibited for decades. Meanwhile, the number of Good News Clubs in public schools
has quietly and steadily swelled. The ministry held 1,155 after-school
clubs in 2000; in 2007, there were 3,956, reaching 137,361 children.
Jaimie Fales, the Fellowship's spokesperson, says that she still hears
people complaining about the good old days before "they took God
out of the schools. I have to remind them, 'Hey, listen, you can have
prayer in public schools! You can have the Bible in public schools!
That's just complaining. We can do it. We just got to get up and *actually* do it! The Supreme Court flung the doors wide open.'" Mathew
Staver, a Liberty Counsel lawyer who represents the Fellowship, has
asserted that the cases "literally turned back the historical clock."

If the ministry longs for an earlier stage of history, it also affirms
a cruder and more elementary kind of faith, one suited to the child's
inchoate cognitive abilities. "We shall no doubt come across analo-
gies between the child and the primitive at every step," wrote the psy-
chologist Jean Piaget, whose work is cited throughout Milford's court
briefs as evidence that a child believes indiscriminately in the "infal-
libility of adult authority." Piaget found that the child does not yet
know the limits of his own mind and confuses "his self with the universe." He believes in an anthropomorphic God—a doting, towering
man who watches his every movement—because it is the only one
he can imagine.

The notion that the young mind allows us access to an earlier historical era is one that has been repeatedly, if carelessly, articulated by
scholars for centuries. Auguste Comte argued that the life of an individual recapitulates human history, beginning in a theological stage
and maturing to scientific thought. The Fellowship, too, equates children with a more primitive phase in our culture. It reaches backward
in time, creating a community that is still vulnerable, prone to magi-
cal explanations, and free of secular learning. Children are predis-
posed to the fundamentalist's literal mode of reading. Unlike adults,
they are not yet suspicious of the way that stories—with their seduc-

tive yet predictable arcs—try to capture our imaginations. They can still surrender to the world of a narrative.

At a ten-day training camp last June in the bucolic town of Cornwall-ville, New York, Josh, Isaac, and half a dozen other seasoned evange-lists supervised the training of thirty missionaries between the ages of eleven and twenty. To learn techniques for presenting the Gospel simply, the young missionaries attended six hours of daily classes in a cavernous barn-shaped dining hall. They were genial, poised, and proudly helpless. When they traveled, they drove in a long, slow line of cars, and only those in the front vehicle knew where they were going. (By the end of the summer, several of the missionaries' cars were dented.) The girls had angelic voices, high and lilting, and fre-quently professed their love: for one another, Jesus, black kids, the color green, Chinese food, the smell of gas. The more time I spent with them, the more I came to feel crass and overgrown (made worse when I got poison ivy on my legs from sitting in a playground). They were always friendly and respectful and rarely asked questions, al-though once, when I responded to an anecdote by calling a coinci-dence lucky, they took care to correct me. There is no such thing as "luck," one girl made clear, curling her fingers into quotation marks.

The missionaries juggled two stories and casts of characters at once: a biblical reality and a far more messy and banal existence. The Lord was both the narrator and the love of their lives. With His guidance, their experiences were no longer fragmented but plotted and saturated with meaning. One of the older trainees, Katharine, a twenty-year-old from an affluent suburb of Hartford, explained that she associated her distaste for men ("As a general rule, I avoid them") with her fear of losing her attachment to this narrative. "Every little girl wants to be a princess," she told me. "I became one when I ac-cepted the love that Christ was offering me. That's one of the reasons I became so wary around guys. Although I had accepted that gift, I didn't want it to become so commonplace that I was willing to trade it for any—I guess what you would call Earth relationships."

The missionaries displayed little interest in works of fiction not in-spired by the Lord, and they had a radical approach to reading. They referred to the Gospel simply as "the Story." The Bible's sentences did not just express love, they *were* love—a gift from the Lord. *Teaching Children Effectively* instructed them to describe heaven as a fairy-tale village that would become the home of every believer, the ultimate happy ending: "There is a street of gold—pure like glass . . . No one is ever sick there. No one ever dies. There is no night. Every person in heaven will be perfectly happy—always." The question that follows so many bedtime stories—"Is it true?"—can at last be answered with certainty. Children are offered the possibility of believing, wholly and unabashedly, an extraordinary tale. They can permanently suspend disbelief. "The Bible is not just on a shelf," one instructor, Jennifer Curtis (affectionately called "the philosopher"), told the class. "Kids are growing up with so many half-truths—but here is a book that is finally all true. The book is alive."

Just after nine one morning in the dining hall, its ten large windows overlooking miles of green hills, the missionaries' textbooks, sweaters, and tote bags splattered on top of portable cafeteria tables, Josh began a forty-five-minute lesson titled "How to Use the EvangeCube." It proved to be one of the camp's liveliest discussions. Josh asked the class whether they had the authority to edit frightening details out of the Story. When many expressed fear that this would violate the sanctity of the Lord's message, Josh asked them to think about how they would describe Hell if mothers were watching. "What are you going to do with a class of suburban five-year-olds? Soccer moms, and they're from Wethersfield, Connecticut. These are rich, educated people."

"We shouldn't water it down," said Jake, a stout boy with blond hair and a thick jaw who had appeared lethargic in previous sessions but now spoke with a new energy. "If it's the truth, it's the truth."

Josh considered the comment. "Yes, we do have to make it clear that there's a punishment if they don't accept Jesus as their best friend. It's not just like, 'Okay, gotta find another friend!' No, there's a punishment." He leaned against a metal music stand that functioned as his lectern. "But does it count if someone is saved based on fear of Hell? Salvation is not just fire insurance."

A Hispanic boy, Tim, raised his hand. Eleven years old, he was the youngest missionary in the group. "It is not wise to make a child afraid," he managed in a wavering voice.

"But you have to let Jesus show them the truth!" interrupted Jake. "Jesus died on the cross for us — you can't say it any other way!"

Josh paced at the front of the room, increasingly ill at ease. He pushed up the sleeves of his blue button-down shirt. "But what is the truth?" he asked. His question was not as existentially charged as it sounded; his uncertainty extended only to whether children must be told all facets of the Story for their salvation to be complete.

"We don't need to worry about which word will go where," suggested a twiggy blonde girl in khaki slacks, a silver necklace, and a padded training bra under her T-shirt that made her chest look like a gym mat. "It should be the Holy Spirit speaking, and He's not going to mess up." (Over the campfire one night, she had said that she prayed to "get smaller and smaller so that God will take over completely.")

A few people said, "Amen." The class seemed exhausted by the discussion and ready to give up all agency. It was an easy method of escape but a slippery one.

"I don't want to hear the word 'save' again," said Josh's fifteen-year-old brother Seth. "We're using that word too much. Let's just tell it the way we want, and let God do his work. If you pray about it ahead of time, you'll be fine."

"We're just tools," another said, sighing. "Jesus will move us around."

One of the most effective missionaries was Oscar, an amiable thirteen-year-old Hispanic boy with small features and shiny black hair that flopped onto his forehead. He had already saved thirty-five children the previous summer. At the Country Village Bible clubs, he talked in a breathless and inspired pant and became friends with his younger students, often borrowing their video games or bikes before class. Of all the missionaries, he had the least trouble speaking what they called "childrenese," and he was usually chosen to tell a Bible story about Jesus healing a crippled man or calming the sea. At the end of the story, he would ask the class to bow their heads and close their eyes. "Boys and girls, if you have never believed on Jesus, you have a problem," he said, unconsciously adopting the cadences of local TV commercials. "But if you'd like to receive Jesus as your savior, you can do it today. You can have a friendship with God that starts right now and goes on forever."

Oscar transformed the poetry of the Bible into something so spare and literal it nearly sounded blasphemous, but the children seemed to comprehend best his version of the Story, purged of abstractions. Each time Oscar counseled a child, he repeated roughly the same script, which he had memorized at training camp. To make the message personal, he asked the child's age and promptly reminded him that "Jesus was your age once, too." Then he asked the age of the child's mother and remarked, "Jesus died at about your mom's age," a detail likely more unsettling than he realized.

On the second day of club, Scott Harris followed Oscar to a shady patch of grass, about ten yards away from the rest of the group, to finish the conversation about Jesus that Isaac started on the basketball court. Sitting cross-legged with his hands between his legs, Scott listened for the second time to the story of Jesus's life, illustrated through the EvangeCube. He was particularly attentive when Oscar arrived at the image of Jesus splayed out on the cross, blood dripping from his wrists. "God really did die for our sins," Oscar said.

"I know," said Scott. "They whipped Him with whips. Spiky whips, and they kept hitting Him."

"Yeah, but Jesus made a way so that we don't have to go there." Oscar pushed his glasses up to his face with his palm. "Because He loves you so much. Nobody else could have come back to life. But He's God. Have you ever seen a dirty shirt? What happens when you put it in the washing machine?"

"It gets clean?"

"Yeah, Jesus wanted us all to be clean. Now you have a choice. If you ask God into your heart, you can become clean."

Scott nodded, his knees bobbing.

"Do you need a little help?"

Scott nodded again, eager to please the older boy.

"Say 'Dear God.'"

Scott pinched his eyes shut. "Dear God."

"Tell God you have sinned."

"I have sinned," he said, a bit too loudly. "Can You please forgive me?"

"When you're all done, just say 'Amen.'"

"Amen."

"Lord, thank You for Scott," Oscar said. "Right now Scott is going to heaven."

His face flushed, Scott stood up and followed Oscar back to the quilt for the final minutes of club. With the other children, he sang a peppy tune called "God Is So Good," and then lined up for cookies and juice.

The week after the clubs ended, I returned to Country Village Apartments to see the children who had accepted Christ as their savior. Although the Fellowship follows up with some children through Good News Clubs during the school year and with others by mail, many the missionaries never see again. The children are left on their own to make sense of the new contract they've struck with the Lord.

While several parents had chosen not to send their children to the clubs — usually with a quick "No thanks, we're not interested" — those who had allowed it were equally trusting when I knocked on their doors. None of them chose to be present for my interviews. Scott, whose family lives in Tennessee, was in Waterbury spending the summer with a family friend who was Catholic but not observant. She lived in a small, dimly lit two-story house crammed with furniture. When I visited, three children from the neighborhood were watching television on her couch, and she was holding an infant in her arms. She did not know whether Scott's family believed in Jesus, nor did it seem a particularly relevant topic of conversation. "I don't think Scott would care if the clubs were Christian or not," she said, stroking the baby's back. "As long as it can hold his attention, it must be doing something right."

Scott and his two friends, Jamal and Lamar Sims, were more enthusiastic. We sat by the oak tree where the clubs had been held and they shared one popsicle I had brought, cutting it into equal sections with a plastic knife. All of them recognized me from club meetings — I imagined that they saw me as one of the Bible teachers, the silent, boring one—and it took several minutes to establish that I was just a writer and that my visit would be devoid of songs and prayers. Because I had not brought a blanket, none of them wanted to sit down. They said there were ants in the grass: Scott sat on a rock, Lamar stood up, and his younger brother, Jamal, who was nine, kneeled on the ground.

While all three children had prayed to Jesus to wash away their sins, Jamal and Lamar, who said they did not come from a religious family, had not appeared particularly moved by the process, and I was surprised by how much importance they later assigned to their conversion. On these long, blank summer days, they had been waiting for a tangible sign that Jesus had, indeed, altered their lives, as the missionaries promised. They were filled with a sense of their own potential.

"I thought we'd start helping people," said Lamar, a handsome twelve-year-old who wore a jersey so large that most of his chest peeked out through the armholes. "If someone was having a baby, we'd just take them to the hospital and leave. We'd want to be good." He walked behind me and leaned against the tree. "Nothing changed." When I asked him if he would consider going back to the club to try again, he became plaintive. "I took my heart out for God. One time should be enough."

Scott was more hopeful about his conversion. He said that it made him feel "smart." "I don't know why, but I'll get a feeling," he said. "God, like, reads your mind. He knows your brain. He crawls up inside you."

At home, in Knoxville, Scott had gone to a "big church with singers," and he said that since the age of six he had been praying—usually that it wouldn't rain, because he didn't like when he couldn't play outside. Disapprovingly, he added that his older sisters "only believe in God when it thunders." I asked Scott if he knew what kind of Christian he was, and Lamar suggested he might be "African American." "No, I'm not," Scott said, shaking his head. "Yes, you are," insisted Lamar. "You're black—that's what you call a black person, 'African American.'"

Scott had been chronicling his spiritual progress through his cut-up knee. At the Bible club, he had listened carefully when Oscar told the story about Jesus healing a paralytic by saying the words, "Your sins are forgiven . . . stand up and walk." Scott assumed the same would happen to him, although he could walk just fine. But it had been a week since his fall, and he touched the scab so much that he kept reopening parts of the wound. "I'd been hoping He'd heal me, but I think He just sits there and watches," he explained, bending his head near his knee and examining the tiny scab particles. "But it is getting better now. I think He takes care of me a week after I do it. See, I busted it open last Wednesday, and nothing happened. But He started healing me a week after. He listens a week late pretty much." He sounded increasingly certain of this impromptu theory.

Having only recently learned to narrate their experiences, children see patterns and correspondences in everything. James W. Fowler, in his 1981 work *Stages of Faith*, a psychological study of religious development, writes that children are more disposed than adults toward "Hierophanies, the giving of signs — both blessed and cursed." Through the passage of time, most of us learn to discard these invisible threads of connection — the signs we once thought were ominous prove meaningless, and moments that felt Promethean pass without memory.

The missionaries attempted to present the Bible as clearly and simply as possible, but it was the rigidity of their lessons that ultimately disoriented the children I spoke to. As they discovered that, in fact, the Lord had not swooped down to heal their wounds and scrapes and disappointments, the new beliefs they had adopted seemed destined to break down, along with whatever was driving them to have faith in the first place. And that original impulse may have been quite simple: something is wrong with me; it is out of my control. Perhaps Jesus's praise for the child is simply an acknowledgment of that primal sentiment — lonely fear in its purest form.

When I asked the three boys if they could imagine the world if God had never existed, they got lost in a mess of apocalyptic plot details.

"The world would be crappy," said Scott, under his breath.

"No one would be living," added Lamar. "We wouldn't be here."

"The dinosaurs would still be killing us!" Jamal said.

"No," Lamar corrected him, "there wouldn't be any dinosaurs. God wouldn't have ever created dinosaurs, because He wouldn't be here."

Jamal looked around the park. His eyes darting, he pulled a clump of grass from the ground. "True, true. The tree wouldn't be right here. There wouldn't be grass. We'd probably be beat up by a lot of people and never die."

"How can we be beat up when we're not even alive anymore? We wouldn't be thinking. We wouldn't even know what's happening."

"We would be in the caves, tortured," said Jamal, as if he hadn't yet processed his older brother's words.

"We wouldn't be alive!" insisted Lamar.

Scott, who had been quiet throughout the conversation, suddenly perked up. "Mary. Mary would be there."

"Who's Mary?" Jamal asked.

"God's mom."

"Oh, yeah," Lamar said. "Then she would have created us. God's mom."

The Fellowship has established a robust presence in the public schools of Southern states; last year, in South Carolina, after-school Good News Clubs in 183 public schools reached 13,524 children. The Connecticut Fellowship has made fewer inroads. In the past few years, it focused its after-school efforts on three districts: two in rural towns in eastern Connecticut and one in Wolcott, near Waterbury. Thomas Smyth, the superintendent of Wolcott Public Schools, received several letters from Josh Guido and the Fellowship's lawyers before approving the clubs. The memos he showed me were rife with such watery sentences as, "We strive to promote positive moral character, provide training, and reinforce values." Smyth had only a vague sense of the club's activities, except that the missionaries had offered to help children with their homework (a task for which they were not trained). "For single moms, that was a big hook," he told me. "Parents wanted the kids to get assistance with homework, even if they had to sit through the Gospel message."

Although after-school clubs are a relatively new piece of the Fellowship's mission, Josh says that they have become the predominant measure of success. "At conferences, everyone is asking how many schools you have," he told me. "No one is asking how many projects you have." Josh prefers holding clubs in city housing developments because he does not have to waste time on legal negotiations, and he can reach more children at once. After every session, missionaries call Josh to report the number of children led to Christ. "When someone says, 'Oh, it's not about the numbers,' often those are the ones who didn't reach many. They'll say, 'It's not about quantity, it's about quality.' I say, 'No, if you were one of the numbers that didn't get reached, you would care.'"

Of course, Josh believed that I, too, should be reached, and he frequently spoke of my soul with thinly disguised homilies ("You go to a gas station, you're lost, and you need directions . . ."). His language would become hackneyed, and I would find myself tuning out. Josh was far more arresting when he spoke of his own beliefs, which felt intimate and mystical, beyond words. He was empowered by the acknowledgment of his own helplessness. His conversations with God were so encompassing that he admitted he would leave friends voicemail messages and accidentally end the call by saying, "In Jesus's name, Amen," confusing the phone message with a prayer. There was little distinction between the spiritual reality he felt and the actual one he lived, and this convergence, I assumed, was why he continued to feel so hopeful about the potential for my salvation. He must have taken comfort in the idea that my resistance to Jesus would make my ultimate submission more beautiful. I imagined that he thought of me as a version of the Samaritan woman at the well in the Book of John who, while waiting for someone to "explain everything," recognizes what she has failed to comprehend. If Josh did not take favorably to this article and decided I was blind, I might be cast in a new role: someone who tests, and ultimately affirms, his faith. Perhaps one of the Pharisees who know not the extent of their foolishness.

The last time I visited Josh at his office in Southington, he was in an expansive mood, looser than I had ever seen him before. We sat in a small, stuffy conference room, at the corner of a long table used for staff meetings. With considerable calm, he told me he was contemplating marriage. When he began speculating about where he and his bride-to-be would live, he became visibly excited. He told me he wanted to move to Laurel Estates, a predominantly black and Hispanic housing development in Waterbury where the ministry had held two Bible clubs the previous summer. He would buy an apartment and "adopt the community." He leaned forward against the desk, with his palms on the table. "In John, it says, 'The Word became flesh and dwelt among us.'" As he often did, Josh offered a Jewish analogue for me; Moses, too, built his tent in the wilderness, and it has always been God's will to reside among his people. "It would just be so exciting to be Jesus to them, to have the kids over every week for pizza and movies." His dream of a simple life would require a total immersion in the narrative. He would become a character, too.

It was not the first time I had heard someone admit to identifying so intensely with Jesus that he felt he could actually become Him. The most devout child I met at all the summer Bible clubs was Edwin Pareles, a tall, articulate nine-year-old with wire-rim glasses who lived in a public-housing complex in Hartford. He attended a Pentecostal church with his father, and he had already heard many stories about Jesus. Still, he called his conversion with Oscar, atop a rusted playground slide, "the most important moment of my life."

After the missionaries had left, I asked Edwin to reflect on his conversion. "I was pretending like I was at the beach with Jesus," he said, sitting on the untrimmed lawn outside his barrackslike brick apartment. "There were some huge waves coming to me, but Jesus said, 'Don't worry about the waves, I'm here.' I felt great because Jesus was with me. I felt I was a grown-up already. I was feeling like I was Jesus."

Edwin had been so inspired by the clubs that he said he, too, wanted to become "the kind of missionary that tells poor people about God." Although he was excited by the prospect of answering abstract questions — "This is philosophical," he asserted proudly — he had a habit of suddenly losing the thread of his thought. He described its loss as something tangible, as if an idea had been placed in his mind by an outside force and then suddenly whisked away. After a long conversation about the books he liked to read (tales of gothic fantasy), he told me, "In my head I'm thinking of a question from the Devil."

His younger brother ran across the lawn in a futile attempt to catch a bee with a Gatorade bottle. I asked Edwin what the question was, and he said he had already forgotten. "Boom! It just erased."

When I visited him the next day, he said he had remembered the question, but this time it came from a dream. It was not clear whether it was a dream at all or just a new thought he wasn't sure was his own. He sat with his knees pressed close to his body on the overgrown lawn in front of his apartment. "The Devil told me the story of Jesus rising is kind of like *Goosebumps*," he said, referring to R.L. Stine's popular horror novellas, Edwin's favorite books. He paused and looked up at me to see if I had followed his logic, which had drawn him, for one fleeting moment, to an unnerving conclusion: the Bible was not inherently distinct in shape from a work of fiction. Jesus was like many triumphant heroes, Satan like many villains. When I asked him what made the Bible feel different, he quickly explained away his anxiety. "Well, there's something about Jesus," he said. "Everyone talks about Him, and then you believe in Him. And when you see Him on the cross, then you *really* believe in Him." Now he was on more stable ground. The afternoon sun reflected off his glasses, and he looked calm and studious. "Jesus died for our sins. All R. L. Stine did was make a book for us. That's the big difference."

The Bible promises to reach out and absorb its readers, to sweep them into its tale. Edwin took comfort in the idea that his future was already written. "Sometimes when my brother is asleep and the TV is off, I imagine God standing in my room," he said. "I hear Him whispering, 'I will come for you, son. I will come.'"

NORA BONNER

■

Burying Jeremy Green

FROM Shenandoah

ON THE PLAYGROUND, we held pretend funerals for Jeremy Green. The boys fought over who got to play the corpse and who got to play the preacher. The girls fought over who got to play his wife and who wouldn't have to play his three-year-old daughter. The other roles we created: his overbearing father, his frazzled mother, his irritating aunt, his twin sister who got straight As in school and never did anything wrong, his bitter younger brother, his loyal best friend, his pregnant lover. The rest of us, the quiet ones, sat back and watched service after service, reenacted for clarity about who this guy was, why he ended his life, and why he chose us for the witnesses.

The fifth graders were the last to enjoy recess at Sojourner Elementary. Our school had three fifth-grade classes, and on the playground we divided: the soccer kids ran up and down the center and everyone else scattered around the edges. Before Jeremy came, we played jump rope or cat's cradle. We sat along the fence and told fortunes with paper we folded into cootie catchers. We chewed gum, forbidden in classrooms, and held contests to see who could blow the biggest bubble. On the playground, we played drinking games with extra cartons of chocolate milk, the rules for which we'd learned from our older siblings. We forced each other to tell secrets and made lists of things we had to do before we died. We learned to wrap our lips around cuss words and wrote our names in the ground with broken glass. This was how Jeremy Green found us.

We played in a lot surfaced with gravel and surrounded by a chain-link fence. Several of the rocks were the size of our fifth-grade fists.

They were dark and iridescent, glittering like they'd exploded in outer space, caught on fire and cooled among the candy wrappers and empty liquor bottles and cigarette butts. Smaller pieces slipped into our sneakers and cut into the soles of our feet. Each September—and Jeremy came during this time—prickly weeds grew over the north side, over the baseball field, and we'd spend the rest of the day picking burrs out of our socks and sticking them on each other's backs so that when we leaned into chairs, they'd dig into our skin. We had no play equipment, just a slab of cement for foursquare, a backstop, and a bench we never used for baseball. Our funerals took place in front of one of those backstops. The kid playing Jeremy would lie down on the bench with his arms folded on his chest like he was some kind of a vampire. His family would sit off to the right, his lover waited behind the backstop for her cue, and the preacher would start us off with a couple of phrases he'd picked up from television eulogies:

"We are gathered here to remember the life of Jeremy Green."

His mother and sister would wail, his father would cough and we'd hum "Amazing Grace" in the background.

"We're shocked by his death, and though we grieve, we are here to remember the good things about the life of Jeremy Green."

His sister walked slowly to Jeremy with a bundle of dandelions and laid them on his chest. He sneezed and brushed them off. Then she turned to us, her eyes on her Velcro tennis shoes, and begged us to remember Jeremy for his intelligence, his sense of humor and his ability to take apart electronic devices and put them back together. "He always wanted to be an inventor," she'd say. "But he just didn't apply himself." Then she'd kneel down by his head, pull out a wad of Kleenex and dab her dry eyes. "It was my fault," she'd confess. "I always made him go away when my friends came over. I never let him play with us." The preacher would then put his arm around her and tell her it was all right, that we all played a part in the death of Jeremy Green.

"Jeremy never wanted to harm nobody." Jeremy's best friend spoke next. "But if anyone tried to mess with me, I could always count on Jeremy to back me up."

At this point, his mother would fling her arms in the air and shout at Jeremy's friend, falling over her husband: "it's because of you that my baby is dead! If it weren't for you, he never would've been arrested!" His father would calm her, telling her to hush. She'd yell: "he never would've gone to prison!"

"Don't try to blame Jeremy on me!" his friend would snap back. "Maybe if you hadn't dropped him on his head so many times he would have actually been somebody when he grew up."

The preacher would urge them to sit back down. They listened to him, and we waited for his aunt.

"Jeremy did my grocery shopping for me. I always asked him to pick me up a bag of cheese puffs. I love those." We laughed. "Then one night he just ran off with my money. I waited all night for those cheese puffs." The preacher tried to interrupt her, to tell her we were just there to remember the good things, but she'd go on, wailing that Jeremy was her favorite nephew, that she loved him like her own son. She loved to bake him his favorite cookies, snickerdoodles, and she loved to take him to hockey games. "I just don't know what happened to him."

His brother would get up and tell us that Jeremy used to be handsome, that he was the prom king, and that he made all the other guys jealous. His grade-school teacher would get up and apologize for always picking on him and giving him a hard time, and his wife would get up and say that he wasn't very dependable, but he sure was funny. His daughter would stay seated and suck her thumb.

The preacher would then call on Jeremy's father to speak last. He'd stand with his hands in his blue jeans pockets and shake his head. "I don't know what to say."

The preacher would beckon him, "Go on, let's hear what's on your mind."

"He was my son."

"Yes."

"He was my baby boy."

"Jeremy was a son," the preacher reminded us, raising his voice in a dramatic lilt. This was his favorite part of the service. "He was a brother, a cousin, a nephew, a friend." His mother wailed. "He was a husband and a father." This was the cue for Jeremy's lover to jump out from behind the backstop and announce that she was pregnant with his second child. We'd gasp. His wife would run at her, and the preacher would hold her back. We'd shriek and egg them on by clapping our hands and chanting for them to fight.

We did this pretty much every afternoon, until one time when Jeremy's lover missed her cue. We found her behind the backstop, clutching the chain link and listening to a distant siren from the main road. We, too, noticed the sound and filed along the fence beside her. The cry grew into a roar, shaking the air and the cool metal beneath our palms. When the sirens diminished, we didn't move. We peered at the now-silent neighborhood through wiry frames in the shapes of diamonds. Cardboard cutouts of skeletons and reindeer hung lopsided in curtain-less windows, deflated snowmen slumped in white piles on untended lawns. Nobody ever went in or out of those houses while we played during recess, and before Jeremy came, it was as though we were the only living creatures for miles; just us on that gravel pit of a playground.

The principal held an all-school assembly in place of recess the day after Jeremy came. Not one of our wooden seats creaked while she spoke to us in strained tones. She said we needed to be careful about what we say, but we should maintain a sense of pride because, on that day, we could all think of ourselves as survivors. She said all of this with her weight pressed into the piano at the bottom of the stage. Behind her, the dusty red curtains were pulled to the side, revealing Woody Guthrie's wheat fields and redwoods painted in loose, bold strokes, leftover from last year's all-school music revue. With her arms folded, unless she was pushing up her glasses, she told us she knew we wanted to talk about it, but begged us, while we were in our classes, not to distract each other with disturbing conversations. Then she walked up the aisle, to address the fifth grade. She spoke just above a whisper when she told us psychiatric doctors would be coming in that afternoon and would be available all week if we needed to talk. Some topics needed special attention, she told us. It would take us a long time to forget, but, she urged us, please don't remind each other.

Some of us did talk to the doctors. We thought we'd be in a closed room, in private, like our visits to the school counselor. Instead, we lined up outside the library. The doctors sat in the corners at wooden tables. They spoke to us in a tense hush and asked us questions: did we talk to our parents about it? Were we having nightmares? Was this the first time we ever saw someone die?

But when we asked questions, they had no answers for us. We wanted more information about Jeremy Green. All we knew for certain came from the five o'clock news: Jeremy had escaped early that morning from the County Correctional Facility, on the other side of town, and ran all the way to our school, just in time for recess. He was twenty-three years old. The stations filled our television screens with his photograph alongside footage of our now-empty playground. We'd studied his faded portrait: the thin dark scar across his left cheekbone, his flat, greasy hair parted to the side, his sunken eyes, his pimply forehead and lanky arms, his crooked teeth. We'd gathered bits of his biography: his life sentence in prison, his wife and his three-year-old daughter, his parents clutching each other on their dilapidated porch, refusing to comment. Though we watched all of this, some of us multiple times because they repeated it on every news station and then they repeated it again at eleven, the story ended before we understood what we had seen.

We were allowed outside again a couple of days later. Some kids weren't ready to face the playground yet, so they optioned to stay in the gym and watch a cartoon version of *The Incredible Journey*. The rest of us searched the gravel for leftover bullets and whispered our survival stories.

"I didn't even know he had a gun until he was already dead."

"He pushed me to the ground."

"He shot at me, but I jumped out of the way, just in time."

"Get real."

"I swear to God."

"I saw him smile every time he pulled the trigger."

"He wanted to die."

"Nobody wants to die."

"He did."

"Then why didn't he just shoot himself?"

We didn't find any leftover bullets or pieces of his shirt that'd snagged and tore on the fence when he tumbled onto the playground. We didn't find any pieces of gravel encrusted with Jeremy's dried blood. We spoke with no evidence. It was as if he'd never come.

When the funerals got old, we played Jeremy's escape from prison. This time, we broke into two teams: prisoners versus guards. The prisoners had to strategize how they would help Jeremy get out of his cell before he got caught, but before he could leave, we had to figure out how he had gotten the gun.

At first we figured he might have grabbed a weapon from his friend's house on the way to our playground, after he'd left the prison. After all, we had no idea how long Jeremy had been on the run. Then someone came up with the idea that Jeremy had stolen it from a prison guard on his way out. This brought the game to a whole different level. We made it so some of the guards carried pencils in their back pockets, which we used for the guns, but the rest of us didn't know which ones had them. We could get shot at any time, and several of our failed strategies ended in a pretend bloodbath.

Each day, the prisoners created a new plan and code word like "rabbit," "Napoleon," "caterpillar," and "Pluto." But those codes were too random to be effective. The guards knew to take action as soon as we started talking about something crazy. Then we started using terms which were harder to detect, words we used all the time, like "glass," "grandma," or "grilled-cheese sandwich." As soon as someone said one of these, we'd attempt to execute our plan of attack.

We marked the barriers for cells along the fence by digging lines in the gravel with our heels. We always started in the evening. The head guard would shout, "Okay, lights out!" and we'd hit the fence behind us to make the sound of heavy levers coming down to switch us into total darkness. We indicated our inability to see by waving our hands in front of our faces. Then we'd start to whisper to each other. Sometimes Jeremy got out because two of us would pretend to be in a fist fight, and the rest of us would shout at each other, distracting the guards. Sometimes he got out because we'd pretend that his cellmate had stolen the key. Sometimes our plans would fail, and the guards would shove Jeremy back into his cell. If one of us got caught trying to steal the gun, a guard would pull out his pencil and shoot us right there on the spot. That's how it worked. We didn't have to shoot anyone to get shot. We just had to show the threat. But sometimes we did succeed, and Jeremy would burst across the field, the pencil in his fist, and the game would be over.

On the day he came, we'd just returned to school after Labor Day weekend. The ground was still damp from a morning thunderstorm. We almost didn't go out. The monitor told us to stay away from the north side because it was full of puddles. All over the playground, the gravel was too wet to sit on. Those of us who weren't playing soccer walked laps around the perimeter.

The fence rattled when Jeremy leaped onto it. At first we thought he was one of us. We thought the soccer ball had gotten over the fence and somebody was just taking a shortcut after tossing it back into the lot. We were supposed to wait for the playground monitor to go and get the ball for us. But she never paid attention. She just sat near the door reading fashion magazines, which is probably why she didn't notice Jeremy right away, either.

He climbed the chain-link in a fury before he dove forward. His white T-shirt snagged on the top of the fence, and he came down, head first, landing not two feet from the baseball bench. He rolled to his feet in one sweeping movement, and when we saw his height, we knew he was an outsider. He rushed out into the center of the soccer game, and we stopped at the sound of nearing sirens. Jeremy whipped out a pistol from his back pocket, cocked it, and stretched his arm up straight in the air like he was going to initiate a race. Then we started to run.

He fired a shot into the clouds, and our playground shrieks turned to deep-throated screams. Some of us ran directly to the steps of the school, but most of us just ran in every other direction away from him. He fired more shots, and we sped up with each one. Some of us ran straight to the north side because it was empty, and it seemed like there was nowhere else for us to go. We doused ourselves in the puddles, sending streams of water into the air and adding to the confusion. We were soaked with mud and sweat, clutching each other's damp hands and bodies, but we kept running around in circles. Four police officers darted onto the playground from the parking-lot entrance, shouting for Jeremy to freeze. He put up his hands and they pumped bullet after bullet into him, even after he had collapsed to the ground.

By then the janitor was out, and a few of our teachers. They shouted our names and pulled us into the school. We tried to crowd by the door to watch them take Jeremy's body away, but we were ushered into the gym, where we'd wait for our parents. Some of us were crying. The rest were too bewildered to show any kind of reaction. At that time we had no idea how to put what we saw into words. We were told Jeremy came to our playground because he wanted to die a dramatic death. This was to comfort us, to assure us that he never intended to hurt us.

In our last game, we acted out the murder Jeremy committed, the one that got him sentenced to life in prison. This time, we were all Jeremy. We'd hop out from behind the backstop and barge across the playground to the slab of cement we designated as his victim's home. The reason for the shooting varied—sometimes the man had beaten him in a game of a pool, assaulted his wife or stolen his child—but in the end, Jeremy was always justified. We played this game until the day we got a new playground monitor. She heard us shouting Jeremy's name and firing his pistols. She didn't tell us to stop, but as soon as we got back into our classrooms, our teachers brought us into the auditorium for another assembly, just for us fifth graders.

The principal walked up and down the aisles and leaned into our seats. She told us how shocked she was at our behavior; that we were the big kids acting like kindergartners. She said kindergartners don't know the difference between what's appropriate to joke about and what's not. Fifth graders were expected to be more sensitive. Then she reminded us that some topics weren't to be discussed without care, that guns weren't funny and that death wasn't a game. In her ultimate act of persuasion, she threatened to take away our recess if she ever heard about us doing this sort of thing again. That was enough for us to do our best to pretend that it never happened.

After a while, Jeremy's name fell from our lips, and we returned to our old playground games. He seemed to be pushed out of our minds with the cold winds that prevented our recesses. He was almost forgotten until, sometime in the following spring, we found his name etched deep into the bench, near the spot where he'd hopped over the fence. We let it sit there for the rest of the school year, until we left, careful never to touch it.

LILLI CARRÉ

■

The Carnival

FROM *MOME*

RANA DASGUPTA

■

Capital Gains

FROM *Granta*

1.

It all comes together on the roads.

Delhi is a segregated city; an impenetrable, wary city—a city with a fondness for barbed wire, armed guards, and guest lists. Though its population now knocks up against twenty million, India's capital remains curiously faithful to the spirit of the British administrative enclave with which it began: Delhiites admire social rank, name-dropping, and exclusive clubs, and they snub strangers who turn up without a proper introduction. The Delhi newspapers pay tribute every morning to the hairstyles and parties of its rich, and it is they, with their high-walled compounds and tinted car windows, who define the city's aspirations. Delhi's millionaires are squeamish about public places, and they don't like to go out unless there are sufficient valets and guards to make them feel at home, and prices exorbitant enough to keep undesirables out.

But in this segregated city, everyone comes together on the roads. The subway network is still incomplete, there are few local trains (unlike Mumbai), and you can't take a helicopter to work (unlike São Paulo)—the draconian security regulations prevent that. So the Delhi roads accommodate every kind of citizen and offer a unique exhibition of the city's social relations.

On the eve of "liberalization" in 1991—when the then finance minister, Manmohan Singh, opened the economy up to global money flows, so bringing an end to four decades of centralized planning—there were three varieties of car on sale in India. The Hindustan Ambassador and Premier Padmini had both been around for thirty years and it took seven years to acquire one—production was limited to a few thousand a year and ownership restricted, in practice, to bureaucrats and senior businessmen. The compact Maruti 800, by contrast, was a recent arrival that had been conceived as a "people's car": with a quota of one hundred fifty thousand a year, it had brought the possibility of private car travel within reach, for the first time, of the middle classes.

Nearly twenty years on, those three originals have all but vanished in the flurry of new brands that liberalization ushered in (though the stately Ambassador remains the preferred conveyance for Delhi's politicians and senior bureaucrats). The new economic regime stimulated more Indian companies, such as Tata, to start building cars, but it also brought in the global giants—Hyundai, then Ford, GM, and Toyota, and sooner or later everyone else—and now, with car markets declining around the world, they are looking to India to take up some slack. India's car consumption is ten times what it was in 1991, and rising rapidly, and the effect in the cities is deadlock. The stricken carriageways are never adequate for the car mania, no matter how many new lanes and flyovers are built—and in Delhi, most cars are stationary much of the time. Hemmed in by the perpetual emergency of roadworks, and governed by traffic lights that can stay red for ten minutes, the situation is unpromising. Delhi drivers, moreover, never confident that any system will produce benefits for all, try to beat the traffic with an opportunistic hustle that often turns to a great honking blockage, smothered in the smoke of so many engines air-conditioning their passengers against the 104-degree heat. The main beneficiaries are foot-bound magazine sellers, who move fast and offer something to while away the time.

Another distraction for unmoving drivers: the endless automobile reveries posted up on hoardings—images of a parallel world where the roads are open, and driving is sexy and carefree.

With so many cars jammed up against each other, each as hobbled as the next, road travel could threaten to undermine the steep gradients of Delhi's social hierarchies. But here the recent car profusion steps in to solve the very problem it creates. The contemporary array of brands and models supplies a useful code of social status to offset the anonymity of driving, and the vertiginous altitude of Delhi's class system comes through admirably, even on the horizontal roads. Car brands regulate the relationships between drivers: impatient Mercedes flash Marutis to let them through the throng, and Marutis move aside. BMW limousines are so well insulated that passengers don't even hear the incessant horn with which chauffeurs disperse everything in their path. Canary-yellow Hummers lumber over the concrete barriers from the heaving jam into the empty bus lanes and accelerate illegally past the masses — and traffic police look away, for what cop is going to risk his life to challenge the entitlement of rich kids? Yes, the privileges of brand rank are enforced by violence if need be: a Hyundai driver gets out of his car to kick in the doors of a Maruti that kept him dawdling behind, while young men in a Mercedes chase after a Tata driver who dared abuse them out of the window, running him down and slapping him as if he were an insubordinate kid.

There is nothing superficial about brands in contemporary Delhi. This is a place where one's social significance is assumed to be nil unless there are tangible signs to the contrary, so the need for such signs is authentic and fierce. And in these times of stupefying upheaval, when all old meanings are under assault, it is corporate brands that seem to carry the most authority. Brands hold within them the impressive infinity of the new global market. They hold out the promise of dignity and distinction in a harsh city that constantly tries to withhold these things. They even offer clarity in intimate questions: "He drives a Honda City," a woman says, meaningfully, about a prospective son-in-law. Brands help to stave off the terror of senselessness, and the more you have, the better. Where the old socialist elite was frugal and unkempt, the new Delhi aristocracy is exuberantly consumerist. With big cars and designer accessories, it literally advertises its supremacy, creating waves of adoration and hatred on every side.

Somewhere around four a.m. on the morning of January 10, 1999, a car sped along Lodhi Road, a broad, leafy artery flanked by Delhi's parks and richest residential areas. At the wheel was a drunk young man named Sanjeev Nanda, who was returning home from a party with two friends. The car was a $160,000 BMW, one of the manufacturer's largest and most luxurious models, which had been privately imported and still carried foreign plates. Later estimates said it was travelling at 140 kilometers per hour; at any rate, it went out of control when it reached a police checkpoint and crashed through the barrier, plowing into seven people and killing six instantly: three policemen and three laborers. Witnesses said that two men got out to see what had happened; when they saw the bodies and the screaming survivors, they got back in the car and drove off in a panic, running over one of the prostrate figures as they went.

Sanjeev Nanda was a charismatic twenty-one-year-old who had just graduated from Wharton Business School. His lineage was deluxe: his grandfather was Admiral S.M. Nanda, chief of India's Naval Staff, who, like several other well-connected figures in the Indian armed services, had made big money in his retirement by setting up as an arms dealer, brokering between foreign arms companies and his former colleagues. The business flourished further under the shrewd eye of Sanjeev's father, Suresh, whose acquisition of Delhi's elegant Claridges Hotel was only a small part of a network of investments and acquisitions he built in India and around the world.

After the accident, Sanjeev sped away to the nearby house of one of his companions, who were also from elite business families. This man's father owned a finance company and was used to grasping complex situations quickly: he immediately ordered his driver to move the BMW off the road and into his compound. The front of the car was covered in a gory mat of blood and flesh, and the guard was given the job of cleaning it up. But it had left a trail of leaking oil as it fled, which the police were able to follow to the house. They turned up in the middle of the clean-up, arrested Sanjeev, and took him, still drunk, into custody.

The case should have been simple, but it melted away under the backstage influence of the Nanda family. Manoj Malik, the only one of the seven victims to survive his injuries, changed his story during the trial to say that it was probably a truck, and not a BMW, that hit him. The only independent witness, Sunil Kulkarni, who had been passing by that night and had described bodies flying over the BMW's roof, withdrew his testimony and said that he had made it under pressure from the Delhi Police, who were supposedly conspiring against Sanjeev Nanda. Sanjeev himself alleged he had not been in the car that night, which was registered in his sister's name, and denied any connection to the incident. The Nanda family tried to dissipate ill feeling by making unofficial payments to the victims' families. The case lost steam and life went on. Out on bail, Sanjeev did an MBA at INSEAD in Fontainebleau, near Paris, became managing director of the family hotel business, and moved into a penthouse at Claridges. Manoj Malik mysteriously disappeared.

Suresh Nanda's business was hit with unfortunate publicity: an undercover investigation into arms procurement corruption carried out by journalists from the news magazine *Tehelka* found that he had paid large bribes to government ministers in return for favorable consideration of his clients' products. He was charged with corruption and let out on bail while the Central Bureau of Investigation looked into his affairs. It emerged that he ran an Internet procurement monopoly that gave him a guaranteed cut of the vast business of government tenders, and the press expressed outrage that he could continue to enjoy this privilege even as that same government had him under investigation. Before long, he was caught offering a bribe of one hundred million rupees ($2.1 million) to a tax official who was offering to hush up the investigation, and he and Sanjeev, who was also involved, were sent to jail for fourteen days.

Then the BMW case took a new turn. The discredited witness, Sunil Kulkarni, in an attempt to show the world what pressure he was under, took undercover television journalists to a secret meeting with representatives of the Nanda family. This operation revealed that the Nandas were paying the lawyers on both sides of the case, who were working together to keep Kulkarni silent. The lawyers were dismissed and the case was finally heard in the Supreme Court. In September 2008, nine years after the incident, Sanjeev Nanda was convicted of mowing down six people while driving in a drunken condition, and sentenced to five years' imprisonment—an extraordinary moment when, contrary to expectations and experience, it was shown that the Indian elite cannot always make its acts disappear.

Contemporary Indian society is transfixed by wealth. A new genre of popular magazine is filled from cover to cover with features about gold-plated bathtubs, diamond-encrusted mobile phones, and super-deluxe vacations, allowing readers to wallow in what they can never afford. Television game shows give weight to the seductive whispers of the market, showing working people in the very moment they are transformed into millionaires. People love to read about the posses-sions, opinions, and talents of India's leading industrialists, some of whom have succeeded in creating quasi-religious cults around them-selves. Criticism of the rich results in astonishing waves of rebuttal by ordinary people who feel it is an attack on their national pride.

But this determined adoration of the rich coexists with something else: something more crepuscular, full of fear and night-time jolts. In a society as stratified as this, it is possible to imagine that the ones at the top enjoy endless freedom — freedom so absolute that the only adequate use of it would be cruelty. For most people, Delhi life re-mains grueling and deprived, the inconceivable promise of the global market unfulfilled, and this feeling of perpetual deficit lets in appre-hensions of a vampiric ruling class, sucking the plenitude away from everyone else. This is the feeling that finds resonance in the story of Sanjeev Nanda, which has become one of Delhi's most popular parables. This story erupts into the public domain with the delicious nausea of something widely felt, but rarely observed: the reckless-ness of this economic system, its out-of-control heartlessness. San-jeev's speeding BMW is a symbol of gleaming, maleficent capital, un-checked by conscience or by the roadblocks of the state. The scene of the impact, a one-hundred-meter stretch of road strewn with organs, severed limbs, and pools of blood, is like a morality painting of the cataclysmic effects of this marauding elite in the world of ordinary people.

In this nightmare version of the rich, they are no longer the pride of the nation but invaders from outside, representatives of transna-tional currents who are never authentically committed to the Indian good. Much was made, in the Sanjeev Nanda story, of his British passport and his imported car, as if his fatal velocity was that of foreign forces whose impact, here in India, could only be catastrophic. The Indian road has not been given over to speed as it has elsewhere; it is a place of innumerable modes of transport, a place of commerce, leisure, and bureaucracy, a place cluttered with history. Even the most powerful men in the country cannot expect that clean lines will open up for them through the Indian reality. Only someone with no connection to that reality could imagine such a thing.

The society that has emerged in post-liberalization India is one consumed both by euphoria and dread. The rich are the emblems for both these sentiments, which is why they never settle into a single meaning. They are the simultaneous saints and demons of contemporary India, and any consideration of them oscillates with powerfully contradictory feeling.

2.

In the Western press, the face of the "new India" is typically urbane. It might be that of the exquisitely suited Azim Premji, chairman of Wipro Technologies, and staple of every Asian power list, who studied at Stanford, inherited a successful vegetable oil company, and turned it into a global technology enterprise. It could be the face of Nandan Nilekani, co-founder of Infosys Technologies, *Forbes Asia*'s "Business Leader of the Year 2006" and author of the recent *Imagining India: Ideas for the New Century*. English-speaking, intelligent, and articulate, these billionaires are the kind of men the West can do business with. They are regularly invited to explain India's economic growth to international business conferences and journals, where they project a rational and understated image of the country. They reassure Western audiences that the "new India" will be no more than an annex of the old West: that the future of India, and therefore, to some extent, of the world, will be intelligible and familiar.

In truth, however, the anglicized class to which Azim Premji and Nandan Nilekani belong is becoming marginalized from Indian society. Immense upheavals are afoot, and English-speaking sophisticates now speak about themselves as harried and besieged. They still enjoy many privileges, but as time goes on they see their values and sensibilities disappearing from the media and the streets, and they are faced with the troubling realization that they no longer rule this society or dominate its imagination—or even understand the first thing about it.

Rajiv Desai, a fan of the Beatles and *The New Yorker*, who spent twenty years working in Chicago before returning to Delhi and setting up one of India's leading PR firms, is quite clear: "Many of my friends are moving to Goa. There are so many people like me who have a second home in Goa, which is the only place you can still find anglicized values. People have intelligent conversation. There's standing room only in the jazz clubs. My house in Goa's not a country home, it's a *second home*, where I go to be myself and preserve my sanity. I can't stay the whole year in Delhi. It's backward. You take your life in your hands on the roads, you see the kind of people there are. It's been taken over by Hindi-speakers and loud Punjabi festivals like *Karwa Chauth* that no one used to make a fuss about twenty years back."

The Indian economy of the turn of the twenty-first century has been far too explosive for the tiny English-speaking class to monopolize its rewards. In fact they have not even been its primary beneficiaries. Their foreign degrees and cosmopolitan behavior prepare them well for jobs in international banks and management consultancies, where they earn good salaries and mix with people like themselves. But they are surrounded by very different people—private businessmen, entrepreneurs, real-estate agents, retailers, and general wheeler-dealers—who are making far more money than they are, and wielding more political power. These people may come from smaller cities, they may be less worldly, and they may speak only broken English. But they are skilled in the realm of opportunity and profit, and they are at home in the booming world of overlords, connections, bribes, political loopholes, sweeteners—and occasional violence—that sends their anglicized peers running for the nearest cappuccino. Over the last few years, provincials have become Delhi's dominant economic group, with many millionaires, and a few billionaires, among their number, and networks of political protection that make them immensely more influential than those who have become rich on a salary.

Saif Rizvi, a sociable young plastic surgeon who grew up mostly in

Saudi Arabia and the United States, is one of many who are affronted by the new arrivals. Prominent Muslims from Lucknow, his family traces its lineage back five hundred years, and Saif has a healthy contempt for Delhi's upstarts: "Oh my God, the nouveaux riches. Yeah, I see them everywhere I go, man, you see the way they walk into the clubs, the way they order their drinks. They're horrible. The only thing those guys have that's nice is their cars. The nicest cars pull up and the most horrible people get out. Horrible bodies, horrible teeth, horrible voice modulation."

Saif moved from New York to Delhi to take over the family clinic when his father was killed by a truck on a road in Uttar Pradesh two years ago, and he is gloomy about his new surroundings. He is alienated by Delhi conversation and he takes refuge in expat social evenings: "I'm not impressed by Delhi since these guys came into money. Now the clubs cater to them, the TV and everything. Everywhere they play Bollywood music, man, that's what these guys like."

A DJ in his spare time, Saif plays the sort of psychedelic trance that gives Delhi's Cambridge- and Berkeley-educated youth a good environment to take MDMA and escape from the city's grind. "The Ministry of Sound set up a club in Delhi and you know what kind of music they played? Bollywood. Can you believe it? The Ministry of Sound is supposed to be cutting edge, and they play Bollywood songs! Just to keep those guys happy!"

Unfortunately for Saif, the laments of disdainful cosmopolites like him carry less weight these days. The city now looks to the Bollywood-loving provincials, who have reaped billions in the early twenty-first century boom, and turned the city's clublike mentality upside down. The rewards of that boom have flowed to them because its implausible escalations rode on the one thing they had that Delhi people did not: land.

In 1957 Prime Minister Jawaharlal Nehru's government consolidated the capital's planning and development agencies into the new Delhi Development Authority. The DDA had sole responsibility for planning and executing the city's expansion and development and, in order to fulfill this, it had the right to acquire land forcibly and at greatly reduced prices. It was a development monopoly, whose exclusivity was guaranteed by laws making it impossible for private individuals or companies to own more than a few acres of land within Delhi's borders.

The DDA was given such enormous power over the landscape of this new capital that one can only be awed, today, by the mediocrity of its achievements. The drab, moldering tower that the agency calls home is fully indicative of the DDA's preferred architectural style; the countless housing developments it has built across Delhi are warren-like and poky, and by now they are leaking and falling down. Nehru Place, the ugly office complex built by the DDA in the 1980s, is in ruins, and has now been mostly abandoned by companies fleeing to new accommodation outside Delhi. Nehru Stadium, which the DDA built for the Asian Games in 1982, has had to be entirely rebuilt in order to serve for the Commonwealth Games in 2010.

Such physical rot is an outward indication of the enormous corruption that gripped the DDA in its heyday of the 1970s and 1980s. Since no one else could own land for development, the agency was able to control the entire construction business — and to charge money for access. It would keep the supply of land low, sitting on its bank of rusty, disused plots and selling building contracts to the highest bidder. Building contractors would then claw the expense of their bribes back, once they were given a contract, by cutting every kind of corner on construction. In a city of Delhi's size and prestige, this racket was big business, and some of the largest fortunes in the city were made by mid-level DDA engineers whose job it was to rubber-stamp new projects — and many of them resisted promotion out of these lucrative positions for years.

But the disaster of the DDA created a set of other, unexpected effects, whose long-term impact was even more momentous. With the city of Delhi completely sealed to private commercial development, a number of individuals began in the 1980s to buy up land in the surrounding states. It was a quiet and laborious process, and most of the people who began it were not from the urban elite. They came from small towns, they understood how to do business with farmers, and they operated in areas that seemed impossibly backward and remote to Delhi businesspeople.

One of these men was Kushal Pal Singh, who came from a small town in Uttar Pradesh, and whose father-in-law's real-estate business was decimated when the DDA was set up. Singh was charged with reviving the business, later called DLF, and in 1979, unable to operate in Delhi, he began to buy up rural land to the south of the city, in the state of Haryana. This is how he describes the process:

> I did everything it took to persuade these farmers to trust me. I spent weeks and months with their families. I wore kurtas, sat on charpoys, drank fly-infested milk from dirty glasses, attended weddings, visited the sick. To understand why this was important, it is necessary to understand the landholding pattern. The average plot size in Gurgaon [one of Haryana's nineteen districts] was four to five acres, mostly held by Hindu undivided families. Legally, to get clear titles, I needed the consent of every adult member of these families. That could be up to thirty people for one sale deed. Getting the married daughters to sign was often tricky because the male head of the family would refuse to share the proceeds of the sale with them. So I would travel to their homes and pay the daughters in secret. Remarkably, Gurgaon's farmers sold me land on credit. I would pay one farmer and promptly take the money back as a loan and use that to buy more land. The firm's goodwill made them willing to act as bankers for DLF. But it also meant I had to be extra careful about interest payments. Come rain or shine, the interest would be hand-delivered to each farmer on the third of every month at ten a.m. We bought three thousand five hundred acres of land in Gurgaon, more than half of it on credit, without one litigation against DLF.

When men like Singh first called Delhi building companies to trudge out into the far-off brushland and build middle-class apartment complexes, the contractors thought they were mad. They drove out in jeeps, lurching over the baked earth, and stood in the naked expanse, where brightly turbaned villagers lived in huts and tended goats, and they wondered which Delhi banker or advertising executive would ever venture there. But by the 1990s, Delhi was caught in a real-estate crisis. Delhi's mega-city population was growing faster than anyone could build, and the city had little space left for new housing developments. The DDA had made almost no provision for commercial real estate, and big companies were operating out of cramped domestic basements. The quaint community markets built in the socialist era were entirely inadequate for exhibiting the products of the new consumer economy. So when Gurgaon opened its doors, proclaiming a "new Singapore" of glass office blocks, gated communities, golf courses, and shopping, it did not take long for the corporate classes to respond. Flush with boom cash, India's banks handed out loans to anyone who asked, and house prices were rising so fast that it made sense for everyone to put their savings into property. Microsoft and its ilk built their Indian headquarters in the thrilling emptiness of the Haryana countryside, and Gurgaon quickly became the largest private township in Asia, a dusty, booming expanse of hypertrophic apartment complexes, skyscrapers, and malls. In 2007 Singh listed his company on the Indian stock exchanges; the 2008 *Forbes* list estimated him to be the world's eighth-richest man, with a fortune of thirty billion U.S. dollars.

Gurgaon was only the largest and most prestigious of many such developments across Haryana and Uttar Pradesh, and Singh's fortune only the most fabulous of countless others. The land surrounding Delhi was an amazing commodity, doubling in value every three or four years, and multiplying its value sixty times with the simple addition of bricks, concrete, and a bit of cheap labor. The new millennium saw a desperate land rush. Hundreds of thousands of acres of agricultural land were sold on to developers. Companies that had previously made their money from other things suddenly switched to real estate, and major banks and financial service firms such as Deutsche Bank and Morgan Stanley queued up to fund them. Small-time developers from drab little towns like Ghaziabad became serious property moguls who bought mansions in Delhi, threw glitzy parties with Bollywood star entertainment, and sent their sons to U.S. business schools to learn how to run billion-dollar businesses. Even farmers walked away from land deals with a few million dollars, and bought hulking SUVs for their sons, who brought them to Delhi and drove with macho glee around the seat of power. Such windfalls were often quickly spent, but the more astute of these families set up real-estate businesses, and took further slices of the pie. Some of the real-estate agents who had set out on their mopeds a few years ago to sell all this new property now received Mercedes and apartments as bonuses. As always, politicians made a killing. Prime Minister Nehru, for whom agriculture was sacrosanct, had cast stringent rules to prevent just such a land grab as this, and Uttar Pradesh's legendarily entrepreneurial politicians made sure that people paid well to have such an august tradition overturned.

This bonanza privileged those whose business methods were catholic. It was nearly impossible to operate at any significant scale without a wide network of paid connections among politicians, bureaucrats, and the police. Moreover, amid such intense competition, the acquisition frenzy sometimes abandoned the delicacy of Singh's recollections. Real-estate mafias grabbed country houses in Haryana and employed senior policemen to silence the owners by filing false criminal charges against them. In Uttar Pradesh, they forced farmers and tribal communities to sell them their land under threat of violence, employed the local police to clear the residents off, and sold it on at a large profit. There was a general escalation of criminality and violence, and the people who came through with new fortunes were a formidable breed. They knew how to hijack state power for their own private profit, and they enjoyed the support of the police and of much-feared extortion gangs. Such people had cracked the muscular equation of contemporary India, and they spurned its liberal platitudes as just so much pious cant. These were the ones who became suddenly and gleefully conspicuous in Delhi, arousing the resentment of people like Rajiv Desai and Saif Rizvi.

During all this action in Haryana and Uttar Pradesh, Delhi's own property prices had reached fairy-tale levels. In 2006, at the height of the boom, industrialists and property moguls were paying almost 1.5 billion rupees (then 33 million dollars) for Delhi mansions. Even retired army officers or journalists, to whom the state had given spacious plots at knock-down prices in the 1950s, suddenly found they were sitting on property worth two or three million dollars—and since they often didn't have much in their bank accounts, they decided to sell. But like everyone else selling property in Delhi, they set the official price low and took the majority of the money in cash so as to reduce the tax bill on their profits. Who could buy property at those prices on those terms? What kinds of people were walking around with, say, a million dollars in cash? It was not the cosmopolitan children of the original Delhi middle class, who worked as PR executives or TV newscasters, and for whom a million dollars of black money was a tall order. These people were moving out of the city into Gurgaon flats. No, the people with the suitcases of cash were, as likely as not, property tycoons, industrialists, politicians, or criminals. The capital of "shining India" was being systematically handed over from its middle classes to a new black-money elite, and it was this group which was increasingly setting the tone—aesthetic, commercial, and ethical—for everyone else.

3.

Tarun Tejpal, editor of *Tehelka*, is a prominent Delhi figure who has devoted the last decade of his life to documenting corruption and violence in the twenty-first-century Indian ruling class. His magazine made its name with a sting operation in which senior government ministers were videotaped accepting bribes in return for their consideration of the products of a fictional British arms company, and boasting openly about other money they had made in this fashion. Another *Tehelka* sting operation helped to put the son of a powerful Haryana politician behind bars after he shot a waitress dead for refusing to serve him a drink: the gunman had been acquitted by the courts, but *Tehelka*'s intervention showed that the witnesses had been paid off by his family. *Tehelka* has published an unparalleled study of the 2002 slaughter of two thousand Muslims in the state of Gujarat—a set of interviews that proved what many suspected: that the state had actively colluded in the event. The magazine has tirelessly documented the ongoing land grab by which vast tracts of Indian territory are seized from farmers and handed over to corporations under the recent Special Economic Zones Act. In a country of complacent, celebrity-happy newspapers, *Tehelka* is a major journalistic achievement, and one might expect Tarun to be quietly satisfied. But he is not.

"No one cares," he says. "There are no ideas except the idea of more wealth. The elite don't read. They know how to work the till, and that's it. There's nothing: we are living in the shallowest decade you can imagine. Rural India, that's eight hundred million people, has simply fallen out of the master narrative of this country. There should have been an enormous political left in India, but people worship the rich and there's no criticism of what they do. They face no consequences; they live in an atmosphere of endless possibility."

"Do you think anything will come of all this money they're making?" I ask. "Do you think they'll try to leave behind a legacy?"

"They don't care about their legacy! This is a Hindu society: I'm back for a million more lives—how much fuss am I going to make about this one? Indian businesspeople might run a school or feed a few orphans, but they're not interested in reform because they are bent on making the system work for them. Hinduism is very pliable. It rationalizes inequality: if that guy is poor it's because he deserves it from his previous lives, and it's not for me to sort out his accounts. Hinduism allows these guys to think that what they get is due to them, and they have absolutely no guilt about it."

There's an incredible energy to Tarun. Messages arrive constantly on his two mobile phones, and he answers them without a break in his tirade. Over the course of the last few years, while managing a weekly magazine, he has somehow found enough spare time to write two novels. The second, *The Story of My Assassins*, has recently come out. It is a devastating portrait of Indian society, a tale of such hopeless horror and violence that the reader is left beaten down and without response.

Tarun is never lost for words, but as we talk I get the feeling that he too is becoming disillusioned. *Tehelka* has got him into a lot of trouble: he has faced death threats for his journalism, and ministers have tried to bury him with tax investigations and libel suits. The magazine runs on a shoestring: advertisers have stayed far away and corporate funders have been advised to pull out. Tarun is a well-connected man from a good army family, but over the last few years many of his connections have turned away. Some have even suggested that he is in the pay of foreign agents and that this is why he writes so critically of the Indian state. All this has left him wondering whether the enterprise of trying to tell the truth as he sees it—"Free, fair, fearless" goes *Tehelka*'s slogan—is simply pointless.

"The dominant mood is frenzied accumulation," he says. "The corporations and the state are in bed with each other, eating and drinking the country out of everything it has. The Ganges is becoming a trickle: the most fertile river basin in the world. But the truth is that no one is interested in what's really going on. We don't even have a vocabulary to talk about it."

To find a reason big enough for such a startling predicament, Tarun burrows into history.

"It all goes back to colonization: we're a damaged people. We were a subordinate race for three hundred years and it's made us envious. Now people are coming into wealth for the first time, they're discovering goodies, and they want them for themselves. They don't want anyone spoiling the party. Their parents were completely different: they weren't extravagant, they never ate out, they were still inspired by Gandhi. This generation has nothing in its head except goodies."

Our conversation is brought to an end by the arrival of Tarun's next visitor. As I leave him I find myself looking for ways out of the sealed box of his hopelessness. I can't disagree with his morose assessment of what is happening around us: it is difficult to live here and not be stupefied by the speed and brutality with which every resource is being fenced in, mined, and commodified. But is it true, as he implies, that north Indian Hindus are simply programmed by their history and religion to be rapacious? *Capitalism* is rapacious, and its new elites, wherever they have been in the world, have usually risen sternly. Is the new Indian elite worse than everyone else? Is it worse, moreover, than the socialist ruling class that went before? It is so common, these days, to hear people indicting the vulgar new India, as Tarun does, by comparing it unfavorably to the more genteel socialist system of the old days. But wasn't the socialist elite just as cruel and corrupt, even as it quoted Shakespeare and Marx? Isn't there much that is positive in the explosive dynamism of the contemporary Indian economy?

I go to have lunch with a psychotherapist, Anurag Mishra. I tell him about a man I recently met who told me a story curiously similar to the Sanjeev Nanda incident.

"His son called him to say he had just killed a man with his car," I say. "The son was in a panic and didn't know what to do. There were injured people lying on the street. The father told him, *Get out of there as quickly as you can.* His son had borrowed his car but he was only sixteen and shouldn't have been driving at all. So he told him to run. Isn't that surprising?"

"Not really. He's an Indian father, and he'll protect his son above everything else. A car accident is a matter of perception, it's a trick of fate, but a father's duty to his son is absolute. Do you think he's going to say, *Confess to what you have done and pay the price?* This isn't a guilt culture. In the Indian psyche, you dissociate yourself from the bad things you have done, and then they're not yours anymore. That's why you can never make any accusation stick to a businessman or a politician. They won't even recognize the crimes you're accusing them of. They'll probably have you beaten up for insulting them."

We are in an Italian-style café. Anurag is talking too much to touch his Caesar salad.

"Delhi is a city of traumas," he says. "You can't understand anything if you don't realize that everyone here is trying to forget the horrifying things that have happened in their families. Delhi was destroyed by the British in 1857. It was destroyed again by Partition in 1947. It was torn apart by the anti-Sikh rampages of 1984. Each of these moments destroyed the culture of the city, and that is the greatest trauma of all. Your entire web of meanings is tied up in culture, and if that is lost, your self is lost."

He tells me stories of clients of his who have been torn apart by returning memories of Partition horrors—memories they had successfully buried for sixty years. He tells stories of the recollections of violence and deprivation that remain frighteningly persistent even in the minds of those who have made good money in the last few years.

"That's why Delhi is by far the most consumerist city in India," he continues. "People buy obscene amounts of stuff here. Delhi has an impoverished symbolic vocabulary: there hasn't been enough time since all these waves of destruction for its symbols to be restored. If I don't have adequate symbols of the self, I can't tell the difference between *me* and *mine.* So people buy stuff all the time to try and make up for the narcissistic wound. It's their defense against history."

"Don't you think it will get boring after a while? If it's as you say, people will surely realize after a while that buying stuff isn't solving anything. Maybe they'll try something else? Maybe their children will rebel?"

Anurag smiles.

"This is very interesting," he says. "You know about the Oedipus complex? Freud said this was the universal condition of young men: they unconsciously want to kill their fathers and sleep with their mothers. That's the source of revolutionary energy—you kill your father symbolically by rejecting all his values and finding new ones. But I don't think this applies to Indian men. I would analyse Indian men in terms of what I call the Rama complex. In the epic poem *Ramayana*, Rama gives up the throne that is rightfully his and submits himself to enormous suffering in order to conform to the will of his father. Indian men don't wish to *kill* their fathers, they wish to *become* them; they wish to empty themselves out of everything that has not come from their fathers."

Like Tarun, Anurag sees the fundamental structures as fixed and preordained, even as the surface of Indian life changes so fast. Once again I struggle to find a way out. Surely it's not enough to say that the business elite is so in thrall to its own wounds and traumas that it cannot restrain its own reckless impulses, for these people are striking primarily for their astonishing boldness, not their limitations. I ask Anurag about his own relationship with money.

"During the British time," he says, "my grandfather was a freedom fighter. After independence he became a Congress politician. My father was a college teacher and member of the Communist Party. Both of them were idealistic and frugal, and I was always taught to think that people with money were bad. They had to be doing something seedy, and probably criminal. At school I envied the boys with money because they had stuff I wanted, but I also thought they must be bad."

We've finished lunch by now and moved out to the café's terrace so that Anurag can smoke one of his beloved cigars.

"I didn't have money for most of my life and it was a big problem for me when I began to practice as a psychotherapist. I didn't know how to relate to myself as someone with money. I didn't really believe that I deserved money, or that I had the right to charge for my services. When I first got money I started eating a lot and I got very fat. I ate bad things, just wanting to fill myself up. I've only made my peace with money quite recently. I've lost all that weight. Now I think it's okay to give myself good things. Like this lunch. I don't have to have twenty bad things: I can have one good thing, and it's better than that excess."

As he talks I realize how complicated it must be for him to watch the unrestrained consumption of the new rich with whom he shares his city. I realize that, for a certain segment of the anglicized middle class, the new rich offend sentiments that are so deep and complex that the only possible response is profound anxiety and revulsion. I realize that there really is no simple way out of the gloom they feel about the present moment; I understand why these conversations always hit dead ends.

If people like Tarun and Anurag refer back so nostalgically to the socialist period it's because, no matter how hypocritical it was, the socialist regime at least took the trouble to legitimize itself in terms they could recognize. This modicum of intellectual correspondence with the ruling class seems positively alluring now that the people who are shaping their world are so adamantly opaque. Where possible, the new Indian elite runs private companies that have no shareholders and no scrutiny—and often it conducts its ground-level operations through a myriad of other companies whose ownership is deliberately obscure. It amasses invisible fortunes and pays very little tax. It does not like to seek funds from public sources; instead it forms alliances with other secretive and cash-rich elites, such as the Russian billionaires. It keeps such a low profile that some of its richest and most enterprising individuals have no entries on Google. It operates behind high walls; it is energized, rather than outraged, by the immense disparities in the world, and it is pretty much indifferent to public outcry or media exposé: you can think whatever you like, there is no dialogue.

I can find little reassurance for someone like Tarun Tejpal. There is nothing trivial about his feelings of outrage and impotence. They are feelings, in fact, that accompany the north Indian business class wherever they go: both Mumbai and Bangalore have significant political movements devoted to protecting local society against the ferocious business acumen of north Indian entrepreneurs. It is true what he says: in these times it is difficult to make any mark on Indian public life through the subtlety or distinction of one's thought. People whose talents and tastes lie in that direction can do what they like; for the time being the rules are set by others.

And perhaps Tarun's are the dominant global feelings, in fact, of the times to come—for the new Indian elite is charismatic and muscular and ultimately well-reared for the age of globalization. In all their grandiose unsentimentality they remind us that a lot of the comfortable myths we have been told about capitalism are simply that. In truth, it is a flailing, terrifying thing.

4.

Monty Chadha makes a timid entrance into the quiet hotel lounge where he has asked me to meet him. He wears a black turban and suit; he is stocky and muscular and speaks with a faint lisp. He is twenty-eight years old.

He is not particularly talkative. I try to break the ice by telling him that we have a friend in common and we talk about her for a while. He relaxes. I ask him about his life.

"Until I was a teenager," he says, "I thought my dad worked for the government. I used to ask, *Why do we have this big house?* They told me, *Your grandfather built it, then we lost the money, and now your dad works for the government.*"

In truth, Monty's father ran a large assembly of businesses across the states of Uttar Pradesh, Haryana, and Punjab. The mainstay of this empire was liquor retail, a business which, in gangster states like Uttar Pradesh, offers rewards only to the shrewd, charismatic, and violent. Other people with Monty's background have told me how they grew up hearing their fathers giving assassination orders over the phone—but at this early point in the conversation Monty is too professional to share such details.

"Of course there were goons around—you can't run this kind of business without a strong arm—but my dad always kept them out of our sight. He believed in discipline. He said, *If you do bad things, like if you get caught for drunk driving, I can't get you off.* A lot of powerful people said to their sons, *I can get you off anything.* It makes for a different kind of mentality. Of course, later I discovered that there was nothing I could have done that my dad couldn't have got me off."

Monty's father is present throughout his conversation as a kind of spiritual touchstone.

"The company was set up by my great-grandfather in 1952. When my father took it over in the 1980s the family was in debt. Now the group has an annual turnover of one billion dollars. My father's will to succeed is phenomenal. If he sets out to do something, he will get it done. If there's someone I want to become, it's him."

Monty speaks about the family business in the first-person plural. He has grown up absorbing business ideas and techniques, and they are a natural part of his speech.

"When our liquor business was at its height we controlled nineteen percent of Indian liquor retail. At that time, the government auctioned liquor outlets to the highest bidder. Later on it introduced a lottery system to prevent monopolies. But we could still grow the business because we had so many employees. In any lottery in our region, out of one hundred entrants, eighty were our men."

Monty was sent to a series of expensive schools, but he was repeatedly expelled, and at the age of sixteen he dropped out for good. He went to London for a year or two to have fun: clubs, parties, and everything else that a teenager with a well-stocked bank account can think of.

When he came back he was put in charge of one of the family's sugar mills. But his heart was not really in it—and the real-estate boom was on. In 2001 the family set up a real-estate business and Monty, twenty-one and entirely untrained, was given the task of building the largest shopping mall in northern India.

"When I was in England I spent a lot of time walking around malls, studying how they were made. There's no point reinventing the wheel. I know more than anyone in India about how you set up a mall, how you arrange your brands. My father had no experience in a professional context, so everything I know about the professional context I've learned myself. I introduced computer systems into the business. I taught myself Oracle programming because the professional contractors were no good. Then I taught myself all about the latest building techniques. Centrestage Mall was built with special prefabricated steel pillars, which had never been used in Indian malls before. Recently, I taught myself finance. I read finance texts online and every time I didn't know a word I looked it up. Six months ago I didn't know anything and now I can conduct finance meetings with Pricewaterhouse."

Centrestage was famous for having Delhi's most luxurious, high-tech nightclub, Elevate. It was Monty's pet project, his personal party zone, with endless champagne for him and his friends—and his nightly arrival there, surrounded by bodyguards, always provided a frisson.

"For a time I was *the man* in Delhi. Loads of people wanted to be my friend. Women wanted to sleep with me. I said to my wife: *if I hadn't been married, things would have been very different.* A lot of people were very fake."

Like many Delhi rich boys, Monty was given a big wedding as a way of winding down his wild years. When he was twenty-two, he married his childhood sweetheart, Shanam Kochar; their reception had six thousand guests and featured dance routines by Bollywood stars Diya Mirza and Shilpa Shetty. Monty still loves parties, and, as I discover during our conversation, he becomes relaxed and witty with alcohol, but there is no doubt that he has by now grown into a fully fledged partner to his father. He's ready to shut down Elevate: he doesn't have time to attend to it any more, and he doesn't want anyone else to run it. He operates five shopping malls across India, and he has another fourteen hundred acres under development. And that is just the beginning. He is moving on to much bigger plans.

"We've just leased seven hundred thousand acres for seventy-five years; we're opening up food processing, sugar, and flower planta-tions."

He is so matter-of-fact that I'm not sure if I've heard correctly. We have already discussed how laborious it is to acquire land in India, buying from farmers five or ten acres at a time. I can't imagine where he could get hold of land on that scale.

"Where?" I ask.

"Ethiopia. My father has a friend who bought land from the Ethio-pian president for a cattle ranch there. The President told him he had other land for sale. My dad said, *This is it, this is what we've been look-ing for, let's go for it.* We're going in there with [exiled Russian oligarch] Boris Berezovsky. Africa is amazing. That's where it's at. You're talking about numbers that can't even fit into your mind yet. Reliance, Tata, all the big Indian corporations are setting up there, but we're still ahead of the curve. I'm going to run this thing myself for the next eight years, that's what I've decided. I'm not giving this to any CEO until it meets my vision. It's going to be amazing. You should see this land: lush, green. Black soil, rivers."

Monty tells me how he has one hundred farmers from Punjab ready with their passports to set off for Ethiopia as soon as all the papers are signed.

"Africans can't do this work. Punjabi farmers are good because they're used to farming big plots. They're not scared of farming five thousand acres. Meanwhile, I'll go there and set up polytechnics to train the Africans so when the sugar mills start up they'll be ready."

Shipping farmers from Punjab to work on African plantations is a plan of imperial proportions. And there's something imperial about the way he says *Africans*. I'm stunned. I tell him so.

"Thank you," he says.

"What is on that land right now?" I ask, already knowing that his response, too, will be imperial.

"Nothing."

Monty is excited to be talking about this. His spirits seem to be entirely unaffected by the recession that currently dominates the headlines. He orders another beer, though we have exceeded the time he allotted me. All of a sudden, I find him immensely charismatic. I can see why he makes things happen: he has made me believe, as he must have made others believe, that he can do anything. I ask him how he learned to think like this.

"I'm only twenty-eight," he says. "Why not?"

He becomes flamboyant.

"We're going to be among the top five food processors in the world. You know the first company I'm going to buy? Heinz."

I'm interested in his *Why not?* Is it on the strength of such a throwaway reason that nearly three-quarters of a million acres of Ethiopia are being cleared and hundreds of farmers shipped across the world? I wonder what the emotional register of this is for him. It seems as if, somewhere, it's all a bit of a lark.

"I sometimes wonder why I work," he says. "I do ask that question. I don't need to work. But what else am I going to do? You can't sit in beach resorts for three hundred sixty-five days a year. So I think of crazy things. I like it when you think up something and it's so wild you're messed in the head and you think, *How can I do this?*—and then you think, *Why not?*"

I feel like pointing out that life holds more possibilities for someone like him than just sitting on the beach. *Messed in the head* sounds like language that remains from his wild days, as if the whole thing is about getting a high. I ask him how he wants to spend his money.

"Currently I drive a BMW 750i. It's good for long drives to the mall I'm building in Ludhiana. The car I really want is an Aston Martin DBS. But I'll buy it later, when I deserve it more. My father wanted to buy me a nice sports car three years ago but I said, *Wait.* I set myself certain goals. By the time I'm forty I want a one hundred sixty-foot boat. I want a nice Gulfstream plane. And I want to be able to run them without it pinching me."

Monty talks as if he were saving up for a motorbike or a fridge, and suddenly he seems strangely banal. This is a man who can dream up Earth-bending forms of money-making, but his ideas of spending it are consumerist in the most ordinary of ways. His middle-class vocabulary seems at odds with his multibillion-dollar international economy, and I wonder if he is deferring his sports car so as not to run out of future acquisitions too quickly. I wonder if the whole enterprise does not teeter on the edge of senselessness, if he is not in fact still waiting for someone to supply him with a meaning for this money around which his life is organized.

Unprompted, he becomes philosophical.

"I'm not religious. I'm spiritual. My basic principle is whatever goes around comes around. It will come back to you, you can be dead sure of that. I live my life in a Vedic way. Disciplined. No idol worship, no stupid acceptance. Also that you don't just let someone hit you and take it from them. You give it back to them."

I'm not sure if this last point flows from the basic principle, but I don't question it. Monty is deadly serious. He is letting me in on his knowledge. He tells me a story.

"I was at a party recently and the waiter was handing out drinks and he moved the tray away a little too soon and this guy hadn't got his drink. So the guy shook up a soda bottle and sprayed it in the waiter's face. I went straight to the host and I had him chucked out of the party. You have to know how to behave. Some people only feel they have money when they can screw someone else, and then they feel, *Okay, I have money.* You have to know how to treat normal people. You see, there are two kinds of rich. There are people who've had money for a long time and they don't give a fuck who you are. They'll be nice to you anyway. Like I'm nice to people. You may get bored being around them, because all they talk about is how they've just got back from Cannes or Saint-Tropez, but they won't kick you out. But the people who've got rich in the last five years, they turn up at a party and the first thing they do is put their car keys down on the table to show they have a Bentley. They don't know how to behave."

Monty is a little drunk, and he's policing boundaries that are clearer to him than to me. It's not the first time he's said that people have to know how to behave. Once again I feel that his stand against the nihilism of the Delhi rich is all the more fervent because he is assailed by it himself. He is intimate with all the thuggish bad boys who have given people like him such a bad name ("It's so sad what happened to Sanjeev Nanda," he says, "he's such a sweet guy") and he is impressed by parables of restraint.

"I have a friend who's a multibillionaire," he says, "and I asked him about the best car to buy for your kids, because I've just had kids, and he suggested a Toyota Innova. He could afford to buy a jet for his kids but he doesn't. They have to earn it. He just buys them an Innova. You see, people say there are bad kids but it's all the parents' fault. It's totally the parents. They have fucked up their kids and once that's happened it can never be undone. One day the guy is driving a Maruti 800, the next day he's driving an S Class, and he buys Beemers for his kids when they're ten years old and they just go crazy. The kids get fucked up."

I've had a number of conversations with people in Monty's economic class and they all talk about Delhi as a kind of El Dorado, where fortunes pour in overnight, almost without your asking. *In this country, at this time,* they say, *you've got to be an absolute fool to go wrong.* But for all the talk of "new money," most Delhi fortunes are not, strictly speaking, new. They have certainly exploded in the last

few years, and small-town powerhouses have indeed turned into met-
ropolitan, and even global, ones. But they rest on influence, assets,
and connections built over many decades, and in that sense they are
wholly traditional. The sudden prominence of a new, provincial elite
should not lead one to think that the economy has become somehow
democratic. People like Monty have always had money, and they see
the world from that perspective. The gruelling, arid Delhi of so many
people's experience is not a city they know.

"Where do you place yourself in the pyramid of Delhi wealth?" I
ask. "There can't be many people turning over a billion dollars?"

"You have no idea," he says, and smiles condescendingly. "This
year's *Forbes* list counted about twenty billionaires in this country.
How many do you think there really are? At least a hundred. Most
people don't go public with their money. They don't want scrutiny.
I would never list my company."

"Who's the most powerful person in Delhi?"

"It all depends on politics. You can have a billion but if you have no
connections it doesn't mean anything. My family has been building
connections for two generations and we know everyone. We know
people in every political party; we never suffer when the government
changes."

"So why do you travel with bodyguards?"

"The UP police intercepted communications about a plan to kidnap me, and they told my father. People want money and they think
of the easiest way, which is to take it from someone who has it. They
can't do anything constructive themselves so they think short term.
We need more professionalism in India. More corporate governance.
Then we'll show the entire world."

For good reason, Monty is grateful to India.

"Since I was fourteen I've realized India is the place. I love this
place, this is where it's at. Elsewhere you may have as much money
as Laxmi Mittal but you're still a second-class citizen. This is your
fucking country. You should do it here."

Monty tells me how he hates America.

"Why should Wal-Mart come in here? I don't mind Gucci and
Louis Vuitton—they do nothing to disturb the social fabric. But keep
Wal-Mart out of here. We were under slavery for seven hundred fuck-

ing years. We've only been free for sixty. Give us another thirty and we will buy Wal-Mart. I tell you, I was at a party the other day and I had my arms round two white people and I suddenly pushed them away and said, *Why are you here? We don't need you guys any more.*"

Twenty-eight years old, well traveled, and richer than most people on the planet, Monty's resentment toward white people is unexpectedly intense. I ask him how the world would be different if it were run by Indians.

"It will be more spiritual," he says. But then he thinks for a moment and says, "No. It will be exactly the same."

I bring our conversation to an end. Monty pays the bill and we walk outside to the quiet car park.

"Thanks," he says, shaking my hand. I don't really know why.

His driver opens the back door of his BMW and Monty gets in. The gates open, the BMW sweeps out, and behind it an SUV full of bodyguards.

Monty lives about two hundred meters away.

I drive home, thinking over our conversation. I ponder a little detail: during my loo break he took advantage of my absence to send a text message to our common friend. Just checking that I really knew her. Somewhere in Monty is something alert and intimidating.

I'm still driving when he sends a text message to me, asking me not to quote certain things he has said. I write back: OK IF YOU ANSWER ONE MORE QUESTION, WHAT DOES MONEY MEAN TO YOU?

He responds straight away: ONE OF THE END PRODUCTS OF MY HARD WORK, IT DOES MEAN A LOT I RESPECT IT IT GIVES ME MORE HARD WORK AND ON THE SIDE A BIT OF LUXURY (:

5.

Driving past Delhi's sole dealer of Bentleys and Lamborghinis, I stop in on a whim and ask to speak to the manager. He's not around and I'm sent to have coffee with the PR girls. They are appropriately attractive and, judging by their diamonds, from the right kinds of families ("I've driven a million Porsches and Ferraris," says one. "They're nice cars. But when you get into a Lamborghini it's something else."). For them, Delhi is a place of infinite money-making and they fall over themselves trying to express this fantastic fecundity.

"When someone comes in here looking to buy a Bentley, we don't ask him what he's driving now. Just because he drives a BMW doesn't mean he can afford a Bentley. We ask if he has a jet or a yacht. We ask if he has an island."

"Are there many people with jets in Delhi?" I ask.

The girls wax apoplectic.

"*Everyone* has one. And not just one—they have two, three, four."

We chat about nice cars and expensive living. A Lamborghini is driven into the showroom: the noise is so deafening that we have to stop talking until it's in place. I ask the philistine's question: what's the point of spending thirty million rupees ($650,000) on a car that can do over three hundred kilometers per hour in a city where the traffic doesn't move? They tell me about the car club that meets at night in the diplomatic enclave, where the roads are straight, wide, and empty.

"You have to have at least, like, a BMW or a Mercedes to join. They meet at midnight and they race their cars. The Prime Minister's office is always calling us to complain."

"Why?"

"Because the Prime Minister can't sleep. These engines make so much noise they keep him awake. So he calls us to complain, but obviously there's nothing we can do."

As I drive away, I cannot help thinking of Prime Minister Manmohan Singh tossing and turning in bed, his snowy hair un-turbaned on the pillow, his dreams interrupted by the rich boys' Ferraris screaming up and down the roads outside. Manmohan Singh is of course the man who, long ago, as finance minister, opened up the economy and set the course for a new market elite.

TAMAS DOBOZY

■

The Encirclement

FROM *Granta*

AT SOME POINT DURING THE LECTURE Sándor would get up, point a finger at Professor Teleki and accuse him of lying—and Teleki would gasp and sputter and grow red in the face and the audience would love it. But it wasn't an act, and Teleki had approached Sándor many times—either personally or through his agent—to ask what his problem was. He even offered him money, which Sándor accepted, only to break his promise and show up at the lectures again—to the point where audiences started expecting him, as if Teleki's presence was secondary, playing the straight man to this hectoring, vindictive blind guy who was the star of the show.

Yes, Sándor was blind. Which only made it more incredible, especially in the early days, that he'd managed to follow Teleki all over North America, from one stop on the lecture circuit to the next. "How the hell can a blind man," Teleki yelled at his agent, "get around the country so quickly?" Nonetheless, Teleki could see it: Sándor in a dark overcoat, black glasses not flashing in the sunshine so much as absorbing it, his cane *tip-tapping* along the pavement through all kinds of landscape—deserts, mountains, prairies—and weather—squalls, blizzards, heatwaves—aimed directly at the place where Teleki had scheduled his next appearance. It was like something out of a bad folktale.

But once Teleki started bribing him the vision changed, and he always pictured Sándor sipping mai tais in the airport lounge before boarding with the first-class ticket Teleki's hush money had bought him, chatting amiably with businessmen and flirting, in a blind-man sort of way, with the stewardesses, though this was as far from the truth as the first vision had been, as Sándor himself explained.

They sat in the bar of the Seelbach Hilton in Louisville and Sándor, with a casual seriousness that always drove Teleki crazy, told him he hadn't spent a cent Teleki had given him and that every single trip had been accomplished through the "assistance of strangers." All he had to do, Sándor said, was step out the door and instantly there were people there, asking if he was okay, if there was anything they could do to help, if there was something he needed. When Teleki said he found it hard to believe that such spontaneous charity could have gotten him from Toronto to New York, to Montreal, Halifax, Boston, Chicago, Calgary, Los Angeles, Vancouver, and Anchorage, in that order, on time for every single one of his lectures, Sándor replied, "You can believe it or not, but that's exactly what happened." He'd found out about Teleki's itinerary, grabbed his coat and suitcase and cane, and walked out of the door into the care of the first stranger he'd met, and from there, "Well, things took care of themselves." Teleki looked at him, then around the Seelbach, wondering if he could get away with strangling Sándor right there.

The point at which Sándor would usually rise from his seat—various people supporting him by the elbows—was when Teleki began to describe the morning of January 18, 1945 in Budapest, the minute he'd stepped off the Chain Bridge, and the order went out to blow it up, along with the Hungarian and German soldiers, the peasants and their wheelbarrows full of ducks, the middle-class children and women and men, suitcases packed, still streaming across it. By then, the bridges were a tangled mass of metal, holes gaping along the causeway, cars stuck in them, on fire, bodies shredded by Soviet artillery and tangled in the cables and railings, thousands of people trying to force their way across in advance of the Soviets, trampling and being trampled on, cursing in the near dark, forced over the sides into the icy river, mowed down by fighter planes, Red Army tanks, machine guns, while behind their backs, in that half of Budapest, the siege went on, fighting from street to street, building to building, the whole place ablaze.

"Tell them how you grabbed two of the children whose parents had died coming across the bridge," Sándor would yell at him at this point. "Tell them how you held them to your chest, telling the Arrow Cross officer you couldn't join the siege effort because your wife had just died. And then tell them how you abandoned those kids in the next street. You tell them that!" Sándor jabbed his cane in Teleki's direction.

"That never happened!" Teleki would shout back. "I never did that."

And the audience would hoot and laugh and clap, egging Sándor on.

It was always something different, another aspect of the story sabotaged. When Teleki got to the part about how he'd gone up to the castle and "volunteered," as he put it, to join the defense under Lieutenant-Colonel László Veresváry, Sándor stood up—someone had handed him a bullhorn—and did a high-pitched imitation of how Teleki, after abandoning the children, had run into an Arrow Cross soldier who saw that he was able-bodied and told him to get up to the castle. "B-b-b-b-but, I'm just looking for fooooood," whined Sándor. "I-I-I-I left my kids a block over and I was about to go back for them. My wife, you see, she died when they blew up the bridge . . ." And here Sándor fell into a fit of such flawless mock weeping that many in the audience turned toward Teleki and copied him. "But the soldier forced you up to the castle anyhow, didn't he?" said Sándor, suddenly serious. "Giving your ass a kick every few feet just to make sure you got there."

"I have no idea what you're talking about," said Teleki, trying to look cool. "And if you don't stop interrupting my talks I'm going to have a restraining order put on you."

But Teleki's agent advised him against this. How would it look, he asked, if Teleki, the great professor of twentieth-century Middle European history, award-winning author of biographies and memoirs, survivor of the siege of Budapest, were suddenly afraid of the rantings of a blind man? Besides, as the agent had explained, it would only provide more publicity for Sándor, which was the last thing either of them wanted. He finally suggested—and he was surprised that Teleki hadn't considered this himself—that he get his act together and take on Sándor directly, since he was after all a historian. Or was he?

Teleki looked at him, wondering whether his agent had been to one of his lectures lately. Had he seen what went on up there? Sándor was killing him, and on the very ground where Teleki was supposed to be the authority. On the other hand, looking again at his agent, Teleki realized that maybe he didn't want him to get rid of Sándor, that maybe—no, *probably*—his agent was actually happy with the way things were working out, eagerly calculating his percentage from the recent "bump" in ticket sales.

"What I mean," said the agent, "is find out who this Sándor guy is. Isn't that something you do? Root around in people's pasts?"

Teleki had not known how to respond to that. Sándor Veselényi was his name; that's as far as they'd gotten during their first few meetings. And he couldn't just walk into the nearest archive and pull out the file with that name and *voilà*, there would be everything from the baptismal record through to the accident that caused his blindness to why he'd decided to make it his life's work to humiliate Teleki. No, it would take years to do that kind of research, just as it had taken years to gather material for each of the biographies and memoirs Teleki had written, to put together the lecture that was now, unfortunately, thrilling audiences more than ever, and which he was contractually locked into.

Not that it wouldn't have been nice—Teleki was the first to admit—to get up at the lectern and to lay it all out the next time Sándor opened his mouth, flashing the slides of Sándor in his fascist uniform, a member of the Arrow Cross, or better yet of Father Kun's murderous band, so unlike the Germans in their rejection of efficiency, in really going out of their way, even to be inconvenienced, as long as it meant slaughtering the Jews *just right*. And for the coup de grâce, for a nice moral twist at the end of the story, something about how Sándor had been blinded by his own desire to seek and destroy, perhaps a shard of glass from an explosion he'd rigged in one of the buildings in the Budapest ghetto—whole families tied up inside.

But Teleki had no information on Sándor—only on himself. He'd get up there with his black-and-white slides, his laser pointer, his tongue tripping up, bogged down, boxed in by English, a language so clunky compared to his own, and try to tighten up his story even further, to make himself appear even *more* authentic, only to have Sándor hobble in on the arms of two businessmen, a mother of three, four old men in outdated suits, and two guys sporting Mohawks.

Teleki spoke on, trying to keep his voice from going falsetto. He focused on the crowd—the usual assemblage of academics, writers, journalists, immigrants, students, amateur historians, senior citizens—and pointed to the picture of himself in the uniform of Veresváry's garrison, expected to keep the Soviets from capturing Buda castle, where the SS and Arrow Cross commanders were wringing their hands in the middle of the siege, encircled entirely by the Red Army, trying to figure out what to do. At night, young men, really just boys, would try to fly in supplies by glider, Soviet artillery shooting them out of the sky. Teleki struck a solemn tone when he told the crowd that the place they were supposed to land—Vérmezö—could be translated as "Blood Meadow."

When Sándor stayed silent, Teleki grew braver, and he told them of what it was like in the final days of the siege, the desperate order of the castle with its German and Hungarian armies, the soldiers too frightened of punishment—usually a bullet in the head—to voice what was on their minds: why SS Obergruppenführer Pfeffer-Wildenbruch hadn't gotten them the hell out of Budapest, why they were clearly sitting around waiting to be slaughtered. Worse still was being under the command of Veresváry, whose soldiers were men like Teleki—refugees or criminals or laborers pressed into service—for whom Veresváry was always willing to spare a bit of whipping from the riding crop he carried around, brandishing it over his head as he strode along the trenches they'd dug and were defending, as if the Soviet bullets whizzing around him were so many mosquitoes. Veresváry would sentence men to death for cowardice, then commute the sentence, then brutalize them so badly over the next several days—screaming and kicking at them while the fusillade continued, a horizontal rain of bullets and mortars—that the men would eventually stand in the trench, ostensibly to take better aim at the enemy, though from the way their guns hung in their hands it was little more than suicide. They stood there until half their faces suddenly vanished in a splatter, or their backs bloomed open, red and purple and bone. This seemed to satisfy Veresváry, who praised them as they fell, pointing to how they slumped, knees buckling, heads thrown back, and said to the rest, "There was a soldier, you chicken-shits. There was a soldier!"

"Was that why you came up with the plan to do away with him? To undermine and to betray and to murder your commander?" asked Sándor, standing up.

"You must be thinking of someone else, Sándor."

"Sure you did. You went from soldier to soldier and then, when you had them on side, you turned around and betrayed them to Pfef-fer-Wildenbruch, telling him you'd heard whispers that there would be a mutiny."

"That's the biggest lie I've ever . . ."

"Look at the next picture. Look at it."

The audience turned from Sándor to Teleki, who was standing there, mouth agape, the remote control in hand, his finger poised above the button, wondering whether Sándor was bluffing, or whether he'd somehow managed to hijack the projector, slipping in a different set of slides.

"Let's see it," someone in the audience yelled, and everyone laughed.

Teleki hit the button and there they were: all those arrested on charges of treason, five battered men with rotting clothes and un-shaven faces standing against the blackened walls of the castle dis-trict, loosely grouped together, as if they were not yet accused and looking to slink off before it happened. It was the picture as Teleki re-membered it, in exactly the place where it always appeared.

"There you are. You're standing just to the left of Pfeffer-Wilden-bruch. That's you right there, you dirty stinking fink! You sold out all your comrades!"

Teleki turned, squinting at the photograph, noting with eye-opening surprise that the guy there did resemble, in a way, what he might have looked like thirty years ago, after seventy or so days of siege—malnourished, frightened to death, desperate.

The audience applauded.

* * *

"The guy can see photographs!" said Teleki to his agent. "He's a complete fraud!"

"Why didn't you say anything at the lecture?"

"I did! But nobody could hear me! They were too busy applauding!"

His agent shrugged. "Maybe he saw the photograph before he went blind. Maybe somebody described it to him."

"Come off it," Teleki said.

"So how come he knows so much about you, then?"

"He doesn't know anything about me! All that stuff . . . he's lying!"

The agent looked at him with a raised eyebrow.

"What? You believe him now, too?"

"The only thing I believe in is sales," replied the agent, recovering quickly. "And sales are excellent," he said. "How would you feel about playing in bigger venues?"

"I'm not 'playing!' I'm trying to inform people, to teach them something!"

What Teleki noticed next was that Sándor's entourage seemed to be growing, as if the people who helped him were no longer dropping him off at the lectures and going on their way, but sticking around, as if something in Sándor's words, the depth of his conviction, had brought them into contact with a higher cause, a belief system. *Great,* thought Teleki. *Just what I need: Sándor becoming a guru.*

In addition, it seemed as though Sándor was now doing more of the talking than Teleki was — bellowing on, jabbing the cane in Teleki's direction, the group of people immediately around him more vociferous in their approval than the rest. By the end of the night, Teleki noted that he'd spoken only three minutes more than Sándor.

But it was not just this that made Teleki decide, then and there, after twelve fingers of Scotch on the balcony of his hotel room, to pack it in, but also what Sándor had said. For the first time since the beginning of their conflict he was seriously doubting whether he knew more about the siege than the blind man, or whether, in fact, his very first guess had been right after all and that Sándor, far from being a disabled person, was some spirit of vengeance, one of those mythic figures who were blind not because they couldn't see, but because they were distracted from the material world by a deeper insight, by being able to peer into secret places. Of course, remembering how he'd seen Sándor walk into pillars or trip over seats, Teleki laughed and dismissed the thought, though it always came back, forcing him up from sleep, the extent of Sándor's information, the way he could retrieve things from the abyss of the past.

For when Teleki had described the last few days in the castle, how Veresváry ordered them to draw up surveillance maps using tele-scopes taken from the National Archives, plotting the streets in the direction of western Buda, Sándor had nodded in his seat. When Teleki said that rumors of a breakout had been swirling for days, Sán-dor rose up, but said nothing. Nervously, Teleki had continued, say-ing the German soldiers, during the Second World War, never sur-rendered, preferring the death of fighting on, of retreat, rather than captivity, for they'd been told of the horrors and torments of Siberia, as if it was possible to imagine a place where death was salvation.

Teleki was sent to Pfeffer-Wildenbruch with the map they'd drawn up. At this point in the story, Sándor began rubbing his hands to-gether, waiting for Teleki to repeat what Pfeffer-Wildenbruch had said that day as he took the documents from Teleki's hand, staring right through him as if he wasn't in the room, as if there was only the Obergruppenführer himself, alone with the choices he couldn't make.

"If I give the order for a breakout," he mumbled, "everyone will die."

It was here that Sándor finally chimed in, mimicking the reply Teleki was supposed to have given: "S-s-s-surely not everyone."

Teleki reached for the volume adjustment on his microphone, continuing with what Pfeffer-Wildenbruch had said to him: "You'll probably be one of the first to die."

"I-i-it's a fitting thing, sir," Sándor interrupted him again.

"I did not say that!" shouted Teleki, turning the volume all the way up.

Someone handed Sándor the bullhorn again. "To face the enemy directly is a fitting thing, Obergruppenführer, sir. Without flinch-ing."

Suddenly Sándor began to play both roles, turning this way and that to indicate when Pfeffer-Wildenbruch and when Teleki was speaking, the crowd watching raptly, oblivious to the "No, no, no!" Teleki was shouting into the microphone.

"Meanwhile," said Sándor, now in the role of Teleki, "while the men are proving their bravery, we could do our duty and escape using the sewers under the castle."

"Our duty?" Sándor carried off Pfeffer-Wildenbruch's fatigue perfectly.

"I-i-i-it would not be cowardice," Sándor stuttered, again playing Teleki. "Such words belong to narcissists, those who worry for their reputations, for how history will regard them. No"—Sándor shook his head as Teleki might have—"we must look beyond our egos, our timid wish for glory. The war effort needs us . . . needs you . . . to survive this. You must sacrifice your pride for the greater good." Then, in a flourish, Sándor removed his glasses, shifting his eyes from side to side, as Teleki had done so many times behind the lectern. "Obergruppenführer, sir, I've heard the men speaking of a plot on Lieutenant-Colonel Veresváry's life. In the sewers, you will need men you can trust . . . To prove my devotion I will give you the names of the conspirators."

"And so," Sándor now said, returning to himself (what Teleki increasingly considered the role of himself), "while men died by the thousands in the breakout, our friend here"—he indicated Teleki—"was splashing through the sewers."

The sewers. Here, Sándor's knowledge was just as extensive. It was called Ördög-árok, "Devil's Ditch," a name in keeping with what was to greet them, descending into waters swirling with suitcases, soggy files, fragments of memoranda, whole suits of clothing from which men and women seemed to have dissolved, a wooden statue of the Virgin face down, her hand entwined with the much smaller one of a body trapped in the waters beneath her. They ran into loose bands of SS. They waited below while men tried scaling the rungs of ladders to sewer gratings above, poking their heads out, followed by the crack of a sniper's bullet, the body falling back and knocking off all who were clinging to the ladder.

They entered aqueducts that grew narrower and narrower, Pfef-fer-Wildenbruch sending Teleki on ahead (or so Sándor said) into places he could move along crouched over, then only on his hands and knees, and finally on his belly, each pipe he went into smaller than the last, until he was overcome by claustrophobia and panicked, inching backwards on his stomach and chest like some worm revers-ing itself—only to find that Pfeffer-Wildenbruch and his party had moved on, leaving him behind. It was at this point that he ran into Hungarian commander Ivan Hindy and two soldiers and his wife, still wearing the finery she put on every day, as befitted her position, the hem of her dress drifting out around her as she whispered to the men on either side, trying to keep the mood light, the conversation agreeable, even as the screams of men rang up and down the sewer. They were holding her by both elbows, but it seemed as if she was holding them, especially the soldier whose arm was in a sling, as if the sound of her voice could keep them going, as if in allowing them to hold her she was lending them strength.

As Sándor's story went—and it was a compelling story, Teleki had to admit, so much so that even he wanted to hear how it would end—Teleki was reluctant to accept Hindy's order to bring up the rear of their little party. And when Hindy, seeing his reluctance, sug-gested that he could go to the front then, Teleki again demurred. "Well, where would you like to be?" And when Teleki said he would prefer to stay in the middle, alongside Mrs. Hindy, everyone laughed, their echoes bouncing off the walls and water until he realized they'd stopped caring, that he was trapped in a group of people tripping along cheerily to capture, trial, execution.

"M-m-m-maybe we should try another few of the sewer gratings," he said, pointing up, waiting for a break in the laughter.

"Would you prefer to go first or second?" Hindy asked, and when Teleki said second they laughed all over again—except for Mrs. Hindy, who reached forward (Sándor reproducing her movement for the benefit of the audience) and tenderly stroked Teleki's cheek.

It was decided that the uninjured soldier would go first, since he was the heaviest and would need two men to lift him within reach of the first rung of the ladder. He would see whether there were snipers present, and draw their fire away from the manhole, hopefully without getting his head blown off. Next would come Teleki, whom the commander could boost up alone, and who'd then help, from above, with the delicate job of heaving up the injured soldier, as well as the voluminous Mrs. Hindy, and finally Hindy himself.

The soldier nodded, taking a long swig from a bottle of Napoleon brandy he said he'd found floating in the sewer, then stepped on to the hands held out to him and reached for the ladder, crawling up it quickly and pushing open the grating. *Click*. There was the sound of a firing pin hitting a dud cartridge. Looking up, they saw the soldier staring directly into the barrel of a Soviet gun, though in the next second he'd swung the bottle of brandy into the Russian's face, rolled quickly out of the hole and run, the Soviet soldier giving his head a shake and then chasing after him. Within seconds, Hindy was holding out his hands for Teleki, who looked at them, placed his foot tentatively into the knitted fingers, then boosted himself up, only to have Hindy remove them the instant he'd grabbed the rung, leaving him dangling there, too weak to pull himself up and too afraid to fall back into the sewer, from where there would be no second chance at escape. Hindy and the injured soldier were laughing again, but not Mrs. Hindy, who was telling them to stop and trying to reach up, to help him, only to be met by Teleki's gaze, desperate and pitiless, as he placed his boot squarely in the middle of her upturned face and pushed off, feeling her nose crack under the sole. And then he was up the ladder, rung over rung, and out of the manhole and running, while they called after him to help pull them out.

Sándor stopped, intending to continue, but the audience had begun booing in Teleki's direction, the sound growing louder and louder until he left the stage.

Strangely, Teleki slept very well that night. There was something about surrender that was incredibly calming, as if the loss of desire could compensate for defeat. But by the middle of the next day he was squirming again, sitting in the café with his agent, who was showing him one article, feature, and editorial after another, all of them reporting on the "creative sabotage" of his lectures. In keeping with Teleki's recent luck, the writers devoted far more space to Sándor than to him, mainly because none of them had been able to dig up a single thing about this blind man tapping his way out of no-where to deliver his long apocalyptic monologues, setting the record straight and exposing the liars. In these articles Sándor was a moral force and Teleki a con man.

"There's one here that speculates on whether you guys are work-ing together," said the agent, pushing across a copy of the *New York Times*.

Teleki glanced at it for a second and then quietly told his agent he was quitting.

"Quitting!" the agent responded. "You can't quit!"

"I think I just need to disappear for a while," said Teleki. "Once this dies down we can talk about what to do next."

"We? There is no we," the agent told him. "Not if you quit!"

Teleki looked at him, and in an instant realized what had hap-pened. "You've been talking to Sándor, haven't you? What, you're rep-resenting both of us?"

His agent looked out the window and then back at him. "You know how often something like this comes around? A sleeper like this?"

"Tonight's my last show," said Teleki, rising from the table.

It wasn't like Teleki to fulfill a contract—or any other kind of prom-ise for that matter—if he didn't want to, and yet he found himself fighting the impulse to just walk away. Maybe he wanted to prove to Sándor that he wasn't afraid, that he couldn't be so easily chased away, that he could take whatever was thrown at him. But there was a more dangerous realization as well, and all that afternoon he seemed on the verge of confronting it, only to get scared and turn away, chan-nelling what he felt into a rage so acute that more than once he was seen talking to himself, having imaginary arguments with Sándor from which he always emerged with the decisive victory.

By nightfall, though, shortly before he was due on stage, Teleki fi-nally admitted to himself that Sándor's descriptions of the man us-ing two children to get out of military service, or exposed by Pfef-fer-Wildenbruch as a totally expendable soldier, or being mocked by Hindy and his men for cowardice was not without a certain com-fort, as if there might be something to gain from having your stories turned inside out, from having the hard moral decision—whether to lie or tell the truth—taken away from you.

And when Teleki took the stage that night, standing on the podium, he was no longer the showman of six months ago, when Sándor had first turned up at his lectures, or even of the day before yesterday, when he'd tried to defend himself. There was something serious in him now, as if having come to the end of all this, having failed to defend himself, he was beyond loss, free, unconcerned for his reputation.

It was in his eyes, the need to survive, irrespective of honor or glory or anything else, as if he was once again looking at what Sándor had begun to describe, standing to interrupt Teleki five minutes into the lecture: the worst of what happened in the siege, all those men forced to take part in a breakout that should have happened months earlier and was now little more than a mass human sacrifice.

He remembered the morning, February 11, when a rumor went around that the radio operators had begun destroying their equipment; remembered the illusions many of the soldiers clung to: that only Romanians were guarding the breakout point; that they'd run the minute they saw the horde of fascist soldiers; that it would be no more than a half-hour march through the empty city to the place where German reinforcements were waiting; that, absurdly, the Russians were no match for the tactical brilliance of the Nazi and Arrow Cross commanders. Like Sándor, Teleki knew that Veresváry had assembled his men at the Bécsi Gate before the march, that they were hit by a bombardment out of nowhere, their bodies ripped open, dismembered, even before they'd had a chance to set out.

He could have followed Sándor word for word in recounting what only a very few men—a mere three percent of the twenty-eight thousand who set out that day—could recount seeing, or refuse to recount, crushed as they were by recurring nightmares of that three kilometers of city, so overwhelming that to begin speaking of it would be to never speak of anything else again. Mortar fire along avenues and boulevards. Flares hanging in the sky overhead. Soldiers screaming in a rush of animal frenzy, all semblance of reason gone as they realized the Soviets were stationed along the route—that they'd prepared for the breakout, that tanks and rockets and snipers were in place to kill every single one of them—now crushed into door-ways, stumbling in the dark, crawling over comrades missing arms and legs and begging to be shot—one last mercy for which no one could spare the time—pushed on by those behind them, a river of flesh squeezed out between the buildings bordering Széna and Széll Kálmán Square, into a night kaleidoscopic with shells, tracer bullets, flares, panzerfausts, the light at the end of machine guns flashing without pause, a city shattered into ever more impossible configu-rations—a maze without discernible routes, choices, even the cer-tainty of dead ends.

There was a pause in the auditorium at the end of this. Then Sán-dor, gathering himself up, began to speak again, his glasses aimed at Teleki. "This is what you saw when you emerged from the sewers. This is what you'd supported—you and the men like you—so eager to support Horthy when he signed with the Nazis, and then, when he was deposed for wanting to break with them, to shift that support to Hitler's puppet, Szálasi, and the Arrow Cross. *Honor!* you said. *Brav-ery! The nation above all!* But it was always someone else who paid for this allegiance, wasn't it? Not you. You slithered out of every situa-tion, every duty you so loudly insisted upon, all those high standards and noble causes you so loudly proclaimed—always the job of some-one else. And at the end of all that, in the aftermath, when you saw the breakout, realized what you'd done . . ."

"You went blind," whispered Teleki into the microphone. "You went blind."

"I'm talking about you!"

"No you're not," said Teleki, and he pushed back the lectern and walked off the raised platform and up the auditorium steps to where Sándor, who drew back as Teleki moved closer, was standing. "This story you've been telling is your own, Sándor."

"It's yours!" Sándor shouted. "You know it's yours!"

And Teleki, in the most inspired performance of his career, threw his arms around the blind man, whispering, "It's okay, it's okay, it's okay," just loud enough to be picked up by the microphone pinned to his lapel.

* * *

He had tightened his hold until Sándor stopped struggling, and all the while he'd continued to whisper soothingly of how this was Sándor's public confession, how he could not have described the things he'd described unless he'd seen them, or known the things he knew unless he'd been there. He said he knew Sándor could still see, and that what had darkened his eyes was not physical in nature, but moral.

Sándor had shouted and hollered and tried to fight him off, but Teleki merely continued to hold him, and the audience had inclined their heads, finally, in sympathy, as if they'd never for a second thought of Sándor as anything other than a refugee from himself, using Teleki's lectures to disclose his conscience in the only way he could—obliquely, by projecting them onto someone else. They even clapped when Teleki finally let go of the exhausted, defeated Sándor and, taking him by the hand, led him from the hall, down the steps, out the back exit off the wings of the stage, where the blind man flung Teleki's hand away, told him he should be ashamed of himself, and stormed off as fast as the tentative tapping of his cane would allow, tripping over the first curb he came to. Teleki smiled.

And he'd continued smiling late into the night, wrapped in his robe in the hotel, drinking the champagne his agent had sent up along with a note of apology Teleki never read, already knowing what it said. He gazed out over the city and wondered what Sándor might be doing now, whom he was with, where he was headed. For that was Sándor's way, Teleki had realized, incapable of functioning, of getting from one place to the next, unless there was someone, preferably a crowd, to help him, as if his blindness was a way of restoring people to some sense of community, as if by helping him they were ultimately helping themselves, as if there was another map of the world, not of nations and cities but of intersections of need, of what draws us together.

Sándor's world, Teleki thought. *His*. And he wondered for a moment what it was like—all those people working together—having long ago learned to count on nobody and nothing, groping his way all alone through the darkest of places.

BRYAN FURUNESS

■

Man of Steel

FROM *Ninth Letter*

A COMMERCIAL CHANGED MY LIFE when I was ten years old. I was watching television in my living room, which really meant that I was tossing a basketball in the air distractedly while slipping in and out of daydreams. Sometimes, during commercials, I would sink so far inside my own head that by the time the show came back on, I would have forgotten what I was watching. But this commercial caught my attention. I don't remember what it was selling, but the product's beside the point; the point is the commercial itself.

It began with strange, warbly music and then, rising from a kind of fog, a simple pencil sketch of a man's face, but then it wasn't a man's face at all: it was a creature with large, almond-shaped eyes and a ridged brow and a pointy chin. This, said a voice—deep and pleasant to listen to—was a creature from outer space, an alien, a traveler from a distant star. "Who knows," said the voice, "what's really out there?"

The basketball fell out of my hands and dribbled away across the carpet. Now a woman looked straight at the camera—into me—and explained how, on an ordinary morning, she'd suddenly felt a blast of burning pain in her hand, when, at that exact moment, a thousand miles away, her son had burned himself on a stove.

"Coincidence?" said the voice.

I shook my head.

Then came the clincher, the part that changed me: a woman stood in her kitchen, looking at a plane ticket in her hand. Something told her it was a bad idea to get on that plane. She stared at the ticket for a long moment before finally putting it down on the table. The camera zoomed in on the ticket as the voice announced that the plane had crashed and there were, sadly, no survivors. My skin prickled.

I turned off the television and stood there listening to the little snaps of the tube cooling off. I was no stranger to disaster, but I had never considered that I might be able to do something about it. In my best announcer voice I said, "No survivors," and gave myself goose-bumps all over again.

That was the day I became a devout listener to my own internal warnings. It turned out there were quite a few, apparently just waiting for an audience.

In those days, I spent a lot of time in the bathroom. I called it my "refuge," a term I had picked up from comic books. Superman had his icy fortress at the top of the world; I had a bathroom with a cheap lock and a loud fan. It wasn't glamorous, but it did afford me the privacy to imagine a tickle fight with my babysitter Missy, who had stopped doing that with me right around the time I started suggesting it; or to stand on the edge of the tub with my back to the mirror so I could see what my butt looked like to other people.

In a larger sense, it seemed important to have a place where I could brood and argue freely with myself, if only in a whisper—a belief I hold to this day.

My father came around every once in a while to knock on the door and ask if I was all right. He probably thought I had an intestinal parasite, an illusion I encouraged by flushing every ten minutes or so and issuing the occasional gratuitous groan. My father wouldn't have understood the importance of a refuge, not in a million years. But I knew he would consider what I did in there to be weird behavior, and so I had to hide it from him. He had become so sensitive to that kind of thing ever since my mother ran away.

Ever since my mother *left*, I suppose I should say, but "ran away" is what we said then, and it's still the first phrase that comes to my mind when I think about her. It's a mean thing to say, I guess, talking about her like she was a kid running down the street, blubbering, with a backpack full of peanut butter sandwiches—but now I think the term carried some hope, too. Adults who leave don't come back, but runaways sometimes do. When I saw the commercial, we'd been waiting nearly six months for her to come back from Hollywood.

But the bathroom—that's what I was talking about. I spent so much time in there that I should not have been surprised to receive my first warning while sitting on the toilet lid. It was morning, I remember, only a few days after the commercial. I was flipping through a ratty issue of *Ironman* while the shower warmed up. That's when I heard the words as clearly as if someone had spoken them inside my own head: *something bad at school today.*

I sat very still, waiting for clarification. In the commercial, the warning had been detailed. *This* plane, *this* crash, don't do *that.* But my warning, the one in my head, was about as specific as a fortune cookie.

To the ceiling fan, I said, "Can I get another clue, please?"

Steam tumbled over the top of the shower curtain. The comic book softened in my hands. When no further instructions came, I stood and turned slowly in a circle, raising my hands to see if that might improve my reception. Then I caught sight of myself in the mirror, arms raised like an orangutan. I pulled them down, embarrassed.

Maybe that wasn't a real warning, I thought. Maybe I didn't have the power. Maybe I shouldn't spend so much time alone in the bathroom.

"Look at me," I said to the mirror. Reluctantly, I met my own eyes. "Do you think Spiderman was on top of his game the minute after he got bitten by that radioactive spider? And what about Batman? He trained for years in the Batcave before he went into the night. And Hulk, well . . . he never really got a handle on his powers."

The lady in the commercial had probably started off small, I thought, with a cloudy vision of a falling teacup, or a voice that suggested that an umbrella might not be a bad idea today. Only with time and practice did she work her way up to transatlantic airline disasters. And yet, here I was, expecting total mastery right off the bat.

I nodded in the mirror, humbled. "You're right," I said. Then I pursed my lips, to see what I would look like if I was about to kiss someone.

*   *   *

I decided to stay home from school that morning. It wasn't hard; I think I just told my father *I don't feel so hot* in a woozy voice. He was susceptible to bad acting, which goes a long way toward explaining why he had married my mother in the first place.

Before he left for work, my father—who meant well but did not know how to deal with a sick child, even a fake one—came into my room with an armful of bottles and tins. Vap-O-Rub, cold cream, Dexatrim, cough drops in oily wrappers, Tinactin, and the giant bottle of aspirin that used to rattle like a snake on the days my mother took to bed: it looked like he had just cleared off an entire shelf of the medicine cabinet.

"Just fluids," I rasped before he had a chance to make a recommendation or concoction. He left and came back with a root beer. *Thank you*, I mouthed. He nodded, pursing his lips so they disappeared under his moustache. When he started backing away, I looked into the middle distance and shot a trembling hand in his direction, like a movie cowboy dying of consumption. I said, "Father . . ."

I guess I wanted him to take my hand, or to pull it down and tuck it under the blankets, saying *There, now,* or some other comforting nonsense, though I should have known it would only weird him out. I watched him struggle for a moment. Then he picked up the root beer and inserted it into my outstretched hand. "Don't spill," he said, and left my room without looking back.

I spent the morning watching reruns of *Gilligan's Island* and *What's Happening Now?* Really, I was waiting for my commercial, but the daytime ads apparently didn't deal in the supernatural. What they dealt was mainly correspondence courses in TV/VCR repair and discount testing strips for diabetics. I saw a world that needed to maintain its machines and sugar levels. By the time *Donahue* came on, I was bored, and itchy with curiosity about the warning. *Something bad at school today*: was it real? And how bad were we talking here? If it was fatal, the warning would have said so, right?

I got dressed and walked to school through the blue light of falling snow, hoping I hadn't already missed the terrible event.

I got to school in time for lunch. I went through the line, got my hot pack, my cold pack, my red box of milk, and joined my classmates back in the room. Everything looked different, though I couldn't say exactly how. Nothing was new, nothing seemed out of place, but everything looked just a little *off*, like when you play around with the contrast knob on the television. Then I understood: the difference was me.

I was seeing the classroom with the brooding wariness of a superhero. Just yesterday the room's only threat was boredom; now it teemed with danger. The rust on the metal edges of the bookshelves screamed of tetanus. The aisles between desks were strewn with pencils as sharp as punji sticks. My own desk, allegedly cleaned with disinfectant every night, bore a pencil sketch of the Chicago Bulls logo that had lasted for three weeks with only slight smearing. And this is where we ate lunch. "My God," I muttered.

The surprise was no longer that something was going to happen to me; it was that I had escaped harm for so long.

As I pried at the top of my milk carton, I pitied my ignorant classmates. I could see, but they were still blind, and probably always would be. *You fools*, I thought, and just then the flap of the carton tore open. Milk spilled across my desk, and, before I could push my chair back, down over my crotch. Timmy Fox, born with a piercing voice and a keen radar for humiliation, jumped up and yelled, "Oh, man! Revie peed his pants!"

I can't say for sure, but there may have been a half-smile on my face as the class hooted and pointed. There could no longer be any doubt: I had a special power.

I began to spend more time in my refuge. Developing my powers of premonition required a good deal of solitary brooding. After turning on the fan and the shower to cover my voice, I liked to look into the mirror and say gravely, *You have an obligation to develop this gift.*

Then I'd make a face of what I imagined to be great turmoil, clenching my hair and shaking my head. *No, no, I just want to be normal.* Then I'd stop and hold my own gaze for a long moment. *You must.*

I repeated this performance until I felt wonderfully burdened with secrets and duties.

A few days after the milk incident, something else happened that confirmed my power, but also its limits. I was waiting for the bus to take me to school when a warning came to me in the image of blood dripping down my finger. The vision was so clear that I actually checked my hands, then jammed them into my pockets for safekeeping. All day long at school I kept my hands in my pockets, even during lunch, when I feigned a stomachache so I wouldn't have to eat my food like a hillbilly in a pie-eating contest. I didn't even take my hands out after Timmy Fox marveled loudly at how I reeeeeeally must love pocket pool.

I'd made it almost home, safe, unharmed, feeling slightly dizzy with hunger but also pretty smart, when I tripped getting off the bus. Because my hands were still in my pockets, I fell like a tree and hit the street with my face.

The bus driver scrambled down from his seat, frightened and angry. "What the hell are you doing, falling like that?"

Dazed, I reached up to touch my throbbing nose. My hand came away bloody. Holding it up to the driver, I said, "Coincidence?"

So I couldn't save myself like the lady in the commercial. So I couldn't alter the course of destiny. Even if my power never got any bigger, I had a heads-up on personal tragedy. I was a dowsing rod to the bad vibrations of the universe: nothing bad should ever catch me by surprise again.

I only wished I had known about my gift earlier so I could have braced myself for my mother's departure. The warning signs were right there, if we'd just understood. The past spring, she'd started spending more and more time in her bedroom, sometimes coming out as late as dinnertime, still in her kimono, which was really just a shiny housecoat she had embroidered with a long, thorny rose. This wasn't every day, understand. On her good days, she was as dynamic as ever, staging tea parties, kaffeeklatsches, cocktail parties, just the three of us, ties and jackets required. On Charade Day, her own holiday she declared sometime in May, she refused to utter a word while the sun was up, even when we were in public, going so far as to act out *sweet potato* for the poor stockboy at the grocery store. "Two words," he said. "First word, rhymes with . . . feet?"

But on other days I would come home from school to hear the television blaring behind the closed door of her room. Once, I cracked the door and saw her sitting propped up against the headboard, eating salted celery and watching *Dark Victory*. On the nightstand was a frog palace of coffee cups and bowls. The smell of spoiled milk lapped over me like a warm sea, and I almost gagged. My mother, though—she was anything but a mess. Her blonde hair was perfectly set, and she was wearing makeup, heavy on the lip liner and eyeshadow.

I thought I was a careful spy, but I guess I wasn't. My mother turned her head, just slightly, and looked right at me. That's when I realized she wasn't eating the celery. Her jaw was moving because she was mouthing the words along with Bette Davis. I closed the door, spooked.

"Every engine sputters once in a while," my father said when I told him about this, and asked if she was okay. "She'll smooth out soon enough."

That was back when my father didn't mind strangeness so much. That was back before I knew how to pay attention to warnings.

I'm sorry, I told myself in the bathroom mirror. My nose was still swollen from hitting the street and my eyes had these little saddlebags. Behind me, the shower thundered away. I reminded myself that Batman had to watch a mugger kill his parents, and Spiderman had to lose his Uncle Ned. My mother's leaving was my Tragic Wake-up Call to My Power and Destiny. I said, *But that's the way it had to be*.

Someone knocked on the bathroom door and I jumped.

"Open up," said my father.

"Can you speak up, please?" I said, holding my hand over my rabbity heart. "It's hard to hear you in the shower."

I nodded at the mirror, congratulating myself on some quick thinking.

He said, "You're not in the shower."

I reached into the shower and adjusted the spray against the wall so it would sound like it was hitting a body.

He said, "Now you just turned the nozzle toward the wall."

How the hell could he tell that? Did he have a power, too? Could he actually see me right now? I stuck my head inside the shower curtain and said, "Can't a guy get some privacy? *Geez*."

There was a pause, long enough that I thought he might have gone away, then he said, "I can hear everything you're saying. Through the vent."

I didn't have to look at the mirror to know that a flush was crawling up my neck. My embarrassment intensified as I thought back to what I'd been saying only a few moments before. *Mr. President, I had a vision . . . no need to thank me for the last one, sir . . . I'm seeing submarines, a bunch of them, coming together just off the coast. On the side of each sub is a picture of a . . . hammer and a sickle. Does that mean anything to you?*

My father said, "Revie, open the damn door or I will open it."

I didn't take him seriously. He was far too gentle and cheap to knock down a door. Later I would push him beyond even that, but at that moment I didn't believe him capable of violence. By the time I heard the metallic click of his Swiss Army knife picking the lock, it was too late to do anything smart, so I jumped in the freezing shower with all my clothes on.

My father tore open the shower curtain and shut off the water. "Son, what is wrong with you?"

I was sitting in the tub, shaking with cold. I'd managed to pry off a single shoe before I realized there would be no good explanation for a pile of wet clothes at the bottom of the tub. *Oh, these? I was just trying to save on laundry detergent.*

He said, "I know what you've been doing. This premonition thing? It's got to stop."

I glared at him in what I hoped was a defiant way, though I must have looked like a drowned rat. Comic books were full of people like him. Fearful, small-minded people determined to limit you to the boundaries of their own tiny lives.

He said, "They're not real, you know."

Clenching my teeth so he wouldn't hear them chatter, I said, "Except they are."

He closed his eyes briefly, then opened them and jerked his thumb toward the door. "Towel off. Get dressed. We're going to the store."

At that moment my powers took another turn. I saw a vision of a falling anvil, and heard the words *Look out below.* "How about I just—"

"I'm not leaving you here alone with the mirror," he said, and hauled me from the tub. I slogged into my room, feeling gut-sick. Disaster awaited me if I went to the store. I remembered when I'd walked around with my hands in my pockets, nervous and scared all day. The waiting, I decided, was the worst part.

I went to my bookshelf and pulled out the Webster's Unabridged. I took it to my closet so my father wouldn't hear, whispered *Look out below* and swung it with all my force onto the crown of my head.

For days my father harped and harped about the premonition business until finally I said *Geez, all right already* and promised I would stop. Which was a lie. Why would I stop, now that I was finally getting a handle on my powers? After clobbering myself with the dictionary, nothing fell on me at the store. And the next day, when I scored my palm with an X-Acto knife—lightly, barely enough to break the skin—I didn't plant my hand on a broken beer bottle like my vision had suggested.

Throwing myself into a briar hedge, dropping from the top of the monkeybars onto my hip, eating half a pinecone, sticking my own head into the toilet (after cleaning it first; I wasn't *crazy*)—when my visions did not come to pass afterward, I came to believe that I had dislodged them with my own ersatz tragedies. An ounce of prevention, etc.

My system worked so well that I started doing harm to myself even when no warnings came. I thought of it as working ahead. If I could just bank enough pain, I thought, there would come a point where I would have clear sailing for the rest of my life, not one twinge or heartache until the moment my spirit left my body in a painless yawn. In one fantasy, I experienced all the pain of my life in a single second, like a lightning bolt.

Then came the day that my powers grew beyond myself. I was sitting behind the wheel of my father's Impala, parked in the driveway. It was evening, and I could see my father in the low light of the front room, watching television. He thought I was out here pretending to drive—a small bit of imagination he tolerated as rehearsal for the day I *would* drive, though it's more likely, I think now, that he needed the occasional break from me—but the truth was that the Impala was my new refuge. Cold as hell on a February night, but at least there were no vents to carry my voice to his ear.

I was playing with the cigarette lighter, pretending my car was jammed in a snowdrift in the Rockies, and I had to keep myself warm until the Mounties or whoever found me in the morning. I'd pull out the lighter, warm a hand over it until the coils darkened, and then plug the lighter back in for another round.

When the vision came, I didn't even recognize it as a warning at first. After all, previous warnings had starred me. But in this one I saw my mother. She had dark hair, bobbed to her shoulders, but it was unmistakably her. She was walking along a darkened street, glancing behind her, and I could tell she was frightened. And then I saw why—a man slipped along in the shadows behind her. He didn't seem to be hurrying, but he was somehow gaining on her.

The noise of her heels echoed off the shuttered storefronts. His shadow lengthened until it was around her like black water. When she looked up the next time, it was into the camera—into me—and I saw that she was asking me why I was letting this happen to her.

A small noise escaped my throat. The lighter popped out. I plucked it from the dash, yanked up my coatsleeve, and applied it to my wrist.

I heard the *shh* of searing flesh before I felt the pain. It took a second to hit me, like my nervous system couldn't believe this was happening, but when it hit, it was unbelievable, the sharpest thing you can imagine. My feet bucked out. My mouth opened all the way, but no noise came out. Waves of light cascaded down over my eyes, like suds going down the windshield in a car wash. Even when I dropped the lighter, my wrist felt like it was still on fire. I writhed in the seat, holding myself at the hand, maybe trying to pry off the arm that was bringing this fire into my body.

Eventually the pain subsided, of course, but only after a long time, and even then, gradually. When I checked my wrist, I expected to see a piece of blackened meat, but what I saw was a shiny, crinkly ring, like a piece of plastic. I wondered if my mother, three thousand miles away, had felt this pain, too. I wondered if she knew I'd saved her.

When I went inside, my father said, "That was a long time to practice driving."

He didn't look up from the television, but I could tell he wasn't
paying attention to that. I said, "I was practicing for a long trip."

"I kept seeing the little light come on, the one from the mirror."

After burning myself, I'd kept checking the lighted mirror in
the flap, to see if my face looked normal enough to go back into the
house without arousing suspicion. But every time I moved, my sleeve
brushed the burn, and my face went pale, my pupils turning into
blasted holes. Finally, I was too cold and tired and afraid I might receive another vision about my mother to care about looking normal.

My father adjusted himself on the couch, then looked over at me.
"You and mirrors," he said. "You have a history."

"A little freaking privacy. Is that too much to ask?"

"Any more premonitions?"

"I told you I stopped."

We stared at each other for a minute. On the television, Lynda
Carter tossed her golden lasso around a man, which meant that he
could struggle all he wanted, but he'd have to tell the truth. My father
said, "Privacy's bad for people. Especially people like you."

And your mother was the part that was left unsaid, but I could hear
it in the air, clear as a warning.

This is how it all came to a head, the night my power was forced out
of hiding.

My father and I were eating dinner, my specialty: spaghetti *à la
sink*. It was basically a giant bowl of spaghetti that we ate directly
over the sink. No dishes, and clean-up pretty much consisted of aim-
ing the sprayer toward anything that fell out of our mouths. I made
this dish at least three times a week.

When the doorbell rang, my father looked up. His moustache was
daubed with sauce, like the end of a paintbrush.

"I'll get it," I said.

Normally a doorbell in the evening meant a sympathetic church
lady with a cellophane-wrapped casserole or some kid hawking
M&M's for band camp. But as soon as I placed my hand on the knob,

I got the sense this was different.

I heard a distant buzzing, like electricity humming through power lines. My heart did this funny tripping thing: *tha-thump, tha-thump-thump-thump.* And the scab on my wrist began itching furiously under the Band-Aid.

Something big wasn't on its way; it was here.

"Who is it?" yelled my father from the kitchen.

I placed both hands on the knob and closed my eyes, trying to get an image of the person on the other side of the door.

The doorbell rang again. My father yelled, "Are you getting it or what?"

Pressing my lips to the gap between door and frame, I murmured, "Place your hand on the knob, please." If I could just see who it was, I'd know how to steel myself.

I heard my father's boots scraping across the kitchen tile. The doorbell started ringing over and over. My heart fell down three flights of stairs. When his boots thunked in the hallway, I squeezed my eyes shut, ready to settle for the most general prediction. "Good or bad, good or bad, good or—"

Whoever was on the porch tried the door and it swung right open.

"—bad," I finished. It wasn't my mother. I cannot say now, for sure, if that's who I really thought was going to be there. But it wasn't. It was Missy, the babysitter from down the street. She was a big girl with a pretty face that shone with good cheer and acne.

"Hope you don't mind me barging in like this, Revie," she said. "It sounded like you were having trouble with the door."

I felt a hand on my shoulder and looked back to see my father wiping at the sides of his mouth. "You're early," he said to Missy, then bared his teeth at her. "Anything in my teeth?"

As Missy squinted, I noticed what I had missed while eating next to him at the sink. He was wearing his good white oxford shirt. His boots gleamed. And was that the crease of an iron in his jeans?

"What?" he said. "I'm going to church."

"It's not Sunday."

"So? Does the Bible say to stay away from church during the week?"

I cocked my head like a television detective. The day wasn't the only cause for suspicion. Even when my mother was around, we hadn't been the most regular churchgoers. And now that she was gone, we didn't go at all. My father was a devout reader of the Sunday *Tribune*, a five-pound monster he read cover to cover with the exception of the Arts & Entertainment section, which he threw in the garbage on account of the link he had made between arts, entertainment, and the destruction of family. Every Sunday I recovered the section and tucked it under my sweatshirt, making my way to the bathroom with the paper's ragged edge rasping seductively against my belly as my father shouted out suggestions for changes to my diet.

"Well," he said. "It's not church-church. It's more of a meeting."

"What *kind* of meeting?"

He looked at Missy, but she suddenly became interested in the floormat. "It's a support group," he said at last. After a moment, he added, "For divorcees."

"Whoa," I said. "You're not divorced. Nobody's divorced here."

"I know that," he said. "Don't you think I know that? But it's not like they offer a group for guys who were—I'm just looking for a little help right now."

He lowered his voice on the word *help* like some people lower their voice on *miscarriage* or *rehab*. He gave Missy a furtive look and finally she stepped forward to steer me into the front room with a suggestion that we play some games. "But you're not divorced," I called over her shoulder. I wasn't exactly cooperating with Missy, but still, I was moving backwards. She was a bulldozer in a sweater. "Yahtzee?" she whispered, her voice tickling my ear. "Uno?" My father shrugged on his coat and I felt everything slipping away from me.

I planted my heels. My voice came out thick and deep. "Look at me."

Missy pulled her hands back as if she'd been shocked. My father stopped buttoning his coat.

All around me was a buzzing noise, loud as a jar of hornets. I said, "Great harm will come to this one if he goes to that meeting tonight."

"Great harm?" said Missy.

My father's hands slapped down against his hips. "Jesus, *this* again?"

I raised my hand toward the corner, where a dusty cobweb fluttered like the softest thing in the world. I knew my sleeve was slipping down to reveal my bandage, but I didn't care. The time for secrecy was over. "I see two drinks on a table. Two people, leaning against one another."

My father said, "It's a church, goddammit, not a pick-up bar."

But I knew all about divorcees. Mr. Ray, our neighbor who liked to point to brown spots in the grass and accuse me of pissing on his lawn, favored the phrase "hot to trot." A bunch of divorcees in one spot, I knew what kind of place it had to be.

"I see the two bodies again," I said. "But something's happened. They're not moving. I think they're . . . broken."

It was satisfying to see Missy raise her hand to her mouth. It was satisfying to see my father squirm. Beyond that, I didn't think about what I was saying.

Now Missy was backing toward the door. "I heard about this kind of thing on a commercial."

"This isn't the real thing, Missy," my father said. "These are just lies that Revie likes to tell himself. He thinks he has these powers, but it's just—I don't want to use the word *crazy*, but—his mother, she pulled the same kind of—I'm thinking of having him tested."

He tried to step in front of Missy, but my father was trim as a whip and stood no better chance against her than I had. She brushed past him, yanked open the door, and turned around on the porch to huff righteously. "You can go if you want to, Mr. Bryson. I can't stop you. But I, for one, will not be a party to your death, you and whoever you're leaned up against."

At the mention of death, I stiffened. That's when I remember the limits of my powers. Once the warning was out there, I could steel myself, I could hasten it, but what good did that do now? What could I exchange for death? Nothing, not all the pain in the world.

My father watched Missy disappear down the hill. He stood for a long time in the open doorway with snow swirling gently around his feet and dissolving on the warm tile. Finally he closed the door softly. I wanted to call out to him, but something was clutching in my throat. When he turned, his face was terrible with anger. Never in my life had I seen him like this.

"You," he said.

I threw a fit going to the car. He carried me in front of him, arms wrapped around my chest and legs like I was a log. I screamed and swung my heels and bucked my head until he shoveled me into the passenger's seat, and when I fled back toward the house, he tackled me in the yard.

It was dark, but the streetlights were on. If Mr. Ray had pulled a curtain aside to check out all the commotion, he would have seen the same scene replayed again and again: the car door flying open, a boy jumping out, a man wrestling him on the lawn, the boy getting stuffed back into the passenger's seat—until my father wedged me into the seat with his foot and tore off the pop-up lock.

My father watched me for a second, breathing hard, then retched a little before limping around to his side. I probably could have slid across the bench seat and tried another escape out the driver's door, but I was sick with exhaustion and doom.

After Missy had left, my father had pulled me into the kitchen and sat me down hard in a chair. Opening the cabinet, he said, "You saw what, two glasses? Well, help me out here, Revie, were they water glasses, shot glasses, pilsner glasses? Or are the details kind of fuzzy?"

If the details were fuzzy, I wasn't about to admit it. When I didn't answer him, he brought down a dusty bottle of Glenlivet and two water glasses, pouring a tall dose into each one. "Bottoms up," he said, draining one and then the other.

"Maybe we should stay here in the house," I said, trying to control my voice. "Just for a week or two."

He made a face as he swallowed, then wiped his mouth with his sleeve. "Oh, no," he said, his voice roughened by the drink. "We got a prophecy to fulfill."

In the car I touched my fingers to my puffy lip. It had its own heartbeat. My left arm felt like it had been torn out and stuffed back in its socket. When my father slid in, I saw blood streaming from his nose. He reached across me, grabbed Wet-Naps from the glove box, and stuffed one into each nostril. They hung down like tusks. He looked demented.

He started to put his seatbelt on, then stopped. "Fuck it, we're going to die anyway, right?"

"The two bodies could just be in a coma," I said quietly, though I didn't believe it.

"Nope, you called down death on this one, my man." He started the Impala and said, "Now tell me what road to take. I don't want to drive around all night looking for the scene of our accident."

As my father laid on the horn and we swept from lane to lane through the snow, passing a station wagon on the shoulder as the woman driver gaped with her mouth open, I waited for my life to pass before my eyes, or to feel that sense of overwhelming peace you hear so much about. When the Impala shuddered with unprecedented speed and my father said, "Wouldn't want to mess it up for you and just get injured," I looked for the Angel of Death to come swooping down in the darkness alongside my window. But I saw nothing, and felt little but plain fear. In the end, all I could do was squint ahead, straining to see the car, the ditch, the bridge abutment that was our end, as though spotting it from the passenger's side would make a bit of difference.

By the time we came flying into the church parking lot and fishtailed up next to the dumpster, my fear had run down into weariness, or maybe that's just how helplessness feels. Not so for my father. He threw the car into park, fumbled with the keys, then left them in the ignition as he punched the steering wheel four or five times. With each blow, a strange squeaking noise came from his throat. *I guess we'll crash on the way home then*, I thought in a detached way.

"A woman needs her privacy," he said in a sharp, mocking way. He tugged the wet naps from his nose and tossed them toward the ashtray. One hit the edge and stuck. The other shot like a meteor into the darkness around my feet. "Otherwise, how's she supposed to keep her mystery?"

He used to say this all the time, whenever I'd pester him about where my mother was, or what she was doing up in the attic, or if she was going to stay in her room all day. Why he was saying it now I had no idea. His voice was high, almost hysterical. I thought he might have snapped.

"Oh, she's so playful, I'd tell people. Such a kidder, what a healthy imagination, it really keeps the marriage alive." He pounded the wheel again and the car honked. A few people straggling through the parking lot looked up at the noise, then ducked their heads again and went down into the church basement through a propped open door that looked like a square of burning light. Above it, in the sanctuary, a single candle burned. "And when she went to her bed, I brought her take-out and turned down the sound on the TV and I said—I said to *you*, do you remember what I said? I said, Give her *space*. Well, I'll be *damned* if I make that mistake again."

He looked at me like it was my turn to say something. But what was I supposed to say? She was gone and we were going to die. I said, "I don't think you have to worry about that."

"I'm talking about *you*. I see your . . . tendencies, where it's all leading. And I will promise you this"—his finger was up, his eyes were white and huge—"the last thing you'll get is space to let that weird stuff grow, I don't care if you do want me dead."

I opened my mouth to tell him I wasn't my mother, but then I stopped. "Wait—you think I *want* you dead?"

"After what you pulled tonight, what the hell am I supposed to think?"

I didn't know how to tell him how much I loved him, so I said, "That's just, well, that's just stupid."

We looked at each other, then we had to look away. We were both miserable. Though he didn't say as much, I was sure of it then and even more sure now. We sat in the car and listened to the ticking sounds it made as the snow came down in the gray light, the world like a snow globe of ashes. I looked into the darkness of the sanctuary and saw the rounded shoulders of the pews, the felt tapestries on the walls, the looming shadow of Jesus. It was strange to see Jesus in the dark like that. He reminded me of a hospital patient after visiting hours, everyone gone, the lights flickering low, the TV shut off by the night nurse, the noise of a get-together downstairs filtering up through the ductwork. He had given his body for those people. They were still as screwed-up as ever, and now he was alone, in the dark.

My father picked up my hand and turned it over. "You did that to yourself, didn't you?"

The bandage on my wrist was half-off from the fight. I looked at the raw flesh, hesitated, then nodded. In admitting it to him, I admitted it to myself, too. These weren't real warnings, they didn't help anyone; it was just something I had done to myself.

He said, "Take off your seatbelt."

I did, and he pulled me to him, on the wide front bench of the Impala. He put his arm around me, making me feel all the heat inside him. Snowflakes landed on the windshield, fat as moths, then burned away. My father put the car in gear and pulled away from the dumpster, toward the street.

He didn't say much to me on the way home. He might not have said anything at all. When I think of this night now, years later, what I remember first isn't the fight in the snowy yard, or my prediction, it's the ride home. And when I think about it, it's like I'm in two places at once, in the front seat with my father, and beside the car, too. I'm flying alongside through the soft, gray streets of town, like a superhero, or an angel of memory. I see dashes of snow in the headlights, and inside the windows of the car, blurred with steam and speed, a father and his boy, two bodies leaning against one another.

ELIZABETH GONZALEZ

■

Half Beat

FROM *The Greensboro Review*

WE STAYED ALWAYS IN THE WOODEN CHAIRS, eyes on the carpet, even though after half an hour it made our rears itch and our
legs ache. It wasn't like we'd never seen a bug before, but the roaches
there were sizable and fast, and the fabrics on the sinking sofa and
armchairs, with their complicated tangles of brown foliage, seemed
murky and threatening. The sofa had black head shadows on the
back, hand shadows on the arms, innumerable blossoming stains on
the seats, and three great butt dents. No kid in her right mind would
sit in such a thing, though the adults often did. Adults would pretend
such a thing was okay.

Sometimes when we couldn't sit any longer, when we felt like there
were firecrackers going off in our legs, we'd step cautiously over to
the big windows at the front of the room and watch the people out on
the street, or climb the stairs, stepping down to the entrance, back up
to the second-floor waiting room, up the next flight—*quietly*—to the
studio hall, back down to the waiting room.

The Mozart Conservatory of Music sat in a neon part of Toledo—sad neon, daytime neon. At some time maybe it had been
more, maybe not. There was no telling, really. You can't exactly ask
someone, was this place always this way or was it nice once? Certainly Miss Wood had real credentials: Juilliard, 1933. We knew this
from the brochure; it was the reason my father brought us all the
way in from Promontory every Saturday morning. We also knew in-
stinctively to pretend the cockroaches didn't exist when any of the

adults were around, even our father. Especially our father. Just as we ignored the messages on the marquee of the Esquire XXX burlesque across the street, which was always advertising LIVE GIRLS LIVE GIRLS through the front windows. Madame Renault, Miss Wood's partner, who had a theater background, called it "the dance hall." That always made Miss Wood roll her eyes. Miss Wood was no-nonsense.

My father explained to us one morning the subtle difference between a burlesque hall and a strip club, the former implying at least a certain level of artistic integrity. He saw art everywhere, or he wanted to, especially in old things. Maybe only in old things. He'd taken a wicked glee the fall before from the fact that Jimmy Carter's campaign bus had to park out there because the Democratic Party headquarters were on the same block. The TV crews had to get creative to shoot the bus from an angle that didn't show LIVE GIRLS LIVE GIRLS over Mr. Carter's head. Riding home from school on the bus that fall, the handful of kids whose parents were Democrats would chant, "Carter, Carter," and we would shout them down with "Peanut farmer!" as if that settled matters somehow. Which was funny, because the richest, most influential people in Promontory were the farmers. But I guess a soybean, to our way of thinking, had an inherent dignity that a peanut lacked, and the fact that this guy talked about his peanuts, about their nutritive qualities and how valuable they might prove against world hunger, made it downright comical. We hooted and clutched our sides, shoved one another into the aisles. A peanut farmer, President of the United States.

So, you never know.

Madame Renault, with her Broadway background, permitted—possibly even encouraged—singing through the nose. That's why my father had us wait for Miss Wood. Madame Renault had not seen a live performance in several decades, but she still wore stage makeup. She plucked her eyebrows all the way out and drew them back in—two fierce black arcs—a full inch higher than they had ever been, so she always looked a little shocked. She was ballerina thin and wore heavy black-heeled dancing shoes, and would clap and stomp in a way that made her limbs look bojangly and loose, like she might come apart if it weren't for the hard strings that held her together. During my lessons, her students' yowling show tunes and her stomping along would come through the walls, only slightly muffled, and Miss Wood would press her eyes shut and breathe, like she was trying to block her out, or maybe fighting a headache.

Miss Wood had long steely hair that she wound into a bun, and she wore muslin dresses with faded flowers and buttons up to the neck, her full slips visible through the worn cotton, peeping out from her hem. She spoke softly, deliberately, but if you missed enough notes she would take your finger and bang it on the key—that's A, A, A. Sometimes she would get so frustrated with me she'd just give up and play. She'd be talking and picking something out on the keys, illustrating some point, and then her hands would take off, crawling blindly, effortlessly up and down the keyboard with their spidery, knowing grace, and you could almost see the music going to waste, pouring down the grimy hallway and out into Toledo, spilling over into the shoe outlet next door, over the heads of the sad people with canes who moved silently through toppling chimneys of odd lots, double-E wides, double-A narrows, sandals in winter, boots in summer.

One morning she came to a lull in the music and stopped, her eyes straight ahead, looking through the wall like she saw it, too. Disappearing down the hall. Her left hand dropped; the right poised over the keys, lilting, ready to continue. This was the time, I'd learned, when I could hit her with a question.

"What was his name?" I asked.

"Who?" Miss Wood said, her head slowly coming down, her right wrist dropping.

"You said you had a suitor once."

"Oh," she said, her eyebrows gathering. "That was Mr. Treski. Louis."

"Did he ask you to get married?"

She looked over at me, a little sharply. "He did. But my mother did not approve." Madame Renault had told my father that much two months ago.

"How come?"

"Because he was a butcher. And he was Polish and Catholic." Her mouth closed decisively. She retrieved her pencil, always freshly sharpened, from the tray, and added, "It was a different time." She brought the book to her lap and began writing instructions on the page in her tremulous scrawl, the pencil scraping against the nubby paper. Her face was downy and pale, softened into uncertain curves, or maybe only looked that way because her eyes were dark brown and watchful and sharp. Her chest rose and fell with her breathing; her heartbeat set her buttons trembling ever so faintly over her chest, at her throat.

Then, next door, *stomp stomp stomp Ma, he's making eyes at me, Ma, he's awful nice to me . . .*

Miss Wood frowned, gave her head a shake. "For next week, I want you to start on Barcarolle. And continue to play through Étude." Then she got out her little star box, even though I'd flubbed Étude in two places. She picked out a green star, lifted it to her tongue and pressed it, fishtailing, to the page until it was fixed in place.

My little brother, John, always took his lesson first, since he couldn't sit in the waiting room for long. When he was done, my father would take him to an antique auction two blocks south, while Ellen and I took voice and piano. That day they came back a little early, during Ellen's voice lesson. My father was toting a long black case, huffing from the stairs, sweating even though it was September and already cold. "You won't believe this," he said. "An alto sax. Two bucks." He set the scuffed, dusty case on the sofa and popped the latches. Inside, nested in black velvet, the sax was intricate, gleaming with the impressiveness that all instruments have, the gravity of a fine thing. He screwed it together, narrating—we'll get a new mouthpiece, some scratches here, they can refinish that—then held it out, triumphant, weighed it in one arm. "Here, try it out," he said, passing the sax to me.

"Daddy," John protested, and my father quieted him, "You're next, you're next," while I worked my hands around it, found places for them. It was unwieldy, heavy in my arms but also soothing to hold, the worn brass warming instantly to my skin, the keys cupping my fingertips. I pushed, and the valves made a satisfying *puh puh puh* sound, like tiny mouths opening and closing.

I passed it carefully to John while my father instructed him: left hand here, right hand here—*don't!*—don't put your mouth on the mouthpiece! Just pretend, Johnny, just pretend. I took my hands away. They smelled bitter, like pennies.

I knew better than to ask my father what he intended to do with it, who would play it. I knew it would wind up in one of the unused rooms upstairs in our house. He just couldn't bear to see an instrument go without a bid, to see it tossed in a variety box or sent to the dump.

The summer before, my father had taken voice lessons from Miss Wood, too, to prepare for an open tryout for the opera chorus. We kept it a secret from my mother until after they turned him down—he had a nice voice, they told him, but too limited a range. At the time I thought it was just a secret for fun, like a birthday surprise, but now that I've reached the age that he was then, I think it was just too big to share, too embarrassing, that for a little while he'd had the nerve to harbor a dream of music for himself.

The opera in Toledo was good, drawing big names like Giorgio Tozzi, Martina Arroyo, and almost Richard Tucker. Almost because, sadly, Tucker died the week before he was due to perform. My father had been stunned. "What some people will do to get out of going to Toledo," he would joke years later, after he'd gotten over it enough to inject a little humor, although it still choked him up sometimes just to think of it, how close he'd come to witnessing greatness.

For me, the opera was sheer spectacle—laughing Musetta riding onstage in a carriage hauled by a real white horse, live camels in *Aida*. They could make the sun set or the moon rise so imperceptibly and magically you didn't even notice it happening, and once they even made it snow—the stage was glowing, a vibrant blue, then the snow began to fall flake by flake, just like a real storm, then heavier and heavier, and the singers left real snow tracks as they wandered the stage, hugging themselves against the cold.

So I understood why my father wanted to join them on that magnificent stage with its sweeping two-story curtains, its outsize scenery, why he wanted to be one of those enchanted people, the men with their round-arm claps on the back, their elaborate courtesies during curtain calls—*after you*—*after you*—the towering bass always going last, the ladies who collapsed between them, sinking into their beautiful gowns, hands to their hearts, then pressed to their lips, while people shouted and threw roses. They were even grander after the performances, those elegant people. Of course my father wanted to be among them. They hailed from another, more beautiful place.

Every week after our lessons, Ellen and I met my best friend, Genevieve, under an old oak tree at the back of my neighbor's empty lot, where I filled them in on the mystery of Miss Wood's lost love. "What's wrong with being a butcher?" Ellen asked after I relayed my latest findings. Her hair blew across her face and she reached up to untangle it from her glasses. Behind us the cornstalks, tan and brittle, clattered in the field. Genevieve pulled her jacket closed, crossed her arms over her knees.

"That's just it," I said. "Just because he was a butcher? Or Catholic? Or what? It doesn't add up."

"There's more to it," Ellen said, squinting.

"Of course there is," Genevieve said.

"I'll find out," I said. "She's warming up to me."

The oak tree was one of our hideouts. It was a lone oak standing between our neighborhood and the fields beyond, so old that when the three of us pressed ourselves against the trunk and stretched out our arms, our fingers barely touched. The neighbors kept the lot empty and mowed and untreated, as people did then, so it was a full acre of ground with nothing better to do than breed clover and dandelion, and draw bees that we caught in jars during the summer.

"Come on," Genevieve said, standing up. "Let's go." She zipped up her jacket and I followed her without another word, because I followed Genevieve everywhere. She was my better half—bigger, older, stronger, smarter. We were blood sisters, spit sisters, cofounders of a dog club, had read in tandem through the entire juvenile and young adult sections of the Promontory Public Library and were now dabbling in adult fantasy, Bradbury and Tolkien and Hesse. We caught snakes together on the railroad tracks, bringing them triumphantly back to the neighborhood in coffee cans, eager to show that we were not afraid. She ducked into one of the rows of corn, hands overhead like a diver, and I stepped in behind, followed by Ellen, who was allowed to tag along, it was understood, only when we felt like it. I kept my head down, brushing the leaves aside, following Genevieve's sneakers down the rows toward the railroad tracks.

Promontory was named after a thirty-foot bank of land, the abandoned shore of an old course of the Maumee River, which had since moved farther north. The river meandered through a great flat plain that had been washed for millennia by floodwaters from Lake Erie, and so you could dig down two, three feet and turn over nothing but rich, loamy black soil just like the potting soil you buy in bags. In spring, the soil sprouted everywhere orderly rows of soybeans and corn, in neat square plots stretching from horizon to horizon, with occasional clumps of trees clustered between the fields like lonely shepherds. As summer came on, the horizon pulled a disappearing act, as the plants rose up to and then higher than the cars, so by midsummer, it was corn and sky. Corn, soybeans, and sky.

I remember the house always first as a ghost, an image from an old photo on glossy paper, fading as the paper slowly lost its magic chemical properties. The photo was passed down from owner to owner, handed to my parents along with the closing papers. Because I was seven when we moved in, I can never be sure how much of my early memory of that gray house is real and how much derives from that milky old picture. If you looked closely at the photo, you could see a few strands of ivy fingering up from the foundation. When we moved in, the house was half-green with it. The leaves made a slapping noise in the wind. Underneath the ivy, the walls were covered with gray stucco sculpted into cruel points. If you got too close, those walls drew blood. You had to be careful when you were down there nosing around under the bushes, smelling the dirt and the mystery bulbs and the deadly things that grew there, lilies of the valley, jack-in-the-pulpit, pokeweed, nightshade.

My parents were restoring the house, which was perched on Promontory's single bank. When it was built, it overlooked a canal. When we lived there, it presided over a limited access highway. The back part of the second floor was a maze of new studs and plywood, while the front rooms upstairs were nearly untouched. The downstairs was a hodgepodge of repairs: cracked, water-stained plaster walls with bands of overlapping brown wallpaper where a drop ceiling had been, plywood patches in the floors. Doors opened onto nothing; holes in the walls and the ceilings were duct-taped shut with sheets of black plastic, which sagged under the weight of crumbling plaster.

The property had been abandoned for some years before we bought it, and neglected for more, and it bore fruit of some earlier time, things nobody grew anymore: earnest catalpa trees with insane sticky bean pods as long as your arm, inedible currants, musky blue concord grapes, tiger lilies, spearmint, violets, hollyhock. Every limb or shrub or tree or weed in the yard bore something. We uncovered an ugly purple mound of leaves; the following summer we had a bathtub full of rhubarb. One afternoon in a fit of pioneer zeal my father tilled a sixty-foot-square garden and, being inexperienced at gardening, planted one hundred tomato plants. We had tomato wars with the neighborhood kids that summer; my mother took up canning. We were relieved when frost came and the plants finally quit. It was as if the ground were claiming us, and not the other way around. At least, it seemed that way to me.

"You must master the metronome before you may abandon it," Miss Wood would say. "That is the difference between improvisation and incompetence."

"But I can't—keep time," I'd plead, "with it ticking. I hear the ticking, I lose the time."

"Practice," Miss Wood would say sternly, and for a moment it was as if she could see me running around the yard, hiding under bushes, lying upside down on the sofa staring at the dust motes in the light rather than practicing. "Just like the notes, Claire. You keep your eyes on them, read them each time, and eventually the letters go away."

I couldn't sight-read yet either. "I keep time better without it," I pouted.

"That is how I learned," Miss Wood said, which was a pretty good closing argument. But I hated even the look of that thing, and whenever Miss Wood turned it on I lost my place, found myself staring up at it, hands paralyzed, neurons misfiring, chaos. The very shape of it was offensive, its tiny stupid head, the tocker waggling back and forth like a finger, *tsk tsk tsk*.

I limped through my piece, restarting once, twice, a third time. The metronome droned on, tripping me up, and then Miss Wood's hands came down. *Appassionata*, the second movement, pastoral and sweet. I could hear her point, the dutiful innocence of the left hand, which marched along, predictable, a steady four beats, while the right hand offered over it a melody, wandering, uncertain, sad. "Hear it?" Miss Wood said, meaning the even tempo of the left, and I nodded. But I also knew that it was all the places where Miss Wood strayed, where she doubled up or hesitated on the right, that made the piece hers, that made it worth hearing. You didn't have to be good or even musically inclined to hear that. You could see it in her hand, the way she'd reach for the next note and then draw up before striking, the way her lips would part so slightly or her eyebrows lift when she pulled these little tricks.

"Miss Wood?" I said when she had stalled, had fallen into gazing, the strings still humming, the metronome mindlessly wagging.

"Do you see?" Miss Wood said, still staring ahead.

I nodded.

"How did you meet him? Mr. Treski."

She leaned forward, stopped the metronome.

"That was a long time ago," she said, pulling down my book, reaching for her pencil.

"You don't remember?"

She blinked at me. I looked quickly down at the piano pedals. She wrote a few words in the book, underlined them. "His father used to make deliveries to our house," she said. "Tuesdays and Saturdays at eight o'clock. One morning, Louis came for the delivery. I was practicing, and I turned and saw him standing in the doorway, listening. After that, we spoke every morning when he came. Only during deliveries — he never called at our house."

"That's all you did? Talk in your living room?"

"Once I visited him at market. My mother had to travel to Detroit to sign some papers after her uncle died. And when Louis asked, I decided to go ahead and see him. But Toledo was not the big city then that it is today, and our neighborhood being what it was, my mother heard about it the moment she came back. She was quite angry. That's when Louis asked me to marry him."

"So what happened?"

"My mother wouldn't hear of it. I was off to Juilliard anyway. She said that time would resolve it, and it did. When I came back from school, he had married a girl from River Park."

I weighed this.

"But you turned him down, right? Before you went away?"

"I told him it was impossible."

"But—would you have married him when you came back, if he hadn't married someone else?"

"It was not an issue," Miss Wood said. "He was married then."

The front windows in our house were original, with wavy glass that made it look rainy when it wasn't. When we were smaller, when we first moved in, Ellen and I would go upstairs in our underwear and scramble around over the boxes and make elaborate forts. We had boxes up there from as far back as Indiana, where I was born—United, Allied, Atlas, Stevens. Mayflower had the best boxes, with green clipper ships on them.

From the road, I always thought those windows out front looked like eyes.

In Promontory I knew all the neighborhood lore, the teenage exploits and the father follies, how it always rained after Kevin Kirby washed his sports car, the time Genevieve's dad erected a snow fence on the wrong side of his driveway and wound up with a big naked green space in the yard and a ten-foot drift the length of his driveway that hung around to torment him through April. I knew all the secrets of the place, which trees were the good climbers and where the best seats were. How my neighbor's pears were best after they fell, scooped up from an early snow on the way to the bus stop, when they were so ripe I would press the waxy skin to my mouth and the pear would rush in, icy wet and sweet, and the juice would run down to my wrist. I'd hear shouting and then I'd run, bangs freezing to my forehead, fringe from my suede purse slapping awkwardly against my leg, chuck the half pear over the bank, give my hands a hasty snow wash, pull myself up onto the bus steps, slipping on the dirty slush.

The following week, I put in a respectable performance, one that seemed to hearten Miss Wood. She pulled the book into her lap, and while she turned the pages back to the start of the piece and reached up for her pencil, I asked, as casually as I could, "So, whatever happened to Mr. Treski? After you came back from college, did you ever see him again?"

She tilted up her chin, then looked back down at the book, and I wasn't sure she'd heard me until she said, "Yes and no." She carefully drew a star on the page, something she did when she was particularly pleased, and wrote some words next to it, then put the pencil down. Her penciled stars always had a tiny loop in each turn. "When I came back from school, he was still making deliveries. He used to come in the back door and put the meat in the icebox for us and leave the bill on the table. I would see his truck pull up in the alley while I was practicing, and then I would see him go again. But after my mother died—she died in '47—I noticed one morning that his truck stayed. I assumed he must need something, so I got up to see what was wrong. But when I stopped playing, he left. After that I noticed he would stay almost every delivery, twenty, sometimes thirty minutes. If I stopped playing, he would leave."

"Did you talk to him?"

"No," Miss Wood said. "That would have been inappropriate. As it was, it was already somewhat inappropriate, since we were alone together in the house."

"Wait a minute. You mean he used to come in and put the meat in your kitchen and sit there and listen to you play, and you never even spoke to him?"

"I never saw him, face to face."

"For how long?"

"Six years," Miss Wood said. "Then he died."

"How did you find out? Did he leave a letter for you?"

"No, no. One day his nephew came for the delivery. He told me that Louis had passed away. A heart attack."

"He didn't leave any — letters — or anything?" I couldn't believe it. It was the worst story I'd ever heard.

She shook her head, opening her little box, fishing for a star to paste next to her handmade one.

"But he did die of a broken heart," I said.

"Oh, Claire," Miss Wood said, almost laughing. Then she looked at me for a moment, trying, I guess, to take me seriously. "I suppose you could say that."

The oak lost its leaves all in a rush, and this was the weekend, a weekend of gusting, turbulent winds that sent them drifting across the field, into Genevieve's yard and beyond. With each rush of wind another batch would come loose and startle around us like a flock of birds. I watched them, waited for a lull to begin. Genevieve yanked down her hat, a green and white one with a big pompon her grandma had crocheted for her, her eyes tearing in the cold, patiently waiting. Ellen shivered, pushed her glasses up on her nose.

"After her mother died, he would come to deliver the meat," I said. "One day, he came in the back door and put the meat in the icebox, and he just stopped. He knew he should go, but he couldn't make himself leave until she finished playing the song she always played on Tuesday and Saturday mornings, when she saw his truck in the alley."

"What song?" Genevieve asked.

"*Appassionata.*"

Ellen gasped. "Just like she plays in —"

"Exactly. In lessons. You know how she always gets to that one part, and stops? One morning he was standing there, listening like he always did with his cap in his hand, and his heart just stopped like a watch. And he died, listening to that song."

"Just like that?" Ellen said, horrified.

I nodded. "So she always plays to that very moment when his heart stopped." I was borrowing heavily from a story my father told, about how Puccini died in the middle of writing Turandot. I looked at Ellen's face but there wasn't any sign of recognition — she was so gullible. "And when she came out she found him there, like he was still listening, just with his eyes closed."

"Didn't he fall?" Genevieve asked.

"He was sitting down," I said.

"You said he was standing up," Genevieve said. "With his hat—"

"He couldn't have stood that long," I said.

"Oh," Genevieve said, but she was eyeing me, her head cocked. Genevieve was the smartest kid in the ninth grade, maybe even the whole school. Not an easy kid to fool.

That evening my mother made a festive dinner, finishing with fruit salad and crème de menthe over ice cream, the menu standing in stark contrast to the atmosphere, the walls exposed lath with dusty plaster oozing from between the slats, the ceiling new blond rafters and plywood with fresh lumberyard stamps, a dispirited light fixture hanging by a long gray wire, solemnly stapled in place. I was pondering Miss Wood, the thousand better endings I could come up with for her story. Miss Wood rushing into the kitchen, throwing her arms around Mr. Treski, a frantic movie kiss. Mrs. Treski dying, and Miss Wood marrying Mr. Treski, and taking him and all his children into her house, teaching his children piano.

Then I saw Miss Wood, hands hovering over the keys, her hair dark, let down over her shoulders, her eyes two black wells as she watched him walk away, week after week after week.

"I guess this is as good a time as any to tell you," my father said. "I got an offer from a company in Texas. Remember last month, when I went down there? It's a great company, right outside of Dallas. You girls won't believe the schools."

"We can't leave," I said. "The house isn't done."

"We'll pay to have it finished," he said, an answer, obviously, ready for everything.

"But you said we were staying here."

"I know, Claire, and I know how much you like it here. But this is an opportunity I can't afford to pass up. I found a house, a brand-new place in a nice development. And wait 'til you see Dallas. You have to see the city at night. It's incredible." He looked back and forth between Ellen and me, gauging. "Dallas is booming," he finally said. "Toledo—Toledo's a ghost town."

John started asking him questions about cowboys and horses and hats, and my father jumped up to fetch some surprises he'd brought for us. My mother sat at the table, looking hopefully at Ellen and me. Ellen turned to me, her mouth opening, but I was already standing up and heading for the kitchen, out the back door.

There was no way to strike a dramatic retreat from the back of the house just then, as it was in the midst of an involved expansion, so I stepped carefully across the two-by-twelve my father had laid over the complicated pit below, future foundation for a back porch or a mud-room of some sort. To the right stood our crazy old garage with its false front of stacked blocks, which made it look like a building from an old Western movie; a single light over the door cast a bright circle on our weedy driveway, the only unpaved one on the street. I walked behind the garage, climbed onto a pallet of bricks, rested my back against the wall and contemplated our yard. Before the pink-streaked horizon the plants were crisp shadows, each stalk and leaf distinct before the fading light. Straight ahead a mound of asparagus swayed, chest high; it had overwhelmed the twisted chicken wire fence and was advancing on the garage. I sat and watched the plants lose their edges and lines, the colors drain away. Somehow, I had missed the signs: my father waking up later and later in the mornings, falling asleep earlier each night with a *National Geographic* in his lap, a sweating scotch on the box next to his chair. Hurrying to work, coming home early. He'd stopped telling work stories a year ago or more, never talked about work at all, had stopped bringing home interesting glassware samples from the lab. The signs were all there, but I guess I had stopped looking.

It was dark when I went in to call Genevieve. "Meet me at the oak tree," I said, and even though it was cold and late and her hair was wet from her bath, and her mother was a stickler for that kind of thing, she didn't even ask what I wanted, she knew me that well.

That night, that swallow-you-whole sky was loaded with stars, and bent so low on every side it felt like it was pressing down on me as I scuffed through the empty lot, knocking loopy, cold-doped bees from the clover heads. Across the way, Genevieve's back door banged shut. I could just make out her figure cutting through the patches of light thrown down by her house, past each familiar bush, ducking under the split rail fence, a shadow person making her way diagonally across the field toward the oak.

At my last lesson, over the garbled shuffle and thump of *Hello, Dolly!*, Miss Wood spent ten minutes writing elaborate notes for my next teacher, who didn't exist and never would. I didn't have the heart to stop her. She wasn't the first person ever to write to people who didn't exist, or to play for a ghost. We were not so different, Miss Wood and I.

I never went back, even though Genevieve invited me for years. The longer I was away, the less I wanted to return and see how small the place must have grown, how sparse the stars, how perfectly ordinary the tract houses, how trim that mysterious house, the jungle of a yard. And even if I managed to come at just the right time of year, and the neighbor's pear tree still stood, and I managed to find a late-season pear in an early snow—would the voices of my friends come wandering down the dark road, calling my name as I bent down to claim it?

ANDREW SEAN GREER

■

Gentlemen, Start Your Engines

FROM *San Francisco Panorama*

SING TO ME, AMERICA, of stock-car racing! Of four hundred miles driven in four hours. Sing to me of Goodyear tires and Sunoco gasoline, of Gatorade Victory Lane and of ServiceMaster Clean, of the Sprint Cup and of Nationwide and Craftsman Truck, of Bud and Bud Light and Bud Light Lime. Sing to me of Jeff Gordon and Jimmie Johnson, of Joey Logano and Juan Pablo Montoya, of Dale Earnhardt and Dale Earnhardt Junior, of Jack Daniel's and Jameson. Sing to me, America, of beer bongs and beads for boobies. Sing to me of Sin City.

Say you find yourself, America, with all your fellow NASCAR fans, gathered around the campfire and throwing menthol cigarettes into its embers, tossing back beers, entranced by the story Lucky tells about Cupcake, the midget stripper he once hired for a bachelor party. You and your husband sit in camping chairs as Lucky's wife Jennifer delivers shots of something they invented called a Cherry Bomb. Say you are a gay man; say tonight is your first wedding anniversary, at least in California where you married while it was legal, and you have chosen to celebrate it here, with strangers, at the Michigan International Speedway. Say Lucky and his friends do not know this. For all you know, they take your two-man tent as simply another strange California way of doing things, your Joey Logano beer coozies (he is the youngest and cutest driver) as one of the whims of NASCAR fandom, and your wedding rings as proof of wives you left behind, as they have left their children. The group toasts with their Cherry Bombs and downs them all together; you and your husband do as well. It tastes like cotton candy. It tastes delicious. Then Lucky tells you about how Cupcake arrived at the party, a much younger girl than he expected, and had the time of her life, giving the groom-to-be a lap dance that took place entirely on his lap. Later he came to understand that this was her first time.

"The variety of human experience," you say, perhaps too loudly, too grandly after all the beers and shots, as the faces turn toward you all at once, "it's vast and wonderful, isn't it?"

There is a pause, and you can hear the beer cans warping slightly in the fire and cracking from the heat. The smell of cotton candy seems omnipresent. Faces glow in firelight, and from somewhere far away, a car alarm goes off.

"Ain't that the truth?" says Lucky, and everyone laughs, and Jennifer pours you another Cherry Bomb. And say this middle-aged man, tanned and big-bodied and happy, just say he murmurs, "Now fellas," nodding at you and your husband very seriously before you down your shots, "since it's your first NASCAR, maybe we should take y'all to Sin City—"

"Oh, Lucky," Jennifer says, shaking her head.

"It's their first time! They gotta see Sin City!"

"What's Sin City?" your dear husband asks, and of course that question can only be answered one way. Lucky looks up at you with a wide grin and shrugs.

"Oh," you interrupt, "oh, we have to get up early for the race tomorrow. We've got pit passes—" In truth, you do not really know what pit passes are.

"Well you gotta see Sin City. You gotta see it to believe it," he says. And within a few minutes he has persuaded the entire group to take you to the secret wild part of NASCAR nightlife, a place found only by chance or by listening for the faint beat of dance music. They call it Sin City, but that's just something they have made up over the years to describe it. There is no real name for what you are trying to find, and now, for you, there is no turning back.

Give me, O America, the strength to tell the tale!

We had come to Michigan in search of NASCAR racing, a weekly event that crisscrosses America and brings with it all the great stars of stock-car racing and their fans, which at the Michigan event numbered above a hundred and twenty thousand on the day of the CAR-FAX 400. Now, I would not call myself a NASCAR fan. In fact, in my first conversation with my husband about the idea, he asked me to tell him what NASCAR stood for, and I answered, "National Stock Car Racing." Then I paused. "Wait, I think I left out some A's there, didn't I? National . . . wait . . . North American Stock Car . . . Association . . . Racing?" Then he asked me what I thought a stock car was. "Oh, well a stock car is like . . . an ordinary car that they've tricked out for racing, with a bigger engine and things, like a turbo Honda Accord." I grinned with pleasure at my answer. Then he asked: "And what direction do the drivers turn?" I figured I had even odds at that one. I guessed they turned right. David nodded his head in amazement.

What NASCAR stands for is National Association for Stock Car Auto Racing. What it is—well, perhaps it's better to say what it's not. It's not what it started as, which was moonshiners evading revenuers in the Appalachian Mountains, modifying their cars with faster engines and learning tricks to take on the rough roads and turns of hill country. In 1948, a man named Bill France came up with the idea of setting a "shiner" race in Daytona Beach, known as the hub of high-speed land records since the early twentieth century. France established a governing body and rules and regulations, and stipulated that the cars be "strictly stock." NASCAR is still run by the France family today. The CEO is Bill's grandson, Brian France, a fact that seems unfair to many fans. Until the fifties, cars ran with virtually no modifications at all, but by the sixties cars were being specifically manufactured for racing. Though they still bear the badges of their putative "stock" models, NASCAR cars are designed from the ground up purely for winning, just as sharks are designed purely for killing.

It is not the Indy 500. It is also not Formula One. As I was informed by my husband, the thrill of NASCAR is that, while the cars are no longer "strictly stock," there is at least a nod toward the originals. NASCAR fans enjoy the idea that these are modified American cars, and while there is no rule to this effect, any deviation brings an uproar; note the fury following the recent inclusion, along with the Chevy Monte Carlo and the Ford Fusion, of the Toyota Camry as an eligible model. Toyota, though not an American company, manufactures the Camry in the states, but I beg you not to visit the numerous forums where the topic of whether Toyota has "ruined" NASCAR usually devolves into whether "Jap" or "redneck" is the more racist term.

Another thrill of NASCAR, apparently, is that the cars have fenders. Unlike Indy and Formula One racing (with their long-necked, big-tired vehicles), this allows cars to scrape up next to each other for seat-hugging suspense without fear of tangled tires. NASCAR also isn't merely a matter of who wins the race: the NASCAR Sprint Cup (as opposed to the Nationwide Series and the Craftsman Truck Series) awards points over its ten-month-long series of thirty-six races, and after twenty-six races the top twelve drivers are awarded a base point level and are now "in the chase" for the Cup. The Michigan CARFAX 400 we were attending was race number twenty-three.

And that is all I know. I am sure I have it completely wrong. I always get this kind of thing wrong, much to my husband's dismay. I am the sort of man who, before attending a baseball game, must yet again have a full explanation of the rules. Nine innings, right? So why are we standing at the seventh? Why does that hitter not have to play in the field? Somehow, I cannot keep this stuff in my head.

Oh, and also: the drivers turn left. When it comes to cars, I cannot get anything right.

This is not for lack of trying. At our house, we subscribe to five car magazines, and one of them is called *AutoWeek*. That magazine arrives, as you've no doubt guessed, weekly. I cannot get through a weekly *New Yorker*, but David gets through *AutoWeek* in no time. In addition, David often purchases copies of his favorite car magazine, a British publication called *CAR*, which is also my favorite car magazine, because it is very glossy and has high-quality photographs of glamorous cars that I can look at in the bathroom. We also travel to auto shows, sometimes three a year, and usually David goes to each show three or four times in order to see all the cars completely, and to get to sit in each one. I try to find interest in all this, I really do. When we go to an auto show, I give David fifteen slips of paper, representing fifteen cars he can make me sit inside, and he has to pay me a slip of paper every time. I do this to prevent him from making me sit in hundreds of cars; I do this to prevent my own untimely death. But I try. I read the car magazines. I listen to his ideas about what cars he thinks everyone we know should get. I look at pictures online of cars he would really like to get himself. I tell him what cars I myself would like to get if I lived in the suburbs, or Germany, or Alaska, or in the 1950s, or on a farm. I listen, I look, I tell. But really, I couldn't care less. Cars, to me, are appliances, just like my microwave. They do their job, sometimes they're pretty, but I don't think about them when they're not around.

David does.

The Michigan International Speedway lies about seventy miles southwest of Detroit, and if you're gay or Jewish or an Obama liberal, you will probably pass through Ann Arbor and pick up four Reuben sandwiches from Zingerman's, visit the Farmer's Market for local greengage plums and apples, discover an astounding invention called Pie Bites (which David plans to market), and visit the local Target for a cooler and cans of Starbucks Espresso & Cream for the morning. Later down the road, you will pick up ice at the liquor store and stand in a walk-in beer cooler and puzzle over the many varieties, all of them light beer, none of which your India-pale-ale-only husband is willing to drink. Finally you will have an argument in the walk-in beer cooler about whether Bud Light Lime is a gay beer or merely a girl's beer, and surely the clerks watch your lovers' spat through the glass of the sealed sound-proof door, faces blocked by stickers of NASCAR drivers. You will also argue over how many beers are needed, and end up buying twenty. Bud Light Lime wins, and you will gaily purchase it from the clerk, confident that you will now have plenty of Bud Light Lime to give away. Turns out you get a free NASCAR poster with every case of Bud.

Husband loads the beer into the cooler. Off you go, confident that everything is taken care of. The notes, the camera, the tickets and camping site. The twenty Bud Light Limes floating in their dream of ice. Of course, twenty will not be nearly enough. Not for NASCAR camping.

The Irish Hills of Michigan host a number of tourist attractions, including the expected Hill of Mystery, shamrock-laded bars and clubs, and numerous BBQ places (one with a gigantic cow bearing the message SAVE A COW, EAT PORK), but none are as attractive as the Prehistoric Forest Amusement Park, which lies with its animatronic dinosaurs frozen over the pathways, forced to endure yet another extinction, this one revealed by the FOR SALE sign out front, and you have a brief fantasy of telling your friends that you've decided to leave San Francisco and open a theme park in rural Michigan, and that the out-of-scale T. Rex will once more attack the meek Diplodocus, and rivers of blood will run again in the Irish Hills. But the fantasy fades as soon as the signs for NASCAR appear.

Tens of thousands of fans camp outside the Michigan International Speedway for each race, but of all the myriad campsites surrounding the track, only one of them offers tent camping. The rest are exclusively for RVs. The cost of a campsite is surprisingly high—one hundred thirty dollars—but it is a flat fee for the week, and considering that many race fans arrive on Wednesday and don't leave until the following Monday, it's not outrageous. Of course, tickets to the Sunday Sprint Cup race are one hundred and ten dollars each, pit passes fifty, tickets to the Saturday Nationwide race fifty as well, and that doesn't count travel costs, RV rental, and food and beverages, so that leaves a family of four spending up to a thousand dollars for a NASCAR weekend, something completely out of the question for most of the people camping there, and a number that makes one wonder how "anti-elitist" the NASCAR circuit can really be. (For the 2010 season, the Michigan International Speedway is lowering weekend prices for all Grandstand seats, with teenagers half off and young kids free.)

To economize, many race fans pay their campsite fee but don't purchase tickets in advance except for the Sunday race. Some are able to borrow tickets, for instance on Saturday when there are two races, or pit passes, which last through long hot hours, from those who have gone earlier in the day and don't plan to use them again. It is crucial to get pit passes, however, in whatever way one can, because for many fans pit-passing allows them their sole moment to meet their favorite driver in the pit and, perhaps, to collect his autograph. It is common to see fans wearing their pit passes around their necks on lanyards, the passes covered with signatures, as a way of showing their status as an autograph-seeker. You and your husband have pre-ordered pit passes. You will, however, fail completely to get anybody's autograph.

And so you arrive at the Northwoods campsite, stopping at the ranger's station to get an entry sticker, and it is there, talking to the rather dykey red-haired ranger Dawn, that you receive the first of many NASCAR shocks: she is absolutely friendly and welcoming. In fact, *everyone* who works here is welcoming: the security guards who search your bags, the teenagers who take your tickets, even Brian at Will Call who sits in a hot booth and listens to a race he never gets to see. Dawn takes the time to make it clear where your site is, how to find the markers, where the shower-trailer is (with hot water!), the Porta-Johns, and the entrance to the track itself. You then enter NASCAR camping proper, past RVs and pop-up trailers, into the tent campsites all aflutter with flags. Canadian flags, NASCAR driver flags (many for 24, Jeff Gordon, and 48, Jimmie Johnson), and yes of course Confederate flags. "But we're in Michigan!" your husband exclaims. "What could a Confederate flag mean to a Michigander? That you wish the South had seceded from the Union? Wasn't this still a territory? I don't get it!" And you tell your husband to be quiet, because you have arrived. Spot P-14. And there, where in every other site campers have erected their tents, you see that yours, in a sweet ironic gesture from the gods, is completely taken up by a tree.

You emerge from your Camry, taking stock of the situation and opening a Bud Light Lime, and a burly suntanned man walks over from another camp, thrusting out his hand and saying, "I like your style! Hi, I'm Lucky!"

I want to make it clear that I have been camping before, and I'm not just talking about Burning Man. I'm trying to say that I've lived in Montana and backpacked for hours into the wilderness, just me and a friend, where we set up our camp beside a little-known hot spring, and while my friend napped I got in *au naturel* and was promptly joined by an enormous female moose. There we sat, me and the moose, enjoying the steaming water, looking out blissfully at the sunset together like a honeymooning couple, while I summoned the courage to call in a wee voice: "Help me!" If I had been wearing pants I would have peed them. But I survived my wildlife encounter, and made a fire, and bear-proofed our foodstuffs, and did all the things one does when one is camping. This is not a story of gay San Franciscans setting up a Moroccan hideaway among all the army-surplus tents, complete with mirrored pillows and a Porta-John covered in veils. I am proud to say it is quite the opposite.

My husband is, in fact, from Montana. That's where we met, thirteen years ago, in the food court of the mall, in front of Orange Julius. Because of this, he does all sorts of guy things, not the least of which is his car obsession, but which include the very straight-male habit of buying the most expensive and elaborate sports equipment available, even for the briefest contact with that sport. David was entrusted with bringing a new tent and sleeping bags; what emerges from his check-in bag is a small miracle in outdoor sciences. He explains to me that the tent weighs only four pounds, the sleeping bags only two, and that they are good down to thirty degrees. The total cost is more than the Comme des Garçons jacket I purchased in Paris, which kept me awake for two weeks with pangs of regret (though it, too, is good down to thirty degrees). David is so pleased to see his tent in action. It springs from his hand, Cat-in-the-Hat–style, and unfurls before us with a titanium spine.

"Quite a setup!" Lucky exclaims. "Where are you two from?"

"California," David says, to Lucky's absolute astonishment. We will come to learn that this is the most astonishing place to be from. "We needed a light tent for a bike trip through Sonoma." This is the first I have heard of a bike trip through Sonoma. But the tent is impressive, and assembled in a flash. By comparison, we will later watch, with our campmates, as ten young Canadian men try to put together an old metal-pole tent. It will take them three hours, though we will consider they are probably stoned out of their minds, and it probably won't help when Lucky sneaks over and steals one of their poles. Just for giggles. Put against these poor suckers, we are practically Grizzly Adams.

"Well what the heck brought you all this way?" Lucky's wife Jennifer asks us. She is a small, attractive woman with a tightly pulled-back ponytail and wire glasses that exaggerate her blue eyeliner. She wears the number 48 prominently on every item of her clothing.

We tried to prepare for this question the night before, while visiting a Detroit gay bar. I suggested saying we were on a road trip across the country, but David said the rental car would give things away. So my husband gives the simplest possible explanation: "We just always wanted to see NASCAR."

Amazingly, this answer requires no further elaboration. Of course it doesn't. We are among NASCAR fans, all of whom have sacrificed and worked hard to come to this event. No enthusiasm is too outrageous. Lucky pats us on the back and introduces us to his mother-and father-in-law, who sit eating beans under a flag-draped canopy.

"Now, this is Andy and David, they came all the way from California!"

The mother asks where in California. "San Francisco," David answers. We wait while this answer makes its presence known. San Francisco means only one thing.

"Well, we're thinking of going out there for a race," the mother offers. There is a NASCAR track in Southern California, outside Rancho Cucamonga.

We will later learn, while sitting by the campfire, that the mother has a son, Jennifer's brother, who just went off to Iraq. He had tried to forestall things, but in order to stay in the Marines he has to see action, and so he put in to go overseas. She is half sick over it, something she admits only while sipping her Jack and Coke. It will turn out that her husband, sitting there eating potato salad, went off to Vietnam one month after their wedding. It is clear this was the worst portion of life she ever had to swallow, and she is terrified of facing another. Both events are on her mind, always.

"Hey David," Lucky calls out, "you going to the Kenny Wayne Shepherd concert tonight?"

"Yep, but first we're gonna see the Nationwide race. Sounds like it already started."

"Yeah, we're ditching," Lucky says. "We got beat by a hot day in the pits."

I offer everyone a Pie Bite, but David cuts in to say we'll come by later and walk with them to the concert.

Lucky responds happily: "It's a deal! Have fun!"

And off we go for our first day at the races.

* * *

The first time I really understood David's obsession was on our first road trip, which happened about a month or so after we started dating. He had told me something vague about an interest in cars, and mainly showed interest in *my* car, an eighties Subaru GL Wagon, which I took, flatteringly, as a sign of the fetishization that comes with early love. Of course he would show an interest in anything of mine! We both lived in Montana at the time, and it didn't seem too strange to talk about how to get places and what you drove; everything was far away and took some thought and planning. I never noticed that the car topic came up more than any other. I lived, you could say, in a cloud of innocence. But it was on a trip we took to Seattle, for a plan to move there I'd made long before David showed up, that I truly saw down to the depths of his soul and glimpsed what swam in the darkness there. It was a few hours outside Missoula, on the long valley highway, in those few years when the speed limit sign read only REASONABLE AND PRUDENT. That was when it happened, when I saw. He presented it very casually, with a smile, perhaps the way a cardsharp might suggest a friendly round of poker. "Hey, I have an idea," he said, letting his left arm drift out the open window. "Why don't you identify the cars as they go by?"

Later I would meet his mother and father, his two sisters, one of whom lived in Canada with two daughters, his brother, who lived out on the streets of Seattle, and various other close and distant friends and relations. But none of those meetings were anywhere near as important as the one that happened that day, with that casual little suggestion. Only now do I understand how beautiful and poignant the moment was, introducing me, in his way, to the *real* love of his life. To cars.

"I can't," I said.

"'Course you can! Look, what's that one?"

I am of course very good at this game now; we hardly need to play it. I've learned all the insignias, but this is cheating; the point is to identify cars by their shape, their color, the obvious details that set them apart from all other makes and models, the way Nabokov could identify some butterflies by their shadows. David, after all, could by the age of five identify the cars passing his house simply from the sound of their motors. This is not expected of me; I am meant only to

be able to follow a conversation about parked cars we pass on our way
to the coffee shop. But back then I couldn't tell a Dodge from a Jag-
uar. And not only that—I was supposed to be identifying cars in the
oncoming lane *as they drove by.* The speed limit, remember, was REA-
SONABLE AND PRUDENT. That meant at least ninety miles an hour.

"I can't do it," I said. "It's like, it's like you're a geologist and you
want me to identify rocks—"

"Well, I guess so—"

"Only you want me to identify the rocks while *throwing them at
me!*" I shouted, somewhat desperately. "What's this?" I said, miming
tossing something at him. "And *this!* And *this!*"

"Come on, here's an easy one. See the grille?"

"Porsche."

"What? Porsche? What? It's a Cadillac! Porsche?"

And on it went. For nine hours. I learned the telltale vertical tail-
light of the Cadillac, the Continental Kit of the Lincoln Continental, the "portholes" distinctive of the Buick brand, the kidney-shaped
grille found on every BMW, and so on. And I saw, every time I mis-
identified a car, his mouth twitch with frustration, because of course
to him it was close to heresy to think a Mitsubishi was a BMW. But I
also saw, when I correctly guessed a make (and I was mostly guessing), a glow of happiness take over his body for a moment. It wasn't
me, the fact that I was learning his world, the things he cared about.
The names themselves caused that pleasure. Ford. Toyota. Audi. It
was the happiness of a gourmet as you described the foods he loved.
Honda. Dodge. Renault. Or an astronomer as you named his beloved
constellations. Volkswagen. Fiat. Saab. Or perhaps a zealot, as you
called forth his gods.

I learned early on in our relationship that if you found my husband staring into space, and wondered if he was perhaps recalling
the past or dreaming of the future or even thinking of you, his life's
great love, you could ask him, "What are you thinking about, honey?"
and he would always turn and give the same answer:

"Cars."

What is the most boring thing you've ever seen? I know, I know, it's
hard to remember, precisely because it was so boring. Boring events,

Thomas Mann once noted, seem interminable to live through, yet these events contract in our memory into no time at all. It is only the intense, sublime experiences of life that, though over in flash, expand to take up most of our remembered past. In just this way I am tempted to skip over the Nationwide Series racing and move straight into Sin City, but I know for a fact we spent three hours watching the race and only about an hour and a half wandering around in search of stripper poles. Isn't it funny how the mind works?

As we arrive at the track that first afternoon, I expect some resistance from my brain. But there is so much else to entertain me—the blow-up dinosaur slide, the T-shirt hawkers, the trailers with driver paraphernalia (where we buy our Logano beer coozies), along with the XXL clientele, each with the one soft-sided six-pack cooler and one transparent bag allowed at the track—that I have not yet confronted the idea that I am about to watch cars. I have already contacted the Michigan International Speedway, intending to have the announcer mention the first wedding anniversary of the somewhat androgynous "Andy and David" (and hoping the camera wouldn't turn to our row), but was told they didn't do announcements of that type. I am a little disappointed, and try not to mention it to David. Our seats are high in the stands (which the lady on the phone recommended), so we have to climb a series of ramps, all the time hearing the *vroom, vroom, vroom* of the cars rushing by. It is exciting, I have to admit. The whole metal structure trembles and there is the very Roman sense of a coliseum crowd come to watch a huge exotic creature, possibly a dinosaur, pacing and roaring its way around the track. And when we finally emerge from beneath the grandstands—spectacular! A red-and-yellow curve of seats pitched at a stomach-churning angle, an oval D track laid out for all to see, little Matchbox cars making their way past each other and a blue sky blazing everywhere overhead. On the infield, rows of RVs and VIP tents are encamped, and Pit Row sits right before us, painted orange, with pit crews at the ready for a crew chief calling in a driver for gas or tires or an adjustment. And the roar! We see that everyone wears thick headsets in gray or yellow, and almost immediately we find ourselves putting our earplugs into our ears. It is absolutely deafening, like a god crying out in agony, the sound of those engines! Earplugs in, all is quiet.

Peacefully quiet. Painfully quiet. And around they go. And around. And around.

And around and around and around and around and around.

Here it is, and I had not known it would come so soon: the most boring moment of my life.

Yet thousands of people are loving it. Wearing their bright headsets, or watching on TV, or listening on radios and loving it. The variety of human experience—it's vast and wonderful, isn't it?

I turn to my husband. He gives me a sheepish smile and offers me another Bud Light Lime. I feel Devil Time hunched over us like a farmer with his chickens, plucking the minutes from our hides. My husband mouths something and mimes frantically. I remove an earplug and he shouts each word over the din: "GET . . . US . . . SCANNERS!"

We saw these for rent at little booths among the stuffed animals (there is a NASCAR groundhog named Digger, with some very gay badger friends, and I now have a T-shirt featuring them in police hats that says BADGERS ON A MISSION), and I ignored them the way I ignore most things I don't understand. But now down the ramp I go, past the tequila stands and Dove Ice Cream Bar carts, throwing myself at the mercy of the woman behind the counter, Stacey, with lemonade hair and caramel tan. "Well, this is the way to go," she tells me, showing me a handheld monitor attached to two bright yellow headsets. "It's the Sprint FanView." This is, in fact, what we had witnessed most of the other fans using: scanners and monitors, most of them Sprint products. (Sprint sponsors the major NASCAR race.) One can rent or buy a scanner at any NASCAR event, which allows one to hear the sportscasters that one cannot hear trackside due to road noise, but also allows one access to the intimate conversations between driver and pit-crew chief about how the tires are doing, fuel levels, the condition of the road, and—most mysteriously and importantly of all—whether the car is "tight" or "loose." The Sprint FanView takes it a step further: it allows you, in addition to rankings and car placement, access to cameras *inside the drivers' cars!* I know David will thank me dearly for being able to sit beside Joey Logano later this weekend. I rent the FanView plus two headsets. It is sixty dollars for the entire weekend. When I arrive with the clear bag of yellow plastic and see David's face, I know it is the best present I have ever given him. It is love. It is the way to go.

It turns out that for me, the key to enjoying any sporting event—for that matter, any dull event where one watches people who are astoundingly skilled at their work, like modern dance—is to have a knowledgeable, enthusiastic companion who, like a guide through a Masonic ritual, will narrate the mysteries. My husband is knowledgeable (he claims not to follow NASCAR, by which he means he only reads the stats in magazines and does not watch it on TV), and damned if he's not enthusiastic, but he is no guide. Here, though, on my Sprint FanView, at last I have found one! Suddenly I can tell who is in the lead (how to guess with them spread out in a circle?) and who is running out of gas, and who has blown a tire and is trying to catch up by sprinting along the straightaways, and who is the outside young kid from Michigan slowly making his way up car after car, unseen by the two leaders (that would be Brad Keselowski, who will go on to win).We get to watch close-ups of pit crews jacking up cars, throwing tires on, tipping gas into the capless tanks, and jumping back as the cars take off. David shows me drivers' views of the track, including Keselowski's (Logano does not race in the Nationwide Series), and animated versions of the very scene we see before us. Most importantly of all, however, my magic headphones explain the rules of the road.

I suppose there are many other sports based on a cumulative point system—all kinds of glorious things exist in this fine world—but I am too ignorant to know much about them. I'm sure, also, that the knowledge I've gained about NASCAR is soon to drain from my mind through the sports-leak I developed as a child when I stepped on a rusty nail, so I should put this down as quickly as I can. It seems that NASCAR drivers can get points in two ways: by their final placement in the race, and by leading a lap. Placement seems obvious: the higher your placement, the greater your points. First place, for instance, gets one hundred and eighty-five points. But (in a lovely little palindrome) forty-third place still gets thirty-four points, which apparently explains why even wrecked cars will try to hump their way through to the finish line. It does give one hope, doesn't it?

A driver can also earn five points for leading any single lap (meaning crossing the finish line first) and five points for leading the most laps in the race. Drivers can lead a lap during both the green and yellow flags, which is why, when other cars are heading into the pits, a driver might forego a pit stop in order to take the lead that lap and gain his extra points. O, but heavens! I haven't explained about the flags!

Don't you really come to NASCAR to see a car crash? I did. So did Brian at Will Call, who when we picked up our tickets told us, "You just missed a great crash!" Can you blame him? After all, the cars drive so close to one another, literally scraping metal, and sometimes follow the outside edge of the track to within an inch of the concrete barrier. I think I explained about the fenders. Because of this, crashes and other problems are bound to occur. This is what actually makes the race interesting to some and manipulative to others. At the least puff of smoke or shred of tire a yellow caution flag goes up, a Chevy Camaro Pace Car arrives, and all drivers are forced to slow to a crawl, keeping their lap positions, while the Servicemaster Clean trucks take to the track and vacuum up any debris (or, as we would learn Saturday, dry it of rain). The green flag comes out when the hazard has been cleared from the track.

There is also a "lucky dog" rule that allows the closest driver who has been lapped by the leader to make up the lap and join the main group. Since 2007, at least seven drivers have taken advantage of the "lucky dog" rule to win a race. To some, these cautions break or even manipulate the action (a few drops of rain seems an unlikely hazard). To others, they are similar to the "leveling" features in most board games, giving bad-luck players a chance and preventing the same dull order of cars from going around and around until the finish.

Because they do go around and around. The first race we witness, the CARFAX 250 Nationwide Series, is two hundred and fifty miles long, which, on a two-mile track like Michigan's, means a hundred and twenty laps. We come in halfway through, so we only have to sit through sixty. That takes about two hours, and we only have six Bud Light Limes with us.

The next day, hung over from our quest for Sin City, we will be watching the race we came for: the CARFAX 400.

That is four hundred miles.

Two hundred laps.

Vroom.

Say, America, that you drink ten Bud Light Limes in a row, on top of two Cherry Bombs and a sip of something pink and curdled involving Malibu Coconut Rum, and decide to go in search of NASCAR debauchery. Perhaps, to get into the spirit of things, you bum a menthol Newport and smoke it until green sparkles appear in the corners of your eyes. Say half a dozen of you, similar substances coursing through your veins, head out from Northwoods through a gap in the chain-link fence while the security guard isn't looking. What would you see?

RVs and pop-ups decorate the dark, rolling landscape, packed together like Chiclets, each strung with Christmas or rope lights or, more elaborately, light-up Budweiser signs and disco balls. Couples, families, or groups of guys are huddled around fires, each encircled (for safety's sake) by rings of dead beer cans piled up in careful structures some three or four cans high. No solo women campers, or groups of women. There are cardboard cut-outs of women, naturally, holding beer signs, loaded with Mardi Gras beads, beside large hand-lettered signs reading BEADS FOR BOOBIES! Some camps are set up as tiki huts, some with simple plywood bars, but most are fold-up chairs around a fire, a cooler for the beer. There are over nine thousand campsites, around fifty thousand campers, and during racing events the city of Brooklyn, which contains this state park, becomes the third largest city in Michigan. South of us the racetrack is afire with floodlights, and the glow of it rises above the trees like the Northern Lights. From time to time, above us float flame-powered red lanterns that drift higher with the air currents, then head west and disappear into the stars. Who knows who is lighting them?

One canopy is decorated with brassieres, and you casually ask where they got them all. "Last night, donations, every one!" says one of the men inside. He then takes you on a tour of each bra, and says a judge came by an hour before, smelling each, and awarded the prizes. First is a red and black lace brassiere, second a pink one, and third something in black. None of the bras are for small women.

"Nice work, gentlemen!" your husband says, and Lucky pats him on the back, saying, "I like your style!" You shoot your husband a glance: *Oh, so we're going to bond over the degradation of women now?*

Suddenly a pretty thirtyish woman appears from between the RVs. "Have you seen two small blond girls?" she asks. She wears her hair in a long braid and is dressed in cut-off jeans decorated with caution tape. She is very drunk.

"Well, no," Lucky says, pondering the idea. "What are they up to?"

"They goddamn ditched us, that's what! Sixteen and seventeen. You see them, Britney and Caitlin, you tell them get the hell home!"

"What's your cell number?" Lucky asks.

"Ain't got a cell. They live here in town. You tell them I called the cops!"

"Will do."

And off she staggers, her long braid swinging. You comment that looking for a Britney or a Caitlin at a NASCAR rally would be like looking for hay in a haystack.

"Ain't that the truth," Lucky says happily.

You have basically spent the night with Lucky and Jennifer, from the Kenny Wayne Shepherd concert until now, far past midnight, in a campground called Juniper Hills where you have no right to be. The concert took place after the Nationwide race, at the water tower where anyone with a race pass could enter the grasslands; thousands of people were gathered around, drinking cans of beer, and every other man seemed to know Lucky. Ahead, on a stage and magnified by monitors, Kenny Wayne Shepherd played his country guitar and rocked his head gently, so his longish blond hair fell over his face. "Who is Kenny Wayne Shepherd?" you had asked on the way over, and Jennifer answered, "Oh you'll recognize him, 'Blue on Black'? 'Deja Voodoo'?" You shook your head. You wondered aloud what would happen to all the crushed beer cans underfoot, and only later saw Onsted Boy Scout Troop 637 moving through the crowd like hyenas, tan and spotted with merit badges, picking up the cans and tossing them into recycling bags, secretly jiggling them to see if they were empty. Men with beer bongs wandered around the audience, offering their services by pointing a finger at your chest. You shook your head. The man beside you took one, and his buddies emptied their beers into the funnel as the man struggled to swallow the foam that overwhelmed him.

Beer bongs are everywhere tonight. You pass a double one strung on a pulley from a tree and watch as it is lowered, filled with beer, then raised again so two strapping young men can stand up to the tubes and, as the umpire shouts and releases the catch, race to the finish. You pass another, deeper in the Brooklyn Trails campground (Lucky is following an instinct northwest, saying he needs to be drunker to find it), and this one is twenty feet high, decorated with rope lights, with a cut-out lady standing beside it and a cartoon bubble reading: LADIES, YOU KNOW WHAT WE WANT TO SEE! Lucky points out that this is the fucker they tried to get him to do the night before, but he doesn't do beer bongs anymore, not since last year in a race when he found out, after finishing his bong, that they'd put whiskey in at the end. He was drunk for days. "No more," he says, "no more, but you should give it a try." David says no thanks, he's had plenty in his time. Then your husband turns to you.

"How about you, Andy? Ever done a beer bong?"

You recognize the little smile on his face. You will never forgive him.

For years I lived under the impression that the first word people said when they thought of me was "fun!" But I discovered, on one drunken night a year ago, that the first word was actually "forbidding." These are very different words. I also recall a townie college boyfriend who said he liked my "British accent," a comment that, after pondering it for twenty years, I can only conclude meant I sounded like Charles Winchester from *M*A*S*H*, the one from Penobscot, Maine. That I sounded like an Ivy League prig. I don't think of myself this way, but I suppose I'm at an age where I no longer get to have illusions about myself. I am an Ivy League prig. I grew up the son of chemistry professors in suburban Maryland, went to a left-wing private school, a left-wing Ivy, and moved promptly to the West Village in New York. I will admit it: Montana baffles me. The South, where my family came from, baffles me. And NASCAR baffles me. "Forbidding," apparently that's me in a word. And let's get down to it, shall we? By "forbidding" they really mean *snob*.

But not David. And this is the main thrust of my defense. David grew up very poor, in a Mormon family in rural Idaho. He was the first to go to college, which he paid for entirely by himself. David has been supporting himself consistently since he was fifteen years old. He has worked every possible job under the sun, and he is always willing to fall back on waiting tables if it becomes necessary. Once in a while he likes to point out that I have no job skills to fall back on when the novel breathes its last breath. I have not had a normal, regular job in at least ten years, and have only once held a salaried position, as an executive secretary for a nonprofit foundation whose name I could not pronounce. My last job? As a contract worker, naming toys for a toy company. Yes, I'm the one who named their floating radio toy "The Sound Turtle."

So say what you like about me. It's all true or possibly true, and I've heard it all. A famous writer, for instance, once provided my recommendation for grad school. It was only after multiple rejections that, puzzled, I broke into the office files and discovered, to my horror, one solitary sentence on his page. *Andrew Sean Greer*, he had written, *is a self-conscious Dudley Do-Right.*

But please, leave my husband out of it. No one would call David "forbidding." Or "self-conscious." Or Dudley anything. The one time David visited my grandparents in rural South Carolina—that's right: *my gay lover visited my Southern grandparents alone*—my grouchy bigoted grandfather's comment was: "That David's a good ol' boy." As even this night at NASCAR is proving, my husband always finds himself loved and embraced. He fits in everywhere. In this way, he will always betray me.

So why is he with me? I ask myself that all the time. Thirteen years. Why does he possibly put up with it? I must be incredibly cute.

It is not so bad, a beer bong. Just a crouching stance, an upward gaze, and people around you yelling "Don't panic! Just relax! Just let it go down!" Some hooting and hollering. And then it comes: the rush of Bud Light Lime—official sponsor, I suppose, of tomorrow morning's hangover. From the height of twenty feet, it is a hard thing to deny. Down it goes—well, about half of it. The rest just dribbles out of your mouth. You look up in fear that you've failed, again, but everyone seems elated. There is no bad beer bong, you're told. Just good and better and best.

"Nice job, Andy!" Lucky says, patting you on the back. Your husband just laughs. And so you are no longer a virgin.

David comes up and whispers: "You are incredibly cute."

Say you wandered drunk for an hour or so among the lit-up RVs and fold-out bars decorated with glowing chili peppers and shots of tequila and found yourself called to, time after time, by people sitting around a fire. "What's your hurry?" they ask, and "Come on in here!" And while you are aware they especially want the girls, there is a certain generosity to their tone. Bring your own beer, of course, but sit in one of our chairs. They don't know you spent last night at a bar called Club Gold Coast, which turned out (to your surprise) to be a hustler bar, where nobody would talk to you and David but the prostitutes, one of whom, Justin, wore a pair of green underwear with BELIEVE IN THIS! spelled in sparkles across the butt and offered to give you a private dance. They don't know any of it, and don't care to know. All they know is that you are here for the racing, and are therefore part of their tribe. Waving at you from a fire, taking you on a tour of the campground, handing you a spare beer. At first it seems like a terrible fraud. But then, of course, you *are* here for the racing. For tonight, you *are* part of their tribe. You and David both. It is certainly a friendlier crowd than Club Gold Coast.

"Hey guys!" a young man implores you. "Come in here and draw on my drunk friend."

"There's always one," Jennifer says.

In you go, all of you, and are given magic markers. The poor guy is in his early twenties, black hair and pale skin, sitting in a chair with his head lolling back, aware of nothing. People have drawn all over his white shirt—mostly obscene imagery—and you merely find a blank spot and write: WASH ME. Lucky writes, directly on the fellow's neck, LUCKY WAS HERE! "Hey!" the friend objects. "Hey, you wrote right on him!" A shrug and a laugh. But there's no real problem here; it's all the price you pay for passing out at NASCAR.

And then there is the glowing sign of a racing car. And there are the women who, indeed, will bare their boobies for beads. And there is the giant Jenga set, each piece half the size of a man, where people are crowded around to watch the action. But nothing more licentious than that; nothing more than anything you might find at Golden Gate Park.

At last you find the secret entrance to Sin City. Here it is, everyone insists, right here where a path leads through the dark junipers. The entrance to Hell.

But there, where we should find lines of drunken fans staggering through the trees, an RV is parked. A dozen folks are gathered around a fire circle, as if the entrance were merely another camping spot, and Lucky asks and discovers that Sin City is closed this year. Not because the rangers found it too outrageous for NASCAR, but because the usual campers didn't come back. They couldn't afford the tickets.

"Recession always hits the partiers first," Lucky notes. "They've got shitty jobs, and they're no good at their jobs 'cause they're always partying. So they're the first fired. Dammit, always the first to go."

Ain't it the truth?

"Sin City's gone!" Jennifer repeats in disbelief. "It's just gone!"

"Sorry, boys!" Lucky says, shaking his head. "Guess you'll have to settle for San Francisco fun." A wide smile. Do they know we're a couple? Of course they do. They knew the instant we stepped out of the car.

Down the street we find a little party going in a brightly lit E-Z UP, where some young girls are playing a strip version of Red and Black, and tell people the news. They nod their heads. "We called that place Purgatory," one comments. He is wearing a rubber mullet. Another says her friends called it Sodom and Gomorrah. Whatever they called it, the economy ate it alive. A reverent hush passes over the crowd.

Drunk from your beer bong, you ask the crowd if Bud Light Lime is a girl's beer.

"No!" the answers arrive in a rush. "No, no, of course not!" The answers all come from girls.

Then you notice the youngsters playing cards. The two teenage boys with them have already lost their shirts, but the girls have everything on, clearly in control of this game. Both are blond, one is very short, but the ringleader is pretty and confident as she yells to her friend: "Hey Britney, tell him to take off his shoes!"

You nudge Lucky and whisper: "Listen to these girls." A moment later, he turns to the ringleader and asks, "Hey, Caitlin, you want another beer?"

"No thanks!"

It's them. It's Britney and Caitlin. You may not have found Sin City, but you have found the wayward girls.

Within minutes the RV owner is shouting, "Party's over, girls!" and shutting off the lights. Lucky has let them know this is a sixteen- and seventeen-year-old who have taken control of their party and are drinking their beers, and Jennifer has pulled the girls aside and told them their mother wants them home immediately and is calling the cops.

Caitlin's face is shaking with fury. Her bleached blond hair is frizzed from the humidity, her lipstick smeared from kissing, and she turns to Britney, her shorter sister or cousin or friend—it has never been clear—and hisses: "That crazy fucking bitch!"

And then, brave and drunk little girl that she is, she turns to the entire crowd and shouts: "This is *my* town! Get the hell out of here!"

Lucky suggests that perhaps the evening is over. You all need to rest up well for the Sprint Cup tomorrow, after all. And what shocks you most, as you and your husband will speak about later, in whispers, in your four-pound tent, is how kind they all have been to you. Lucky and Jennifer and the others. There was not a moment of wariness or suspicion; that was all on your side. These people walked over the instant you arrived and led you around every moment of the day, from concerts to dinner to drinks, wanting nothing other than to show you hospitality, the NASCAR way, with the wish that you would return to the same campground beside them. Lucky and Jennifer, telling now about the strippers he once hired who poured red wax over each other until it hardened into molds like armor breast-plates. Somehow the image sticks with me. Laughing, walking away from Britney and Caitlin, who can still be heard screaming at us all: "Get the hell out of my town!"

And tomorrow, at last, is the Sprint Cup.

America, how beautiful you are in multitudes! One hundred twenty thousand of you, fanned across the metal bleachers, wearing T-shirts boldly numbered with your favorite drivers, or, in most cases, wearing no shirts at all, pale and tanned and sunburned in fascinating shadows of yesterday's clothing, tattooed with feathered cow skulls across your backs and barbed wire around your biceps and Celtic spirals on your shoulders—who knows what it all means to you?—lathering each other with sunblock or sun oil, watching the camouflaged roofless Humvees make their way around the track, each carrying one of the drivers you adore, waving at you with a smile.

"And today!" the announcer says, "The Canadian National Anthem will be performed by Amy Rivard! You know her from the TV show *What's Up Canuck?*! A big welcome to . . . Amy Rivard!"

How beautiful in families, gathered together with your headsets daisy-chained along the row, connected at last to dad's bought-not-rented scanner, each with your legal six-pack cooler and transparent bag, with Buds and Bud Lights kept cold in coozies with those same glorious numbers—48! and 24! and 88! Your big pale girls in tank tops and little wire glasses, their white hair tied up high in the heat, and tall tan lanky boys with boxers showing and a heart-shape of sweat already forming on their shirtfronts, and dads hunkered down over their FanViews, and moms standing and rooting for their drivers, then turning and asking if anybody *wants* anything, waiting for headsets to be removed and repeating loudly "*Anybody WANT anything?*" before heading out for a cigarette.

"And today!" the announcer says, "the national anthem will be performed by Chris Young! You know him as Nashville's rising star . . . and *Country Weekly*'s Hottest Bachelor! A big welcome to . . . Chris Young!"

How beautiful in Pit Row, earlier that morning, under the sweltering sun, as you gathered by the cars you loved, and wrote messages on the white concrete barriers, and paid a dollar for a yellow Joey Logano lugnut, watching as a crewman painted putty on the wheels and placed new lugnuts, lovingly, on the soft adhesive so they could be thrown onto the car and bolted quickly. How lovely standing on the track itself, shimmering in the heat, taking pictures of yourself against the vertiginous slope of the asphalt, the announcer's tower, the climb of the stadium behind you in yellow and red. How glorious standing by the fence, waiting for each driver to arrive, as they always do, and sign your pit pass for you—for of all the sports, these stars are the most accessible to fans, the most touchable, the most *real*.

"And today!" the announcer says, "We are being assisted by the A-10 Warthogs from Selfridge Air Force Base! Here they come!"

We sit in giddy expectation, hats in hands, hands still over our hearts from the National Anthem. Our drivers are there; Joey Logano has just gotten into his car after the last words. Embraced by our campmates, enlarged by the event itself, barely touching fingers in an encoded sign of love—and a sign floats overhead: BILLY WILL YOU MARRY ME? AMANDA, and why didn't I think of that? An airplane banner, brilliant. Amanda is more of a romantic than I, who can only think of irony when planning an anniversary. NASCAR indeed. And what is that roar behind us? A squadron of fighters, flying up from the horizon in strict V formation. The heart drops.

Look up! Look up, here they come!

"And today!" the announcer says, "Our Grand Marshals are Jordan and Jacob Vanderstel of Hudsonville, Michigan!"

The screen cuts to two boys in baseball caps, one wearing Gordon's number and the other Jimmie Johnson's. They are in wheelchairs. Apparently both have muscular dystrophy. They wave to the crowd.

How wonderful what we are about to watch, over four hours of race cars zooming through the miles, the crowd braving three rainstorms, waiting out the long stretches as the ServiceMaster trucks dry up the track, the caution when Robby Gordon blows a tire, watching Dale Earnhardt Jr. work his way car by car up the stretch, making up time on the straightaways and hugging the outer groove, calculating the fuel consumption, as Jimmie Johnson, after leading nearly every lap of the race, is forced to pit two laps shy of the finish and allows Brian Vickers to pull into the lead just a second and a half ahead of Jeff Gordon. How wonderful to see my husband bent over his FanView, watching the image of each car along the track, each driver, each pit stop, his childhood fantasies come true—of seeing cars not as vehicles but as creatures of grace and power. How nice it will be to have a good shower in a hotel, and a good dinner and a beer back in Detroit, but for now the Bud Light Lime is cold and right. The hot dogs are right. The crowd is right, and somewhere out there

Lucky and Jennifer are in their seats, the western ones with the sun at their backs, the same seats they get year after year, with friends beside them, standing to watch the cars get in their row from qualifying. A man leans in with the green flag. I see David laughing soundlessly and he grabs my hand, turning to me and mouthing "HAPPY ANNIVERSARY!" and I mouth back "HAPPY ANNIVERSARY!" We listen as, in the high bland tone of sick children called on to do their best, the Vanderstel brothers shout:

"Gentlemen, start your engines!"

How lovely to be married in America.

EMMANUEL GUIBERT, DIDIER LEFÈVRE, *and*
FRÉDÉRIC LEMERCIER
(TRANSLATED FROM FRENCH BY ALEXIS SIEGEL)

■

The Photographer

FROM *The Photographer*

In July 1986, Didier Lefèvre left Paris for Afghanistan. He was twenty-nine and his task was to document a Doctors Without Borders mission. It was his first major assignment as a photojournalist. Lefèvre traveled with a band of doctors and nurses into the heart of Northern Afghanistan, where the war between the Soviet Union and the Afghan mujahideen was raging. Years later, Lefèvre's photos were paired with drawings by Emmanuel Guibert to tell the story of Lefèvre's adventures. The book was called The Photographer *and it was designed by Frédéric Lemercier. What follows is a portion of that volume.*

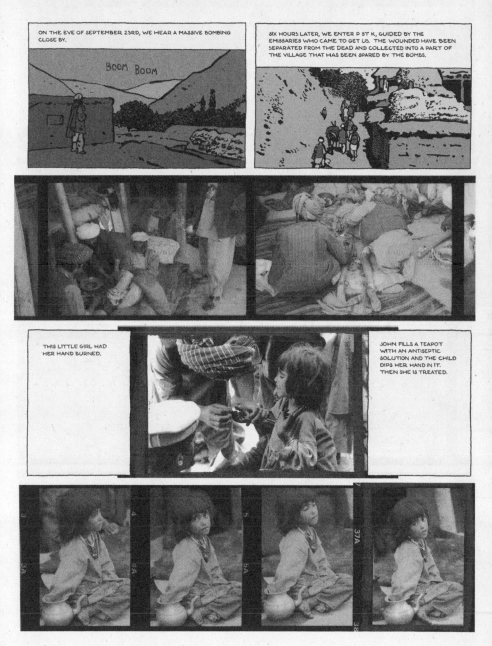

ON THE EVE OF SEPTEMBER 23RD, WE HEAR A MASSIVE BOMBING CLOSE BY.

BOOM BOOM

SIX HOURS LATER, WE ENTER P ST K, GUIDED BY THE EMISSARIES WHO CAME TO GET US. THE WOUNDED HAVE BEEN SEPARATED FROM THE DEAD AND COLLECTED INTO A PART OF THE VILLAGE THAT HAS BEEN SPARED BY THE BOMBS.

THIS LITTLE GIRL HAD HER HAND BURNED.

JOHN FILLS A TEAPOT WITH AN ANTISEPTIC SOLUTION AND THE CHILD DIPS HER HAND IN IT. THEN SHE IS TREATED.

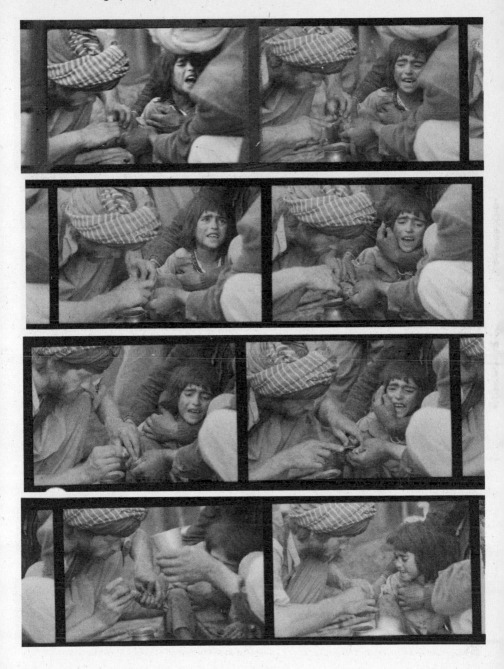

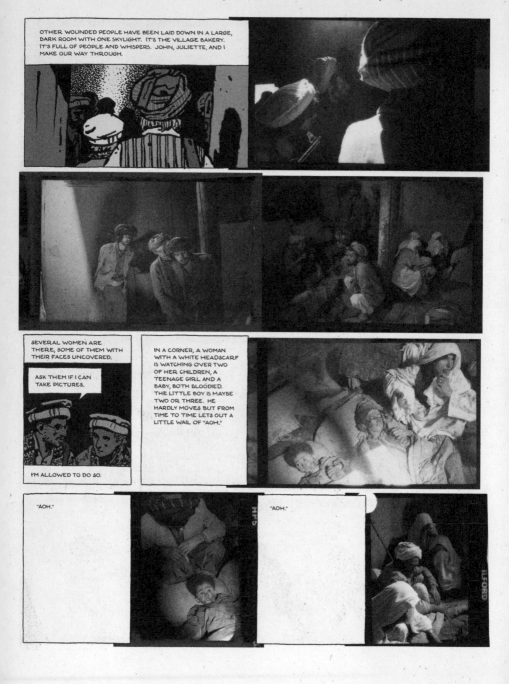

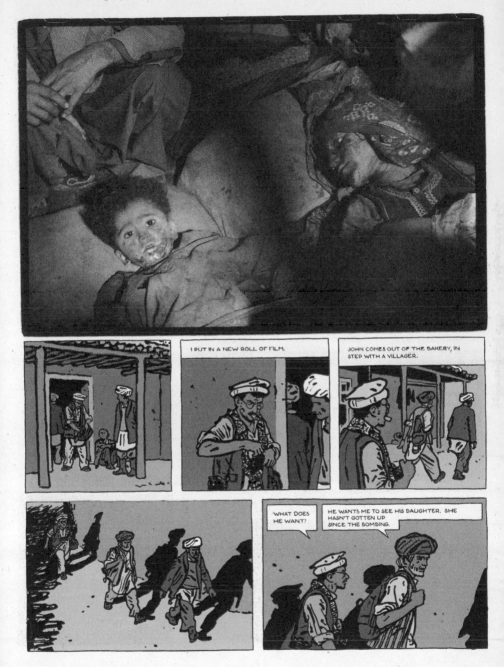

THEN ON HORSEBACK, ON A DONKEY'S BACK, ON A MAN'S BACK, OR CARRIED ON STRETCHERS, THE WOUNDED START OUT ON THE LONG AND ARDUOUS ROAD UPHILL TO ZARAGANDARA.

WE GET BACK. THE TEAM DEALS WITH THE INFLUX OF WOUNDED. WHILE THE MOST SERIOUSLY INJURED ARE TREATED BEHIND BLANKETS, THE OTHERS WAIT.

THE BROTHER OF A GUY WITH A WOUNDED KNEE RAISES A RUCKUS. HE DEMANDS THAT THE LOCAL BONESETTER TAKE CARE OF HIS BROTHER. REGIS IS ABSOLUTELY OPPOSED TO IT.

THAT'S COMPLETELY MORONIC!

THIS GUY DOESN'T HAVE A BONE OUT OF JOINT, HE HAS AN OPEN WOUND. IF HE TRIES TO RE-SET THE KNEE HE'S GOING TO DESTROY IT!

THE BONESETTER ARRIVES. REGIS BARS HIS WAY.

THE BROTHER INSISTS. THINGS TURN NASTY.

IN THE END REGIS IS FORCED TO LET THE BONESETTER GO OVER TO THE PATIENT.

AND IN NO TIME FLAT, THE BONESETTER HAS CAUSED IRREPARABLE DAMAGE.

THE POOR GUY'S KNEE HAS LITERALLY EXPLODED.

PERFECT! I HOPE YOU'RE PROUD OF YOURSELVES!

THERE ARE SOME THINGS THEY KNOW HOW TO DO AND OTHERS NOT AT ALL. I HAVE THE SAME KIND OF FIGHTS WITH THE LOCAL MIDWIVES, THE MATRONS. THEY MAKE HORRIFIC BLUNDERS SOMETIMES.

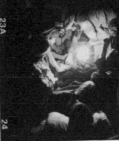

NIGHT HAS LONG SINCE FALLEN, BUT THE TREATMENTS CONTINUE.

JOHN, WHO HASN'T STOPPED BENDING OVER PATIENTS, HAS A TERRIBLY SORE BACK.

AS IF THERE HADN'T BEEN ENOUGH, ONE MORE PATIENT IS BROUGHT TO US. UNCHARACTERISTICALLY, THE MUJ' BRINGING HIM ARE GUFFAWING.

WHAT'S SO FUNNY IS THAT THE GUY HAS A BULLET IN THE ASS. AND IF HE CAUGHT A BULLET IN THE ASS, THAT MEANS HE WAS TURNING HIS BACK TO THE ENEMY, THE COWARD! THAT CRACKS UP THE AFGHANS.

THE WOUND IS VERY DEEP. ROBERT INSERTS GAUZE WICKS TO PROBE AND DISINFECT IT. A MORE DETAILED EXAMINATION WILL HAVE TO WAIT UNTIL A SHORT WHILE LATER, WHEN THERE'LL BE DAYLIGHT AND WE'LL HAVE SLEPT A BIT.

SLEEPING A BIT. THAT'S WHAT'S IN STORE FOR RÉGIS, WHOSE ALARM RINGS EVERY TWO HOURS SO THAT HE CAN CHECK UP ON AMRULLAH AND THE OTHER WOUNDED, TREAT THEM, FEED THEM, AND WATCH OVER THEM.

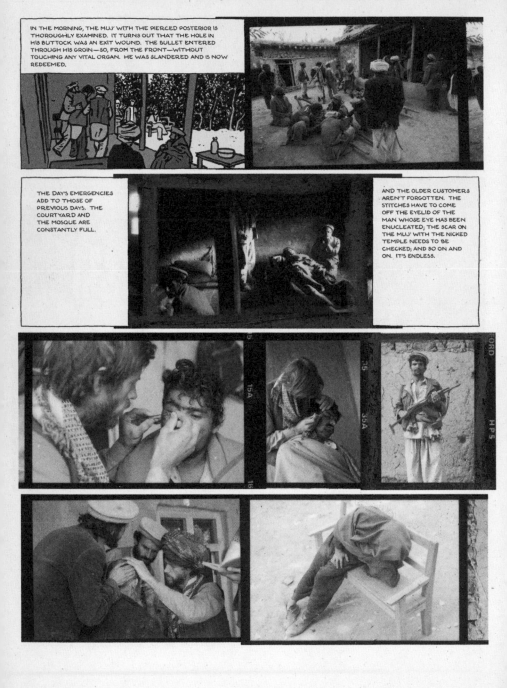

IN THE MORNING, THE MUJ' WITH THE PIERCED POSTERIOR IS THOROUGHLY EXAMINED. IT TURNS OUT THAT THE HOLE IN HIS BUTTOCK WAS AN EXIT WOUND. THE BULLET ENTERED THROUGH HIS GROIN—SO, FROM THE FRONT—WITHOUT TOUCHING ANY VITAL ORGAN. HE WAS SLANDERED AND IS NOW REDEEMED.

THE DAY'S EMERGENCIES ADD TO THOSE OF PREVIOUS DAYS. THE COURTYARD AND THE MOSQUE ARE CONSTANTLY FULL.

AND THE OLDER CUSTOMERS AREN'T FORGOTTEN. THE STITCHES HAVE TO COME OFF THE EYELID OF THE MAN WHOSE EYE HAS BEEN ENUCLEATED; THE SCAR ON THE MUJ' WITH THE NICKED TEMPLE NEEDS TO BE CHECKED; AND SO ON AND ON. IT'S ENDLESS.

THE NEXT DAY, THE MUJ'
BRING IN AMRULLAH ON A
STRETCHER.
AMRULLAH, 16, HAD THE
LOWER PART OF HIS FACE
TORN OFF BY SHRAPNEL
FROM AN ARTILLERY SHELL.

HE'S IN A HALF-COMA
AND IS BETTER OFF THAT
WAY. HIS WOUND IS
HORRIFYING. EVERYONE
IS PETRIFIED AT THE
SIGHT OF IT, EXCEPT
THE DOCTORS, WHO
IMMEDIATELY START
TREATING HIM.

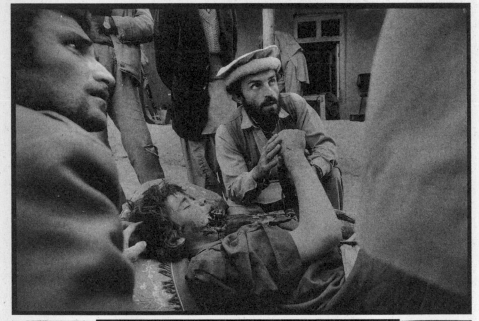

AMRULLAH IS
TRANSFERRED FROM
THE STRETCHER TO THE
"OPERATING ROOM," ON
THE TERRACE.

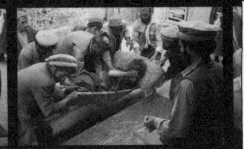

DO THE DOCTORS BELIEVE
THAT THEY CAN REPAIR
SUCH A DISASTER? THEY
CERTAINLY INSPIRE THAT
BELIEF IN US. AGAINST ALL
ODDS, DESPITE THE DUST,
THE LACK OF SPACE, THE
BARREN CONDITIONS, WE
PLACE OUR TRUST IN THEM.

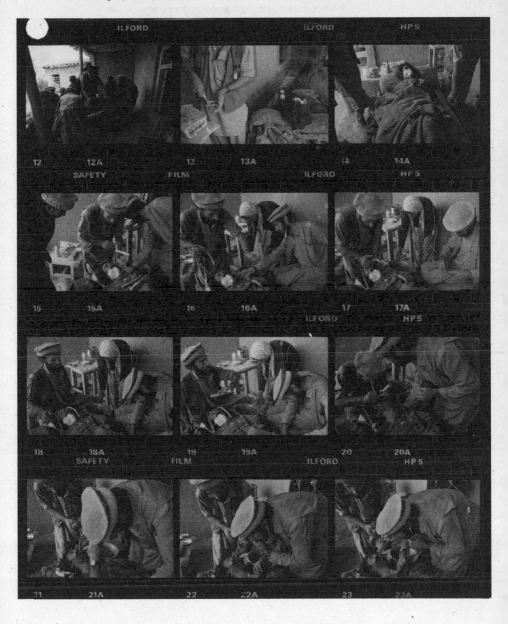

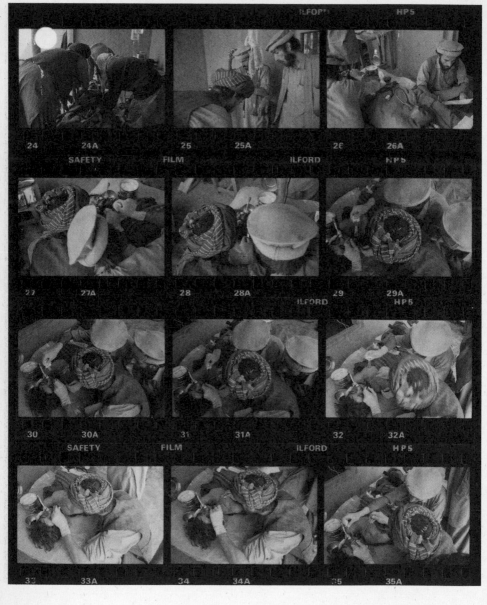

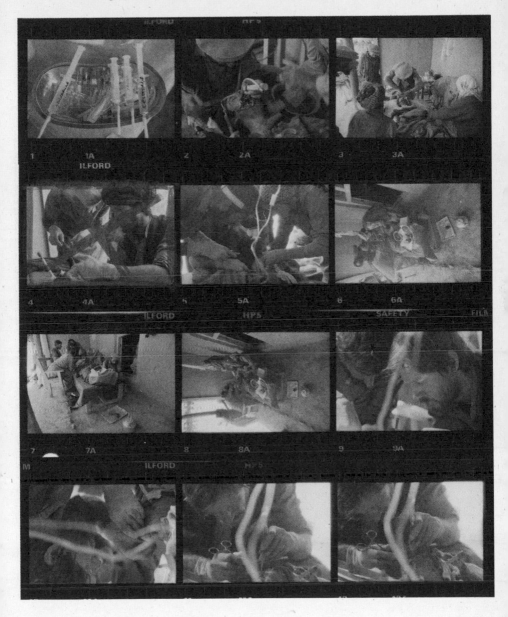

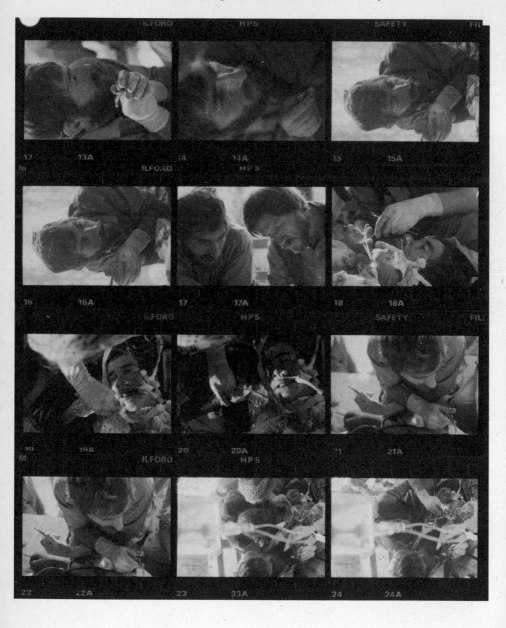

THE OPERATION CONTINUES LATE INTO THE NIGHT. I PHOTOGRAPH IT AT LENGTH, DOING MY BEST TO MAKE MY PRESENCE INCONSPICUOUS. WITHOUT THE DOCTORS' INTERVENTION, AMRULLAH MIGHT HAVE BEEN DEAD BY NOW. BUT HE ISN'T. HE IS RESTING.

I GO TO DO THE SAME. OUR ROOM SEEMS LARGER THAN USUAL, BECAUSE REGIS AND EVELYNE ARE WATCHING OVER AMRULLAH. EVERY DAY, I FEEL LIKE TELLING THEM HOW MUCH I ADMIRE THEM. I KNEW THEY'D JUST LAUGH AT ME FOR SAYING IT, BUT WHAT THEY'RE DOING IS PRETTY DAMN IMPRESSIVE.

SO, HAVING MADE SURE EVERYONE IS ASLEEP AND NOBODY CAN HEAR ME, I SAY OUT LOUD:

BRAVO.

AND FALL ASLEEP.

ETGAR KERET

(TRANSLATED FROM HEBREW BY NATHAN ENGLANDER)

■

What, of This Goldfish, Would You Wish?

FROM *Tin House*

YONATAN HAD A BRILLIANT IDEA for a documentary. He'd knock on doors. Just him. No camera crew, no nonsense. Just Yonatan alone, a little camera in his hand, asking, "If you found a talking goldfish that granted you three wishes, what, of this goldfish, would you wish?"

Folks would give their answers, and Yoni would edit them down, make clips of the more surprising responses. Before every set of answers, you'd see the person standing stock still in the entrance to his house. Onto this shot he'd superimpose the subject's name, his family situation, his monthly income, and maybe even the party he'd voted for in the last election. That, together with the wishes, and maybe he'd end up with some real social commentary, a testament to the massive rift between all our dreams and the often unpromising realities in which we live.

It was genius, Yoni was sure. And, if not, at least it was cheap. All he needed was a door to knock on and a heart beating on the other side. With a little decent footage, he was sure he'd be able to sell it to Channel 8 or Discovery in a flash. Either as a film or as a bunch of vignettes, little cinematic corners, each with that singular soul standing in a doorway, followed by three killer wishes, precious, every one.

Even better, maybe he'd cash out, package it with a slogan and sell it to a bank or cellular phone company. Maybe tag it with something like, "Different dreams, different wishes, one bank." Or, "The bank that makes dreams come true."

No prep, no plotting, natural as can be, Yoni grabbed his camera and went out knocking on doors. In the first neighborhood, the kindly folk that took part generally requested the foreseeable things: health, money, bigger apartments, either to shave off a couple of years or a couple of pounds. But there were also the powerful moments, the big truths. There was one drawn, wizened old lady that asked simply for a child. There was a Holocaust survivor, a number on his arm, who asked very slowly, and in a quiet voice—as if he'd been waiting for Yoni to come; as if it wasn't an exercise at all: he'd been wondering (if this fish didn't mind), would it be possible for all the Nazis left living in the world to be held accountable for their crimes? There was a cocky, broad-shouldered lady-killer who put out his cigarette and, as if the camera wasn't there, wished he were a girl. "Just for a night," he added, holding a single finger right up to the lens.

And these wishes were just from one short block in one small, sleepy suburb of Tel Aviv. Yonatan could hardly imagine what people were dreaming of in the development towns and the collectives along the northern border, in the West Bank settlements and Arab villages, the immigrant absorption centers full of broken trailers and tired people left to broil out in the desert sun.

Yonatan knew if the project was going to have any weight, he'd have to get to everyone, to the unemployed, to the ultrareligious, to the Arabs and Ethiopians and American ex-pats. He began to plan a shooting schedule for the coming days: Yaffo, Dimona, Ashdod, Sderot, Taibe, Talpiot. Maybe Hebron even. If he could sneak past the wall, Hebron would be great. Maybe somewhere in that city some beleaguered Arab man would stand in his doorway and, looking through Yonatan and his camera, looking out into nothingness, just pause for a minute, nod his head, and wish for peace—that would be something to see.

Sergei Goralick doesn't much like strangers banging on his door. Less so is he amenable to it when those strangers are asking him questions. In Russia, when Sergei was young, it happened plenty.

The KGB felt right at home knocking on his door. His father had been a Zionist, which was pretty much an invitation for them to drop by any old time.

When Sergei got to Israel and then moved to Yaffo, his family couldn't wrap their heads around it. They'd ask him, What are you looking to find in a place like that? There's no one there but addicts and Arabs and pensioners. But what is most excellent about addicts and Arabs and pensioners is that they don't come around knocking on Sergei's door. Like that, Sergei can get his sleep, and get up when it's still dark. He can take his little boat out into the sea and fish until he's done fishing. By himself. In silence. The way it should be. The way it was.

Until one day some kid with an earring in his ear, looking a little bit homosexual, comes knocking. Hard like that—rapping at his door. Just the way Sergei doesn't like. And he says, this kid, that he has some questions he wants to put on the TV.

Sergei tells the boy, tells him in what he thinks is a straightforward manner, that he doesn't want it. Not interested. Sergei gives the camera a shove, to help make it clear. But the earring boy is stubborn. He says all kinds of things, fast things. And it's a bit hard for Sergei to follow; his Hebrew isn't so good.

The boy slows it down, tells Sergei he's got a strong face, a nice face, and that he simply has to have him for this movie picture. Sergei can also slow down, he can also make clear. He tells the kid to fuck off. But the kid is slippery and somehow between saying no and pushing the door closed, Sergei finds that the kid is in his house. He's already making his movie, running his camera without any permission, and from behind the camera still telling Sergei about his face, that it's full of feeling, that it's tender. Suddenly the kids spots Sergei's goldfish flitting around in its big glass jar in his kitchen.

The kid with the earring starts screaming "Goldfish, goldfish," he's so excited. And this, this really pressures Sergei, who tells the kid, it's nothing, just a regular goldfish, stop filming it. Just a goldfish, Sergei tells him, just something he found flapping around in the net, a deep-sea goldfish. But the boy isn't listening. He's still filming and getting closer and saying something about talking and fish and a magic wish.

Sergei doesn't like this, doesn't like that the boy is almost at it, already reaching for the jar. In this instant Sergei understands the boy didn't come for television, what he came for, specifically, is to snatch Sergei's fish, to steal it away. Before the mind of Sergei Goralick really understands what it is his body has done, he seems to have taken the burner off the stove and hit the boy in the head. The boy falls. The camera falls with him. The camera breaks open on the floor, along with the boy's skull. There's a lot of blood coming out of that head, and Sergei really doesn't know what to do.

That is, he knows exactly what to do, but it really would complicate things. Because if he brings this kid to the hospital, people are going to ask what happened, and it would take things in a direction Sergei doesn't want to go.

"No reason to take him to the hospital anyway," says the goldfish, in Russian. "That one's already dead."

"He can't be dead," Sergei says, with a moan. "I barely popped him. It's only a burner. Only a little thing." Sergei holds it up to the fish, taps it against his own skull to prove it. "It's not even that hard."

"Maybe not," says the fish. "But, apparently, it's harder than that kid's head."

"He wanted to take you from me," Sergei says, almost crying.

"Nonsense," the fish says. "He was only here to make a little nothing for TV."

"But he said . . ."

"He said," says the fish, interrupting, "exactly what he was doing. But you didn't get it. Honestly, your Hebrew, it's terrible."

"Yours is better?" Sergei says. "Yours is so great?"

"Yes. Mine's super-great," the goldfish says, sounding impatient. "I'm a magic fish. I'm fluent in everything."

All the while the puddle of blood from the earring kid's head is getting bigger and bigger and Sergei is on his toes, up against the kitchen wall, desperate not to step in it, to get blood on his feet.

"You do have one wish left," the fish reminds Sergei. He says it easy like that, as if Sergei doesn't know—as if either of them ever loses count.

"No," Sergei says. He's shaking his head from side to side. "I can't," he says. "I've been saving it. Saving it for something."

"For what?" the fish says.

But Sergei won't answer.

That first wish, Sergei used up when they discovered a cancer in his sister. A lung cancer, the kind you don't get better from. The fish undid it in an instant—the words barely out of Sergei's mouth. The second wish Sergei used up five years before, on Sveta's boy. The kid was still small then, barely three, but the doctors already knew. Something in her son's head wasn't right. He was going to grow big but not in the brain. Three was about as smart as he'd get. Sveta cried to Sergei in bed all night. Sergei walked home along the beach when the sun came up, and he called to the fish, asked the goldfish to fix it as soon as he'd crossed through the door. He never told Sveta. And a few months later she left him for some cop, a Moroccan with a shiny Honda. In his heart, Sergei kept telling himself it wasn't for Sveta that he'd done it, that he'd wished his wish purely for the boy. In his mind, he was less sure, and all kinds of thoughts about other things he could have done with that wish continued to gnaw at him, half driving him mad. The third wish, Sergei hadn't yet wished for.

"I can restore him," says the goldfish. "I can bring him back to life."

"No one's asking," Sergei says.

"I can bring him back to the moment before," the goldfish says. "To before he knocks on your door. I can put him back to right there. I can do it. All you need to do is ask."

"To wish my wish," Sergei says. "My last."

The fish swishes his fish tail back and forth in the water, the way he does, Sergei knows, when he's truly excited. The goldfish can already taste freedom. Sergei can see it on him.

After the last wish, Sergei won't have a choice. He'll have to let the goldfish go. His magic goldfish. His friend.

"Fixable," Sergei says. "I'll just mop up the blood. A good *sponga* and it'll be like it never was."

That tail just goes back and forth, the fish's head steady.

Sergei takes a deep breath. He steps out into the middle of the kitchen, out into that puddle. "When I'm fishing, while it's dark and the world's asleep," he says, half to himself and half to the fish, "I'll tie the kid to a rock and dump him in the sea. Not a chance, not in a million years, will anyone ever find him."

"You killed him, Sergei," the goldfish says. "You murdered someone—but you're not a murderer." The goldfish stops swishing his tail. "If, on this, you won't waste a wish, then tell me, Sergei, what is it good for?"

It was in Bethlehem, actually, that Yonatan found his Arab, a handsome man who used his first wish for peace. His name was Munir; he was fat with a big white mustache. Super photogenic. It was moving, the way he said it. Perfect, the way in which Munir wished his wish. Yoni knew, right while he was filming, that this guy would be his promo for sure.

Either him or that Russian. The one with the faded tattoos that Yoni had met in Yaffo. The one that looked straight into the camera and said, if he ever found a talking goldfish he wouldn't ask of it a single thing. He'd just stick it on a shelf in a big glass jar and talk to him all day, it didn't matter about what. Maybe sports, maybe politics, whatever a goldfish was interested in chatting about.

"Anything," the Russian said, "not to be alone."

■

Fed to the Streets

FROM *L.A. Weekly* ·

MY PARTNER TAKES A LONG DRAG on his cigarette and scratches the back of his head. I stand with hands in pockets, my head cocked to one side. We are silent. We are staring. We face the object in front of us almost as if we are at an altar praying, so deep is our reverie.

The rig is new. New! Crisp, clean walls with our company's logo and colors painted on both sides, bordered by gleaming chrome and perched on tires with fresh tread. No scratches, no dents, no scrapes. Shining like an egg in the sun. The sirens and brakes haven't yet experienced Code-3 driving; the inside compartments, newly stocked, have not heard screaming, gasping, puking, crying; the gurney hasn't yet been contaminated with Code Yellow or Code Brown; and blood has not yet dripped onto the floor.

My eyes slowly scan the rig from top to bottom, soaking in every detail. I feel, strangely, a little sick to my stomach. Is this sparkling new ambulance mocking us? I don't want to be reminded of what our last rig went through. I don't want to think about what this one is about to go through. I don't want to remember the particularly bloody trauma call two months ago, and how my partner had complained for weeks because blood had seeped between the metal floor plates that lock the gurney in place. I don't want to think of the smells I occasionally noticed in the back—old, lingering smells. We survived all that, the rig, my partner and I. We got through it together. Now, here's this ridiculous rookie rig, all clean and eager and unaware.

The station phone rings, the loudspeaker blaring right behind us. In the old days I would have jumped, panicked, bolted for the passenger seat, grabbed the radio and my map book, stared at my pager for the address and type of call. But these are not the old days, so says the fresh ambulance in front of us. I toss the keys to my partner, who drops his cigarette, crushes it. I let out a long sigh. Then we slowly walk to the doors and get in.

First call of the day. It begins.

Fumble

You are young, eager, a rookie, and you don't yet know that this job does not mean saving lives. You haven't yet figured out that ninety percent of all 911 calls are BS, so every time you hear dispatch say your rig number over the radio, your heart does a front flip into your mouth, all that extra weight just sitting on your parched tongue. You scramble with the Thomas Guide. You aren't good at mapping yet. Your partner may or may not hate you, and the firefighters all but roll their eyes at you as you fumble, fumble, fumble.

Your first call, the first real call, is a two-vehicle accident and an overturned truck whose wheels are still spinning as you arrive first on scene. Your partner checks the truck while you squat next to the crinkled, folded car. Your patient sits slightly dazed amid the chaotic mess. Your patient asks for water, asks if he can call his fiancée, asks if he can go home. But you don't answer his questions or say much, because as soon as your eyes connect with his against the backdrop of What He Just Went Through.

There's light behind him

Every bit of medical information you ever had flies out of your head. You used to know the difference between pleural effusion and pericardial tamponade, but at the moment you don't know your own name, much less how to make an assessment. Your eyes are locked with his, he seems calmer than you feel, despite the blood on his face and arms, the pieces of glass still stuck to him.

Does he know can he feel

Your brush jacket is too big and the helmet keeps slipping down over your eyes. You feel like a little kid playing dress-up, and it doesn't help that you could swear you see something that doesn't make any sense.

I swear I can see I swear I can see

Already you know you are too sensitive for this job, not tough enough, too trusting. You've been laughed at before for dutifully taking the blood pressure of a patient obviously faking an illness. But patients appreciate that you are all sympathy and that you actually listen to what they're saying. What you need to learn is how to focus on what needs to be done in the short time you have.

I can see does he know

And it's frustrating because you know you have potential, you know you could be good at this job but you just can't put the pieces together fast enough.

I can see his

Or detach yourself like you know you need to.

There's so much light

Because in this job to help someone you kind of need to ignore them, don't you.

I can see so much

The fire truck and the paramedic squad are pulling up lights and sirens and you open your mouth to tell him that he can't have water because it's an airway compromise, that he has to go to the hospital because he may have sustained serious internal injuries, that the paramedics are here to help him. But what comes out instead is, "I can see your guardian angel. You're going to be fine."

Half-mast

"Baby girl," he says. He is unable to keep his eyes open, but he's trying; his eyebrows are pulled up like ship sails trying to catch a breeze. "Baby girl, I'm not okay." I nod sympathetically, fighting the twitch his words induce in my stomach, and the flush in my cheeks. It's not that he's so good-looking, necessarily, but his low tone is personal and intimate, and there's something about those two words and the way he says them that is getting to me. If he had called me baby, babe, sweetheart, chick, darling, lady, queen, hot stuff, foxy—I've heard them all—I would've rolled my eyes, stiffened and put on my tough-girl act, but his soft, sad crooning is making me wish I had someone to go home to at the end of this shift.

I awkwardly pat his shoulder. "What happened, sir?"

When we pulled him out of the bushes twenty minutes earlier he was alone, had no wallet or ID, and was utterly incapable of answering any questions, this comical, towering six feet three inches, spilling over both ends of the gurney. Now at the hospital, the largest rag doll I've ever seen is coming to life.

He shudders slightly and his eyebrows relax, eyelids drifting shut. "I lost all my money," he says sadly. "I gambled it away."

I nod even though he can't see. "What did you take?"

He tries to remember. He'd been drinking for twelve hours straight, and took seven pills given to him by friends throughout the night. One or two of the pills were Ecstasy, but other than that, he can't remember a thing. Which, it sounds like, was the point.

"Baby girl," he says again. He is fumbling for my hand now, and as he grasps it I really am blushing, amused and caught off-guard by my vulnerability. He rolls his head to look at me. It's a fluid, slippery motion only drunks are capable of, and for a minute it looks like his head will keep rolling right off the gurney. With supreme effort he keeps his eyes open, and then peers at me solemnly.

"Baby girl, I'm sorry."

GSW

The only time I've ever dreamed about a patient, I held the potent images in for as long as I could and was scared to share them. Some things are precious. The patient was a GSW: gunshot wound. The patient was found lying facedown in the street, with a river of blood coming out of his head. The patient was about twenty-five years old; the patient was a heavily tattooed John Doe; the patient was presumably a gang member.

Police were on scene long before we were, and they didn't bother to call it in because they assumed he was dead. They staged out the area, put up the caution tape, and started hunting for clues, witnesses, the killer, and the weapon. At some point someone noticed that blood bubbles were popping out of his mouth, that he was still breathing.

For those of you who want to know, it looks exactly like the movies. I had trouble watching graphic movies before I drove an ambulance, and I can't watch them now. Funny, I guess, that most people can't do this kind of work, but can watch those movies without a problem.

We descended on him eagerly—a true case of trauma is a rare and coveted event—and the police officers watched with bemused interest. One even got a notebook ready in case the guy regained enough consciousness to reveal his or his assailant's name. It was my first GSW and I was very much a rookie at the time, but even I could've told the cop to put his notebook away.

The bullet had gone through the patient's occipital lobe, and the larger exit wound showed that it had shot out of his left temporal lobe. The part of his brain that controlled his breathing remained, amazingly, intact. Once we had treated, packaged and begun our transport to a trauma center, there was nothing to do but sit and watch him breathe. I matched his respirations with the bag-valve mask to help push extra O_2 in. His vitals were fine, but we all knew we were looking at a dying man, or a comatose one. His body had yet to admit the obvious.

When we went over a bump in the road, the trauma dressing slipped from his forehead, and a large geyser of blood and brain gushed from the exit wound. I yanked my left hand out of the way and slid my foot away from the new pool of blood. My right hand continued to bag him with oxygen as I reached for a new multitrauma dressing. *I saw brain*, I kept thinking.

I had the strangest feeling while watching him. His body was still warm and strong. His clothes had been cut off and he lay there oozing with life, impossibly alive. *Somebody loved him*, I thought. His mother, his girlfriend, his brother, his friend. Somebody thought he was invincible. He had thought he was invincible, clearly. The muscle memory in his body reeked of it.

Later, when it was over, when I had changed into a fresh uniform and finished my report, I took a nap in the ambulance, my arms crossed over my chest, my sunglasses on. I looked tougher than I felt. I was shaken to my boots. He died amid the tools, machinery and impersonal language of the ER. All that yelling across his body, but nothing anybody did seemed related to him. And where was he in the midst of it all? Forgotten. A John Doe, dead. A policeman's empty notebook page.

My partner didn't think he was worth saving. His opinion was that all gang members were a cancer on society, and they should be rounded up and allowed to kill each other, so the rest of us could be free of them. He had two years' experience on me and ordered me around constantly. That day I was too numb and exhausted to tell him what I was convinced of: that it wasn't our job to decide who lived or died. That I didn't ever want it to be my job to decide. If a person lay dying in front of me, I would try to help.

I didn't think I'd be able to fall asleep sitting in the rig, but in the end I did. I slept and I dreamed. In my dream there was a clean white room: white walls, tile floor. John Doe was lying on the floor, still naked but cleaned up: no sign of blood or brain or even the wound for that matter, and his skin and tattoos were gleaming. His eyes were closed, he wasn't yet dead but not alive either, and whatever life existed in him was in the form of a kind of coiled-up and angry tension: some part of him refused to let go.

I got underneath him very carefully. Curled up in a ball, my head lowered, my breathing labored, I inched his torso into a sitting position by leaning my body weight into his back and pushing the ground away. It was slow, meticulous work and he was unnaturally heavy. His arms were relaxed at his side and his head was tilted back resting on my serpentine spine. His mouth was ajar and through the open channel of his throat came a kind of smoke or light. Every time I nudged him, his body relaxed a little more, and that strange substance slid out, curling up into the air around him.

That smoke, that light was grateful to be going. It was grateful to be going, and the more it left him, the lighter and more relaxed his body became. No tension, no ugliness, no holding on. Just a body on a tile floor, with smoke and light in the air around it, and me crouched underneath.

I want to be that grateful when I go.

Our Phantom Limbs

We drive her home in the middle of the night, but she can't remember her zip code or any cross streets. The hospital face sheet only has a numeric address, and there are so many streets with that name in the Thomas Guide, running east, west, north, south, and diagonal—what side of the city did she live on? Then I have the bright idea to call someone who knows her. I pull over on the big vacuous street, a half-mile from the hospital, and set my hazards blinking. Once in a while a car zooms by and the rig slowly rocks from side to side. My partner in the back is digging through the patient's purse and finds a tattered piece of paper with a phone number on it; I dial it on my phone, forgetting that it's the middle of the night, not recognizing the New York area code, and wake the woman up. Her voice, brittle and paper-thin over the bad connection, grows with warmth and volume as the conversation progresses; she didn't know her sister was in the hospital. She helps me out with the address, then, with a choke in her voice, says, "Tell her to call me when she gets home. Please?"

I assure her, hang up, put the paper slip back. I drive again, my hands at a perfect ten and two on the wheel. I know where I'm headed, easy does it, this is a simple transfer, I'm just tired, no problem, but before I know it, one tear rolls down, and then another. Ridiculous, I say out loud. I wipe my face and say it again, softer and under my breath. Ridiculous. I hope my partner doesn't see or hear me being a fool up front, but then I stop caring about that and give myself over to it. The tears flow steadily now; I have no idea where they're coming from or why. Something about that concerned voice on the phone, and the empty, dark streets, and the sad, lonely character in back, the one who doesn't remember where she lives, who didn't tell her sister about her medical problems, who is now a double amputee.

When we get to the house and struggle to fit her through the narrow, cluttered hallways in her new wheelchair, she tells us to lock the door on our way out; there are seven dead bolts and nothing inside worth stealing. I remind her, with a sense of responsibility and my own familial guilt: call your sister, okay? She looks at me, nods reluctantly, and, just before we squeeze ourselves out and into the night, gasping for fresh air, I see her pick up the old rotary receiver and stare at it.

WeThemUs

We eat fried chicken, potato chips, burritos, pizza. We microwave a frozen dinner and follow it with ice cream. We drink coffee, soda, energy drinks, liquid crack. If caffeine via IV were available, we would jab it into our veins; if filling meals existed cheaper than five dollars, we would consume them unapologetically. We smoke cigarettes right outside the hospital, chew tobacco and spit it into cups, careful not to stain our uniforms. We get scattered sleep but have perfected catnapping: we know how to park the rig in the shade, lean the seat back, and even in our sleep, we can filter noises from the radio, only waking when Dispatch calls our rig number. We fry our brains on television and video games during the day at station. We sleep as hard as we can for as long as we can, knowing we will never make it through the night, knowing there will always be at least one call. We know how to stumble out to the rig with a half-buttoned shirt, peer sleepy-eyed at the map book, flip on lights and sirens, drive relentlessly fast, and get on scene within time. Get there and have the shirt tucked in, gloves on, equipment ready. Get there and be alert, helpful, polite. Stumble back to sleep when it is done. In the morning there is coffee. In the morning there are bags under our eyes. In the morning we have dry skin, wrinkled uniforms, our first cigarettes. Meanwhile, the firefighters are switching out crews and the fresh ER hospital staff are just arriving, pouring coffee, hearing stories of the night before.

Our patients have diabetes, heart problems, chronic respiratory disease, renal failure, hypertension. Often they have spent years killing themselves slowly with their vices; their lists of medicines are long, their trips to the doctor often. Their pain scares them, wakes them in the night, and their fear of dying lives under their skin like a parasite. They feel it is unfair, their poor quality of life. But they remember to bring their cigarettes to the hospital even when their ambulance ride is spent wheezing. They sit and watch TV on tiny beds, complaining of nonfatty, compartmentalized food, even as their feet grow bluer from pooling, noncirculating blood. They stare blankly at the doctor when he advises them to exercise.

And we, the emergency medicine providers, the first responders, the paper pushers and gurney loaders, we hand off these patients to caffeine-ridden nurses, stressed-out and sleep-deprived doctors, overweight administrators. We hand them over and we roll our eyes and cluck our tongues: Here we go again, this frequent flyer is back, same chief complaint of chest pain. She survived this time, but we know one day she won't. One day we will be pulling her through hospital doors in a flurry of action: chest compressions, ventilations, IV bag in tow, the paramedic pushing atropine and epinephrine through the narrow tube. If it is someone we like, we will feel frustrated, sad, helpless. Come back, come back, we lost you this time, your heart finally up and quit. We told you, we tried to tell you, now there is nothing we can do.

All the same, we refuse to think of our own mortality.

Somehow it feels like the only way we can survive this job is to have these same vices as an outlet, as if the cigarettes and caffeine and cheap fast food are just as necessary as the gloves and uniform and gear. As if being able to choose what we put in our body makes our poor choices irrelevant. We think our youth will save us, but we are only throwing useful artillery to the enemy, only turning a blind eye to the shrinking distance between us and our patients.

Come back, come back!

Chief Complaint

The patient I am treating has myriad infectious diseases and is spouting off a narcissistic soapbox tangent about what's wrong with her life, her health, my clumsy efforts to help. Meanwhile, the rig is lurching because my partner is tired and resents this patient's intrusion on his sleep cycle. It is three a.m. on a Monday night, Tuesday morning, whatever. I peer out the back of the rig at the streams of light. The police car is probably still behind us—should I have insisted that an officer ride in back with me? A moment ago, she'd been crawling up my arm, literally, demanding to see my pen and wanting to know what I'd done with her children—why had I killed them, why was I taking her to the graveyard, when she just wanted to go home.

I pictured the pen being driven into my throat, so I gulped away my sleepiness and threw my forearm into her sternum with my weight behind it to sit her back on the gurney. I looked at her with an icy strength I didn't feel and said in my best warning voice: "Hey, be nice to me and I'll be nice to you. I promise not to take you to the graveyard. Now *relax.*"

My paperwork is sprawled about the rig. I'd take wrestling a psych patient over filling out paperwork any day. Name, DOB, Social Security number, medical-insurance ID, height, weight, age, medical history, allergies, meds . . . on and on. She's changed her mind three times about her home address, not to mention having given six digits for her phone number, so I give up. The most important part of the paperwork, medically speaking, has yet to be filled out. In a few minutes, I will give a report to the triage nurse, explaining who the patient is and what's wrong with her, and I still don't know what I'll say. She's violent, diseased, angry, but there is no apparent drug use. She's probably a psych patient who is noncompliant with her meds . . .

Does it hurt anywhere? I ask loudly, interrupting her rant. Where is your pain? "Fuck you. Where are my kids, you bitch . . ." and off she goes. Okay. Chief complaint: pissed off. Chief complaint: threatened an officer outside a 7-Eleven, then insisted she had severe pain that has now vanished. Chief complaint: probably doesn't have a home, so the hospital is as good a place as any. Chief complaint: bilateral full-bodied "fuck you" pain with good circulation, sensory and motor.

I'm going to die this way, I think suddenly. I'm going to catch Hep C from a patient, or tuberculosis, or, at the very least, MRSA. I will get slammed in an ambulance crash, crushed by a burning building, shot by a gangbanger, blown up by a terrorist, exposed to a hazmat leak. I make minimum wage, risk my life in a war zone, and for what?

I'm almost tearing up, I'm so self-involved. The car lights are getting blurry and the paperwork is forgotten. I look back at her to find her quietly studying me. I have treated her before, I realize with a start, when I first started doing this. I have a painful, blindingly self-aware moment: here I sit, another burnt-out EMT, with a wrinkled uniform and scuffed boots. My boots! When was the last time I polished them? Her eyes are momentarily clear and lucid and she smiles. "You're very pretty," she says.

Thanks. The rig stops and my partner ambles around the side to open the backdoor. His face is miserable as he puts on a fresh pair of gloves.

We're here, I say.

No Complaints

Let me tell you a secret: in our job, it's better when there are things to do. The worst kind of patient is the one we can't help. Want to know the most infuriating chief complaint out there? Abdominal pain. We hate treating abdominal pain in the field. When someone has abdominal pain, whether it's mild indigestion or a life-threatening aortic aneurysm, the treatment is the same: drive to the hospital. That's it. They could have an ulcer, blood in their GI tract, kidney stones, a bladder infection, appendicitis; they could have internal bleeding from a bruised solid organ or the swollen infection of a hollow one. They could be throwing up bright-red blood or vomiting "coffee grounds"—digested blood. This could have been going on for weeks or hours. The most you can do on your way to the hospital is get an accurate description of where in the body the pain is occurring, signs and symptoms, and severity. The triage nurse takes it from there, but God forbid you finish your assessment on the rig and still have even one minute to go on your ride to the ER. That's one more minute of sitting there, listening to someone scream their head off, ask for pain medicine, tell you they're going to throw up. You can sympathize with their pain, hand them a basin, tell them no pain medicine is allowed until some tests are performed at the hospital, but what it feels like you're saying is: I'm useless, I can't help you; just sit tight in this overrated taxi and we'll get you there.

At least, that's what I thought.

I get a call for an unconscious male outside a shopping mall. That description, of a "man down," is the vaguest one out there; it can mean anything from a medical cause (syncopal episode, seizure, low- or high-blood-sugar diabetic, stroke, heart attack, drunk, or drug overdose) to a traumatic one (assault, stabbing, gunshot wound). He could be sleeping or he could be dead.

This patient is none of the above. When asked what hurts the most, where his pain is, what his reason was for calling 911, he says the same thing over and over.

"I can't function."

We walk him to the rig and sit him on the gurney inside and the paramedic and I climb in the back. The barrage of questions begins. Pain in your head, chest, abdomen? Difficulty breathing? Is there ringing in your ears, is it difficult to see, can you squeeze my fingers and wiggle your toes? Do you have heart problems or diabetes, do you feel confused, weak, dizzy? Have you fallen, been hit or bruised, can you describe how you're feeling, do you have any pain, and has this happened to you before? What have you had to eat or drink, what medications are you taking, what kind of medical problems do you have? Drugs, alcohol? Anxiety, stress, panic attacks?

"I can't function."

He's alert and oriented, knows where he is/what day it is/his name, but to every other question he says the same thing. He can't function. He's not taking meds, he ate lunch not that long ago, he feels "warm" from sitting in the sun, he doesn't want to hurt himself or anyone else, and one more thing: he can't function.

At first it's kind of funny, then it's annoying, then it's sad. The paramedic sits there, asking, asking, going through his store of medical information, the mental checklist. Interrupting, I report the guy's vitals one by one: his breathing, pulse and blood pressure are fine; his lungs are clear bilaterally. His blood is fully oxygenated and traveling to the farthest reaches of his body. His pupils are PERL (pupils equal, round, and reactive to light), his skin signs are normal, he's not altered in any way, and his blood sugar is perfect.

There is a moment of silence and we all sit there. If there were a clock, we would have heard its ticking. The paramedic is frustrated, but I am somewhat in awe. This man walked out of a shopping mall on a Thursday afternoon. He didn't make a purchase. He probably walked toward his parked car, or the bus stop, and then just stopped dead in his tracks, not knowing if he wanted to go home, stay put, or return to the mall to buy something. Not knowing if he was hungry, thirsty, tired, lonely, restless, anxious, sick, or crazy. He only knew he didn't know. It's not a medical complaint, and there isn't a thing we or the hospital can do, but all the same, he can't function. What do you do when you can't function? You call 911. Who else are you going to call?

Something criminal happens, and 911 sends the police; if there is a fire, the fire trucks arrive; he has a medical problem and here are the paramedics and EMTs; and when things are real bad, you get all of the above. But when someone's mind starts to go, there is no system in place. If you can't function in this society, you'd better have friends and family, because otherwise, you are shit out of luck.

In the end we take him to the hospital. I sit in the back and don't say a word. I keep thinking of a clock for some reason, the one that would be ticking because it is so quiet. The one we don't have.

Cracked

Hail Jesus God our Father please save him, save my baby let him live please . . .

I glance in the rearview mirror. I have only a blocked view of what is happening in the back, but I hear all kinds of noise, not to mention the patient's wife is sitting in the passenger seat praying her head off. My hands are gripped tight to the wheel and I am still pouring sweat from struggling with the 280-pound patient. The one who went from dead to combative as we loaded him on a backboard and attempted to walk him down a steep flight of stairs to the ambulance waiting below. The one found pulseless, his last dying breath escaping out of his lungs as his eyes went limp.

Someone had bagged him with oxygen immediately and I had jumped on compressions. Locked my arms, leaned my full weight into the heels of both palms, pushed down to a depth of two inches, then released completely, counting to thirty at a rapid rhythm similar to that of the disco song "Staying Alive." Compressions are simple enough to do but horribly grotesque, too. They don't tell you in CPR classes that you will hear the sound of ribs separating from sternum, followed by strange squelching noises that emanate from the chest cavity. Luckily, that didn't happen with him. Luckily, his heart had a shockable rhythm and between two shocks, drugs pushed through an IV, and immediate CPR, he had actually come back.

All the while his wife had been yelling at him in an unbelievably commanding voice, "Breathe, big man! Breathe baby!" I had thought at the time, with complete absurd sincerity, that we should bring her to every full arrest from now on, who wouldn't do what she says?

Four percent or less. That's how often someone actually ends up living after CPR is initiated. It's rare to get pulses back, it's uncommon to regain spontaneous breathing, but for someone to go from dead to awake is nothing short of exceptional.

Now I see huge arms flailing around and hear the paramedic's voice, not as commanding, saying "Calm down, sir. Try to relax." I turn to the wife needing to confirm a suspicion I've had since we first got on scene. She starts her story of what happened, but before she really gets through it I cut to the chase: history of drug use?

Her eyes get real wide and she uses her booming voice to say, "He does crack cocaine!"

I nod my head, fighting the inappropriate urge to laugh. So the patient in the back is a crack overdose who just got loaded up with voltage and pure adrenaline. No wonder he's swinging and frothing at the mouth.

Please God let him go to rehab, he's been clean for two years God don't let him die for this mistake, please God praise Jesus let him live let him live . . .

After we get his pulse back our next step is to transport him immediately. Because he is big we have to four-point the backboard, and unfortunately the way out is so tight that we have to lift his feet up over the banister and carry him down the stairs head first, all of us squeezed together, shuffling our steps, trying to move as smoothly as possible. Halfway down the stairs, all that blood in his brain, his eyes open and he starts yelling and flailing and fighting us. He probably has no clue what happened to him. There he is, a born-again newborn, and his first view of the world after dying is a very strange angle of the night sky, our sweaty faces, and a beeping EKG monitor we have balanced on his chest.

We're finally at the hospital and I fly out of the ambulance to open the back doors. That's when I see that the walls, ceiling, floor, and doors are all splattered with a clear fluid that smells faintly of alcohol. Two paramedics, my partner, and our deer-in-headlights student riding with us today pile out like clowns from a circus car looking exhausted and overwhelmed. Someone tells me that our patient threw up four times en route to the hospital as I stand there, stunned, looking at the mess. Also, our patient managed to free himself from the backboard, and the slamming I had heard was that of the board swinging and hitting the rig walls.

"Everyone okay?"

Yes. Even on her first day in the field our student knew to get out of the way of projectile vomit.

We walk into the emergency department with our patient very much alive, sitting crazy-eyed on the gurney, a rubber airway assist still dangling out of his nose. The awaiting ER team that usually greets full arrests looks bewildered.

"Is this him?"

"Yup, it's him. He came back."

We move like a confused school of fish to get the patient into a room, unload him on to a hospital bed, disentangle wires, hang up the IV bag, hook him to the hospital's pulse ox, and so on. The lead paramedic's voice calls out over the scuffle of activity. He is looking at his run sheet for reference: "Good evening everybody, we have a twenty-eight-year-old male overdose found pulseless, v tach with agonal breathing. Epinephrine was administered . . ."

The medic continues and the last I see of our patient as the swarm closes in are his terrified eyes. He looks no closer to understanding what has happened to him.

Does he know? The biggest secret of all, has he realized it? We are selfish human beings just like everybody else. Ours is a gritty, gory, glorified service job that is up to its ears in the mucked up beauty that is human life. We do this job to help people, but we also do it for the adrenaline rush, the lifestyle, the stories, and the feeling of being needed. We do it because the human body is amazing and capable of so much, and because shifting the balance in a person's life is heady, addictive, and gratifying.

Hopefully, when he realizes we narrowly saved his life tonight, he won't mind how terribly impersonal it was.

Eyes

You avoid looking at your patient, you have learned this much on the job at least: patient is ninety-five, female, complains of chest pain. The live-at-home nurse called 911 because she wasn't sure how severe the old woman's condition had become. They both speak Russian, you half-listen to the firefighters struggle with the language barrier while you hook up the twelve-lead EKG. Move the ninety-five-year-old breast out of the way, line up V4 with the midclavicular line, line up V6 with the midaxillary line, the rest is easy. Ma'am, we're going to take a picture of your heart, you say, knowing that she's not listening. Hold still for us, okay?

She is strong and angry; you feel it coming off her in waves. Feel it but don't see it; you still won't look at her. She is not the boss of the scene, the lead paramedic is, so you turn to him with the first copy of the EKG readout, which you wish you understood better but don't. He looks at it, nods. You start to put her on oxygen but he shakes his head. Thumbs over his shoulder. Do that on the rig, we're going to load her up and go.

Ah. Sack-of-potatoes time, you were waiting for this. She is old and weak, with light bones; there is a fairly easy path from the bed to the gurney waiting in the hall. You nod to your partner: we'll GS her, you say. You still don't know what GS stands for, but you get behind her, put your arms through her armpits, and grab her wrists. Your partner scoops up her legs: one, two, three, lift. The whole time, she is complaining loudly in Russian, and then before you can get to the gurney the ninety-five-year-old flesh-and-bones package wrapped in your arms starts writhing and her complaints grow louder. All of it too fierce for that frail frame.

Almost there, but the paramedic stops you. There has been a shift in the air, but you missed the turning point. You were busy negotiating with the carpeted stairs, the thick table legs, the vase your partner almost elbowed. The paramedic's face and voice have softened. Put her back, he says. You blink at him, feel the thin layer of sweat under your uniform, and start the shuffle back. She has slipped down and it's increasingly awkward. You hear the paramedic talking to the nurse while the firefighters pack up their gear and you strain to make out the words.

Okay. It's her choice. If she wants to die in her home, that's her choice.

Strangely elated, with respect, you place her on the bed. You know you can look at her now, so you do. She is propped up on frilly pillows, hands clasped, coal-black eyes burning fiercely into yours, white hair in a tight bun. Reserved, dignified, powerful. Go away, her eyes say. I am the boss of me.

Beautiful, you think. Thank you, you almost say, but stop yourself. You slip the image of her gorgeous face into your pocket along with the second copy of the EKG printout you'll study later, and almost skip out the door.

Under the Radar

On my partner's last day there is a heat wave, and my company sets a new record: 198 calls in less than 12 hours. Everyone is calling 911 today, everyone can't breathe, or has a splitting headache, or stood up and felt dizzy, or has chest pain. Everyone is hot and uncomfortable and anxious; the lines at the hospital in our district are flowing out the door. Firefighters are pouring sweat even with the air conditioning flooding the back of the rig, and the EMTs lining the hospital hallways look ready to pass out. Only the emergency room triage nurses remain unflappable.

"I have so much food sitting at station," I complain to him as we drive to our umpteenth call. "I don't want to have to buy lunch."

He doesn't say anything, just nods slightly in acknowledgement. But we both know I'll be lucky to get to eat at all today. By now he's familiar with my low-blood-sugar bitchiness; he'll probably help find me food at the hospital—one of those awful prewrapped sandwiches, or a little package of graham crackers—just to fend it off.

We work really well together. I've been trying to be unflappable myself today, and I'm failing at it: I'm terribly sad to see him go. Having a good partner is like breathing, blinking, or swallowing: so natural you don't even notice. Having a bad one is like an acute case of the hiccups. He and I have worked together now for about four months, and he's my third regular partner. We've only had a couple minor hiccups.

The scene of our umpteenth call is a residential street with a church on the corner, and when we get there we have trouble finding our patient. As the fire department pulls up, I'm looking at my pager for patient details: forty-eight-year-old male, behavioral. I start scanning this peaceful intersection for someone who fits the description. This kind of situation always amuses me. It feels odd to be standing on a street corner next to a large lit-up vehicle, with gloves and uniforms on, looking at pedestrians with questioning eyes: *Is it you? Are you sick or injured? Do you need us?* I think healthy people probably get nervous when they see that question in our eyes.

One of the firefighters spots a regular standing arm in arm with another man, both of them silently watching us. The firefighter walks over and calls him by name, asks him if he called 911.

It takes me a while to place this frequent flyer although I know I've seen him before. Then I realize the last time I saw him, his miserable drunken face had been attached to a limp body that was crumpled at the bottom of a set of concrete stairs. He had smelled bad and looked worse, the stairwell had reeked of urine, and the worst part was, he kept apologizing. *He needs help,* I had thought as I hoisted him up and over to the gurney, mentally trying to squeeze my nostrils shut, *but not the kind I know how to give.* Getting sober momentarily wasn't going to fix his problems. But we had taken him to the hospital anyway, where everybody knew him. That kind of patient usually gets returned to the same hospital, by ambulance, within twenty-four hours of getting released.

Today he looks different. Today his eyes are clear, not bloodshot. He is standing tall, his arm firmly wrapped around the other man's elbow with an air of proud possession. His thick beard looks distinguished instead of vomit-flecked and grubby, and face is more handsome than I remember. In fact, standing sober in the hot sun, he looks beautiful.

I don't hear the conversation he has with the firefighter, but it becomes quickly clear that he has no interest in going to the hospital. They exchange goodbyes and the firefighter turns to us, saying what we already know but are happy to hear: "You're cancelled."

My partner and I put the gurney away and take our gloves off, wiping the new sweat from our faces. We climb into the ambulance and he reaches for the radio. "Wait," I say. "Not yet."

I want thirty seconds. I want a moment, this moment, to be under the radar. Dispatch thinks we're on scene still, and as soon as we tell them that we're cancelled the madness of the day will begin again.

He understands. He releases the brake and turns off the rotating red and amber lights; he puts the rig in drive, and we coast, slowly, silently. There is a feeling of suspension. We are in a bubble, a 3.5 ton bubble, gliding down the street.

Sometimes I have the reverse situation. Instead of trying to locate the sick person who blends in with a healthy-looking crowd, I see sick people everywhere. I see a kid riding a bike recklessly without a helmet, or an overweight person eating a triple cheeseburger. I see people stumbling around drunk in the middle of the day, driving like maniacs, chain-smoking cigarettes, getting into fights, and I think, *We'll be coming for you later.*

My partner turns right at the stop sign. Facing us and half a block down is the busy street loaded with speeding cars that will take us anywhere we might need to go: our station, the next call, or another district to provide coverage.

It's time.

I reach for the radio serenely; there is the feeling of suspension still. We are off the map, off the charts, in a submarine floating under the battlefield. I click the side button and in a clear calm voice tell dispatch that we have been cancelled on scene and are available. And with that, the bubble pops, my serenity becomes a lingering memory, and it's like someone has pressed the fast forward button. We are off, lights and sirens. We are entered back into the system, we are fed to the streets.

TÉA OBREHT

■

The Tiger's Wife

FROM *The New Yorker*

I. The Tiger

Having sifted through everything I have heard about the tiger and his wife, I can tell you that this much is fact: in April of 1941, without declaration or warning, the German bombs started falling over the city and did not stop for three days.

The tiger did not know that they were bombs. He did not know anything beyond the hiss and screech of fighter planes passing overhead and the missiles falling, the bears bellowing in another part of the fortress, and the sudden silence of the birds. There was smoke and a terrible warmth, a gray sun rising and falling in what seemed like a matter of minutes, and the tiger, frenzied, dry-tongued, ran back and forth along the span of rusted bars.

He was alone and he was hungry, and that hunger, coupled with the thunderous noise of bombardment, had burned in him a kind of awareness of his own death, an imminent and innate knowledge that he could neither dismiss nor accept. He did not know what to do with it. His water had dried up, and he rolled around in the stone bed of his trough, making that long sad sound that tigers make.

After two days of pacing, his legs gave out and he was reduced to a contraction of limbs, lying in his own waste. He had lost the ability to move, to produce sound, to react in any way. When a stray bomb hit the south wall of the citadel, sending up clouds of smoke and ash and shattering bits of rubble into his skin, his heart should have stopped. The toxic, iridescent air; the feeling of his fur folding back like paper in the heat; and then the long hours during which he crouched at the back of his pen, watching the ruptured flank of the citadel wall: all of these things should have killed him. But something, some sudden flickering of the blood, forced him to his feet and he made his way through the gap in the wall.

The tiger's route that night took him past the waterfront, where the remains of the merchants' port and the Jewish quarter spread in flattened piles of brick down the bank and into the waters of the Danube. The river was lit by fires, and those who had gone into it were washing back against the bank where the tiger stood. He considered the possibility of swimming across, and under optimal circumstances the tiger might have attempted it, but the smell rising off the bodies turned him around, sent him back past the citadel hill and into the ruined city.

People must have seen him, but in the wake of the bombardment he was anything but a tiger to them: a joke, an insanity, a religious hallucination. He drifted, enormous and silent, down the alleys of Old Town, past the smashed-in doors of coffeehouses and bakeries, past the motorcars flung through shopwindows. He went down the tramway, up and over the fallen trolleys in his path, beneath the lines of electric cable that ran through the city and now hung broken and black as jungle creeper.

By the time he reached Knez Petrova, looters were already swarming the boulevard. Men were walking by him, past him, alongside him, men with fur coats and bags of flour, with sacks of sugar and ceiling fixtures, with faucets, tables, chair legs, upholstery ripped from the walls of ancient Turkish houses that had fallen in the raid. He ignored them all.

Some hours before sunrise, the tiger found himself in the abandoned market at Kalinia. Here the scent of death that clung to the wind separated from the pools of rich stench that ran between the cobbles of the market square. He walked with his head down, savoring the spectrum of unrecognizable aromas—splattered tomatoes and spinach that stuck to the grooves in the road, broken eggs, bits of fish, the thick smell smeared around the cheese counter. His thirst insane, the tiger lapped up water from the leaky fountain where the flower women filled their buckets, and then put his nose into the face of a sleeping child who had been left, wrapped in blankets, under the pancake stand.

It was dawn by the time the tiger left the city, but he did not go unobserved. He was seen first by the gravedigger, a man who was nearly blind, and who did not trust his eyes to tell him that a tiger, braced on its hind legs, was rummaging through the churchyard garbage heap, mouthing thistles in the early-morning sunlight.

The tiger was noticed, too, by the city's police chief, who would go on to shoot himself three days later, and who mentioned the tiger in his last letter to his fiancée. "I have never seen so strange a thing as a tiger in a wheat field," he wrote, "even though, today, I pulled a woman's black breasts and stomach out of the pond at the Convent of Sveta Maria." The last city dweller to see the tiger was a farmer who was burying his son in a garden two miles north of the city, and who threw rocks when the tiger got too close.

The tiger had no destination, only the constant tug of self-preservation in the pit of his stomach, some vague, inborn sense of what he was looking for, which carried him onward. For days, then weeks, there were long, parched fields and stretches of marshland clogged with the dead. Bodies lay in piles by the roadside and hung like pods from the branches of trees. The tiger waited for them to fall, then scavenged them until he got mange, lost two teeth, and moved on. He followed the river upstream through the flooded bowl of the foothills, swollen with April rain, sleeping in empty riverboats while the sun, pale in the blue mist of the river, grew dimmer.

By early autumn, he had spent four months in the swamps, gnawing on decaying carcasses that drifted by, stealing the occasional bird's egg, and snatching frogs and salamanders along the creek bed, until one morning, in the grip of an early frost, he came across a boar. Brown and bloated, the hog was distracted with acorns, and for the first time in his life the tiger gave chase. It was loud and poorly calculated. He came on with his head up and his breath blaring like a foghorn, and the boar, without even turning to look at its pursuer, disappeared into the autumn brush.

The tiger did not succeed, but the attempt was something, at least. He had been born in a box of hay in a Gypsy circus, and had spent his life feeding on fat white columns of spine in the citadel cage. For the first time, the impulse that made him flex his claws in sleep, the compulsion that led him to drag his meat to the corner of his solitary cage, was articulated into something other than frustration. Necessity drew him slowly out of his domesticated clumsiness. It strengthened and reinforced the building blocks of his nature, honed his languid feline reflexes, and the long-lost Siberian instincts pulled him north, into the cold.

II. The Village

I'm told that the tiger was first sighted on the Galinica ridge, above my grandfather's village, during a snowstorm at the end of November. Who knows how long he had already been hiding up there, but on that particular day the herdsman Vladiša lost a calf in the blizzard, went up the mountain to retrieve it, and, in a thicket of saplings, came across the tiger, yellow-eyed and bright as a blood moon, with the calf, already dead, hanging in its jaws.

People did not believe poor Vladiša, even when they saw him running down the hill, white as a ghost, arms in the air, with no calf. They did not believe him when he collapsed in the village square, breathless with terror, and managed to stutter out that they were all done for, that the Devil had come to Galina, and call the priest quick. They did not believe him because they didn't know what to believe—what was this orange thing he was screaming about, its back and shoulders scorched with fire? They would have been better equipped to react if Vladiša had told them that he had meant the witch Baba Roga and, in that same instant, her skull-and-bones hut on its one giant chicken leg had come tearing down the hillside after him.

My grandfather and his own grandmother, Mother Vera, were among those who were summoned to the square by Vladiša's shouting. My grandfather was nine, and he ran out of the house in just his shirtsleeves. Mother Vera came out after him with a coat in her hands, cuffing him across the ear and forcing him into it, while the blacksmith and the fishmonger and the man who sold buttons propped Vladiša up in the snow and gave him water.

Vladiša was saying, "The Devil, I tell you! The Devil has come for us all!"

To my grandfather, the Devil was many things. The Devil was the hobgoblin whom you met in the pasture, and who asked you for coins—deny him and he would turn the forest around, and you would be lost forever. The Devil was Night, Baba Roga's third horseman, who rode a black charger through the woods. Sometimes, the Devil was Death, who waited for you at a crossroads or behind some door you had been repeatedly warned against opening. But as my grandfather listened to Vladiša, who was sobbing about orange fur and stripes, it became clearer and clearer to him that this devil on the mountain was something else.

Mother Vera's people had always been shepherds, and when my grandfather fell to her care she was determined to make him continue the legacy. When he turned eight, my grandfather started taking the sheep to pasture in the green, quiet fields above Galina. With sixty sheep to one boy and all the tree shade he could want, my grandfather taught himself to read that first summer. He read the alphabet book, that staple of childhood learning. Then he read *The Jungle Book*, a gift from the village doctor. For weeks, my grandfather sat in the long-stemmed grass and pored over the brown volume with its soft pages. He read about the panther Bagheera, Baloo the bear, the old wolf Akela. Inside the cover was a picture of a boy, thin and upright, thrusting a stick of flame into the face of an enormous square-headed cat.

"But that's Shere Khan," he said to the crowd, and everyone who had come running from the village turned to look at him. The doctor, however, was there, too. "You may be right," the doctor said. "Where's that book I gave you?" My grandfather ran inside to get it, and came back out with the book open to the dog-eared page with his favorite picture, the one of Mowgli and Shere Khan. He held it out to the terrified cowherd. Vladiša took one look at it and fainted, and that was how the village found out about the tiger.

III. The Meat

If the tiger had been a different sort of tiger, a hunter from the beginning, he probably would have come down to the village sooner. His long journey from the city had brought him as far as the ridge, and even he could not be certain why he had chosen to remain here. But the ridge—with its bowed saplings and broken trees underfoot, the steep flank of the mountain studded with caves, the wild game wide-eyed and reckless with the starvation of winter—trapped him between his new, broadening senses and the vaguely familiar smell of the village below.

All day long, he walked up and down the length of the ridge, letting the smells drift up to him, puzzled by the feeling that they weren't entirely new. He had not forgotten his time at the citadel, but his memory was heavily veiled by his final days there and the days afterward, his arduous trek, the burrs and splinters of glass stinging his paws, the dense, watery taste of the bloated dead. By now, he had only an indistinct sense, in another layer of his mind, that long, long ago someone had thrown him fresh meat twice a day and sprayed him with water when the heat grew unbearable. The smells from below meant something related to that, and they made him restless and agitated as he wandered the woods, impulsively sprinting after every rabbit and squirrel he saw. The smells also made him more and more aware of his hunger, of his lack of success as a hunter, of the length of time since his last meal, the calf that had blundered into him that bitter afternoon when he'd seen the man turn and run. The taste of the calf had been familiar; the shape of the man had been familiar.

And, some nights later, there was a new smell. He had sensed it here and there in the past—the momentary aroma of salt and wood smoke, rich with blood. It came up to him almost every night, in darkness, and he stood there in the freshly fallen snow, with the trees arching in low around him, breathing it in and out.

One night, he went down to the valley and stood at the pasture fence. Across the field, past the barn and the empty pigpen, past the house with its snow-packed porch, stood a smokehouse. There was the smell, almost close enough. He did not return for two days, but when he did he found meat. Someone had been there in his absence.

One of the fence planks had been ripped down, and the meat lay under it, dry and tough but full of the smell that frenzied him. He dug it up and carried it to the woods, where he gnawed on it for a long time. Two nights later, he had to venture closer to find the next piece; it was waiting for him under a broken barrel that had been left out in the field, just yards from the smokehouse door. A cautious return some nights later to the same place, a bigger piece. Then two pieces, then three, and, eventually, a whole shoulder right at the threshold of the smokehouse.

The following night, the tiger came up the smokehouse ramp and put his shoulders in the doorway, which was thrown wide open for the first time. He could hear the sheep bleating in the stable, some distance away, terrified by his presence; the dogs, fenced up, barking furiously. The tiger sniffed the air: there was the smell of the meat but also the thick, overwhelming smell of the person inside, the person whose scent he had found on and around the meat before, and whom he could see now, sitting in the back of the smokehouse, a piece of meat in her hands.

IV. My Grandfather

For a while there was no trace of the tiger, and the town went nervously about its business. The end of the year was marked by heavy snowstorms, knee-deep drifts that moved like sand in and out of doorways and buried the mountain passes and, along with them, any news of the war. The season provided the townspeople with the best possible excuse for staying indoors, and the tiger, they hoped, would not survive the winter.

They had almost managed to convince themselves that it had all been a joke, that Vladiša had seen a personal ghost or perhaps had some kind of seizure up there in the mountains. But the village dogs—sheepdogs, thick-coated herders with yellow eyes—knew for certain that he was up there, could smell the big-cat stink of him, and it drove them crazy. They bayed and pulled at their tethers, filling the night with a hollow sound, and the villagers, swaddled in their nightshirts and woollen socks, shook in their beds and slept fitfully.

But not my grandfather. My grandfather still carried wood from the timber pile, collected eggs, brought water back from the well every evening. Mother Vera's back and stiff joints were his responsibility, and, besides, he was hoping, all the time hoping, for a glimpse of the tiger. So much so, in fact, that he carried his brown volume with the picture of Shere Khan everywhere he went. And while he never went far that particular winter, it must have been tangible, the excitement of a nine-year-old boy, because it brought him to the attention of the girl who lived in the butcher's house.

She was a small-wristed, olive-skinned girl of about sixteen, and my grandfather, not the most observant boy, had seen her occasionally, on market days, but had never noticed her with any particular interest until that winter, when she blocked his path and took the book out of his breast pocket. She smiled at him and opened it to the dog-eared page, running an ungloved finger through the knots of dark Turkish hair that curled around her face. My grandfather had his cap down around his ears, and in the muted hush of his own head he heard himself say, "That's what the tiger looks like."

The girl did not say anything, and it occurred to him that she might be embarrassed because she couldn't read—so he launched into an explanation of Shere Khan and his complicated relationship with Mowgli. He talked quickly, and the girl, who still hadn't uttered a word, continued to smile, and then, after a few minutes, handed the book back to him and went on her way. My grandfather puzzled over this all day, and when he asked Mother Vera about her she cuffed him and said, "Don't bother her, that's Luka's wife. That girl's a deaf-mute, and a Muhammadan besides—you stay away from her."

Luka, the town butcher, owned the pasture and the smokehouse on the edge of town. He was a tall man with wavy brown hair and thick red hands, and he wore an apron that was perpetually soaked in blood. My grandfather could remember only one encounter with Luka, during a winter storm when Mother Vera had sent him out to buy a leg of lamb. The front room of the shop had been filled with the smell of meat, and my grandfather had stood and looked around at the hams and sausages hanging from the rafters, soup bones and square bacon slabs in the cold counter window, the skinned red lamb with its sharp little teeth lying on the block while Luka cleaved the bone of the leg away. My grandfather was leaning in to look at jars of something brined and white and lumpy behind the counter when Luka nodded to him and said, "Pigs' feet. Delicious. Taste a lot like little boys' feet, actually," which sent my grandfather home crying.

He couldn't remember whether he had seen the girl when he had gone to the butcher's shop; perhaps she hadn't been married to Luka then. And he did not see her again until the day before Christmas Eve, when he went out after dark to fetch water for Mother Vera's bath.

My grandfather wore his wool coat and hat, and carried the empty bucket to the well, which stood at the center of the village. He had just put the bucket down and grabbed the rope when he looked up and saw a thin light at the edge of the pasture. My grandfather tried to see through the darkness: he could see the butcher's house, with the fire dying inside, which meant Luka was probably fast asleep, but the light was not that. It was the smokehouse: the door was open and there was light inside.

My grandfather did not go there looking for trouble. It merely occurred to him that some travellers or some Gypsies had found shelter for the night and that they shouldn't be there—Luka would be angry, or they might come across the tiger. It was the latter thought that drove him to pick up his bucket and press on to the smokehouse, partly because he wanted to warn the intruder about the tiger, partly because he was filled with a frantic, inexplicable jealousy at the thought of some drifters seeing his tiger first. Carefully, he crossed the empty fold and picked his way through the pasture.

My grandfather crept up the ramp to the smokehouse and stood in the doorway, looking in, and realized there was a lot less light than he had initially supposed. He could hardly see inside, where the hollowed-out hogs and cattle hung in rows, to the little room in the front corner, where the butcher's block stood. The smell was wonderful, and he suddenly felt hungry, but then there was a different smell that he hadn't noticed before, a thick, dark musk, and just as he realized this the light went out. In the sudden darkness, he heard a low, heavy sound, like breath, all around him, a single, deep rumble that strung his veins together and spread through his skull. He dove into the butchering room and crawled under a tarp, where he sat in a shuddering heap.

Something in the darkness moved, and the butcher's hooks, hanging along the rafters, clinked against one another, and my grandfather knew that it was the tiger. The tiger was walking. He could not make out the individual footfalls, the great velvet paws landing one in front of the other, only the over-all sound of it, a soft, travelling thump. He tried to quiet his own breathing, but found that he couldn't. He was panting under the tarp, and the tarp kept drawing in and rustling around him, pointing him out. Then he could sense the tiger just beside him, its big red heart clenching and unclenching under its ribs, the weight of it groaning through the floor. My grandfather's chest was jolting, and he could already picture the tiger bearing down on him, but he thought of *The Jungle Book*—the way Mowgli had taunted Shere Khan at Council Rock, torch in hand, grabbing the Lame Tiger under the chin to subdue him—and he put his hand out through the tarp and touched the coarse hairs passing by him.

And, just like that, the tiger was gone. My grandfather felt the big, hot, rushing heart brush past and vanish. He broke out in a sweat, sitting there with his bucket between his knees. He heard the sound of footsteps, and moments later the deaf-mute girl was kneeling at his side in the little room, digging him out of his tarp, brushing the hair from his forehead with worry in her eyes. Her hands, sweeping over his face, carried the heavy smell of the tiger, of snow and pine trees and blood.

And then Mother Vera's voice, screaming in the distance: "My child! The Devil has taken my child!"

My grandfather eventually learned that Mother Vera, sensing he had been gone a long time, had stepped out and, from the stairs of their little house, had seen the tiger taking off across the field. She was still screaming when the doors of the houses around the square opened, one by one, and the men spilled out into the streets and gave chase to the edge of the pasture. Loud voices, and then light and men filling the smokehouse doorway, even Luka the butcher, looking furious in his nightshirt and slippers, a cleaver in his hand. The deaf-mute helped my grandfather to his feet and led him to the door, where he could see the dark field swimming with shadows: the villagers, the snowdrifts, the fence. But not the tiger. The tiger was already gone.

"He's here, here he is," my grandfather heard someone say, and suddenly Mother Vera was clutching at him with her cold hands, out of breath and stuttering.

Outside, in the snow, were footprints. Big, round, springy footprints, the even, loping prints of a cat. My grandfather watched as the grocer Jovo, who had once killed a badger with his bare hands, knelt down in the snow and pressed his hand into one of them. The tracks were the size of dinner plates, and they ran—matter-of-factly and without pause—down from the woods and across the field, into the smokehouse and back.

"I heard something in the smokehouse," my grandfather was telling everyone. "I thought one of the animals had escaped. But it was the tiger."

Nearby, Luka stood looking out through the smokehouse door, holding on to the arm of the deaf-mute, whose skin had gone white around his grip. She was looking at my grandfather and smiling.

He appealed to the deaf-mute. "You came out because you heard him, too, didn't you?"

"The bitch is deaf. She didn't hear anything," Luka answered, before he led her across the field into the house and closed the door.

V. The Blacksmith's Gun

There was only one gun in the village, and for many years it had been kept in the home of the blacksmith. It had been fired only once, in the direction of a sheep rapist, and never by the blacksmith himself. Now, my grandfather learned, the gun would be used to kill the tiger. He watched the men prepare for the hunt the following morning, in the gray hours before dawn. My grandfather did not know what to make of his encounter in the smokehouse, but his throat was tight when the blacksmith emerged from his house with the gun under his arm. With him were two other men: Luka and Jovo. They had dogs with them, too—a short, fat hound with floppy ears and an old red sheepdog with one eye.

It was Christmas Eve, and the entire village had turned out to watch the hunters depart. People stood in a long line by the side of the road, their hands held out to touch the gun for luck as it went by on the blacksmith's arm. My grandfather stood guiltily beside Mother Vera with his sleeves drawn down over his hands, and when his turn came he touched the barrel with the tip of one sleeve-covered finger, and only for a moment.

That afternoon, as my grandfather waited for the hunters to return, he drew in the hearth dust with the same finger and hated the men on the hill. He hated Luka already, for the pigs' feet and for the way he called his wife "bitch," but now he hated the other men, and the dogs, too, because he believed, fully and wholeheartedly, that the tiger would have spared him, even if he had come in a moment earlier or later, even if he had come in to find the tiger's eyes burning at him from the other side of the smokehouse. He could already see the men coming back, the tiger slung upside down on a pole between them, or just the tiger's head, in one of their carry-sacks, and he hated them.

He probably would not have hated them had he known what is easy to guess: that the blacksmith was terrified. Climbing up Galinica, knee-deep in snow, the gun a dead weight against his ribs, the blacksmith was convinced that this was the end for him. Like everyone in the village, he had faith in the rituals of superstition. He gave money to beggars before traveling. He had spat on his children when they were born. But, unlike his fellow-villagers, he was renowned for having a deficit: he had been born in a lean year, and, to make matters worse, an estranged aunt had once lifted him from his crib and praised heaven for what a gorgeous, fat, rosy baby he was—thereby sealing forever his fate to be generally impoverished, crippled, struck down and taken by the Devil at some unexpected time, in some terrifying way.

Of course, it hadn't happened yet. But he could not imagine anything more terrifying than a tiger. And there he was—thirty-nine years old, happily married, with five children—on his way to meet the Devil. Like his companions, the blacksmith did not know what to expect. He hoped that they would not meet the tiger at all. He hoped to find himself at home that night, eating goat stew and preparing to make love to his wife.

The day was intermittently gray and bright. A freezing rain had fallen during the night, and the trees, twisting under the weight of their ice-laden branches, had transformed the forest into a snarl of crystal. The dogs plodded along, running to and fro, sniffing at trees and pissing wherever they could, seemingly unaware of their purpose on this trip. Luka was bracing himself up the mountain, using his pitchfork as a staff, and talking, too loudly for the blacksmith's taste, about his plans to raise the price of meat if the Germans came through in the spring. Jovo was eating cheese, throwing slices of it to the dogs, and calling Luka a filthy collaborator.

It was late afternoon when they came across the tiger in a clearing by a frozen pond, bright and unreal, as if carved from sunlight. The dogs saw him first, sensed him, perhaps, because he lay partially obscured in the shadow of a tree. The blacksmith felt his organs clench as the first of the dogs, the bravely stupid, half-blind shepherd, reached the tiger and immediately went end over end as the big cat lashed at and then pinned him with all its enormous weight.

Jovo seized the other dog and held it in his arms as they watched the tiger crush the thrashing shepherd. There was blood on the snow already, from something that the tiger had been eating, something that looked like a pork shoulder, something that Luka was observing keenly as his grip on the pitchfork tightened.

Later on, in the village, Luka and Jovo would praise the blacksmith for his strength and resolve. They would talk about how bravely he had raised the gun to his shoulder. Over and over, they would tell the villagers about how the blacksmith had fired, how the bullet had struck the tiger between the eyes, sending up a tremendous rusty spurt. The noise that the tiger had made: a sound like a tree breaking. The tiger's invincibility: how they had watched while it got to its feet, despite the bullet lodged in its skull, and cleared the pond in a single bound before bringing the blacksmith down in a cloud of hellish red; a snap like thunder—and then nothing, just the blacksmith's gun lying in the snow and the dead dog across the pond.

In reality, at that moment, the blacksmith stood stone still, staring at the yellow thing in the bracken. Seeing it there, crouched at the pond's edge with the body of the red dog under it, the blacksmith suddenly felt that the whole clearing had gone very bright, that brightness was spreading across the pond and toward him. Luka shouted to the blacksmith to hurry up and shoot, idiot, and Jovo, whose mouth had dropped open, had now taken off his hat and resorted to slapping himself in the face with it, while the remaining dog, shivering like a bulrush in a high wind, cowered under his free arm.

After uttering a little prayer, the blacksmith did actually raise the gun to his shoulder and did cock it, sight, and pull the trigger, and the gun did go off, with a blast that rocked the clearing and spasmed through the blacksmith's knees. But when the smoke had cleared and the noise of it had died down in his ribs the blacksmith looked up to discover that the tiger was on its feet and moving swiftly to the frozen center of the pond, undeterred by the ice and the men and the sound of the gunshot. Out of the corner of his eye, the blacksmith saw Luka drop his pitchfork and break for cover. The blacksmith fell to his knees. His hand was rummaging through the clots of yarn and the buttons and crumbs that lined the bottom of his pocket, searching for the encased bullet. When he found it, he stuffed it into the muzzle with shaking hands that seemed to be darting everywhere with the sheer force of terror, and fumbled for the ramrod. The tiger was almost over the pond, bounding on muscles like springs. He heard Jovo muttering, "Fuck me," helplessly, and the sound of Jovo's footsteps moving away. The blacksmith had the ramrod out and he was shoving it into the muzzle, pumping and pumping and pumping furiously, his hand already on the trigger, and he was ready to fire, strangely calm with the tiger there, almost on him, its whiskers so close and surprisingly bright and rigid. At last, it was done, and he tossed the ramrod aside and peered into the barrel, just to be sure, and blew his own head off with a thunderclap.

No one would ever guess that the gun had misfired. No one would ever guess that Luka and Jovo, from the branches of the tree up which they had scrambled, had watched the tiger reel back in surprise and look around, puzzled. No one would ever guess, not even after the blacksmith's clothed bones were found in disarray, many years later, that the two of them had waited in that tree until the tiger had pulled the blacksmith's legs off and dragged them away, had waited until nightfall to climb down and retrieve the gun from what was left of the blacksmith. No one would guess that they had not even buried the unlucky blacksmith, whose brain was eventually picked over by crows, and to whose carcass the tiger would return time and time again, until he had learned something about the taste of man, about the freshness of human meat, which was different now, in snow, than it had been in the heat of summer.

When Luka and Jovo returned from the mountain, carrying with them the gun of the fallen blacksmith—about whose fate they lied through their teeth, and whose final moments they played up to such an extent that stories of the blacksmith's skill and fortitude were being told in surrounding towns long after the war had ended—my grandfather was relieved to discover that the hunt had not been successful. In the long afternoon and night while the hunters were away, he had contemplated his encounter with the tiger in the smokehouse. Why had the girl been there? Had she been there the whole time? What had she been doing?

He knew for certain that her purpose had not been to harm the tiger, that she had smiled knowingly at him when it became obvious that the tiger had escaped. My grandfather considered what he would say to the girl when he saw her next, how he could ask her, knowing she could not reply, about what she had seen, what the tiger was like.

My grandfather felt certain that he would see her at the service to honor the blacksmith. Sunday afternoon, he stood at the back of the church and scanned the frost-reddened faces of the congregation, but he did not see her. He did not see her outside afterward, either, nor later that week at the Wednesday market.

VI. The Butcher

What my grandfather didn't know was that, in addition to the gun, Luka had brought something else back from the mountain: the pork shoulder that the tiger had been eating when the hunters had come upon him in the glade. My grandfather did not know that, after Luka had entered his quiet house at the edge of the pasture and slowly placed the blacksmith's gun by the door, he had swung that pork shoulder into the face of the deaf-mute girl, already kneeling in the corner with her arms over her belly. My grandfather didn't know that Luka, after he had dislocated the deaf-mute's shoulder, had dragged her into the kitchen by her hair and pressed her hands into the stove.

People now, they give a thousand explanations for Luka's marriage to the girl, who was only thirteen the day they wed. She was the bastard child of a notorious gambler, some say, who was forced on Luka as payment for a tremendous debt, a shameful secret that followed him back from those years he spent as a *guslar* in Turkey, before his father died and he was summoned home to Galina to take over the family trade. According to others, he purchased her from a thief in Istanbul, a man who sold girls at the souk, where she had stood quietly among the spice sacks and pyramids of fruit until Luka found her.

Whatever Luka's reason, there is general agreement that the girl's presence in his life was intended to hide something, because a deaf-mute could not reveal the truth about the assorted vices he was presumed to have, his gambling, his whoring, his predilection for men. He thought he had found someone to put between himself and the village, someone whose appearance, at least, if not her disability, would discourage the townspeople from making contact—because she would remind them too much of the last war, of their fathers' fears, the stories they'd heard of sons lost to the Sultan. Never mind, the villagers thought, that he had found a wife who could never demand anything of him, or reproach him for being drunk, or beg for money.

But, in finding her, Luka had stumbled into an unwelcome complication. He had underestimated the power of her strangeness, the village's potential for a fascination with her, and now people were talking more than ever. The secrecy she had been intended to afford him had turned his life into a public spectacle. The villagers were constantly chattering now, gossiping, speculating, and flat out lying about where she'd come from and how he had found her, asking after the bruises on her arms, why they were rarely seen in public together, why she'd yet to bear him a child—every possible answer leading only to further questions, further humiliations. It was worse than the first winter of their marriage, when he had brought her with him to church on Christmas, and the entire congregation had whispered afterward, "What does he mean by bringing her here?" Worse even than the following Christmas, when he had not, and they said, "What does he mean by leaving her at home?"

And now they were talking about the smokehouse. In the two days since the tiger was spotted in the village, there were whispers every-where. "What had she been doing," they were asking on street cor-ners, "in the smokehouse with that tiger? And what did it mean," they wanted to know, "that Luka couldn't keep her in his bed?"

For weeks, he had suspected that the smokehouse was missing meat, but he had second-guessed his own judgment, refusing to be-lieve that she had the audacity to steal from him. And then he had seen the tiger, and the sight of that pork in the big cat's jaws had stunned him—that little Gypsy, he had thought, that emasculating Muhammadan bitch, sneaking out and giving his meat to the Devil. She was making him look like an idiot.

Hitting her had never helped before, but it made him feel that he was doing something, interrupting her thoughts, at the very least, if he could do nothing to interrupt the town's. In a way, her silence had always terrified him. She was like an animal, he thought, as silent and begrudging as an owl. The injustice of it: that judgment that he knew was there but couldn't make her voice or put away, reinforced now to such an extent that she spent her nights away from him and stole from him, and the whole village had seen it. They were saying what she couldn't—or at least that's what he thought—and so he beat her. With his hands, his feet, his belt, he beat her.

The night he returned from the hunt, he took her outside and tied her up in the smokehouse. He told himself that he wanted only to punish her, but while he was eating his supper and getting ready for bed he understood that some part of him was hoping that the tiger would come for her, that it would come in the night and rip her apart, and in the morning he would awake to find nothing.

VII. The Wife

If you go to Galina now, people will tell you different things about Luka's disappearance, but, of course, no one will ever tell you that days went by before anyone began to suspect a thing. People didn't like Luka—they didn't visit his house, and his eerie docility as he stood in the shop, covered in blood with his hands on the meat, made them universally uncomfortable. The truth is that even after the baker's daughter went to buy meat, and found the shutters of the butcher's shop closed and the lights out, it took several days before anyone tried again.

At the time, most people assumed that Luka had simply left, that he had given up on the village and decided to brave the snowed-in pass and make for the city while the German occupation there was still new. In fact, the whole situation did not strike anyone as particularly unusual until the deaf-mute girl appeared in town two weeks later, with a fresher, brighter, slightly fuller face and that smile which suggested something new about her.

My grandfather had just returned from the timber pile and was pounding the snow from the bottoms of his shoes, when he saw the deaf-mute girl coming down the road, wrapped in Luka's fur coat. It was a cloudless winter afternoon, and villagers were leaning against their doorways. At first, only a few of them saw her, but by the time she reached the square the whole village was watching her as she made her way into the fabric shop. A few minutes later, my grandfather saw her cross the square with a parcel of Turkish silks under her arm, followed by a small procession of village women, who, while keeping their distance, were too intrigued to maintain the illusion of nonchalance.

It wasn't long before they were talking about her, and my grandfather was listening. They were talking about her on every village corner, on every village doorstep, and he could hear them as he came and went from Mother Vera's house. Truths and half-truths drifted like shadows into conversations he was not intended to overhear.

At the greengrocer's, in line for pickling salts:

"I seen the deaf-mute today."

"The Muhammadan?"

"I seen her coming down from that house again, alone as you please."

"Where was Luka? She's driven him away, hasn't she?"

"Of course not. Isn't it plain? That tiger's got him. That tiger's got him, and now she's all alone, nobody bothering her, no one but the tiger."

Then, two days later, at the well:

"You hear? That tiger got Luka in the smokehouse."

"Sure he did. All strung up, ready for him."

"How do you mean?"

"Well, you don't think it was an accident, do you? That Luka, he never was none too clever. Still, that's what comes to you when you marry one of them Muhammadans from God knows where. Like a Gypsy, that girl. Probably strung him up with his own meat hooks, left him there for the tiger."

"That can't be true."

"Well, you believe it or don't. But I'm telling you, whatever happened to that Luka was no accident. And that baby—that's no accident, neither."

"What baby?"

"Haven't you seen her? Haven't you seen her coming into town? That girl's got a belly out to here, are you blind?"

"There's no belly."

"Oh, there's a belly—and I'll tell you something else. That belly ain't Luka's."

At the timber pile:

"I heard she carved him up, right in his own smokehouse, and then in comes the tiger for dinner, and she feeds him strips of her dead husband like it's feast day."

At church, holding Mother Vera's hand:

"That tiger. I seen him crossing the pasture by moonlight, big as a horse. Wild eyes in that tiger's head, I'm telling you. Froze me right down to my feet."

"What were you doing out so late?"

"That doesn't matter. Point is, that tiger came all the way up to the door of Luka's house, and then he gets up and takes off his skin. Leaves it out on the step and goes in to see his wife."

"Imagine that."

"Don't have to, I seen it."

Who came up with that name for her? I can't say. It was only recently, after years of coming back to Galina in search of answers, that I learned about it. Up until the moment of Luka's disappearance, she was known only as "the deaf-mute girl" or "the Muhammadan." Then suddenly—after that first walk into town, when she wrapped herself in Turkish silks and admired herself in the fabric-shop mirror with the whole village staring in at her from the snow, after her belly had fully swollen, after it was clear that Luka wasn't coming back—she was referred to as "the tiger's wife."

Almost half a century later, on our weekly walks to the citadel zoo to see the tigers—always the tigers—my grandfather never referred to her as such. In fact, he rarely spoke of her at all, and when he did, it was to say, "I once knew a girl who loved tigers so much she almost became one herself." Because I was little, and my love of tigers came directly from him, I thought he was talking about me, making up a story in which I could imagine myself—which I did, for years. I did not even question or consider the reality of the girl until after my grandfather's death, when a letter of condolence arrived from the village, from an old man who called himself Jovo, who mentioned the tiger and that winter, and who said he could still see my grandfather with *The Jungle Book* in his pocket, running after the girl when no one else would go near her.

I was twenty-seven then, coming slowly out of the aftermath of the latest war, the second of my lifetime, my grief intensified by the realization that I had somehow misinterpreted my grandfather's preoccupation with tigers, and I couldn't understand why Jovo, of all the stories he must have known about my grandfather, could think to mention only this one. It drew me in—not immediately but over the course of months and then years, during which I gradually realized that she stood in the back of my mind like a person in a dream, a person whose face you cannot see.

I pulled her life together as well as I could—from the few stories that my grandmother reluctantly gave up, from the anecdotes of old villagers who were unwilling to talk, from the household myths of people who were overeager to talk—and I still don't know who or what she was. I cannot tell you for certain what happened to Luka, though I tend to side with those who say that he awoke, on the night he had left the girl to the tiger, to find her kneeling at the foot of his bed, her wrists skinned raw, holding the blacksmith's gun against his mouth.

In the end, even I find myself making things up to explain what can't be accounted for, just as the villagers have done these past seventy years. The girl's presence in town, smiling, unbruised, unafraid, coupled with Luka's sudden disappearance, invited endless speculation—stories that spread from door to door, never confirmed but always based on the same common denominator, always stemming from her secret, silent world with the tiger, from the loneliness that had drawn them together, both of them strangers in the same foreign land, she the relic of an old war, he barely a survivor of the one that had just begun.

The truth is that the people of Galina had no idea what they were witnessing, but with that ignorance they crutched their way over to something, a necessary something that justified a shared moment in a time that was otherwise completely inexplicable—a tiger that seemed to come from nowhere, a valiant but dead blacksmith, a vanished butcher, a war delayed by the weather. Something that eased the villagers' anxiety about the way things could come and go, even beyond the certainty of death; something they could cling to through the darkest nights of that winter, through the melting of the passes and the arrival of the Germans, who brought with them a real knowledge of change. By the end, so many details had piled up that the events themselves no longer mattered. All that remained was a story and its infinite variations—those of the village and of Jovo; that of the blacksmith's great-great-grandson; my grandfather's; and this one, which is mine—a hundred different wives for a single, solitary tiger, whose own disappearance no one had noticed, even after he had long since moved on.

T. OTT

■

Breakdown

FROM *MOME*

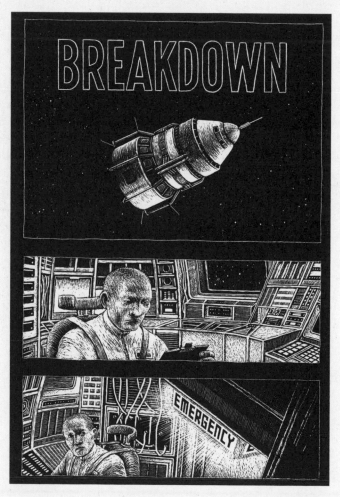

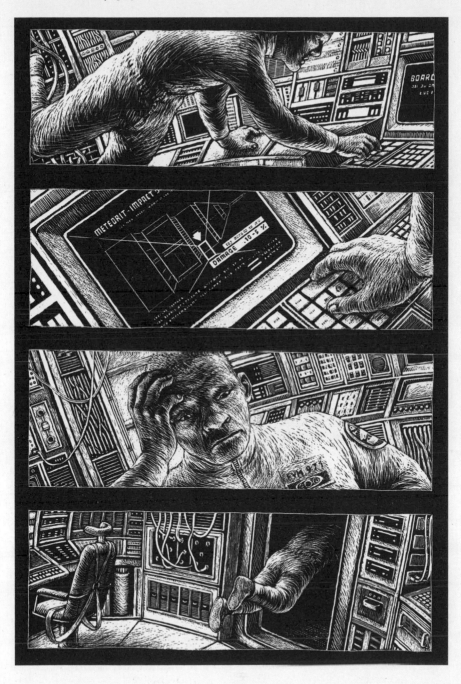

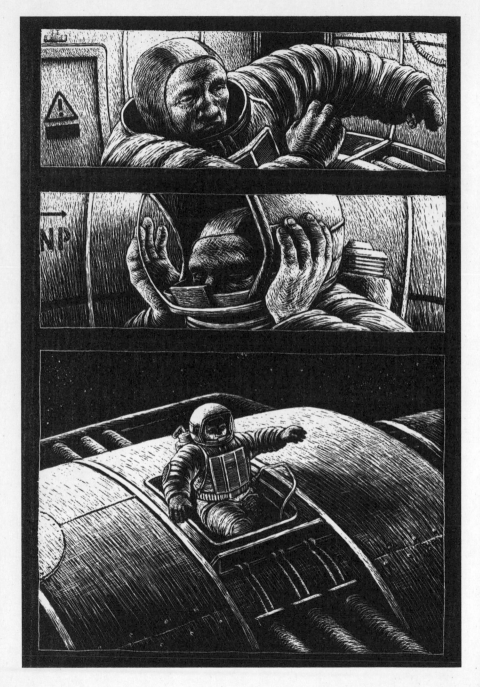

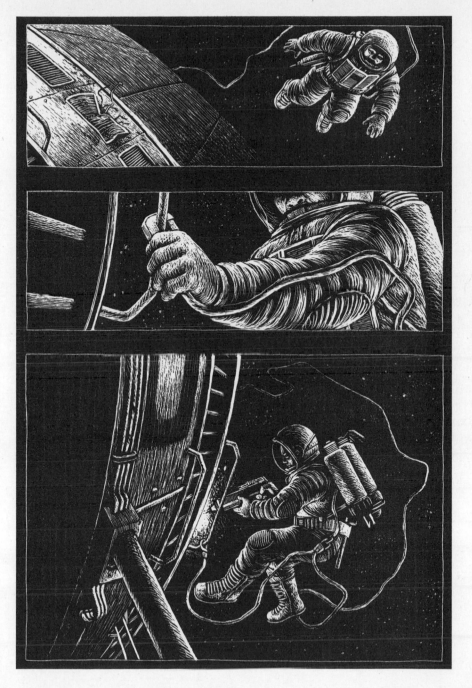

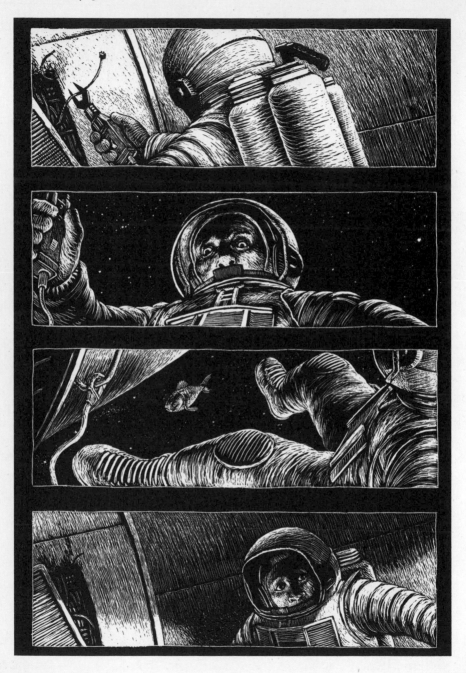

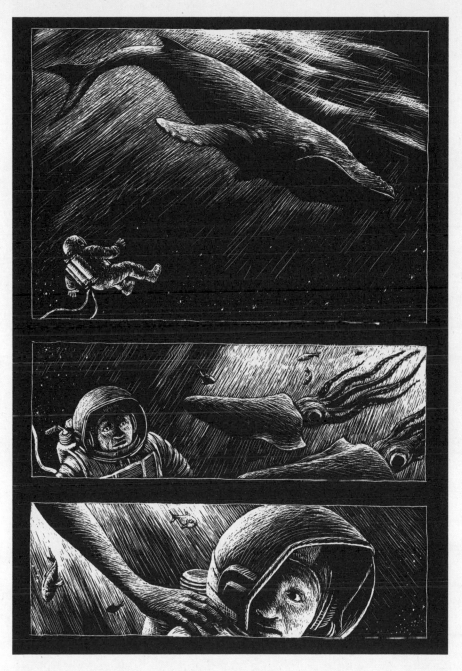

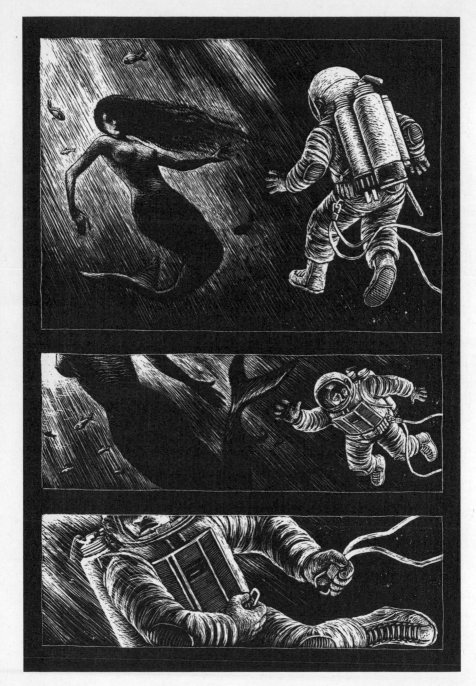

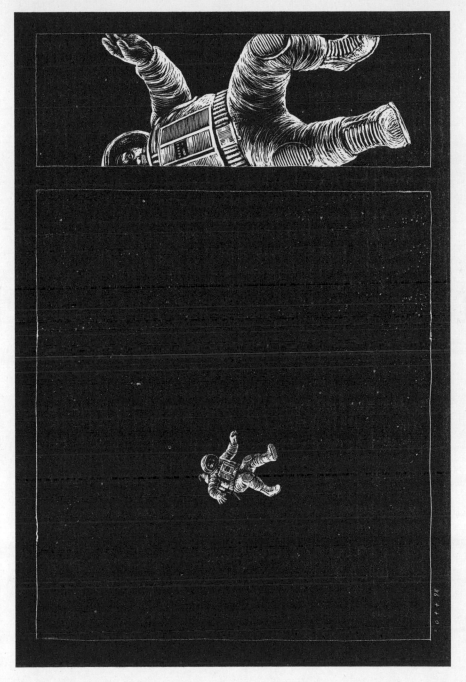

PATRICIO PRON

(TRANSLATED FROM SPANISH BY MARA FAYE LETHEM)

■

Ideas

FROM *The Paris Review*

ON APRIL 16, 1981 at approximately three p.m., little Peter Möhlendorf, whom everyone called *der schwarze* Peter, "black Peter," went home from the village school. His house was on the eastern edge of Sterberode, a town of some five thousand inhabitants outside the East German town of Magdeburg whose main economic activity is farming—asparagus, mostly. His father, who was in the basement of the house when little Möhlendorf arrived, would later say that he heard him come in and then could infer from the sounds in the kitchen, which was above the basement, what he was doing: he flung his backpack beneath the staircase landing, went to the kitchen, took a carton of milk out of the refrigerator, and poured himself a glass, which he drank standing; then he put the carton back in the refrigerator and went out into the backyard. Anyway, that was what he did every day when he came home from school and it could be that his father hadn't really heard the noises he later would say he heard but rather had heard Peter come home and from that had guessed the rest of the series of actions. However, what his father did not know, as he listened or thought he listened to the noises his son was making above his head, was that little Peter was not going to return home that night or the nights that would follow, and that something incomprehensible and frightening was going to open up before him and the rest of the townspeople, and it would swallow everything up.

Peter Möhlendorf was twelve years old and had brown hair. He was shy and didn't usually play with the other children. In fact, he seemed actively to avoid them. The only exception he seemed to allow himself was when the children played soccer. He would go to the field behind the remains of the medieval wall, which were later leveled by the authorities of the so-called Democratic Republic of Germany to build a highway that was never built because the government of the so-called Democratic Republic of Germany fell two months after construction began; the management of ruins is the only thing that government really seemed to have devoted itself to, from its creation to its collapse on October 3, 1990. Peter used to stand near the field, waiting for one of the players to get tired or injured so that the others would let him play in his place. Usually, before that could happen, the owner of the ball would kick some player off his team and signal to little Peter to join the game, because Peter was good.

When Peter didn't come home on the evening of April 16, his father went out to look for him. Möhlendorf walked to the field and questioned the players there, of which there were very few at that hour, but they all said that they hadn't seen him that day. Möhlendorf searched the streets that led to the school, but the building's caretaker told him that Peter had left with the rest of the kids and that the building was empty. Möhlendorf went by the homes of some of the children in his son's class but he wasn't there or anywhere else.

Night had already fallen when Möhlendorf gathered some neighbors together beneath a street lamp and explained the situation. His opinion — expressed nervously and immediately dismissed by the other parents — was that little Peter had gotten lost. It was hard to believe that a boy could get lost in such a town, a town so small that there wasn't enough traffic to cause an accident. Some time later, when events began to happen very quickly and the hours of searching had to be filled up with talk, each parent remembered what they had thought at that moment: Martin Stracke, who was tall and red-headed and repaired electrical appliances, said that he had thought little Peter was playing a joke and that he'd come home as soon as it started to get cold; Michael Göde, who was blond and a gym teacher at the town high school, had thought that little Peter had had an accident, probably in the forest, which was the only place that held any potential for danger in or near the town. For my part, I hadn't thought of anything except my own son, but later, when I heard the other parents' confessions, I lied and said that that night I thought that Peter had gotten lost in the woods. My lie was taken for the truth, which may explain the events of the night of April 16, since, after discussing Peter's disappearance beneath the street lamp for a while, we all went to our homes to look for jackets and flashlights and then we went out to search for Peter in the woods. I'll never know why we did that, because no one that night suggested the idea that Peter had gotten lost there; my later invention justified our actions and that was why everybody had accepted it. It gave meaning where there had been none.

The woods are on the outskirts of Sterberode and continue until they are silhouetted against the Harz mountain range, dividing the region in two. They are dense and dark, the kind of woods that inspire legends told lightly by those who live in cities and in the mountains, but that those who live near the woods fear and respect. That night we scoured the woods like madmen, without mapping out a route or spreading ourselves usefully through the area. Time and time again my flashlight drew a circle in the darkness and in it I found Martin Stracke's red head of hair. On other occasions I was the one who fell into the cone lit up by someone else's flashlight. Michael Göde was the first to quit, because he had to teach the next day. The next was Stracke. At one point my flashlight illuminated Möhlendorf's face and his flashlight illuminated mine and we remained that way for a little while, like two rabbits dazzled on the highway, about to be run over by something we couldn't even sense. Then we returned to town without saying a word.

The next morning we continued the search, helping the two policemen from the local garrison of the Volkspolizei, whom Möhlendorf had apprised of the case. We didn't find anything, but when we left the forest that evening, we saw little Peter's mother running along the road that comes from town. Her lips were moving but we couldn't understand anything because the woods absorbed all the sounds and pushed them toward the tops of the trees, where only the birds could hear them. When she was close enough, the woman told her husband that she had seen Peter crouched on the hill behind their yard. She had called to him but Peter seemed not to hear her and hadn't come into the house. When she approached him, Peter ran away.

Like those nights when one upsetting dream is followed by another that brings relief only until we find that it, often no more than a reflection or prolongation of the first dream, is much more upsetting, the news from Möhlendorf's wife was at first a relief to us. After all, Peter was still alive. But at the same time it raised new questions about why he had ignored his mother's call, where he had spent the night, and why he hadn't come home.

When we arrived back in town, two boys from Peter's class came out to meet us and told us that they had seen him around the field, but he was no longer there. That night I heard Möhlendorf's wife, who lived right next door, crying for hours.

The next day Frank Kaiser, the town tailor, visited Möhlendorf to tell him that he had seen Peter that morning with the eldest of the Schulz children running into the forest. A few hours later Martin Schulz, an asparagus gatherer who always wore his shirt sleeves rolled up, no matter how cold it was, told us that his son had disappeared.

In the following days other children disappeared: Robert Havemann, twelve years old; Rainer Eppelmann, six; Karsten Pauer, twelve; and Micha Kobs, seven. One of the Pauers, who was present when his brother left home, said that he was in his room studying and watching his brother play in the yard when he saw Peter and the other children appear among the trees of a neighboring property; he said that no one spoke, that his brother was squatting, scratching at the ground with a spoon, and then he lifted his head and saw the others, threw the spoon to one side, walked toward them, and then they all ran off together.

Our fears from that point on shifted: we were no longer worried about Peter's disappearance, but rather the way he seemed to have gained influence over the other children in the town and was dragging them along with him. Added to the anguish of the parents whose children had left them was the anguish of those who feared their children would be next. Many stopped sending their kids to school and there were those—but this was only known later—who locked them in their rooms to keep them from escaping, but the children always managed to get out anyway, imbued with an intelligence and a strength whose source was unbeknownst to us and that emerged as soon as Peter and the other children appeared on the horizon, slightly crouching in wait.

The authorities of the so-called Democratic Republic of Germany sent policemen with two dogs and some soldiers of the Volksarmee to search through the woods for the children, but they never found them. While the police, soldiers, and parents searched through the forest hearing only the whining of the dogs, telling ourselves what we said we remembered thinking the night that little Peter had disappeared, Peter struck our homes and more children joined up with him: Jana Schlosser, seven years old; Cornelia Schleime, thirteen; Katharina Gajdukowa, nine. His growing influence with the rest of the children, his ability to vanish in a small town in a relatively accessible region—with the exception of the woods, which were and are still today tangled and dark—and his ability to go without food and shelter were surprising and disheartening to us but they also introduced a parenthesis in our more or less common and miserable lives, and this parenthesis seemed to offer a new normality comprised of disappearances that, in their proliferation, we feared would eventually make us indifferent to them.

One afternoon I was at home fixing a pigeon cage I had. The pigeons flew over my head and the head of my son, who disinterestedly handed me the tools I asked for. My son was telling me the plot of a film he said he had seen: in it, a woman believed that her son was dead; the viewer believed what the woman was saying until learning that the woman's husband thought she was crazy and that they had never had any kids. The woman then ran away from her husband and met up with a man she remembered who had memories of her son; then the viewer changes his mind for the third time and thinks that the woman really did have a son. I asked my son how the movie ended. He said that he didn't remember, but that he thought that the woman finally understood that her husband was right and that she was crazy and that it was just a coincidence that she had found another crazy person who believed the same thing she did. She had never had any children, said my son, and that was the correct ending for the film because, more or less, all kids, imaginary or not, were just an idea of their parents and, like ideas, could be forgotten or set aside when another better idea arrived.

I was about to say something in response, or ask him why he made up these stories—I knew the state channels and I knew that, even if such a movie did exist, they would never have shown it—but then my son paused while handing me a tool and the tool fell to the floor. On the hill at the back of our yard, in the yellow glow of the dusk, I saw the silhouettes of Peter Möhlendorf and the other children; they were crouching like animals. My son looked at them, and they, stock-still, looked at him; I thought they would say something, that they would call to him, but they didn't speak a word. My son took a step toward them and I said something or just wanted to say it but the sound of the pigeons as they flew in circles around their cage was so loud no one could hear anything. In that moment the pigeons all plummeted from the sky until they hit the bars of the cage and the sound of their feet scratching the metal made me think of rain, an unexpected rain that had fallen on us all. And I thought of the film that my son had told me about and I said to myself: He too is just an idea. We are all ideas thought up by our parents, and we vanish before or after them. A small bell, which my wife had hung up that day, rang as the wind moved it. A car passed slowly in front of the house and didn't stop. My son then did something I wasn't expecting: he looked at the ground and took me by the arm, as if I were the one who was going to run away and join up with the other children—if indeed they still were children—and distance myself from him. Then I saw that Peter had stood up somewhat on the hill and his clothes seemed to become transparent when the setting sun hit him. I couldn't see his face because he was in the shadows, and yet I think I remember—but it could just have been an illusion—that he smiled and that his smile didn't explain anything, not a thing. Then he disappeared behind the hill. My son trembled furiously beside me and the pigeons slipped on the metal as if it were ice.

A couple of days later, when the disappearance of the children had become just another of so many inconveniences that we could say nothing about and that were a substantial and incomprehensible part of life in the so-called Democratic Republic of Germany, little Peter Möhlendorf came back home. His father, who was sitting in the kitchen in front of a topographical map of Sterberode and the woods, lifted his head and saw him pass by on the way to his room. A moment later Peter came back into the kitchen with new clothes on, took a carton of milk out of the fridge and poured some into a glass, drank it standing up, then put the carton back in the fridge and didn't go out to the backyard; he just stood there looking at his father in silence.

That night or the next the rest of the children returned to their homes. None of them seemed to be hurt; none of them seemed to be unusually hungry, or cold, or sick. None of them ever spoke about their disappearance or what they had done during that time away. Little Peter Möhlendorf never explained to anyone what had made him flee his house for those days and perhaps he never was able to explain it to himself. He was an outstanding student in high school and his classmates remember him as someone applied but accessible, who perhaps smoked too much. Peter Möhlendorf studied engineering at the University of Rostock and now lives in Frankfurt an der Oder. He has two children.

EVAN RATLIFF

■

Vanish

FROM *Wired*

1.

AUGUST 13, 6:40 P.M. I'm driving east out of San Francisco on I-80, fleeing my life under the cover of dusk. Having come to the inter-state by a circuitous route, full of quick turns and double backs, I'm reasonably sure that no one is following me. I keep checking the rearview mirror anyway. From this point on, there's no such thing as sure. Being too sure will get me caught.

I had intended to flee in broad daylight, but when you are going on the lam, there are a surprising number of last-minute errands to run. This morning, I picked up a set of professionally designed busi-ness cards for my fake company under my fake name, James Donald Gatz. I drove to a Best Buy, where I bought two prepaid cell phones with cash and then put a USB cord on my credit card—an arbitrary dollar amount I hoped would confuse investigators, who would scan my bill and wonder what gadgetry I had purchased. An oil change for my car was another head fake. Who would think that a guy about to sell his car would spend sixty dollars at Oil Can Henry's?

I already owned a couple of prepaid phones; I left one of the new ones with my girlfriend and mailed the other to my parents—giv-ing them an untraceable way to contact me in emergencies. I bought some Just for Men beard-and-mustache dye at a drugstore. My final stop was the bank, to draw a $477 cashier's check. It's payment for rent on an anonymous office in Las Vegas, which is where I need to deliver the check by midday tomorrow.

Crossing the Bay Bridge, I glance back for a last nostalgic glimpse of the skyline. Then I reach over, slide the back cover off my cell phone, and pop out the battery. A cell phone with a battery inside is a cell phone that's trackable.

About twenty-five minutes later, as the California Department of Transportation database will record, my green 1999 Honda Civic, California plates 4MUN509, passes through the tollbooth on the far side of the Carquinez Bridge, setting off the FasTrak toll device, and continues east toward Lake Tahoe.

What the digital trail will not reflect is that a few miles past the bridge I pull off the road, detach the FasTrak, and stuff it into the duffle bag in my trunk, where its signal can't be detected. Nor will it note that I then double back on rural roads to I-5 and drive south through the night, cutting east at Bakersfield. There will be no digital record that at four a.m. I hit Primm, Nevada, a sad little gambling town about forty minutes from Vegas, where fifteen dollars cash gets me a room with a view of a gravel pile.

2.

Officially it will be another twenty-four hours before the manhunt begins. That's when *Wired*'s announcement of my disappearance will be posted online. It coincides with the arrival on newsstands of the September issue of the magazine, which contains a page of mugshot-like photos of me, eyes slightly vacant. The premise is simple: I will try to vanish for a month and start over under a new identity. *Wired* readers, or whoever else happens upon the chase, will try to find me.

The idea for the contest started with a series of questions, foremost among them: how hard is it to vanish in the digital age? Long fascinated by stories of faked deaths, sudden disappearances, and cat-and-mouse games between investigators and fugitives, I signed on to write a story for *Wired* about people who've tried to end one life and start another. People fret about privacy, but what are the consequences of giving it all up, I wondered. What can investigators glean from all the digital fingerprints we leave behind? You can be anybody you want online, sure, but can you reinvent yourself in real life?

It's one thing to report on the phenomenon of people disappearing. But to really understand it, I figured that I had to try it myself. So I decided to vanish. I would leave behind my loved ones, my home, and my name. I wasn't going off the grid, dropping out to live in a cabin. Rather, I would actually try to drop my life and pick up another.

Wired offered a five thousand dollar bounty—three thousand of which would come out of my own pocket—to anyone who could locate me between August 15 and September 15, say the password "fluke," and take my picture. Nicholas Thompson, my editor, would have complete access to information that a private investigator hired to find me might uncover: my real bank accounts, credit cards, phone records, social networking accounts, and email. I'd give Thompson my friends' contact information so he could conduct interviews. He would parcel out my personal details online, available to whichever amateur or professional investigators chose to hunt for me. To add a layer of intrigue, *Wired* hired the puzzle creators at Lone Shark Games to help structure the contest.

I began my planning months in advance. I let my hair and beard grow out, got a motorcycle license, and siphoned off extra cash whenever I visited an ATM, storing it in a hollowed-out book. One day over lunch, a friend from Google suggested software to hide my Internet address—"but all of these things can be broken," he warned—and how best to employ prepaid phones. I learned how to use Visa and American Express gift cards, bought with cash, to make untraceable purchases online. I installed software to mask my Web searches and generated a small notebook's worth of fake email addresses.

I shared my plans with no one, not my girlfriend, not my parents, not my closest friends. Nobody knew the route I was taking out of town, where I was going, or my new name. Not even a hint. If I got caught, it would be by my own mistakes.

Friday afternoon, August 14, I arrive in Vegas wearing a suit and sporting my normal brown hair, a beard, and a pair of rectangular tortoiseshell glasses. Carrying enough electronic equipment to stock a RadioShack, I drive straight to a dreary two-story office complex among the strip malls on South Pecos Road and hand over the cashier's check, securing a tiny windowless office. There I set up two laptops, flip on a webcam to track any activity in the office, and leave.

At CarMax, a used-auto outlet, I then sell my Civic for three thousand dollars. The next day, the first official one of my disappearance, is spent dyeing my hair and goatee jet-black and locking down the security on my laptops—including a third one that I'll carry with me.

At five a.m. on Sunday morning, the graveyard shift clerk at the Tropicana hotel hands over my one hundred dollar cash deposit, barely looking up. If she had, she might have noticed that the man checking out of room 480—wearing a pair of oversize Harry Potter-style glasses, hazel-colored contact lenses, slicked-back hair, and a belt with two thousand dollars cash hidden in an underside pocket—bears surprisingly little resemblance to the one who checked in two days before.

3.

When Sarah Manello heard from a friend about the search for Ratliff, she couldn't resist. A researcher based in Rochester, New York, Manello had long worked with private investigators, digging up information for defense attorneys and tracking down missing people. She quit a few years ago after growing increasingly dissatisfied with the industry's tactics. But her skills remained intact. The initial question she posted on Twitter, under the handle @menacingpickle, was private investigation 101: what was Ratliff's middle name?

The first trickle of discussion among Manello and other hunters appeared by the morning of August 16, thirty-six hours after news of the hunt was posted on Wired.com. The next day it had grown into a deluge. On Twitter, anonymous users dedicated to Ratliff's pursuit sprouted by the hour: @VanishingActo1, @FindEvanRatliff, @EvanOffGrid, @FinderofEvan, @FindThatMan, among others. They organized around the Twitter tag #vanish, which, when placed in a post, allowed the growing horde of investigators to exchange theo-

ries, clues, and questions. They created Web sites and blogs and fly-
ers and even a telephone tip line. A programmer in St. Louis, Michael Toecker, started a Facebook group called "The Search for Evan
Ratliff." A week later it would have nearly a thousand members. (A
countergroup designed to help Ratliff, founded by a banker in Cin-
cinnati named Rich Reder, garnered a few dozen.)

What drew all these people? Some of them were lured by the
$5,000 bounty. Others were intrigued by the technical challenges of
online tracking or the thrill of stakeouts. Some felt that a public dare
needed to be answered. For many, Ratliff's flight evoked their own
fleeting thoughts of starting over. "It was an adventure," says Matty
Gilreath, a grant manager at UC San Francisco, referring to the dozens of hours he spent on the pursuit. "I'm grateful for my career. But
there are other things I'd like to do, and this brought up a lot of is-
sues about reinventing yourself."

From the *Wired* offices, Thompson began doling out information
from Ratliff's accounts onto a blog—starting with the final credit
card purchases and the FasTrak data. The would-be hunters dissected
it as quickly as Thompson could post it. Using two FedEx tracking
numbers from Ratliff's credit card bill, Manello managed, in a few
aboveboard telephone calls, to find out where the packages had gone
and who had signed for them. Hunters scoured the pictures on Ratliff's Flickr page, writing software code to extract information about
the camera used and search for other photos it had taken. They combined the FasTrak data with other clues to build maps of possible
routes.

Within days, they knew that Ratliff was a borderline-obsessive
U.S. national soccer team fan and a follower of the English team
Fulham. That he had celiac disease, a condition under which he ate a
diet entirely free of gluten, a protein found in wheat. That he and his
girlfriend had bought an apartment in Brooklyn (in fact, the hunters posted a scan of Ratliff's signature from the deed). That he had
recently attended a wedding, sporting a beard, in Palo Alto. They
knew of his purchases at Best Buy and Oil Can Henry's and bom-
barded both businesses with calls.

What had started as an exercise in escape quickly became a cross between a massively multiplayer online game and a reality show. A staggeringly large community arose spontaneously, splintered into organized groups, and set to work turning over every rock in Ratliff's life. It topped out at 600 Twitter posts a day. The hunters knew the names of his cat sitter and his mechanic, his favorite authors, his childhood nicknames. They found every article he'd ever written; they found recent videos of him. They discovered and published every address he'd ever had in the U.S., from Atlanta to Hawaii, together with the full name and age of every member of his family.

They discovered almost every available piece of data about Ratliff, in fact, except his current location.

4.

If you are looking to launch a disappearance, I cannot recommend any location more highly than a big-city Greyhound bus station. A mode of transportation Americans have seemingly left to the poor and desperate, it reeks of neglect and disdain. But for anonymity in the post-9/11 world—when the words "I'll just need to see a photo ID" are as common as a handshake—bus travel remains a sanctuary untouched by security. At the station in Las Vegas, I paid cash for a ticket under the name James Gatz, no ID required. Six cramped hours later I was in Los Angeles.

I hopped a city bus to Venice Beach and checked in to 15 Rose, a quaint European-style hostel that I'd found online. The laid-back day manager sympathized with my story of losing my credit cards and driver's license and showed me to a clean, spare room with free Wi-Fi. So began what I thought might be a few pleasant days on the beach: no phone calls to return, no deadlines to hit. Just my new life, stretching leisurely out before me.

When I flipped open my laptop and saw my private information spilling onto the Web, however, I got my first taste of a soon-to-be-permanent state of fitful anxiety. I'd signed up for it, of course. But actually living the new, paranoid reality felt different. Absurd ideas suddenly seemed plausible. They'd contacted my cat sitter; would they kidnap my cat?

Email was choking the inbox of the account *Wired* had made public, eratliff@atavist.net. Most of the messages consisted of efforts to subtly or not-so-subtly trick me into revealing my location by replying or visiting a Web site designed to trap my Internet protocol (IP) address, which maps to a physical location. I also started getting what I came to think of as little plea bargain offers: "Send me a picture and the code word and I'll split the $5K 50/50."

Fortunately, while I was shocked by the intensity of the pursuit, I had anticipated the tactics. To keep my Web surfing from being tracked I often used a piece of free software called Tor, designed to protect the Internet activities of dissidents and whistleblowers around the world. Tor masks a computer's IP address by diverting its requests through designated routers around the world. So when I logged in to Gmail from IP 131.179.50.72 in Los Angeles, the logs showed my request originating from 192.251.226.206 in Germany.

But as my friend from Google had reminded me, no security is unbreakable, so I'd added another layer: Vegas. I used the laptop I carried with me to log in remotely to my computers there, using free software from LogMeIn.com. The Vegas machines, in turn, were running Tor. Anyone clever enough to untangle those foreign routers would get only as far as a laptop sitting in an empty office on South Pecos Road.

Meanwhile, in LA, I meticulously kept up my physical disguise. One afternoon, a few blocks from my hotel, I had a chance to test it. A camera crew, fronted by an Internet news correspondent named Amanda Congdon, was corralling passersby for man-on-the-street interviews about their views on swine flu. I volunteered myself as an interview subject. A few days later, I found my interview on the SometimesDaily.com site, Venice Beach in the background. It was time to get out of LA.

5.

On August 20, a sixteen-year-old high school student in Portland, Oregon, named Jonathan Mäkelä saw a link to the story about the *Wired* contest on Hacker News. Mäkelä was a casual participant in the online community 4chan, whose pranks sometimes involved tracking down documents concerning unsuspecting targets. Mäkelä had grown fascinated by how much intel could be legally dug up online. Here was a guy, Ratliff, who invited people to use that same intel to find him. Now that was interesting.

Mäkelä began using a Twitter account under an anonymous handle, @socillion, and started pulling apart Ratliff's IP addresses. He quickly marshaled a collection of online tools with which he could peg IPs to a physical location and Internet service provider, often triangulating between several sites. By now, other hunters had determined that Ratliff's IPs—which Thompson published several times a day after logging in to Ratliff's email—appeared to be useless nodes from the Tor network. But Mäkelä meticulously verified that each was indeed a Tor node. He shared his information with the crowd and then got feedback in return. Eventually, he figured, the target might make a mistake.

Mäkelä quickly became one of the most active investigators, posting ideas to Twitter at least a dozen times a day. But this public collaboration, he soon realized, was itself a problem. The hunters were benefiting from their collective brainpower, but Ratliff could follow their thoughts just as easily. "Groups need to take this private," he posted to Twitter on August 20, "otherwise we are guaranteed never to win." Mäkelä set up a secure chat room and gave the password to only those he could verify weren't Ratliff.

6.

My plan involved leaving L.A. for good by midday Friday, August 21, and heading east. But before I left, I wanted to give my investigators a parting diversion, something to keep them fixated on the West Coast. So at 11:55 p.m. Thursday, I inserted my bank card into an ATM in nearby Santa Monica, deposited the three thousand dollar car check, and took out $300 cash, the maximum single-day withdrawal. Figuring that as long as I was revealing my location to the world, I might as well pad my reserves, I withdrew another three hundred dollars at 12:01. Then I treated myself to a credit card purchase: a thirteen dollar vodka martini at the nearby Viceroy hotel.

Friday, I woke up at dawn and found the hostel Wi-Fi down. Blind to my pursuers, I decided to risk a last jog; I donned a baseball cap and trotted down along the water's edge. As I turned around to head back, a helicopter came up the beach from the opposite direction, flying low. It stopped and hovered between me and a group of surfers floating idly on their boards.

I'm not sure when the thought entered my head, but when it did, it lodged there: was it possible that someone had seen my ATM transactions, called up a friend with a helicopter, and sent them out to scan the beach for me?

The correct answer was no. Deep down I knew this. But there the chopper was, hovering. I jogged a little bit farther, and it seemed to ease toward me, staying not-quite-directly overhead. I stopped to see if it would pass over. It didn't. The beach was empty. I jogged up to a lifeguard stand, putting it between me and the helicopter, and waited. A few seconds later, the nose crept around the building and back into my line of sight.

In that moment, reason evaporated. I took off toward the boardwalk, a lone figure sprinting across the sand at dawn. Seen from the air, I must have appeared, at this point, worth following. Whatever the reason, the helicopter kept coming. I reached the pavement and turned down a side street, bolted up one alley and down another, and finally ducked under a tree, lungs burning. I could still hear the thump-thump of the blades. I waited, my thoughts spinning out into ever-wilder fantasies. Were they radioing a ground team to drive by and yell "fluke"? Had they already staked out my hotel? Really? All for five thousand dollars?

A few minutes passed and I heard it drift away. I took off again down the alley and ducked into a convenience store. There was an old pay-by-the-minute Internet terminal, and I slipped in a dollar. The ATM transactions hadn't even posted to my account yet.

7.

When Thompson posted Ratliff's ATM transactions online, late the morning of August 21, the pursuit kicked into high gear. For the first time, Ratliff had pegged himself to a specific place, and hunters hit the streets to try to nab him. Mäkelä pinpointed the exact location of the ATM in Santa Monica. One man set about frantically calling restaurants in the area, asking whoever picked up the phone to scan the crowd for someone who met Ratliff's description. Manello called the car dealer in Vegas, then she found a bookstore owner who claimed to have seen him.

In the private chat room that Mäkelä ran as Socillion, however, the consensus seemed to be that Ratliff had moved on. They discussed and discarded strategies ranging from the clever to the outlandish to the completely illegal. Somehow, they had to figure out how to get ahead of him. "Right now, Evan is controlling us," a participant named AtavistTracker wrote. "Evan's had over two months to plan this. We need to alter that plan. I like disinformation."

"Me too," Socillion replied. "Fight with his tools."

8.

By the end of the first week, the deception had already begun to wear me down. Lying about your identity involves more than just transgressing some abstract prohibition against deceit. It means overcoming a lifetime of built-up habits, from a well-rehearsed life story to the sound of your own name. When I convinced people that I really was James Donald Gatz, I occasionally felt a mischievous thrill. Most of the time, however, I felt awful. The people I encountered weren't credulous; they were just nice.

I left L.A. with a band called the Hermit Thrushes, trading gas money for a spot onboard a converted retirement-home shuttle van that served as their tour bus. An indie rock group composed of college grads from Philadelphia, they'd responded to an ad I posted on craigslist, under the name Don, needing a ride to Austin or New Orleans. We rattled along from show to show: L.A. to Tempe to Las Cruces, up to Lubbock and Tulsa, east to Fayetteville, then north toward Chicago. The band played whiskey bars, coffee shops, and rowdy house parties. We crashed on living room floors or crammed into the seats of the bus, and, once, on the grass at a rest stop in Texas.

The band was serious about its music but unperturbed about

much else, and I settled into a role somewhere between lazy roadie and moneyed patron, pulling one hundred dollar bills from my belt at gas stations. On board, I staked out the bus's backseat, where I could use my laptop without anyone looking over my shoulder. With a one hundred fifty dollar wireless broadband card from Virgin Mobile, the only nationwide service that didn't require a credit check, I had almost uninterrupted online access.

So I passed the long hours on the road building up an online life for my new identity. I'd opened a Facebook account under "GatzJD" and a Twitter account under @jdgatz (which I kept open to the world for days, cataloging my location for posterity, before panicking and locking it from public view). For the average person, populating an online social network account is as easy as finding your friends, connecting to their friends, and watching the virtual acquaintances pile up. As Gatz, though, I had no actual friends. Instead, I set about finding people who would accept my friendship automatically, and soon my profile was overrun with multilevel marketers and inspirational speakers. Enough, I thought, to convince potential real acquaintances who didn't look too hard that I wasn't friendless.

I'd been set to depart the tour in Lubbock, Texas, but the band was cool and I was safe, so I kept going. On the afternoon of August 26, the bus finally pulled into St. Louis, where the band had a college radio gig scheduled and I had a plan to get to the train station. A half hour later, listeners to KWUR heard the Hermit Thrushes dedicate their show to a mysterious single-named traveler, Don, headed for New Orleans.

9.

On August 24, a former Microsoft group program manager in Seattle named Jeff Reifman read about the hunt in *Wired*. Reifman, self-employed these days, had recently launched a series of grant-funded Facebook applications to study the engagement of young people with the news. From a technical standpoint, the contest seemed intriguing.

On August 27, working on a desktop in his living room, he created Vanish Team, a Facebook app dedicated to information and discussion about Ratliff. He announced it on Twitter, and people began clicking over to check it out. Reifman was late to the party, however; most of the real intel swap stayed on Twitter or in Mäkelä's secure chat room.

Down in Portland, Mäkelä was learning that it wasn't secure enough. One night, as a San Diego–based hunter was making the drive to Las Vegas—where the chat room believed Ratliff was headed—an insider emailed Ratliff to tip him off.

When Thompson posted the anonymous email on the *Wired* blog, it was the hunters' turn to be paranoid. Mäkelä moved to another chat room, and then started another, jettisoning all but a few of his most trustworthy correspondents. One of the people he kicked out, after a set of heated exchanges, was Reifman.

10.

From St. Louis I took a bus to Carbondale, Illinois, and caught a train south to New Orleans. To get around Amtrak's mandatory government ID requirements, I booked online, using my real name, and picked up the ticket from a machine at the station. I still might need an ID on the train, so to obscure myself to anyone who might get into the Amtrak database, I booked under my middle name and misspelled my last name ever so slightly, leaving out the *l*.

I'd chosen New Orleans months before, distant enough from the coasts to provide obscurity but familiar to me from trips I'd taken years before. Showing up in a city with no friends, no contacts, no credit cards, and no ID is itself a discomfiting experience, and having a basic grip on the layout eases the alienation. After four days in a vacation condo, rented from an absentee landlord who accepted PayPal, I found a cheap one-bedroom apartment around the corner. The next day I signed my well-practiced J. D. Gatz scrawl on the lease. The landlord, after a friendly chat, was ready to hand over the keys. He would, he said, just need to see my driver's license.

I'd been working for months to establish James Donald Gatz as a separate identity. The name itself—the one that Jay Gatsby sheds to start over in *The Great Gatsby*—was easy for me to remember. More important, due to the prolific amount of Gatsby analysis online, it was basically un-Googleable. The middle name was my own, but Mr. Gatz received an entirely new birthday: July 1, 1976, shaving about a year off my age.

He also got a "research firm," Bespect LLC, registered in the state of New Mexico and complete with a logo—a bespectacled cartoon man with a mustache—and a Web site at Bespect.com. Gatz's Pay-Pal account was funded using gift cards. I'd even ordered up a gift card with his name on it that looked to the casual eye like a real credit card.

My new landlord glanced at the business card and flimsy home-laminated "visiting scholar" credentials that I slid across the table. "Bespect.com, eh?" he said. "Interesting. These will do." He turned around, photocopied them, and dropped the copy in a folder along with my lease.

At this point, my new life seemed, superficially at least, satisfactory. My days were spent jogging along the Mississippi, haunting the coffee shops and jazz bars of my adopted neighborhood, and exploring the city by bike. I located a soccer bar and even got a one-night job selling beer and nachos for tips during a Saints game at the Superdome.

The gnawing flaw in the idyllic life of J. D. Gatz was that I did all of these activities alone. It wasn't just that I had no friends. It was that the interactions I did have were beyond superficial. They were fake. My online social networks were populated with strangers; my girlfriend was thousands of miles away; my family knew about me only from news reports and online speculation.

I'd always prided myself on being comfortable with solitude, but this wasn't normal solitude. It was everyone-is-out-to-get-me isolation. What to the hunters felt like an intricate puzzle felt real enough to me—and there was no one around to laugh and tell me otherwise. Instead there was just me, staring into my laptop all day, wondering if it was safe to go out and get the paper.

For the first time in my life, I couldn't sleep. One night I awoke at four a.m. drenched in sweat, having dreamed that a childhood friend turned me in.

11.

Out in Seattle, Reifman wasn't generating solid leads. Through a convoluted set of clues, some of which later turned out to be inaccurate, he developed a theory that the target had headed to San Diego. Reifman posted it to the Vanish Team site, but nothing came of it.

He decided to try a different tack. Instead of using the Vanish Team application to gather news about Ratliff, he'd use it to track him. He installed 38 lines of new code. It was rudimentary and unlikely to work if Ratliff had set up Tor, his anonymity software, correctly. But it gave Reifman a tool to easily pick out the IP addresses of Facebook visitors to Vanish Team. Ratliff might be among them. He'd be the guy without many friends.

12.

In constructing a proper disguise, there is no place for vanity or pride. Altering your appearance, after all, is not about convincing people. It's about misdirection, diverting their attention from the physical features you are unable to change and toward the ones you can. Success often involves making yourself look older, fatter, nerdier, sleazier, or otherwise more unpleasant than you were before. The goal is to be overlooked, ignored, or, sometimes, noticed and then dismissed with a chuckle.

It was the last to which I aspired as I walked through security at the Memphis airport, on Saturday morning, September 5, barely resembling the face on the real ID I showed at the security line. My hair was shaved clean on top with a razor but left short-cropped on the sides and back, in the manner of advanced male pattern baldness. The bald spot had been enhanced with tanning cream, compensation for the sudden paleness of my newly shorn dome. I wore a borderline-creepy mustache, above which a new set of prescriptionless glasses were backed by brown prescription contacts. I twirled a fake wedding band on my finger. A hands-free cell phone headset dangled from my ear.

Unable to completely abandon the hobbies of my previous life, I was headed to Salt Lake City for the U.S. World Cup qualifying soccer match against El Salvador. The logistics had been complicated: a train to Memphis, followed by a flight to San Francisco (which needed to be under two hundred fifty dollars, the maximum gift card available) that stopped in Salt Lake.

The greater problem would be avoiding the hunters. They had long speculated that I might attend the game, and I'd seen stakeout rumors on Twitter. So I bought two fully refundable tickets to Salt Lake on my credit card for September 4, originating in L.A. and Portland—misdirections I knew they'd discover and that I hoped would lead them to the airport on the wrong day. I'd anonymously emailed a prominent hunter a link to the Venice Beach "swine flu video" to fix my previous appearance in their minds. Finally, I'd unmasked my computers' address in Las Vegas several times, turning off Tor while visiting Web sites that I knew were trapping IPs.

But it was my disguise that gave me confidence as I breezed off the plane in Salt Lake City, dressed in a suit and tie, jabbering loudly to imaginary business contacts on my hands-free. I met an accomplice, an old friend also dressed as a low-rent sales rep; we dodged a suspicious lurker at the baggage claim. Then we checked in to a downtown hotel and changed into our game-day disguises. For him: a red, white, and blue afro wig. For me: waving stars and stripes painted atop my head, augmented with a bulky pair of American flag sunglasses and a red clown nose.

Walking to the stadium, we passed several people who seemed to be doing nothing other than scanning the crowd. "I've already seen a few people that I thought could be him," one man murmured as we passed a few feet away.

13.

For the hunters, it was again time to put boots on the ground. But where? Mäkelä, jumping on the real IP address, called a technician at an ISP in Las Vegas who happily revealed the address on South Pecos Road. The hunters puzzled over the businesses listed there, wondering if Ratliff somehow had a friend among them.

For now, though, the action was headed for Salt Lake City. One woman bought a refundable ticket to get through security and stake out departure gates at the Portland airport. A man did the same for arrivals in Salt Lake City, waiting for seven hours over two days. Mäkelä generated a map of all the known gluten-free eateries in the area, and hunters hit pregame parties. All that turned up were look-alikes.

That Friday afternoon in Seattle, Reifman was sorting through more Facebook profiles. Recalling Thompson's statement that Ratliff would not just be hiding but trying to make new friends, Reifman had decided to expand his search to include Vanish Team visitors with up to fifty Facebook friends. He pulled up the profile for a James Donald Gatz, who seemed to be visiting Vanish Team regularly. The name didn't ring a bell, but the photo looked familiar. Then he realized where he'd seen that look before: the swine flu video. He flipped back and forth between the two, and soon he was positive. Gatz was Ratliff.

At first, he was giddy. All he needed to do was friend one of Gatz's friends or convince one to reveal their new pal's location. Looking through the profile, though, he realized that Ratliff had populated his account with what amounted to Facebook automatons. Reifman tried sending messages to a few, telling them about the hunt. No luck.

He decided to try Twitter. Eventually, he typed in "jdgatz" and found the account, locked from public view. Friends of @jdgatz could see his posts, but the general public, including Reifman, couldn't. With a simple Google search for "jdgatz," Reifman located an archived, unprotected version of jdgatz's posts from the previous week. Gatz, at least at that point, had been revealing his location as he moved around. Maybe he'd do it again.

Currently, though, gaining access to Gatz's daily feed would require his permission. Not wanting to spook the target, Reifman tried to enlist the help of one of Gatz's current connections, who would already have access. Again, most were multilevel marketers or autoreply bots. But he managed to find three real people among them: a Hawaii real estate agent, a Segway aficionado in New Zealand, and a blogger in Atlanta. Reifman convinced all three to keep him apprised of whatever Gatz wrote.

At four a.m. on Sunday, Reifman's girlfriend came downstairs and found him staring into the screen. "What are you doing?"

"I think I've found Evan."

14.

The morning after the soccer game, I caught a flight to Atlanta via Denver. After landing at Hartsfield Airport, I rushed off the jetway, a businessman in a hurry. Safely a few gates away, I opened my laptop for a routine check of the *Wired* blog. Headline: "Evan Ratliff will arrive in Atlanta in five minutes." I slammed the laptop shut and took off.

All of the Hartsfield terminals funnel out to a single exit. But as a former Atlanta resident, I knew one other way out, a solitary revolving door from the T Gates leading to a remote part of baggage claim. It was eerily empty when I got there. I slipped out, hustled to the public transit station at the far end, and caught a train into town. Only later would I learn that a hunter in Atlanta arrived minutes after I'd left, sprinted to the trains, and frantically canvassed the passengers.

I crashed for a few hours at the house of a friend—one of only a few I was willing to reach out to, knowing that Thompson was posting interview transcripts of his talks with them. The next morning I caught the first Amtrak train out, sinking down in my seat for the twelve-hour ride back to New Orleans. A few times en route I opened my laptop to check on reports of the hunters scurrying furiously around Atlanta. On Twitter, the guy running the Vanish Team Facebook application kept announcing new scoops, exhorting people to check out his site. Each time, I'd click over to Facebook, using James Gatz's account. What scoops? Vanish Team seemed like all bluster.

At this point, I'd stopped logging in to my Vegas computers for anything but the riskiest Web surfing. This was partly out of a growing laziness; the whole process took longer than dialup circa 1993. I also figured that I could freely visit Facebook pages like Vanish Team. Anyone who built an application to use on a corporate site, I assumed, would need cooperation from the company to track their users.

Once back safely in New Orleans, I decided to redouble my efforts to socialize, both online and in real life. For starters, I opened up my @jdgatz Twitter feed to the public—maybe I could connect with some local friends. I searched for New Orleans businesses I might follow. One was a local gluten-free pizza place I'd wanted to go to called NakedPizza.

15.

By Monday, Jeff Reifman had mentioned the @jdgatz account to a few active hunters, including Sarah Manello and Mäkelä, with whom he'd patched things up. When Ratliff opened his Twitter feed to the public, Reifman created two fake accounts of his own—crafted to look like automated Twitter bots, so as not to raise Ratliff's suspicion —and started following the account.

Then Monday night, Reifman noticed James Gatz logging in from a new IP address: 74.180.70.233. According to the database Reifman was using, the address pointed to Jacksons' Gap, Alabama. After he emailed his select group of trusted hunters, Mäkelä ran the address through his own little triangulated system and discovered where it actually originated from. Two minutes later he sent a one-line response to Reifman: "That IP is in New Orleans."

Reifman flipped over to the @jdgatz Twitter feed and noticed that the number of accounts Gatz was following had gone up by three—all New Orleans businesses. He looked up NakedPizza's Web site and fired off an email explaining the hunt. "I have accurate information that Evan has arrived in New Orleans and plans to go to NakedPizza Tuesday or Wednesday," he wrote. A few minutes later, he followed up. "I forgot to mention," he said, "that we know Evan has shaved his head either partially (male pattern bald) or fully." Reifman informed his fellow hunters, and Manello spent the evening dialing fifty hotels near the restaurant, asking for a James Gatz.

The next morning when Jeff Leach, cofounder of NakedPizza and a tech-savvy entrepreneur, got the email, he thought at first it was a scam. But he passed it along to his business partner, and after delving into the hunt information online, they concluded it was real. Leach decided to help.

16.

Tuesday, September 8, seven a.m.: Just seven days to go. I awake in my apartment in New Orleans, relieved to find no online indication of anyone wise to my location. Aside from a few random new followers to my Twitter feed, all of whom seem like automated bots, nobody seems to be paying attention to my fake accounts either.

I use a gift card to book a flight to New York City on September 15, the final day of my disappearance, and hatch plans to surprise Thompson in his office using a fake security badge. I've been communicating sporadically with my editor through a public blog—I'd post something, he'd read it, delete it, and then post his response. Before Salt Lake City, I'd boasted that I could survive the month, "just by keeping my head down and being careful with my phones and IPs."

Now *Wired* has decided to up the stakes, offering me four hundred dollars for each of a series of challenges I complete. And I could use it. As much as any other factor—personal gall, or endurance, or discipline—staying on the run requires an abundance of cash. I've already nearly spent the three grand I brought with me. Besides, I made it through the Salt Lake City gauntlet and survived a near miss in Atlanta. I can do this.

The first two challenges—clues to which are embedded, with the help of Will Shortz and Lone Shark Games, for the hunters to find in the *New York Times* crossword puzzle—are to go to the fiftieth story of a building and to attend a book reading. Checking online, I identify only two buildings in downtown New Orleans of fifty stories or taller, and I choose One Shell Square. At the security desk, back in my businessman disguise, I step up and announce that I'm here to visit the law firm occupying the upper floors. "Just sign in here. And we'll need to see your ID."

"Well, I've lost mine. Will a business card and a credit card do?"

In two minutes, I'm on the fiftieth floor, video camera rolling. Later, as I wander home through the French Quarter, a street vendor sidles up beside me with some friendly unsolicited advice. "Hey buddy," he says, gesturing to my haircut. "You gotta shave the rest of that off, man."

That same morning, Leach, of NakedPizza, calls Reifman, and the two begin comparing notes. Leach searches through his Web site's logs, finding that IP address 74.180.70.233—aka James Gatz—visited NakedPizza.biz late the previous evening.

By eleven a.m., Leach has briefed all of his employees on the hunt. If they see the target, he explains, they need to say "fluke" and take a photo. He creates a folder on the company network with pictures for them to study. One is a Photoshopped mock-up of Ratliff, bald.

Brock Fillinger, also a cofounder, whose own pate is clean-shaven, heads over to stake out the tours at Old New Orleans Rum, another business Ratliff was following on Twitter and that Reifman had contacted. "Hey," the woman behind the desk says as Fillinger lingers nearby, "are you that *Wired* writer?"

Snide street comments aside, I've already decided to shave the rest of my head and mustache. My acquisition of actual friends will require looking less creepy. I change into casual clothes, grab a fedora, and ride my bicycle to the barber.

At 5:20 I'm completely bald, and I'll have to hustle to make it across town for the book reading I plan to attend.

At 5:48, Leach and Fillinger are watching both entrances to the Garden District BookShop. They're expecting someone "wigged up," someone who looks like he doesn't quite belong. But the reading started promptly at 5:30, and there is no sign of Ratliff.

Leach sends a text message to Fillinger. This looks like a bust. They meet up out front, ready to move on.

It's surreal, in those moments when I stop to think about it. Scores of people have studied my picture, stared into those empty eyes in the hopes of relieving me of thousands of dollars. They have stood for hours, trying to pick out my face in a crowd. They've come to know me like we've been friends for years. It's weirdly thrilling, in a narcissistic kind of way, but also occasionally terrifying.

I almost ride past the bookshop before I see the sign, tucked into a tiny shopping center. I stop at the corner and pull out my bike lock. Two men stand on the stairs outside, facing the street. They glance over at me.

My first impulse is to ride away. But at what point do I separate caution from self-delusion? Not every out-of-place person is looking for me.

Tired from the bike ride, tired of the corrosive suspicion, I decide to walk past them on the sidewalk, making no move toward the bookstore. Just a local, heading down the street to visit a friend.

"Hey," Leach calls out from the stairs, taking a hesitant step toward me. I freeze and stare back helplessly. "You wouldn't happen to know a guy named Fluke, would you?"

17.

At first I was angry: at myself for getting caught and losing the money, at *Wired* for tempting me with the challenges. But that was soon replaced by the thrill of being redeposited in my own identity, with a family, a partner, friends, and a past I didn't have to hide. I packed up my apartment, rented a car, and visited my parents in Florida. Then I bought a plane ticket home.

Leach and Reifman had agreed to split the prize money, but they both ended up giving it all to Unity of Greater New Orleans, a charity helping the city recover from Hurricane Katrina. Socillion started his junior year of high school. The online chatter dissolved as quickly as it had formed.

And what of our original questions? Had I shown that a person, given enough resources and discipline, could vanish from one life and reinvent himself in another? I thought I had, though only up to a point. Obviously the smarts and dedication of the hunters had overwhelmed my planning and endurance. Along the way they'd also proven my privacy to be a modern fiction. It turns out that people—ordinary people—really can gather an incredible dossier of facts about you. But a month later, life was back to normal and no one was taking any interest.

More than all that, I'd discovered how quickly the vision of total reinvention can dissolve into its lonely, mundane reality. Whatever reason you might have for discarding your old self and the people who went with it, you'll need more than a made-up backstory and a belt full of cash to replace them.

For weeks after the hunt ended, I still paused when introducing myself and felt a twinge of panic when I handed over my credit card. The paranoid outlook of James Donald Gatz was hard to shake. Even now, my stomach lurches when I think back to the night I got caught. "You wouldn't happen to know a guy named Fluke, would you?"

Right after it happened, I rode my bike back to my apartment and sat in the air-conditioning, unsure what to do. Finally I got online and logged in to the hunters' private chat room for the first time. Rich Reder, founder of the Facebook countergroup designed to help me stay hidden, had infiltrated the room and sent me the password. Just a little too late.

I found Mäkelä there, still logged in. I asked him why he was hanging around a chat room dedicated to catching a guy who'd already been caught. "Just lurking," he wrote. "Working out the moles."

After a while I signed off, closed my laptop, and walked down the street to J. D. Gatz's local dive bar. I ordered a whiskey and tried to tell the bartender how I abandoned my life and then got it back. For the first time in weeks, someone didn't seem to believe my story.

DAVID ROHDE

■

Seven Months, Ten Days in Captivity

FROM *New York Times*

THE CAR'S ENGINE ROARED AS THE GUNMAN punched the accelerator and we crossed into the open Afghan desert. I was seated in the back between two Afghan colleagues who were accompanying me on a reporting trip when armed men surrounded our car and took us hostage.

Another gunman in the passenger seat turned and stared at us as he gripped his Kalashnikov rifle. No one spoke. I glanced at the bleak landscape outside—reddish soil and black boulders as far as the eye could see—and feared we would be dead within minutes.

It was November 10, 2008, and I had been headed to a meeting with a Taliban commander along with an Afghan journalist, Tahir Luddin, and our driver, Asad Mangal. The commander had invited us to interview him outside Kabul for reporting I was pursuing about Afghanistan and Pakistan.

The longer I looked at the gunman in the passenger seat, the more nervous I became. His face showed little emotion. His eyes were dark, flat, and lifeless.

I thought of my wife and family and was overcome with shame. An interview that seemed crucial hours earlier now seemed absurd and reckless. I had risked the lives of Tahir and Asad—as well as my own life. We reached a dry riverbed and the car stopped. "They're go-ing to kill us," Tahir whispered. "They're going to kill us."

Tahir and Asad were ordered out of the car. Gunmen from a sec-ond vehicle began beating them with their rifle butts and led them away. I was told to get out of the car and take a few steps up a sand-covered hillside.

While one guard pointed his Kalashnikov at me, the other took my glasses, notebook, pen, and camera. I was blindfolded, my hands tied behind my back. My heart raced. Sweat poured from my skin.

"Habarnigar," I said, using a Dari word for journalist. "Salaam," I said, using an Arabic expression for peace.

I waited for the sound of gunfire. I knew I might die but remained strangely calm.

Moments later, I felt a hand push me back toward the car, and I was forced to lie down on the back seat. Two gunmen got in and slammed the doors shut. The car lurched forward. Tahir and Asad were gone and, I thought, probably dead.

The car came to a halt after what seemed like a two-hour drive. Guards took off my blindfold and guided me through the front door of a crude mud-brick home perched in the center of a ravine.

I was put in some type of washroom the size of a closet. After a few minutes, the guards opened the door and pushed Tahir and Asad inside.

We stared at one another in relief. About twenty minutes later, a guard opened the door and motioned for us to walk into the hallway.

"No shoot," he said, "no shoot."

For the first time that day, I thought our lives might be spared. The guard led us into a living room decorated with maroon carpets and red pillows. A half-dozen men sat along two walls of the room, Kalashnikov rifles at their sides. I sat down across from a heavyset man with a patu—a traditional Afghan scarf—wrapped around his face. Sunglasses covered his eyes, and he wore a cheap black knit winter cap. Embroidered across the front of it was the word "Rock" in English.

"I'm a Taliban commander," he announced. "My name is Mullah Atiqullah."

* * *

For the next seven months and ten days, Atiqullah and his men kept the three of us hostage. We were held in Afghanistan for a week, then spirited to the tribal areas of Pakistan, where Osama bin Laden is thought to be hiding.

Atiqullah worked with Sirajuddin Haqqani, the leader of one of the most hard-line factions of the Taliban. The Haqqanis and their allies would hold us in territory they control in North and South Waziristan.

During our time as hostages, I tried to reason with our captors. I told them we were journalists who had come to hear the Taliban's side of the story. I told them that I had recently married and that Tahir and Asad had nine young children between them. I wept, hoping it would create sympathy, and begged them to release us. All of my efforts proved pointless.

Over those months, I came to a simple realization. After seven years of reporting in the region, I did not fully understand how extreme many of the Taliban had become. Before the kidnapping, I viewed the organization as a form of "al Qaeda lite," a religiously motivated movement primarily focused on controlling Afghanistan.

Living side by side with the Haqqanis's followers, I learned that the goal of the hard-line Taliban was far more ambitious. Contact with foreign militants in the tribal areas appeared to have deeply affected many young Taliban fighters. They wanted to create a fundamentalist Islamic emirate with al Qaeda that spanned the Muslim world.

I had written about the ties between Pakistan's intelligence services and the Taliban while covering the region for the *New York Times*. I knew Pakistan turned a blind eye to many of their activities. But I was astonished by what I encountered firsthand: a Taliban ministate that flourished openly and with impunity.

The Taliban government that had supposedly been eliminated by the 2001 invasion of Afghanistan was alive and thriving.

All along the main roads in North and South Waziristan, Pakistani government outposts had been abandoned, replaced by Taliban checkpoints where young militants detained anyone lacking a Kalashnikov rifle and the right Taliban password. We heard explosions echo across North Waziristan as my guards and other Taliban fighters learned how to make roadside bombs that killed American and NATO troops.

And I found the tribal areas—widely perceived as impoverished and isolated—to have superior roads, electricity, and infrastructure compared with what exists in much of Afghanistan.

At first, our guards impressed me. They vowed to follow the tenets of Islam that mandate the good treatment of prisoners. In my case, they unquestionably did. They gave me bottled water, let me walk in a small yard each day, and never beat me.

But they viewed me—a nonobservant Christian—as religiously unclean and demanded that I use a separate drinking glass to protect them from the diseases they believed festered inside nonbelievers.

My captors harbored many delusions about Westerners. But I also saw how some of the consequences of Washington's antiterrorism policies had galvanized the Taliban. Commanders fixated on the deaths of Afghan, Iraqi, and Palestinian civilians in military airstrikes, as well as the American detention of Muslim prisoners who had been held for years without being charged. America, Europe, and Israel preached democracy, human rights, and impartial justice to the Muslim world, they said, but failed to follow those principles themselves.

During our captivity, I made numerous mistakes. In an effort to save our lives in the early days, I exaggerated what the Taliban could receive for us in ransom. In response, my captors made irrational demands, at one point asking for twenty-five million dollars and the release of Afghan prisoners from the American detention center at Guantánamo Bay, Cuba. When my family and editors declined, my captors complained that I was "worthless."

Tahir and Asad were held in even lower esteem. The guards incessantly berated both of them for working with foreign journalists and repeatedly threatened to kill them. The dynamic was not new. In an earlier kidnapping involving an Italian journalist and his Afghan colleagues, the Taliban had executed the Afghan driver to press the Italian government to meet their demands.

Despite the danger, Tahir fought like a lion. He harangued our kidnappers for hours at a time and used the threat of vengeance from his powerful Afghan tribe to keep the Taliban from harming us.

We became close friends, encouraging each other in our lowest moments. We fought, occasionally, as well. At all times, an ugly truth hovered over the three of us. Asad and Tahir would be the first ones to die. In post-9/11 Afghanistan and Pakistan, all lives are still not created equal.

As the months dragged on, I grew to detest our captors. I saw the Haqqanis as a criminal gang masquerading as a pious religious movement. They described themselves as the true followers of Islam but displayed an astounding capacity for dishonesty and greed.

Our ultimate betrayal would come from Atiqullah himself, whose nom de guerre means "gift from God."

What follows is the story of our captivity. I took no notes while I was a prisoner. All descriptions stem from my memory and, where possible, records kept by my family and colleagues. Direct quotations from our captors are based on Tahir's translations. Undoubtedly, my recollections are incomplete and the passage of time may have affected them. For safety reasons, certain details and names have been withheld.

Our time as prisoners was bewildering. Two phone calls and one letter from my wife sustained me. I kept telling myself—and Tahir and Asad—to be patient and wait. By June, our seventh month in captivity, it had become clear to us that our captors were not seriously negotiating our release. Their arrogance and hypocrisy had become unending, their dishonesty constant. We saw an escape attempt as a last-ditch, foolhardy act that had little chance of success. Yet we still wanted to try.

To our eternal surprise, it worked.

On October 26, 2008, I arrived in Afghanistan on a three-week reporting trip for a book I was writing about the squandered opportunities to bring stability to the region. I had been covering Afghanistan and Pakistan since 2001 and was inspired by the bravery and pride of the people in those two countries and, it seemed, their popular desire for moderate, modern societies.

The first part of my visit proved depressing. I spent two weeks in Helmand Province, in southern Afghanistan, and was struck by the rising public support for the Taliban. Seven years of halting economic development, a foreign troop presence and military mistakes that killed civilians had bred a deep resentment of American and NATO forces.

For the book to be as rigorous and fair as possible, I decided that I needed to get the Taliban's side of the story.

I knew that would mean taking a calculated risk, a decision journalists sometimes make to report accurately in the field. I was familiar with the potential consequences. In 1995, I was imprisoned for ten days while covering the war in Bosnia. Serbian authorities arrested me after I discovered mass graves of more than seven thousand Muslim men who had been executed in Srebrenica.

My detention was excruciating for my family. Promising I would never put them through such an ordeal again, I was cautious through thirteen subsequent years of reporting.

I flew from Helmand to Kabul on Sunday, November 9, to meet with Tahir Luddin, who worked for the *Times of London* and was known as a journalist who could arrange interviews with the Taliban.

After making some inquiries, Tahir told me that a Taliban commander named Abu Tayyeb would agree to an interview the next day in Logar Province. We could meet him after a one-hour drive on paved roads in a village near an American military base.

Tahir had already interviewed Abu Tayyeb with two other foreign journalists and said he trusted him. He said Abu Tayyeb was aligned with a moderate Taliban faction based in the Pakistani city of Quetta.

The danger, he said, would be the drive itself. "Nothing is one hundred percent," he told me. "You only die once."

I felt my stomach churn. But if I did the interview, the most dangerous reporting for the book would be over. I could return home with a sense that I had done everything I could to understand the country.

"Yes," I told Tahir. "Tell him yes."

That night, I had dinner with Carlotta Gall, a dear friend and the Kabul bureau chief for the *New York Times*, and asked her if the interview was a crazy idea. Carlotta said she had never felt the need to interview the Taliban in person and preferred phone conversations. She recommended that we hire a driver to serve as a lookout and end the meeting after no more than an hour.

I also met with a French journalist who had interviewed Abu Tayyeb twice with Tahir. In the fall of 2007, she spent two days filming him and his men as they trained. In the summer of 2008, she spent an evening with them and filmed an attack on a police post.

She pointed out that I was more vulnerable as an American, but she said she thought Abu Tayyeb would not kidnap us. She said she believed that he was trying to use the media to get across the Taliban's message.

I slept poorly the night before the interview. I got out of bed early and put on a pair of boxer shorts my wife had given me on Valentine's Day emblazoned with dozens of "I love you" logos, hoping they would bring good luck.

I left two notes behind. One gave Carlotta the location of the meeting and instructed her to call the American Embassy if we did not return by late afternoon. The other was to my wife, Kristen, in case something went wrong.

I walked outside and met Tahir and Asad Mangal, a friend he had hired to work as a driver and lookout. As we drove away, Tahir suggested that we pray for a safe journey. We did.

Dressed in Afghan clothes and seated in the back, I covered my face with a scarf to prevent thieves from recognizing me as a foreigner. Most kidnappings in and around Kabul had been carried out by criminal gangs, not the Taliban.

From the car, I sent Carlotta a text message with Abu Tayyeb's phone number. I told her to call him if she did not hear from me. If something went wrong along the way, Abu Tayyeb and his men would rescue us. Under Afghan tradition, guests are treated with extraordinary honor. If a guest is threatened, it is the host's duty to shelter and protect him.

We arrived at the meeting point in a town where farmers and donkeys meandered down the road. But none of Abu Tayyeb's men were there. Tahir called Abu Tayyeb, who instructed us to continue down the road.

Moments later, I felt the car swerve to the right and stop. Two gunmen ran toward our car shouting commands in Pashto, the local language. The gunmen opened both front doors and ordered Tahir and Asad to move to the back seat.

Tahir shouted at the men in Pashto as the car sped down the road. I recognized the words "journalists" and "Abu Tayyeb" and nothing else. The man in the front passenger seat shouted something back and waved his gun menacingly. He was small, with dark hair and a short beard. He seemed nervous and belligerent.

I hoped there had been some kind of mistake. I hoped the gunmen would call Abu Tayyeb, who would vouch for us and order our release. Instead, our car continued down the road, following a yellow station wagon in front of us.

The gunman in the passenger seat shouted more commands. Tahir told me they wanted our cellphones and other possessions. "If they find we have a hidden phone," Tahir said, "they'll kill us."

"Tell them we're journalists," I said. "Tell them we're here to interview Abu Tayyeb."

Tahir translated what I said, and the driver—a bearish, bearded figure—started laughing.

"Who is Abu Tayyeb? I don't know any Abu Tayyeb," he said. "I am the commander here."

They are thieves or members of another Taliban faction, I thought. I knew that what we called the Taliban was really a loose alliance of local commanders who often operated independently of one another.

I looked at the two gunmen in the front seat. If we somehow overpowered them, I thought, the men in the station wagon would shoot us. I did not want to get Asad and Tahir killed. My arrest in Bosnia had ended peacefully after ten days. I thought the same might occur here.

One of the gunmen said something and Tahir turned to me. "They want to know your nationality," he said. I hesitated and wondered whether I should say I was Canadian. Being an American was disastrous, but I thought lying was worse. If they later learned I was American, I would instantly be declared a spy.

"Tell them the truth," I told Tahir. "Tell them I'm American."

Tahir relayed my answer and the burly driver beamed, raising his fist and shouting a response in Pashto. Tahir translated it for me: "They say they are going to send a blood message to Obama."

By the time I met face to face later that day with Atiqullah, our kidnapper, I still did not know which Taliban faction had abducted us.

A large man with short dark hair protruding from the sides of his cap, he appeared self-assured and in clear command of his men. He also seemed suspicious of us, which worried me. I knew many Taliban believed all journalists were spies.

With Tahir translating, we explained that we had been invited to Logar Province to interview Abu Tayyeb, the Taliban commander. I said I had worked as the *Times'* South Asia correspondent from 2002 to 2005. I described articles I had written during the war in Bosnia and told him that Serbian Orthodox Christians had arrested me there after I had exposed the massacre of Muslims.

Atiqullah remained unmoved. He denied our request to call Abu Tayyeb or a Taliban spokesman. He controlled our fate now, he announced. Atiqullah handed me the notebook and pen his gunmen had taken from me and ordered me to start writing.

American soldiers routinely disgraced Afghan women and men, he said. They forced women to stand before them without their burqas, the head-to-toe veils that villagers believe protect a woman's honor. They searched homes without permission and forced Afghan men to lie on the ground, placing boots on the Afghans' heads and pushing their faces into the dirt. He clearly viewed the United States as a malevolent occupier.

He produced one of our cellphones and announced that he wanted to call the *Times'* office in Kabul. I gave him the number, and Atiqullah briefly spoke with one of the newspaper's Afghan reporters. He eventually handed me the phone. Carlotta, the paper's Kabul bureau chief, was on the line. I said that we had been taken prisoner by the Taliban.

"What can we do?" Carlotta asked. "What can we do?"

Atiqullah demanded the phone back before I could answer. Carlotta—the most fearless reporter I knew—sounded unnerved.

Atiqullah turned off the phone, removed the battery and announced that we would move that night for security reasons. My heart sank. I had hoped that we would somehow be allowed to contact Abu Tayyeb and be freed before nightfall. As we waited in the house, I thought Carlotta would be calling my family and editors at any minute to inform them that I had been kidnapped.

We were taken to a small dirt house and then spent the remainder of the day trapped in a claustrophobic room with our three guards. Measuring roughly twenty feet by twenty feet, its only furnishings were the carpet on the floor and a dozen blankets. The following morning, I awoke before dawn to the sound of the guards performing a predawn prayer with Tahir and Asad.

One of our guards introduced himself as "Qari," an Arabic expression for someone who had memorized the Koran. He later said he was one of the "fedayeen," an Arabic term the Taliban use for suicide bombers.

Food arrived at mealtimes, and no one was beaten. Yet Tahir grew increasingly worried. "These guys are really religious," he whispered to me at one point. "They're really religious. They're praying a lot."

Confined to the room for most of the day, I found it increasingly suffocating. By now, I was sure my family had heard the news.

Several hours after sunset, we were hustled into a small station wagon.

"We have to move you for security reasons," said Atiqullah, who was sitting in the driver's seat, his face still concealed behind a scarf. Arab militants and a film crew from Al Jazeera were on their way, he said.

"They're going to chop off your heads," he announced. "I've got to get you out of this area."

As we drove away, I asked for permission to speak. Atiqullah agreed, and I told him we were worth more alive than dead. He asked me what I thought he could get for us. I hesitated, unsure of what to say. I was desperate to keep us alive.

I knew that in March 2007, the Afghan government exchanged five Taliban prisoners for the Italian journalist after the Taliban executed his driver. Later, they killed his translator as well. My memory of the exchange was vague, but I thought money was included. In August 2007, the South Korean government had reportedly paid twenty million dollars for the release of twenty-one Korean mission-aries after the Taliban killed two members of the group.

"Money and prisoners," I said.

"How much money?" Atiqullah asked.

I hesitated again.

"Millions," I said, immediately thinking I would regret the state-ment. Atiqullah and one of his commanders looked at each other.

Over the next hour, the conversation continued. Atiqullah promised to do his best to protect us. I promised him money and prisoners.

As we wound our way through steep mountain passes, Atiqullah asked for the names and professions of my father and brothers. I told him the truth. Given the unusual spelling of my last name, I thought he could easily find my relatives online.

My father was a retired insurance salesman, I said. One of my brothers worked for an aviation consulting company. A stepbrother worked for a bank. I thought being forthright was helping convince him that I was a journalist, not a spy.

For the next four days, we lived with Qari, the suicide bomber, in an-other small dirt house. On one afternoon, he allowed us to sit outside in a small walled courtyard.

He even let Tahir play a game on a cellphone. But when Tahir asked for the phone a second time, Qari shouted that we planned to send a text message to the Kabul bureau of the *Times*. Suddenly en-raged and irrational, he denounced us as liars. He picked up his Ka-lashnikov, pointed it at Tahir's chest and threatened to shoot him.

Tahir stared back, unmoved. *Pashtunwali*—an ancient code of honor practiced by ethnic Pashtuns in Afghanistan and Paki-stan—prevented each man from showing fear and losing face.

Asad and I stepped in front of Tahir. We begged Qari to put down his gun. "Lutfan, lutfan," I said, using a local expression for please. Qari lowered his weapon but motioned for Tahir to step into an outer room.

Through the wall, I heard Tahir begin praying in Arabic. I heard a thump and Tahir cried out, "Allah!" A second thump and "Allah!"

Several minutes later, Tahir walked back into the room, crawled under a blanket, and began moaning. Qari had beaten him on the back with his rifle.

Qari unnerved me. Earnestly reciting hugely inaccurate propaganda about the West I had seen on jihadi websites, Qari seemed utterly detached from reality. Other guards joked that he had mental problems.

In my mind, Qari and Atiqullah personified polar ends of the Taliban. Qari represented a paranoid, intractable force. Atiqullah embodied the more reasonable faction: people who would compromise on our release and, perhaps, even on peace in Afghanistan.

I did not know which one represented the majority. I wanted to believe that Atiqullah did. Yet each day I increasingly feared that Qari was the true Taliban.

The following day, Atiqullah arrived to move us again. During the ride, he said we would be taken to a place where I could receive bottled water and we could call our families. He promised to protect me.

"I will not kill you," he said. "You will survive."

I insisted that he promise to save Tahir and Asad as well. "You will not kill the three of us," I said. "It has to be the three of us."

Initially, Atiqullah refused. For days, I raised the issue over and over, remembering that under the Pashtunwali code a promise of protection should be ironclad. At one point, I suggested that he cut off my finger instead of harming Tahir and Asad.

Later that day, he finally promised to protect all three of us. "I give you my promise," he said, as I lay down in the back of the station wagon. "I will not kill any of the three of you."

Then, he said, "Let's kill Asad first," and laughed.

The following afternoon, a new commander arrived. A bone-thin man with a long beard and one arm, he got into the driver's seat and guided us through barren, rock-strewn territory, steering the car and shifting gears with lightning-quick movements of his one hand.

At sunset, he stopped the vehicle, and Atiqullah announced that we would have to walk through the mountains. A large American base blocked the path in front of us, he said. The one-armed commander gave me a pair of worn loafers, and another guard gave me his jacket.

As we walked, I understood why Western journalists had grown enamored of the anti-Soviet Afghan resistance fighters in the 1980s. Under a spectacular panorama of stars, we wound our way along a steep mountain pass. Emaciated Taliban fighters carried heavy machine guns with little sign of fatigue. Their grit and resilience seemed boundless.

I thought about making a run for it but had not had a chance to talk it over with Tahir and Asad. I also knew that the half-dozen guards would quickly shoot us.

As the hike continued, I grew suspicious. Atiqullah—who had promised to carry me if needed—proved to be in poor shape. On one of the steepest parts of the ascent, he stopped, sat on a rock, and panted.

Nine hours after we set out, the sun rose and the hike dragged on. Asad approached me when the guards lagged behind, pointed at the way ahead and whispered, "Miram Shah." Miram Shah is the capital and largest town in North Waziristan, a Taliban and al Qaeda stronghold in Pakistan's lawless tribal areas. North Waziristan was the home of some of the Taliban's most hard-line members. If we were headed there, we were doomed.

After eleven hours, our hike finally ended. The guards lit a fire, and we warmed our hands as we waited for a vehicle to pick us up.

Exhausted and anxious, I told myself that Asad was wrong. I told myself that we were walking into southern Afghanistan, not Pakistan. I told myself we would survive.

The next day our journey continued in a car. A young Taliban driver with shoulder-length hair got behind the wheel. Glancing at me suspiciously in the rearview mirror, he started the engine and began driving down the left-hand side of the road.

It was some sort of prank, I hoped, some jihadi version of chicken—the game where two drivers speed toward each other in the same lane until one loses his nerve.

Which lane he drove down showed what country we were in. If he continued driving on the left, we had crossed into Pakistan. If he drove on the right, we were still in Afghanistan.

A mile down the road, traffic signs appeared in Urdu.

We're in Pakistan, I thought to myself. We're dead.

Atiqullah had lied to us. We were not in southern Afghanistan. We were in Pakistan's tribal areas, an isolated belt of Taliban-controlled territory. We were now in "the Islamic emirate" — the fundamentalist state that existed in Afghanistan before the 2001 American-led invasion. The loss of thousands of Afghan, Pakistani, and American lives and billions in American aid had merely moved it a few miles east, not eliminated it. It was November 18.

Through seven years of reporting in the region, I had pitied captives imprisoned here. It was arguably the worst place on Earth to be an American hostage. The United States government had virtually no influence and was utterly despised.

Since 2004, dozens of missiles fired by American drones had killed hundreds of militants and civilians. The Taliban had held Afghan, Pakistani, and foreign hostages in the area for years, trading lives for ransom and executions for publicity.

"We're in Pakistan," I said out loud in the car, venting my anger.

Atiqullah laughed, and the driver appeared surprised.

"How does he know it's Pakistan?" the driver asked.

"Because you're driving down the left-hand side of the road," I answered.

"How do you know that?" he asked. "When were you in Pakistan before?"

Atiqullah smiled and appeared amused by the conversation. He knew I had been to Pakistan many times on reporting trips.

I was one of dozens of journalists who had written articles detailing how al Qaeda and the Taliban had turned the tribal areas into their new stronghold after being driven from Afghanistan in 2001. I had watched the Pakistani government, then led by President Pervez Musharraf, largely stand by as the Taliban murdered tribal elders and seized control of the area.

Now, an abstract foreign policy issue was deeply personal. When my wife and family learned that I was in the tribal areas, their distress would increase exponentially. They would expect that I would never return.

We arrived in a large town, and I spotted a sign that said "Wana" in English. Wana is the capital of South Waziristan, the most radical area of the seven administrative districts that make up the tribal areas. We stopped in the main bazaar, and I was left alone in the car with the young driver.

Desperate rationalizations swirled through my mind. Our captors wanted a ransom and prisoners. Killing us got them nothing. The three of us would survive. They were all delusions, of course. Simply getting us this far was an enormous victory for them. We would be held here for months or killed.

Outside the car, dozens of Pakistani tribesmen and Afghan and foreign militants milled around. Each carried a Kalashnikov assault rifle on his shoulder and had a long, thick beard.

A man with a large turban stopped, peered at me in the back seat and asked the driver a question in Pashto. The driver looked at me and said a sentence that I thought included the word for martyr. I told myself the driver had said I was on my way to heaven.

Atiqullah got back into the car, and I felt relief. He had kidnapped us, but more and more I desperately viewed Atiqullah as my protector, the man who would continue to treat us well as other militants called for our heads.

We arrived at last at our first Pakistani home, in Miram Shah, the capital of North Waziristan. Two large sleeping rooms looked out on a small courtyard. One even had a small washroom, separate from the toilet, for showering.

On the first day there, I went to the bathroom and returned to find Tahir with a fresh cut on his calf. It looked as if someone had drawn a line across his leg in red ink. A local Waziri militant had taken out his knife and tried to cut off a chunk of Tahir's calf, saying he wanted to eat the flesh of an Afghan who worked with Westerners. One of Atiqullah's guards had stopped him.

All day, a parade of random Pakistani militants stopped by the house to stare at us. I felt like an animal in a zoo. Among them was a local Taliban commander who introduced himself as Badruddin. He was the brother of Sirajuddin Haqqani, who led the Haqqani network, one of the most powerful Taliban factions in the region. Miram Shah was its stronghold.

Their father was Jalaluddin Haqqani, an Afghan mujahideen leader whom the United States and Pakistan backed in the 1980s when he battled the Soviets. In the 1990s, the United States ended its relationship with the Haqqanis and many other hard-line Afghan fighters. With Pakistan's help, the Taliban movement emerged and the Haqqanis joined them.

Badruddin, a tall, talkative man who appeared to be in his early thirties, said he was preparing to make a video of us to release to the media. He smiled as he showed me a video on his camera of a French aid worker, Dany Egreteau, who had been kidnapped a week before us as he walked to his office in Kabul. He was in chains and appeared to have welts on his face. He implored his family and friends to save him.

"It's a nightmare," he said. "I really beg you to pay."

I asked if Tahir and I could speak alone with Atiqullah, and I told him we should not make the video. The American and Afghan governments were more likely to agree to a secret prisoner exchange, I said, than a public one.

Trying to reduce their expectations, I told him it would be far easier to get prisoners from the main Afghan-run prison outside Kabul, known as Pul-i-Charkhi. If the Taliban demanded prisoners from the American-run detention centers at Guantánamo Bay, Cuba, and Bagram, Afghanistan, they would never succeed.

I was not worth that much, I told him, and he should compromise. I did not say it, but I also wanted to spare my family the pain of seeing me in a video. To my surprise, Atiqullah agreed.

"I am one of those kinds of people," he said at one point. "I am one of those people who like to meet in the middle."

Tahir, Asad, and I would be allowed to call our families that night to prove we were alive, he said. Atiqullah told me to emphasize during the call that he wanted to reach a deal quickly. He continued to cover his face with a scarf. To me, that meant he did not want to be identified because he planned to release us.

I spent the rest of the day nervously scribbling a list of things I wanted to say to my wife, Kristen, whom I had married just two months earlier. I added items and then crossed them out. I wanted to ease my family's fears that I was being tortured, but I also wanted to do everything possible to free the three of us. I wasn't sure I would have another chance to speak with her.

Late that night, Atiqullah and Badruddin drove us out of town. Atiqullah stopped the car in a dry riverbed and turned off the engine. He left the headlights on, and we used them to see the number pad on a small satellite phone. Atiqullah and Badruddin ordered me to tell Kristen that we were being held in terrible conditions in the mountains of Afghanistan. I dialed my wife's number.

"Hello?" she said.

"Kristen?" I said. "Kristen?"

"David," she said, "it's Kristen. I love you."

She sounded calm.

"Kristen?" I asked.

"Yes?" she said.

"I love you, too," I said. "Write these things down, okay?"

"Okay," she said.

She sounded remarkably composed.

"I'm—we are being treated well," I said.

"Being treated well," Kristen repeated.

"Number one," I said.

"Uh-huh, number one," Kristen said.

"Number two," I said. "Deal for all three of us, all three of us, not just me. The driver and the translator also. It has to be a deal for all three of us."

"Deal for all three of us," she repeated. "The driver and the translator as well. Okay."

"Do not use force to try to get us," I said.

"Do not use force," Kristen repeated.

"Four," I said.

"Yes," Kristen said.

"Make a deal now or they will make it public," I said. "They want to put a video out to the media."

Kristen repeated my words back to me.

"It will make it a big political problem," I said.

Atiqullah told me to tell her that this was my last call.

"They said I can't call you again," I said. "They want a deal now and I can't call you again."

"You cannot call me again," she repeated. "I love you. I love you, honey."

"I love you, too," I said. "Tell my family I'm sorry."

"Your family is here, Lee's here with me," she said, referring to my older brother.

"I'm sorry," I said, "I'm sorry."

"It's going to be all right," Kristen said calmly. "I love you. I am praying for you every day."

Kristen said she wanted to make sure she understood what the Taliban wanted.

"What is the deal?" she asked.

Atiqullah told me to tell her that he would call the *Times*' Kabul bureau with demands. "We are very concerned about you," Kristen said. "And we love you, and we're praying for you."

The satellite phone beeped and abruptly went dead. Kristen was gone.

Standing in the remote darkness of Waziristan at the mercy of Taliban militants, I felt at peace. I had spoken to my wife for the first time in nine days. I had expected panic or tears, but she sounded collected and confident. Her words "It's going to be all right" would linger in my mind for months. Her composure would sustain me.

Atiqullah and Badruddin then told me to call the *Times*' bureau in Kabul. But instead of ordering me to make specific demands, they instructed all three of us to exaggerate our suffering.

"We are in terrible conditions, Tahir is very sick," I told Chris Chivers, a close friend and *Times* reporter, who answered the phone. I was ordered to tell Chris that Atiqullah was not with us — even though he was, in fact, standing beside me.

Tahir then spoke to Chris and asked him to tell his family he was alive and in good health.

"They keep telling me that if things go wrong they will repeat the story of Helmand," Tahir said, "so I am just afraid they are going to kill me."

Tahir was referring to the 2007 kidnapping of an Italian journalist in Helmand Province that ended in the beheadings of an Afghan journalist and a driver working with him.

Asad then spoke with an Afghan reporter in the bureau.

"I am fine, I am okay," he said. "Tell my family that we are in the mountains but we are okay."

The conversation dragged on, with Atiqullah continuing to direct me about what to say. When he ordered me to tell Chris that they would kill the driver and translator first, I refused.

"Kill me first," I told Atiqullah, "Kill me first."

Chris overheard me and interrupted. "Nobody needs that, David," he said. "Nobody needs to die."

"They are threatening to kill the driver and the translator," I explained to Chris. "I have to tell you, I have to tell you. I don't want to tell you."

"We understand that they are making those threats," Chris said, "but that will not make our job easier."

Chris said that if the Taliban killed anyone it would make government officials angry and make any deal even more difficult.

"Please don't let them kill the driver and the translator," I said. "Please don't let them kill the driver and translator.

"I am sorry about this," I added. "I apologize to everyone."

"David, this is not your fault," Chris said. He urged me to tell Atiqullah to keep calling.

"Okay, all three of us, Chris," I said as Badruddin and Atiqullah ordered me to end the call. "It's gotta be all three of us. I gotta go."

As Atiqullah drove us back into Miram Shah, I felt relief. Kristen had sounded calm. Chris had said the *Times* was doing all it could. I felt I had fought for Tahir and Asad.

We arrived at a new house, and I was again surprised by the good conditions. It had regular electricity, and we could wash ourselves with buckets of warm water. I received a new set of clothes, a tooth-brush, toothpaste, and shampoo. Guards allowed us to walk in a yard, and the weather was surprisingly warm. We received pomegranates and other fresh food and Nestlé Pure Life water bottled in Pakistan.

The tribal areas were more developed and the Taliban more so-phisticated than I expected. They browsed the internet and listened to hourly news updates on Azadi Radio, a station run by the Ameri-can government. But then they dismissed whatever information did not meet their preconceptions.

Atiqullah said he needed to return to Afghanistan, but two of his men stayed behind to guard us. "I will return in seven to ten days," he promised, then disappeared.

That week, to help us pass the time, we received a shortwave radio and a board game called checkah, a Pakistani variation of Parcheesi. To my amazement, the guards even brought me English-language Pakistani newspapers. Delivered to a shop in Miram Shah, the news-papers were only a day or two old. Instead of beating us as I expected, our captors were at least trying to meet some of our needs.

But as in so much of our seven months in captivity, reasons for optimism would be overtaken by harsh realities.

For the next several nights, a stream of Haqqani commanders overflowing with hatred for the United States and Israel visited us, unleashing blistering critiques that would continue throughout our captivity.

Some of their comments were factual. They said large numbers of civilians had been killed in Afghanistan, Iraq, and the Palestin-ian territories in aerial bombings. Muslim prisoners had been phys-ically abused and sexually humiliated in Iraq. Scores of men had been detained in Cuba and Afghanistan for up to seven years without charges.

To Americans, these episodes were aberrations. To my captors, they were proof that the United States was a hypocritical and duplici-tous power that flouted international law.

When I told them I was an innocent civilian who should be re-leased, they responded that the United States had held and tortured Muslims in secret detention centers for years. Commanders said they themselves had been imprisoned, their families ignorant of their fate. Why, they asked, should they treat me differently?

Other accusations were paranoid and delusional. Seven years after 9/11, they continued to insist that the attacks were hatched by American and Israeli intelligence agencies to create a pretext for the United States to enslave the Muslim world. They said the United States was forcibly converting vast numbers of Muslims to Christianity. American and NATO soldiers, they believed, were making Afghan women work as prostitutes on military bases.

Their hatred for the United States seemed boundless.

Ten days passed, but Atiqullah did not return as promised. Badruddin now seemed to be in charge.

He moved us to a far smaller, dirtier house. The space we were allowed to walk in was the width of a city sidewalk and ringed by high walls. The food was unclean and made me sick.

Our first night there, the Taliban commander who owned the house promised to update us every three days on negotiations for our release. But we would not see him again for months. The guards stopped taking Tahir to a local doctor for digestive and skin ailments.

And it was increasingly clear that Tahir and Asad would be separated from their families for Id al-Adha—a major Muslim holiday that marks Abraham's willingness to sacrifice his son to show his devotion to God.

Alarmed by the worsening treatment, Tahir and I began a hunger strike in early December. At first, the guards panicked and begged us to eat. We refused.

After two days, the guards said Atiqullah had called and told them that a deal for our release was nearly complete. He said he was waiting for approval from President Hamid Karzai of Afghanistan, who was on a foreign trip. The French aid worker in the video I was shown had been released, they said. We would be next.

Fearing that our continued defiance would anger our captors and scuttle the deal, we began eating again.

Instead of releasing us, Badruddin moved us to yet another house. It was larger than the previous one but felt more like a prison. Twenty-foot-high concrete walls surrounded a small courtyard where I spent my days walking in circles. For the first time in my life, I began praying several times a day, and I found that it centered me.

We started preparing our own meals. The food was cleaner and fresher, but cooking for ourselves gave a worrying sense of permanence to our imprisonment.

Badruddin visited us several days later and promised that negotiations were continuing. But he was increasingly casual. Any sense of urgency about our release seemed to be fading. Before leaving, he told me the Taliban would not kill me.

"You are the golden hen," he said, clearly expecting me to lay a golden egg.

I asked him to promise not to kill Tahir and Asad. Speaking directly to me in broken English, he said the Taliban had decided to kill Asad if their demands were not met in a week. After he left, Tahir and I decided not to tell Asad.

I panicked over the next two days, frantically trying to think of ways to save our young driver. Since the three of us had arrived in Pakistan on November 18, I had spent hours each day talking politics, religion, and survival with Tahir, but I could barely communicate with Asad.

I spoke little Pashto, he spoke little English. I came up with a routine when a newspaper arrived. I showed Asad photos and tried to explain what they were about. He laughed, but I felt like a monster. Asad was an impoverished, hard-working father of two—and I was going to get him killed.

On the third day after Badruddin's visit, I told one of our guards that I was willing to make a video—or do anything they wanted—to save Asad. The guard said he would check with Badruddin. The following day, the guard announced that it had all been a misunderstanding. There was no deadline to kill Asad. I didn't know what the truth was but felt enormous relief.

Several days later, Badruddin arrived to make the video. He promised us that it would go only to our families, but what he instructed us to say made me think it would be released publicly. As guards pointed assault rifles at our heads, I called for President Bush and President-elect Obama to meet the Taliban's demands.

"If you don't meet their demands," I said, "they will kill all of us."

Tahir and Asad then made similar statements. Badruddin departed, and I told myself that our families would at least know we were alive.

As December dragged on, tensions in the house steadily grew. Qari, the guard who had nearly shot Tahir, tore the checkah board to shreds after he repeatedly lost. Then, Tahir and Asad ripped up two other checkah boards out of frustration as well. Qari began spending hours alone reciting the Koran and seemed increasingly distant and unstable. I worried that the situation was slowly spinning out of control.

Several days before Christmas, Atiqullah finally returned. He announced that he had spectacular news. "We are here to free you," he said, wearing no scarf over his face for the first time. "We have come here to release you."

At first, I was euphoric. My confidence in Atiqullah had not been misplaced. Here was a more moderate and reasonable Taliban leader who would persevere and release us.

Then, later that night, the conversation turned menacing.

The American military had mounted an operation to arrest Abu Tayyeb on the morning that we were to interview him, Atiqullah said, referring to the Taliban leader we had been traveling to meet when we were kidnapped.

Shocked, I told Atiqullah I knew nothing about a military operation.

I had sent text messages from my cellphone to Saudi Arabia before the interview, Atiqullah claimed, to tip off the American military about Abu Tayyeb's location. Again, I told him I had no idea what he was talking about.

Finally, he announced that I was a spy, along with other employees of the *Times* in Afghanistan. His men had prepared a suicide attack on the paper's Kabul bureau, he said, which he could set off with a single phone call. His men had nearly kidnapped Carlotta Gall, our bureau chief, but she had left an interview just before they arrived.

"She was probably given information," he said, seemingly convinced that all journalists were intelligence operatives.

Our imprisonment, I thought, had reached a low point. My colleagues in Kabul were now in danger. Atiqullah's talk of our imminent release seemed farcical.

The following morning, Atiqullah insisted that there was, in fact, a deal. At one point, he said we would be exchanged within "days." He toyed with me, asking which flights I would take back to the United States and how many television cameras would be at the airport. He asked me what I would say to my wife when I saw her.

By this point, I began to doubt everything he said. Then I learned that he had lied to us from the beginning.

In conversations when our guards left the room, Tahir and Asad each separately whispered to me that Atiqullah was, in fact, Abu Tayyeb. They had known since the day we were kidnapped, they said, but dared not tell me. They asked me to stay silent as well. Abu Tayyeb had vowed to behead them if they revealed his true identity.

Abu Tayyeb had invited us to an interview, betrayed us, and then pretended that he was a commander named Atiqullah.

I was despondent and left with only one certainty: we had no savior among the Taliban.

That morning, Badruddin arrived at the house in Miram Shah and announced that he was taking us out of town to a snow-covered hillside to shoot the final scene of a video that would be released to the news media. He was determined to make it look as though we were being held in the frigid mountains of Afghanistan, not in a bustling city in Pakistan.

On the way, we ran into a Pakistani Army supply convoy. A nervous looking Pakistani soldier pointed a rocket-propelled grenade at our pickup truck. It was late January. The Taliban guard beside me loaded his rifle and ordered me to put a scarf over my face. A group of Pakistani civilians standing nearby moved out of the way, anticipating a firefight.

Badruddin Haqqani was in the driver's seat of our vehicle. Obeying the guard, I covered my face. The soldier was in the lead vehicle of the convoy. After surveying the road, the soldier got back in his truck, and the convoy rumbled forward.

I hoped that the Pakistanis might somehow rescue us. Instead,

I watched in dismay as Badruddin got out of the truck and calmly stood on the side of the road. As trucks full of heavily armed government soldiers rolled by, he smiled and waved at them.

After the convoy disappeared, Badruddin seemed amused.

"Do you know who that was?" he asked me.

"No," I said, trying to play dumb.

"That was the Pakistani Army," he said.

He explained that under a cease-fire agreement between the Taliban and the army, all civilians were required to get out of their cars when an army convoy approached. For Taliban vehicles, though, only the driver had to get out. The practice, I realized, allowed the Taliban to hide kidnapping victims and foreign militants from the Pakistani Army.

As we continued our journey, we passed a half-dozen checkpoints that had been abandoned by the Frontier Corps, a militia that had been the Pakistani government's primary security force in the tribal areas until 2001. Badruddin said that under the cease-fire agreement, only unarmed militia members could stand at the checkpoints.

As we drove, I occasionally saw members of the militia standing on the side of the road without guns. Some casually chatted with local tribesmen.

The trip confirmed suspicions I had harbored for years as a reporter. The Haqqanis oversaw a sprawling Taliban ministate in the tribal areas with the de facto acquiescence of the Pakistani military. The Haqqanis were so confident of their control of the area that they took me—a person they considered to be an extraordinarily valuable hostage—on a three-hour drive in broad daylight to shoot a scene for a video outdoors.

Throughout North Waziristan, Taliban policemen patrolled the streets, and Taliban road crews carried out construction projects. The Haqqani network's commanders and foreign militants freely strolled the bazaars of Miram Shah and other towns. Young Afghan and Pakistani Taliban members revered the foreign fighters, who taught them how to make bombs.

Over the winter, I would come to know the reality the Haqqanis had created. Some nights, commanders and their fighters visited the houses where we were being held. Conversations were dominated by their unwavering belief that the United States was waging a war against Islam.

It was a universe filled with contradictions. My captors assailed the West for killing civilians, but they celebrated suicide attacks orchestrated by the Taliban that killed scores of Muslim bystanders. They bitterly denounced missionaries, but they pressed me to convert to their faith. They complained about innocent Muslims being imprisoned by the United States, even as they continued to hold us captive.

Yet in our day-to-day existence, when commanders were absent, some of our guards showed glimpses of humanity. Those moments gave us hope that we might somehow be able to talk or reason our way out of captivity.

In early February, our guards told us that Badruddin had sent the video to Afghan and foreign media outlets but that only Al Jazeera had broadcast it. The news frustrated Tahir and Asad, who had hoped that the video would be widely broadcast and would stimulate negotiations.

I was not surprised. I had heard before our abduction that the Afghan and foreign news media had struck an informal agreement not to publicize the kidnappings of journalists in Afghanistan if their organization requested it.

The October 2008 kidnapping of a Canadian journalist in Kabul, Melissa Fung, had been kept quiet. Keeping the kidnappings out of the news, it was hoped, would decrease the expectations of hostage-takers that they could garner vast amounts of publicity or ransom for journalists.

After news outlets declined to show the video, we asked our guards to call Abu Tayyeb, the Taliban commander who had abducted us outside Kabul and concealed his identity. He agreed to return to Miram Shah and said he would try to negotiate a ransom with my family.

Tahir, Asad, and I had received comforting letters from our families through the International Committee of the Red Cross. But I hadn't spoken to my wife, Kristen, in three months.

Finally, on February 16, Abu Tayyeb drove me to a remote location and allowed me to call her. The Taliban told me to give her the number of their cellphone and have her call us back. They were demanding seven million dollars at that point but were too cheap to pay for the phone call.

"This is my last call," I said to her, repeating what they had told me to say. "This is our last chance."

Abu Tayyeb promised that he would reach a settlement with my family. Then, as he had many times before, he left without doing so. My conversations with him during his brief visit left me doubtful that he would ever compromise in a case involving an American.

One morning, he wept at news that a NATO airstrike had killed women and children in southern Afghanistan. A guard explained to me that Abu Tayyeb reviled the United States because of the civilian deaths.

One evening, Abu Tayyeb declared that the Taliban treated women better than Americans did. He said women in the United States were forced to wear revealing clothes and define themselves solely as sex objects. The Taliban protected women's honor by not allowing them to appear in public with their faces unveiled.

My captors saw me—and seemingly all Westerners—as morally corrupt and fixated on pursuing the pleasures of this world. Americans invaded Afghanistan to enrich themselves, they argued, not to help Afghans.

They ignored the fact that the United States helped build hundreds of miles of paved roads in Afghanistan and more than a thousand schools and health clinics. My captors denied widespread news reports that the Taliban burned down scores of newly built schools to prevent girls from getting an education.

I argued that the United States was not the menacing, predatory caricature that they believed. I also tried to counter their belief that all Americans were astonishingly rich. Nothing I said, though, seemed to change their minds.

One day, I received a copy of *Dawn*, an English-language Pakistani newspaper, that featured an article on the perilous financial state of the *New York Times*. I saved the newspaper until commanders stopped by for visits.

Showing them the headline "*New York Times* Struggles to Stay

Afloat," I explained that the American newspaper industry—as well as the American economy—was in a free fall. They listened to what I said and nodded. Then, they ignored me.

We were held for much of the winter in a building the Pakistani government had constructed to serve as a health clinic. It was part of an American-backed effort to win the hearts and minds of the local population.

Our guards spent their days there listening to radio broadcasts and shouting "God is great!" at reports of the deaths of Afghan and American soldiers.

Most of the guards were Afghan men in their late twenties and early thirties. Some had grown up as refugees in Pakistan. All had limited educations from government schools or religious institutions, known as madrasas. Some did not make it past junior high school. None had seen the world beyond Afghanistan and Pakistan.

They all had relatives or friends who had been killed by Soviet or American troops. They grew up in a culture where teenage boys reached manhood and made a name for themselves by showing their bravery.

I tried to get to know one of the guards, who was preparing to be a suicide bomber. A young man in his twenties with a slim build and brown eyes, he said he had studied engineering in high school. He never attended college but was relatively well educated compared with the other fighters.

When I asked him why he wanted to die, he replied that living in this world was a burden for any true Muslim. Heaven was his goal, he said. Earthly relationships with his parents and siblings did not matter.

He spoke a smattering of English, and my own beliefs seemed to interest and amaze him. During our six weeks together, he asked me a series of questions. Was it true, he asked, that a necktie was a secret symbol of Christianity? Was it true that Christians wanted to live one thousand years?

As the weeks passed, our captivity became increasingly surreal.

My Taliban guards slept beneath bedspreads manufactured by a Pakistani textile company and emblazoned with characters from the

American television show *Hannah Montana* and the movie *Spider-Man*. My blanket was a pink Barbie comforter.

My captors railed against the evils of a secular society. In March, they celebrated a suicide attack in a mosque in the Pakistani town of Jamrud that killed as many as fifty worshipers as they prayed to God. Those living under Pakistan's apostate government, they said, deserved it.

One commander declared that no true Muslim could live in a state where Islam was not the official religion. He flatly rejected my compromise suggestion that strict Islamic law be enacted in Afghanistan's conservative rural south, while milder forms of Islam be followed in the comparatively liberal north.

Citing the Taliban's interpretation of Islam, he said it was every Muslim's duty to try to stop others from sinning. If one person in a village commits a sin, those who witness it and do not stop him will also be punished by God.

After we had been held for months in captivity, my kidnappers demanded that I stop washing the group's dishes because they did not want to catch my diseases. They believed that problems I was having with my stomach stemmed from my being an inherently unclean non-Muslim, not from unhygienic water.

Their rigidity was the opposite of the tolerant attitudes I had found among the vast majority of Muslims I had met in Afghanistan and Pakistan.

Pressing me to convert, one commander ordered me to read a passage of the Koran each day and discuss it with him at night. He dismissed my arguments that a forced conversion was not legitimate. He and the guards politely said they felt sorry for me. If I failed to convert, they said, I would suffer excruciating pain in the fires of hell.

At one point, a visiting fighter demanded to know why I would not obey. He said that if it were up to him, he would take me outside and offer me a final chance to convert. If I refused, he would shoot me.

I realized that he and other fighters might be exaggerating their views to frighten me. The virulence I saw among the Haqqani foot soldiers was not as monolithic as it sometimes seemed.

One young fighter showed a different side. He refused to carry out a commander's order to kidnap a foreigner working in Afghanistan. During one visit, he suggested that I read a passage in an English-language Koran to comfort myself.

"Allah tasketh not a soul beyond its scope," it said. "For it is only that which it hath earned, and against it only that which it hath deserved. Our Lord! Impose not on us that which we have not the strength to bear! Pardon us, absolve us, and have mercy on us, Thou, our Protector, and give us victory over the disbelieving folk."

During our months in Miram Shah, patterns emerged. When certain commanders visited, the atmosphere was tense, and discussions centered on what they saw as Western injustices against Muslims. When we were alone with the guards who lived with us, moments of levity emerged.

They searched for ways to break the monotony. After dinner on many winter nights, my guards sang Pashto songs for hours. My voice and Pashto pronunciation were terrible, but our guards urged me to sing along. The ballads varied. On some evenings, I found myself reluctantly singing Taliban songs declaring that "you have atomic bombs, but we have suicide bombers."

On other nights, at my guards' urging, I switched to American tunes. In a halting, off-key voice, I sang Frank Sinatra's version of "New York, New York" and described it as the story of a villager who tries to succeed in the city and support his family. I sang Bruce Springsteen's "Born to Run" and described it as a portrayal of the struggles of average Americans.

I realized that my guards, too, might have needed a break from our grim existence. But I felt like a performing monkey when they told me to sing for visiting commanders. I knew they were simply laughing at me.

I intentionally avoided American love songs, trying to dispel their belief that all Americans were hedonists. Despite my efforts, romantic songs—whatever their language—were the guards' favorites.

The Beatles' song "She Loves You," which popped into my head soon after I received my wife's letter from the Red Cross, was the most popular.

For reasons that baffled me, the guards relished singing it with me. I began by singing its first verse. My three Taliban guards, along with Tahir and Asad, then joined me in the chorus.

"She loves you — yeah, yeah, yeah," we sang, with Kalashnikovs lying on the floor around us.

Two deafening explosions shook the walls of the compound. My guards and I dived to the floor as chunks of dirt hurtled through the window.

"Dawood?" one guard shouted, saying my name in Arabic. "Dawood?"

"I'm okay," I replied in Pashto. "I'm okay."

The plastic sheeting covering the window hung in tatters. Debris covered the floor. Somewhere outside, a woman wailed. I wondered if Tahir and Asad were alive. A guard grabbed his rifle and ordered me to follow him outside.

"Go!" he shouted, his voice shaking with fury. "Go!"

Our nightmare had come to pass. Powerful missiles fired by an American drone had obliterated their target a few hundred yards from our house. Dozens of people were probably dead. Militants would call for our heads in revenge.

Outside, shredded tree leaves littered the yard, but the house and its exterior walls remained intact. Tahir and Asad looked worried. No one was hurt, but I knew the three of us might not survive for long.

It was March 25, and for months the drones had been a terrifying presence. Remotely piloted, propeller-driven airplanes, they could easily be heard as they circled overhead for hours. To the naked eye, they were small dots in the sky. But their missiles had a range of several miles. We knew we could be immolated without warning.

Our guards believed the drones were targeting me. United States officials wanted to kill me, they said, because my death would eliminate the enormous leverage and credibility they believed a single American prisoner gave the Haqqanis. Whenever a drone appeared, I was ordered to stay inside. The guards believed that its surveillance cameras could recognize my face from thousands of feet above.

In the courtyard after the missile strike, the guards clutched their weapons and anxiously watched the sky. Fearing a direct attack on our house, they ordered me to cover my face with a scarf and follow them outside the compound. I knew that enraged Arab militants or local tribesmen could spot me once I was outside, but I had no choice.

They hustled me down a hillside to where a station wagon was parked between rows of trees. Opening the rear door, they ordered me to lie inside and keep the scarf on so passers-by could not see my face.

I lay in the back of the car and silently recited the Lord's Prayer. In the distance, I heard men shouting as they collected their dead. If many people had been killed, particularly women and children, we were sure to die. For months, I had promised myself that if they taped our execution I would remain calm for my family and declare our innocence until the end.

After about fifteen minutes, the guards returned to the car and led me back to the house. The missiles had struck two cars, killing a total of seven Arab militants and local Taliban fighters. I felt a small measure of relief that no civilians had been killed. But I knew we were still in grave danger.

Two weeks earlier our captors had moved us from Miram Shah to a remote town in South Waziristan. I had seen on a receipt from a local shop that we were in Makeen, a stronghold of the leader of the Pakistani Taliban, Baitullah Mehsud. The region teemed with Uzbek, Arab, Afghan, and Pakistani militants.

For the next two hours, I did my best to placate the guards. I did not walk in the yard. I did not speak unless spoken to. I praised God for saving us.

Later, I learned that one guard called for me to be taken to the site of the attack and ritually beheaded as a video camera captured the moment. The chief guard overruled him.

The Taliban assailed the drone attacks, and my captors expressed more hatred for President Obama than for President Bush. They bitterly criticized the Obama administration for increasing the missile attacks in Pakistan's tribal areas and the number of American troops in Afghanistan.

A stalemate between the United States and the Taliban seemed to unfold before me. The drones killed many senior commanders and hindered their operations. Yet the Taliban were able to garner recruits in their aftermath by exaggerating the number of civilian casualties.

The strikes also created paranoia among the Taliban. They believed that a network of local informants guided the missiles. Innocent civilians were rounded up, accused of working as American spies, and then executed.

Several days after the drone strike near our house in Makeen, we heard that foreign militants had arrested a local man. He confessed to being a spy after they disemboweled him and chopped off his leg. Then they decapitated him and hung his body in the local bazaar as a warning.

The house in Makeen was the crudest we had inhabited in Pakistan. Perched on a hilltop, it had no running water. It had fleas and a courtyard littered with trash.

Makeen was colder than Miram Shah, and frequent rain and frigid temperatures created miserable conditions. Hailstorms were common and viewed as punishment from God by our captors.

I was given daily chores by guards who were half my age. The tasks were demeaning, since elders are treated with reverence in Pashtun culture, but I did not care. The chores helped me pass the time and appeared to give the guards the sense I was loyal.

Twice a day, I filled a barrel in the bathroom with water, which we used to flush the toilet, and methodically swept the dirt floors. It was a Sisyphean task, but cleaning gave me the illusion of control when in reality I had none.

Rarely allowed outside the house, I saw my world shrink to a few dozen square feet. My daily focus simply became survival.

Tahir struggled as well, telling me at times that he could no longer remember the faces of his seven children.

"This is not life," he said. "I want to die."

With each passing month, we felt increasingly forgotten and at the mercy of the young guards who lived with us. The chief guard was the younger brother of Abu Tayyeb. He began pocketing some of the money given to him to buy our food and supplies. He dared us to try to escape so he could end our captivity with "one bullet." He complained that mujahideen were dying in the drone strikes yet enormous attention was being wasted on one American prisoner.

When I showed him several dozen flea bites on my stomach and arms, he bought a pesticide and suggested that I put it on my sleeping bag. Fearing it would make me sick, I declined. When the bites continued, I showed another guard. His response was to show me his own stomach, which had no bites on it.

"I never get sick while I'm on jihad," he said.

After long conversations between Tahir and me prompted the guards to accuse us of planning an escape, we spoke less. Some days, we talked only a few minutes. Increasingly, I became lost in my own thoughts, and my memories of the world I had known began to fade.

Trying to stay connected, I listened to the BBC's shortwave radio broadcasts for hours at a time. The news broadcasts raised my spirits, but they also gave me the sensation of being in a coma. I could hear how the world was progressing but could not communicate with anyone in it.

The video image was grainy but I immediately recognized the hostage's face. "Hello, Peter," an off-camera questioner said. "How are you?"

"Fine," answered Piotr Stanczak, a soft-spoken forty-two-year-old Polish geologist kidnapped by the Taliban in September 2008. Two masked militants holding assault rifles stood on either side of him. A black sheet with jihadi slogans hung on the mud-brick wall behind him.

In mid-March, one of our guards arrived with a DVD player. After that, watching jihadi videos became the guards' favorite pastime. Playing along with his captors in the video, Stanczak called for the Polish government to stop sending troops to Muslim countries and to break relations with the Pakistani government.

I had never met Stanczak but had read about his ordeal in Pakistani newspapers. When I realized the video would end in his beheading, I stood up to leave. I did not want to watch it—or give the guards the satisfaction of seeing me watch it.

"I would say people of Pakistan is very good, people is very good," I heard Stanczak say as I walked out of the room.

The videos were impossible to avoid at night, when I was confined

to the room the guards were in. They were little more than grimly repetitive snuff films. The Taliban executed local men who had been
declared American spies. Taliban roadside bombs blew up Afghan
government trucks and American Humvees. The most popular videos documented the final days of suicide bombers.

As I silently watched, the guards repeatedly asked me what I
thought of seeing American soldiers killed on the screen in front
of us.

"All killing is wrong," I said.

The guards would watch for hours at a time. Over all, the videos
created an alternate, pro-Taliban narrative of the war in Afghanistan.
A recurring theme was that the United States and NATO underre-
ported the number of foreign troops dying in Afghanistan.

The videos were not limited to the conflict in Afghanistan and Pakistan. Images of dead Palestinian, Kashmiri, and Iraqi civilians delivered the message that vast numbers of Muslims were being slaughtered across the globe.

The constant images of death seemed to be cynical efforts by Taliban commanders to numb their young foot soldiers to the prospect
of sacrificing their lives. Death, the message went, was not a distant
fate. Instead, it was a friendly companion and a goal.

The guards shared a book that glorified martyrdom, promising saccharine fruit juices, sumptuous food, and seventy virgins in
heaven. One of the guards read haltingly, pronouncing each word out
loud as if he were an elementary school student.

I feared that the videos were brainwashing our driver, Asad. After
we moved to Makeen, he seemed more friendly toward the guards
and began carrying a Kalashnikov they had given him. He also
stopped smoking, which the guards said was forbidden under Islam.
He was only doing what he needed to do to stay alive, I told myself.

In late April, a surprise visit by Abu Tayyeb raised our hopes that our
freedom was being negotiated. Dressed in an expensive white tunic,
he strode into our compound just before dinner.

"Dawood," he asked, "what would you say if I told you that you
could start your journey back to New York tomorrow?"

"That would make me incredibly happy," I said.

He told me to get a notebook and pen and ordered everyone to leave the room except for his deputy commander, Tahir, and me.

"Your family has been very slow," he said. "Write this down."

"This is my proof-of-life video," he dictated. "Maybe another video will come that will be very bad."

He paused and tried to think of his next line.

"If this message does not help," he said. "I cannot say what will happen to me."

I quickly realized that Abu Tayyeb had not shown up to complete a deal. His visit was another effort to extort money from my family. Five months into our captivity, he had refused to lower his demands below a five million dollar ransom as well as an exchange of prisoners.

Calmly sitting across the room from me, he dictated more lines.

"If you don't help me, I will die," he said. "Now the key is in your hand."

He paused again for a moment.

"Please save me, I want to go home," he said. "Don't you want me to stay alive with you? Hurry up. Hurry up."

Then he told me I would need to cry for the video. I stared at Tahir. If I refused, the Taliban might kill him or Asad to drive up a potential ransom payment. I hated the thought of my wife and family seeing such a video, but Tahir was the father of seven children, and Asad the father of two. I agreed to make it.

The deputy commander, a man in his fifties, placed a scarf over his face and picked up a .50-caliber machine gun. He pointed it at my head, and one of the guards turned on a camera.

During the filming, I tried to convey that I was reading a prepared statement by intentionally looking down at the pad of paper. I sobbed intermittently but no tears flowed from my eyes.

After the first take, Abu Tayyeb announced that I hadn't cried enough. He ordered me to read the message a second time. Standing behind the guard holding the camera, Abu Tayyeb waved his hands in the air, as if he were a film director, motioning for me to sob louder.

I tried to cry in an exaggerated fashion so that my family would recognize that none of it was real.

Later that night, Abu Tayyeb announced that the Afghan government had agreed to free twenty prisoners in exchange for our release.
The problem, he said, was that my family would not agree to pay the
five million dollar ransom.

"My family does not have five million dollars," I told him angrily.
"Why do you think we have been here for so long? Do you think
they're sitting on five million dollars and just playing a game? If they
had the money, they would offer it."

Abu Tayyeb continued. He smiled and told me I was a "big fish."
He said my brother was the president of a company that manufactured jumbo jets. If my brother would sell one plane, he explained,
my family could pay the ransom.

He had clearly looked up my family on the internet. My brother
was, in fact, the president of a small aviation consulting company,
but it consisted of six people and manufactured nothing.

Abu Tayyeb claimed that the American government paid ten million dollars for the release of John Solecki, a United Nations worker
kidnapped in Pakistan in February. As I had for months, I told him
that the American government didn't pay ransom.

Ignoring me, he said that the head of the FBI's office in New York
had traveled to Afghanistan to secure my release. He vowed to force
the United States government to pay the five million dollars.

"You know where the money will come from," he said. "And I
know where the money will come from."

I told him that he was delusional and that he should just kill me.
Tahir refused to translate my words. "Don't provoke him," he said.

I told Abu Tayyeb we would "be here forever" if he did not reduce
his demands.

"You are a spy," Abu Tayyeb declared. "You know that you are a
spy."

I told him that he was absolutely wrong and that I was a journalist.
Then I tried to shame him in front of his men.

"God knows the truth," I said. "And God will judge us all."

Abu Tayyeb disappeared the following morning. We spent the next
six weeks in a new house in a remote village in North Waziristan.

Each week, we received bits of information about the negotiations.

First, our captors informed us that an agreement had been reached on the twenty Taliban prisoners who would be exchanged for our release. Then they said that not enough money was being offered along with the prisoners. Finally, they told us that only sixteen of the twenty prisoners had been agreed upon.

In late May, we were taken back to Miram Shah, where we were informed of a final deal. All that was needed, they said, was for the two sides to agree to where the prisoner exchange would take place. The next day, they announced that there actually was no agreement.

In early June, Abu Tayyeb reappeared and announced that the American government was offering to trade the seven remaining Afghan prisoners at Guantánamo Bay, Cuba, for us. I told him that was ridiculous.

For months, Abu Tayyeb had been vastly exaggerating my value. He falsely claimed that the American diplomat Richard Holbrooke had freed Serbian prisoners in 1995 to win my release in Bosnia.

He insisted that I was best friends with Mr. Holbrooke, now the Obama administration's special representative for Afghanistan and Pakistan.

"Then why I am still sitting here after seven months?" I asked him.

He smiled. If I made one more video, he said, we would be released. Ashamed of my previous video and convinced that Abu Tayyeb was lying yet again, I refused.

"This is all about you," I said, raising my voice. "You are demanding millions of dollars so you can make yourself look good to the other commanders. You are the problem."

He declared that he was doing everything "for the jihad." Visibly angry, he again told me to make the video and then left the room.

Thirty minutes later, he returned and said that making the video was not a choice but an order. The half-dozen guards in the room stared at me.

Once again, Abu Tayyeb repeated his order, and I said no. I knew it was reckless, but standing up to him felt enormously liberating after months of acquiescing.

Sensing that Abu Tayyeb and his men were about to beat me, Tahir and Asad told me to make the video. "Just do it," Tahir said.

I finally relented, but I was determined to turn it into an opportunity to console our families, not worry them. No guns were pointed at my head. I refused to cry. I spoke to the camera calmly and said the three of us were well.

At the end of the video, I included a message I had wanted to relay since the day we were kidnapped.

"However this ends, Kristen and all my family and friends should live in peace with yourselves," I said. "I know you have all done absolutely everything you can to help us."

I stood in the bathroom of the Taliban compound and waited for my colleague to appear in the courtyard so we could make our escape. My heart pounded. A three-foot-tall swamp cooler—an antiquated version of an air-conditioner—roared in the yard a few feet in front of me. I feared that the guards might wake up and stop us. I feared even more that our captivity would drag on for years.

It was one a.m. on Saturday, June 20. We were still in Miram Shah. After seven months and ten days in Taliban captivity, I had come to a decision with Tahir to try to make a run for it. We had concluded that our captors were not seriously negotiating for our release, and never would.

Tahir and I had decided that I would get up first that night and go to the bathroom without asking the guards for permission. If the guards remained asleep, Tahir would follow. Twenty feet away, on a shelf outside the kitchen, was a car towrope we planned to use to lower ourselves down a fifteen-foot wall ringing the compound. I had found it two weeks earlier and hidden it beneath a pile of old clothes.

Several minutes went by, but Tahir did not come out of the room. I stared intently at the entrance to the living room where we slept side by side with the guards—roughly fifteen feet away and directly across the courtyard from the bathroom—and waited for Tahir to emerge. I had pulled his foot to rouse him before I crept out of the room. He had groaned and, I assumed, awakened.

As the minutes passed, I wasn't sure what to do. I stood in the darkened bathroom and wondered if Tahir had changed his mind. If the guards caught us, they might kill me, but they would definitely kill Tahir. Part of me thought it was wrong even to have agreed to do this. After seven months in captivity, I wondered if we were capable of making rational decisions.

Even if we made it over the wall, we would have to walk through Miram Shah to get to a nearby Pakistani base. The town teemed with Afghan, Pakistani, and foreign militants. Whoever caught us might be far less merciful than our current guards. Once on the base, we might encounter Pakistani military intelligence officials or tribal militia members who were sympathetic to the Taliban, people who would hand us back to the Haqqanis.

Yet I desperately longed to see my wife and family again. And I hated our captors so vehemently that I wanted them to get nothing in exchange for me. I pushed ahead.

Following a backup plan that Tahir and I had discussed that afternoon, I stepped out of the bathroom and picked up a five-foot-long bamboo pole leaning against the adjacent wall. I walked to the living room window and peered inside to make sure the guards were still asleep.

Beside me, the swamp cooler covered up the noise I made. Inside the room, a ceiling fan hummed. I opened the window, pointed the pole at Tahir's side, and poked him. I quickly walked back to the bathroom, leaned the pole against the wall, and stepped inside.

Still, Tahir did not appear. I was convinced that he had changed his mind. It wasn't fair of me, I thought, to have expected a man with seven children to risk his life.

Then, like an apparition, Tahir's leg emerged from the window. His upper body and head followed and, finally, his second leg. As he stood up, I rushed out of the bathroom to meet him and kicked a small plastic jug used for ablutions. It skidded across the ground, and I motioned to Tahir to freeze, fearing that the noise would wake the guards.

Tahir and I stared at each other in the darkness. No guards appeared from the living room. Taking a few steps forward, I whispered in Tahir's ear. "We don't have to go," I said. "We can wait."

"Go get the rope," he said.

Inside the living room, Asad was sound asleep with the guards.

Several weeks earlier, we decided we could no longer trust Asad, who had begun cooperating with the guards and carrying an assault rifle they had given him. That afternoon, Tahir and I made a gut-wrenching decision to leave without him, fearing that he would tell the guards of our escape plans—as he had before.

Our rupture with Asad had become the darkest aspect of an already bleak captivity. Over the many months, the solidarity the three of us shared immediately after the kidnapping on November 10 frayed under the threat of execution and indefinite imprisonment.

In December, Tahir and Asad expressed fury at me for exaggerating what our captors could receive for us in ransom. After being told that crews were on their way to film our beheadings, I had blurted out that our captors could receive prisoners and millions of dollars if we were kept alive.

I repeatedly apologized to Tahir and Asad, saying I had been trying to save us. But they called me a fool.

Over the course of the spring, Tahir said Asad told the guards that Tahir once had encouraged him to escape on his own. He said Asad told the guards that I was an American spy.

Finally, Tahir said he had whispered to Asad "We should escape" one night two weeks earlier. Asad did not respond. Days later, a guard announced that he had heard that Tahir was trying to escape.

Yet I also knew that Asad was under enormous pressure. As the driver, he would probably be the first one killed by the Taliban. He could be cooperating with the guards in order to survive.

Still, I did not trust him. If Tahir and I spoke with Asad about escaping for a second time, he could once more inform the guards. At the very least, we would squander an opportunity we might never have again. At worst, Tahir and I would be killed.

When we'd again been moved to Miram Shah in early June, I'd swept the floors and picked up trash, as I had done when we arrived in each new place, to create a sense of order. It was then that I found the car towrope beside some wrenches and motor oil. The discovery, I thought, was the first stroke of good luck in our seven months in captivity. Thinking we might be able to use the rope during an escape, I hid it under an old shirt and pants.

In the days that followed, I tried to think of ways we could flee.

When the guards let us sit on the roof with them at dusk, I noticed that the compound was surrounded by a five-foot-high wall. If we could hoist ourselves over it, I thought, we could use the rope to lower ourselves to the street.

At the same time, Tahir surveyed the area around the house when the guards took him with them to buy food and watch cricket games once or twice a week. He determined that the compound was closer to Miram Shah's main Pakistani militia base than any other house we had been held in.

Tahir and I kept our conversations brief about how we could escape, worrying that the guards or Asad would overhear us.

On the afternoon of June 19, electricity returned to Miram Shah for the first time since nearby fighting cut power lines a week earlier. It was a fortuitous development. Electricity meant the swamp cooler and ceiling fan would help conceal any noise we made when we fled.

Already angry at new lies the guards had told us that morning about the negotiations, we agreed to try to escape that night. Tahir would keep the guards up late playing checkah. If they were tired, they would sleep more soundly. Our plans for how to get over the wall were in place. Unfortunately, we disagreed about what to do after that.

Tahir said the Pakistani militiamen who guarded the military base would shoot us if we approached them at night. He said we should hike fifteen miles to the Afghan border. I responded that we would never make it that far without being caught. Going to the Pakistani base was a risk we had to take. If we could surrender to an army officer, I said, he would protect us.

As we continued to argue, the guards returned to the room, and Tahir and I had to stop speaking. For the rest of the evening, we were never alone again. Our plan had no ending.

Tahir kept the guards up late as we had discussed. By roughly eleven p.m., everyone was in bed. I lay awake, trying to listen to the guards' breathing to figure out whether they had fallen asleep.

I blinked over and over in the darkness but saw no difference when my eyes were open or closed. It was as if I were blind. I turned around at times to look at the orange light on the swamp cooler to make sure I could still see.

Anxious, I tried to calm myself by praying. In February, a Taliban commander who had been pressing me to convert to Islam told me that if I said "forgive me, God" one thousand times each day our captivity might end. I had done as he had suggested, with no results. But I did not care.

The prayers soothed me and passed the time. Each day, I would stare at the ceiling and say "forgive me, God" one thousand times while the guards took naps. Counting on my fingers, it took me roughly sixty minutes to reach one thousand.

That night, waiting to make sure the guards were sound asleep, I asked God to forgive me two thousand times.

In truth, I expected the escape attempt to fail quickly. I thought a guard would wake up as soon as I tried to leave the room. I would say I was going to the bathroom, walk to the toilet, return a few minutes later, and go back to sleep. I would feel better the next morning for at least having tried.

Instead, to my amazement, our plan was actually working. After Tahir and I made it to the courtyard, I retrieved the rope and we crept up a flight of stairs leading to the roof.

Tahir tied the rope to the wall surrounding the roof. Placing his toe between two bricks, he climbed to the top and peered at the street below.

"The rope is too short," he whispered after stepping down.

I shifted the knot on the rope to give it more length, pulled myself up on the wall, and looked down at the fifteen-foot drop. The rope did not reach the ground, but it appeared close.

I glanced back at the stairs, fearing that the guards would emerge at any moment.

"We don't have to go," I repeated to Tahir. "It's up to you."

I got down on my hands and knees and Tahir stepped on my back and lifted himself over the wall. I heard his clothes scrape against the bricks, looked up, and realized he was gone.

I grabbed his sandals, which he had left behind, and stuffed them down my pants. I climbed over, momentarily snagged a power line with my foot, slid down the wall, and landed in a small sewage ditch. I looked up and saw Tahir striding down the street in his bare feet. I ran after him.

For the first time in seven months, I walked freely down a street. Glancing over my shoulder, I didn't see any guards emerge from the compound, which looked smaller than I had expected.

We headed down a narrow dirt lane with primitive mud-brick walls on either side of us. Makeshift electrical wires snaked overhead in what looked like a densely populated neighborhood.

We walked into a dry riverbed and turned right. I kept slipping on the large sand-covered stones and felt punch-drunk. I caught up to Tahir and handed him his sandals.

"My ankle is very painful," Tahir said, as he slipped them on and continued walking. "I can't walk far."

A large dark stain covered his lower left pant leg. I worried that he had ripped open his calf on his way down the wall. At the same time, my left hand stung. I noticed that the rope had made a large cut across two of my fingers.

"Where are we going?" I asked Tahir as we quickly made our way down the riverbed, afraid someone would see or hear us.

"There is a militia base over there," Tahir said, gesturing to his left. "I don't trust them."

Neither did I. Earlier, Tahir had told me there was a checkpoint maintained by a Pakistani government militia near the house. Turning ourselves in there would be a gamble, I thought. I still believed that our best chance was to surrender to a military officer on the Pakistani base in Miram Shah.

"We have to go to the main base," I said.

"Impossible," Tahir said, continuing down the riverbed. "The guards said that Arabs and Chechens watch the main gate twenty-four hours a day."

The Taliban would recapture us, Tahir believed, before we got to the base. I started to panic. We had made it over the wall but did not know where we were going.

Despite his ankle, Tahir seemed determined to hike fifteen miles to the Afghan border. As we walked, we argued over which way to go.

"We have to go to the Pakistani base," I told Tahir.

Striding ahead, he didn't respond. Dogs began barking from one of the walled compounds to our right.

"We can't make it to the border," I said. "We have to go to the base." Tahir continued walking, but after a few minutes he complained about his ankle.

"There is too much pain," he said.

We stopped and I pulled up his pant leg. His calf had not been cut. The dark stain on his pants was from the sewage ditch we had both landed in outside our compound.

"There is another gate," Tahir said, changing his mind. "Come."

I waited for Taliban fighters to emerge from the darkness, but none did. Tahir told me to put a scarf I was carrying over my head.

"If anyone stops us, your name is Akbar and my name is Timor Shah," he said. "Act like a Muslim."

My sense of time was distorted, but it seemed as though we had been walking in the darkness for five to ten minutes. I did not feel free. If anything, I was more frightened. I worried that an even more brutal militant group would capture us.

We left the riverbed and walked down an alleyway between compounds for about fifty yards. We arrived at a two-lane paved street.

"This is the main road in Miram Shah," Tahir whispered.

To our left was a vacant stretch. To our right stood a gas station with four pumps and several shops. Dim light bulbs hung outside and illuminated the area. I silently questioned why Tahir was leading us down the center of the road where we could be easily spotted.

Suddenly, shouts erupted to our left and I heard a Kalashnikov being loaded. Tahir raised his hands and said something in Pashto. A man shouted commands in Pashto. I raised my hands as my heart sank. The Taliban had recaptured us.

In the faint light, I saw a figure with a Kalashnikov standing on the roof of a dilapidated one-story building. Beside the building was a mosque with freshly painted white walls. The building and mosque had concertina wire and earthen berms in front of them.

"If you move," Tahir said, "they will shoot us."

Then, Tahir said words I could scarcely believe.

"This is the base."

We had made it to the Pakistanis.

I held my hands high in the air and dared not move an inch. A nervous Pakistani guard could shoot us dead as we stood in the street. With my long beard, scarf, and clothes I looked like a foreign suicide bomber, not a foreign journalist.

Another voice came from inside the building. It sounded as if the guard was waking up his comrades. One or two more figures appeared on the roof and aimed more gun barrels at us.

The Pakistani guard on the roof intermittently spoke in Pashto with Tahir. I heard Tahir say the words for "journalist," "Afghan," and "American."

My arms began to burn, and I struggled to slow my breathing. I desperately tried not to move my hands.

"Tell them we will take off our shirts," I told Tahir, thinking the Pakistani guards might fear that we were suicide bombers who wore vests packed with explosives.

Tahir said something in Pashto, and the man responded.

"Lift up your shirt," Tahir said. I immediately obliged.

The guard spoke again.

"He is asking if you are American," Tahir said.

"I am an American journalist," I said in English, surprised at the sound of my own voice in the open air. "Please help us. Please help us."

I kept talking, hoping they would recognize that I was a native English speaker. "We were kidnapped by the Taliban seven months ago," I said. "We were kidnapped outside Kabul and brought here."

"Do you speak English?" I said, hoping one of the Pakistani guards on the roof understood. "Do you speak English?"

The guard said something to Tahir.

"They are radioing their commander," Tahir said. "They are asking for permission to bring us inside."

Tahir pleaded with the guards to protect us under the traditional honor code of Pashtunwali, which requires a Pashtun to give shelter to any stranger who asks. He begged them to take us inside the base before the Taliban came looking for us.

About two or three minutes passed. The Pakistani guards stood behind sandbags on the roof. Above us, stars glittered in a peaceful, crystal clear sky.

For the first time that night, it occurred to me that we might actually succeed. Escape—an ending I never dreamed of—might be our salvation. I held my hands still and waited.

Several minutes passed, and Tahir and I grew nervous. "Please allow us in the mosque," Tahir said. "Please let us inside."

The Pakistani guard on the roof said they were waiting for the senior officer to arrive. Tahir asked what we should do if the Taliban drove down the road. The guard said that we should dive behind the dirt embankment, and that they would open fire on anyone who approached. But they still declined to let us on the base.

Tahir complained to me about the pain in his arms as he held them in the air. His ankle hurt as well.

"Please wait, Tahir," I said, encouraging him to keep his hands in the air. "Please wait. We're so close."

Tahir asked for permission to sit on the ground, and the Pakistani guard granted it. Tahir sat down and groaned. He seemed exhausted.

Soon after, the Pakistani guard said we could walk toward the mosque. With our hands in the air, we crossed over the surrounding berm unsteadily. As the loose soil gave way, we both nearly lost our balance. I worried that we would be shot if we slipped and fell.

"Lie down on the ground," Tahir said. "If you move, they will shoot us."

Soon after, a senior Pakistani officer arrived, and Tahir told me to stand up. The officer stood a few feet from us on the other side of the concertina wire. He spoke with Tahir in what sounded like a reassuring tone.

"He is a very polite person," Tahir said. "We are under their protection. We are safe."

In one moment, the narrative of our captivity reversed itself. The powerlessness I had felt for months began to fade. We were achingly close to going home.

I thanked the officer in Pashto, Urdu, and English, desperate to win his trust.

"How are you?" the senior officer said in English.

"How are you?" I replied, trying again to demonstrate that I was an American.

At this point, Tahir and I had been standing outside the concertina wire for fifteen or twenty minutes. We still needed to get inside the base.

We offered to take off our shirts, and the officer told us to do so. I watched Tahir step unsteadily over the concertina wire and into the base.

"Come," Tahir said. "Come." I followed Tahir inside, and the senior officer and several Pakistani guards shook my hand.

"Thank you," I said to them in English, over and over. "Thank you."

The politeness of the Pakistani guards amazed me. I knew we could still be handed over to the Taliban, but I savored the compassion we were receiving from strangers. For the first time in months, I did not feel hostility.

They let us put our shirts on and drove us in a pickup truck toward the center of the base. I stared at Tahir and slapped him on the back. We were both in shock.

"Thank you," I said. "Thank you."

I asked Tahir to tell the guards that I wanted to call my wife, Kristen. I needed to somehow communicate to the outside world that we were on a Pakistani base. If we could get word to American officials, it would be extraordinarily difficult for the Pakistanis to hand us back to the Haqqanis.

We arrived in the center of the base, and I got out of the back of the truck. A row of well lit, white, one-story offices sat fifty feet away on the other side of a neatly manicured lawn. It was the first green grass I had seen in seven months. I walked across it and relished the sense of openness and safety. The guards brought us to a clean, modern office with a large desk and couches along the walls.

After several minutes, a young Pakistani captain who spoke perfect English introduced himself as the base commander. He looked as if he had just gotten out of bed.

After explaining our kidnapping and escape, I asked him if I could call my wife. He hesitated at first and then said he would try to find a phone card to make a long distance call.

As we waited, Tahir spoke in Pashto to the various militia members on the base. A doctor cleaned and bandaged the cuts on his foot and my hand. Tahir laughed and his face beamed as he spoke. I had never seen him so happy. But after several minutes, his face darkened.

"David, I feel terrible about Asad," Tahir said. "What have we done?"

I looked out the window in the direction of Miram Shah and wondered whether the guards who had been holding us captive had awakened yet. When they did, they would be furious.

"We had no choice," I said, trying to rationalize abandoning Asad. I wondered if our escape could prompt our captors to kill him. I prayed that they would be merciful.

About an hour later, a soldier arrived with a phone card, and I wrote my home number on a white slip of paper. The captain dialed the phone on his desk and handed me the receiver.

The phone in my apartment back in New York rang repeatedly and no one answered. Finally, the answering machine picked up and I listened to my wife's cheerful voice ask callers to leave us a message. Our escape still seemed like a dream. The machine beeped, and I spoke in an unsteady voice.

"Kristen, it's David," I said. "It's David. Please pick up."

I repeated the words several times. Fearing that the tape on the answering machine would run out, I finally blurted out, "We've escaped."

Someone picked up the receiver in New York.

"David," a woman's voice said. "It's Mary Jane."

My mother-in-law had answered.

"We've escaped and are on a Pakistani military base," I told her.

Fearing retaliation by the Taliban, I asked her to call the *Times* immediately and tell them to evacuate Tahir's and Asad's families from their homes in Kabul, as well as the people in the newspaper's bureau there.

I spent the next several minutes describing our exact location. I gave her the names of the tribal area, town, base, and commanding officer. I told her she needed to contact American officials and ask them to help evacuate us. I wanted the Pakistani officer to hear that the American government would soon know we were on his base. At the end of the conversation, I apologized to her for all of the pain and worry I had caused.

"Just come home safe," she said.

Thirty minutes passed, and the captain agreed to let me make another call to try to reach my wife. With each passing minute, I began to believe that we were finally safe and would return home.

The phone rang. This time, Kristen picked up.

"David?" she said, breathlessly. "David?"

"Kristen," I said, savoring the chance to utter the words I had dreamed of saying to her for months.

"Kristen," I said, "please let me spend the rest of my life making this up to you."

"Yes," she said. "Yes."

■

Tent City, U.S.A.

FROM GQ

Introduction, Purpose, and Methodology

An *in situ* study was conducted of a tent city near downtown Fresno, California. The objective of the Study was to explore this unusual community of homeless people and learn something of its inhabitants. The Fresno location was chosen based on its size (the Study Area extends over several city blocks) and substantial population (approximately three hundred individuals).

The project methodology was simple: the Principal Researcher (PR) would set up a tent within the tent city and observe the inhabitants.

Description of Study Area

It is difficult to convey the sobering effect of entering the Study Area for the first time.

On occasions during the Study, when use of a notebook seemed problematic, the PR would switch on a portable tape recorder. On the tape from day one, as the PR enters the Study Area, there may be heard: a long silence, an audible exhalation, a whispered profanity.

The PR had previous experience in the ghettos, slums, and shanty-towns of various Third World cities, including Jakarta, Nuevo Laredo, Peshawar, Bangkok, and Kathmandu. It was observed, however, that the PR was feeling more fear here in Fresno than he had felt in any of those foreign locales. Wild shouts could be heard; the air smelled of wood fire and dust; dogs roamed the Study Area; mysterious figures stared out from asymmetrical doorways; in the distance, under a highway overpass, a cramped, smoky, Stygian neighborhood seemed to exude menace.

At first glance, the Study Area presented as a junkyard, but one in which people were living. Tents of various vintage were observed. In addition, the following materials had been used to construct dwellings within the Study Area: Plyboard. Blue plastic tarp material. Tree limbs. Lengths of string, wire, and rope. Large wooden cable spools. Shopping carts. Construction pallets. A piece of inverted signage reading: lt. governor bustamante, working for families. Rocks, bags of dirt, and an office chair had been used to secure a tin roof. The yard of one house boasted a number of well-tended houseplants, including several cacti. This house also had a white metal screen door neatly mounted into its frame and an American flag flying above it on a tilted pole. At a nearby house, dozens of branches from an artificial Christmas tree had been inserted at regular intervals into the siding, decoratively.

In short the Study Area did not conform to the PR's expectations. Based on a pre-Study survey of existing media information, the PR had expected the tent city to be populated by middle-class individuals recently made homeless by the economic downturn, beaten but not destroyed, a kindly Steinbeckian gathering of stoic types, possibly playing guitars, who would welcome the PR, gratified that someone had come to document their plight.

The PR left the Study Area and drove around Fresno for several hours, seeking a more Steinbeckian tent city. Although promising pockets of poverty were observed, no Steinbeckian tent city was found.

At approximately two p.m., the PR returned to the Study Area. Overcoming some initial fear-related resistance to exiting the vehicle, the PR exited the vehicle.

A squat reddish woman was observed in a chair, blunt legs thrust out into the road.

This was Wanda.*

---

* All names have been changed.

Wanda: A Modest Proposal

Wanda was a woman of uncertain ethnicity between thirty and fifty years of age whose face consisted of a series of sun-darkened red-and-purple rounded structures, like rosy cheeks, but located in places on her face where cheeks would not normally be found. Nevertheless, Wanda exuded a wry joviality, as if aware that there were comic aspects to the fact that she was seated, sunburned and barefoot, on a street of houses made of garbage, wearing what appeared to be a set of maroon hospital scrubs.

How are you? the PR inquired.

Could be better, Wanda responded.

Wanda reported that she had recently been hit by a train. (The Study Area was located illegally on railroad land, and its western border was a busy switching yard.) She'd been trying to cross the tracks with her bike. That train could have at least honked, she said. Wanda inquired as to whether the PR would give her a hundred dollars. The PR demurred. Wanda asked whether the PR would give her a kiss. The PR demurred. Wanda stated that the PR "looked rich." The PR protested that he was not rich. Wanda looked pointedly at the project research vehicle, a late-model rental minivan. Wanda showed the PR her train-injured foot, which was red, glazed, and infected. Her big toe was bent at a right angle, as if someone had snapped the big toe at the joint and set it ninety degrees from the correct orientation.

The PR expressed his desire to put up a tent of his own.

Wait, you staying here? Wanda said. How long you staying?

Maybe a week? the PR said.

You married? Wanda said.

Twenty-one years, the PR said.

I'm a rape you, Wanda said.

Meet the Neighbors

The PR's tent was new. He had never assembled it before. All day he'd been worrying about this moment of confused fumbling, and now it was happening. Several more poles than expected tumbled out of the bag. The instructions were observed to be blowing away. The PR felt the eyes of the entire Study Area upon him.

Suddenly, a burst of competence appeared in the form of Valerie, who feverishly began assembling his tent. Valerie was a small woman in her late forties, a grandmother, she said, of seven and a half, wearing John Lennon–esque glasses, baggy men's clothing, and a khaki-colored baseball cap pulled low over broad, friendly features that made her look, someone would later say, "like John Denver on the cover of *Rocky Mountain High*."

Valerie stated that the PR was welcome to stay here, near her compound. The compound was a large, corral-like enclosure defined by a fence of pallets stood on end and draped in black plastic tarping. Inside were: multiple tents; a blue Rubbermaid cart; a sun-faded Little Tikes playhouse; a table made of a cable spool, with ad hoc patio umbrella; a bike frame; and two couches. Entry was gained by lifting/ sliding a pallet laid across a gap in the fence.

Valerie was joined by a diminutive handsome Tibetan-looking man with a long black ponytail and little wool cap with short front brim that gave him the look of someone who should be playing a wood flute in a park in New York City.

This was Ernesto.

As he helped Valerie assemble the tent, Ernesto urgently offered the PR several pieces of advice.

Ernesto's Advice

The PR looked good. Too good. Ernesto himself tried to look not too good. The PR better park that van somewhere else. There were crackheads living up in here. After dark the crackheads would break into the van and steal everything. Even the van. This was not a good place. These were not good people. The PR better take off his wedding ring. They'd come in the night and steal it, taking the finger if necessary. The PR would see tonight how wild it got. A friend of Ernesto's had stayed out here once, to learn about the homeless. After two weeks, he was dead.

They killed him? the PR said.

He killed his own self, Ernesto said. It made him so sad to see how the people are living. He stayed a couple nights. Then two weeks later, he kill himself. I don't want that to happen to you.

The PR observed with some interest that his reaction to the clarification that Ernesto's friend had not been murdered, but had only killed himself in despair, was relief.

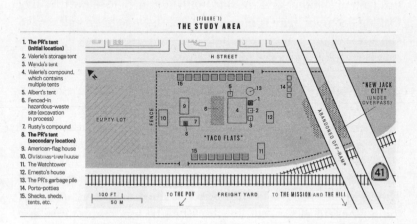

(FIGURE 1)
THE STUDY AREA

1. The PR's tent (initial location)
2. Valerie's storage tent
3. Wanda's tent
4. Valerie's compound, which contains multiple tents
5. Albert's tent
6. Fenced-in hazardous-waste site (excavation in process)
7. Rusty's compound
8. The PR's tent (secondary location)
9. American-flag house
10. Christmas-tree house
11. The Watchtower
12. Ernesto's house
13. The PR's garbage pile
14. Porta-potties
15. Shacks, sheds, tents, etc.

Origins of the Study Area

An overview of the Study Area is presented in Figure 1.

As shown, the Study Area consisted of two subcommunities: one under the overpass, another out in the open. Per Albert, who lived in a tent at Valerie's front gate, the community under the overpass had been named, by its residents, New Jack City. Or as Albert said he sometimes called it, New Crack City.

The open area (where the PR's tent was located) was called Taco Flats. That is in actuality something that I baptized it, said Albert. Me and Valerie were the first ones here. Then your people from Mexico, the paisas, they came here. There was, uh, what's his name? Juachi. And Mundo. There was Sinaloa. And eventually, you know, it was like the old saying, If you build it, they will come. And they sure as heck did. But she was the first one here.

Valerie confirmed that she was the founder of Taco Flats.

Valerie: A Settler's Tale

My husband and me started out underneath the bridge. Two weeks after that, we got our tools stolen and shit like that. So we came down here, got it all flattened down, put our tents up. We were like: Fuck this. So we put up all these tents and shit—my ex-husband gave me that tent, my brother gave me that tent, the church gave me that one, that big one right there is my husband's. That one there's all torn to shit but I'm gonna take it over there and sew it at the women's center. And everybody just moved in beside me.

And Yet Not

This version of events was later contradicted by a woman named Large Jo, a blond oracular woman of sixty always found in a certain shady location on G Street in her wheelchair who said that if anyone had a right to Taco Flats, it was the paisas. They were there first. They'd worked hard, built nice places, framed them out and everything. She had pictures of Pancho when he was framing the first house in Taco Flats. The white guys didn't come in until the paisas had been there awhile.

As will be seen, truth was relative within the Study Area. Truth is relative everywhere but was even more relative within the Study Area. Anything anyone ever claimed during the Study was, at some point, directly contradicted by something someone else claimed. Stories within the Study Area, as will be seen, were rife with exaggeration, omission, or fabrication. It is postulated that this was related to the hardship of material conditions within the Study Area, as well as the prevalence of mental illness within the Study Area. The relation between mental illness and residency within the Study Area is worthy of further study. In some cases, mental illness seemed to be the reason for residence within the Study Area. In other cases, residence within the Study Area seemed to be causing mental illness in individuals who, in a less stressful setting, might not have been mentally ill at all.

The View from the Project Research Center

The day was windy. Following setup, as the PR ferried his things—sleeping bag; mini reading light; roll of toilet paper; approximately twenty (20) moist towelettes; eight (8) bags organic instant oatmeal; useless plastic tent-stake hammer; a copy of *The Savage Detectives* by Roberto Bolaño—from minivan to tent, the tent was observed to be rolling away across the Study Area. An aggressive young man of about eighteen, noticing the PR emerging from the minivan, confronted him angrily. Who was he? What was he doing here? The PR pointed out the rolling-away tent and indicated that it was his. The young man and the PR watched the tent go. The PR's willingness to admit ownership of the rolling tent seemed to convince the angry young man that the PR belonged here.

During this incident, the tent was damaged in several places. The PR, recalling Ernesto's warnings, used his fingers to create, from an existing scuff mark, a security eyehole. In the dwindling light, through the eyehole, a pile of garbage could be observed near the tent. In a heap of discarded clothes sat a white plastic lawn chair, one leg bent beneath it, evoking a racehorse with a broken leg, photographed in midfall. Also in the pile were two mattresses, one of which was hot pink. Also visible was a ribbonlike length of VCR tape fluttering maniacally in the wind; no VCR casing was observed. Also visible were a white plastic fork, a single huarache sandal, and a piece of thin green plastic tubing, like a miniature garden hose.

Business Time

The security eyehole provided initial data on Study Area activities.

Vehicles would enter the Study Area and sit idling in the empty zone of hard dirt and vestigial asphalt that separated Taco Flats and New Jack City. A shadowy figure would shuffle out to the car. The shadowy figure might lean into, or enter, the car. A short while later, the shadowy figure would dash off in the direction from which he or she had come. The car would then drive away.

The wind, if it blew just right, would lift the front window flap, affording the PR a view of a fortresslike structure behind Ernesto's house—which, in time, he would learn was called the Watchtower. A man's head could be observed sticking out above the roof, as if he had been beheaded and his head placed on the roof. When a car entered the Study Area, this man would emit an angry-sounding cry which, to the PR, came to seem like a sort of Study Area anthem: Hey! Hey! Hey!

If the vehicle slowed near the PR's tent, this meant the driver had chosen to make his purchase from the group affiliated with the man whose head was sticking out of the roof, i.e., from Taco Flats. If the vehicle proceeded into the empty zone, this meant the driver had chosen to make his purchase from New Jack City, whose men were also continually barking: Hey! Hey! Hey!

That is, a spirited capitalist competition appeared to be occurring between the two locales.

A Comfort Station Indeed

Sometimes an individual would enter the Study Area on foot, and a brief transaction would occur on what would have been the lawn of the PR's tent, had the PR's tent had a lawn. Observing the illicit transactions occurring on his nonlawn gave the PR a giddy, powerful feeling. The dealers didn't even know he was in there, taking notes.

Soon, however, he became aware of an urge to urinate.

A row of porta-potties had been placed, by the city of Fresno, approximately fifty yards from New Jack City. A person wishing to attain the porta-potties thus needed to walk directly toward New Jack City, and nearly enter New Jack City, thus making himself easy prey for those crackheads who all evening had been wondering where the individual who had arrived at the Study Area in a luxurious rented minivan had gone.

Still, he couldn't very well pee in his tent. Earlier, Valerie had kindly given him a bottle of water. Could he pee in there? It was a little early in the Study, the PR felt, for such an extreme manifestation of cowardice.

As the PR crossed the empty zone, he observed himself to be walking in a deliberately shuffling gait, with a slight fake limp, in an attempt to appear more homeless.

The PR lingered inside the potty. It felt safe. Safer than the tent. The potty had a door with a lock. It didn't smell nearly as bad as he'd expected. Someone had been in here with some disinfectant or something. Well, he couldn't stay here all night, could he? If the potty were only larger, and a bit cleaner, he could lie down. He could go back, fetch his sleeping bag . . .

The PR reluctantly left the porta-potty and started back across the empty zone.

A gold Mercedes entered the Study Area, passed in front of the PR, and sat idling in the empty zone. It was a beautiful car and appeared to shimmer in the combined moonlight/streetlight. Several shadowy figures left the area under the bridge and raced toward the Mercedes.

The PR made for his tent.

How you getting by, kiddo? Wanda said, as the PR rapidly approached.

Okay, said the PR. Everyone seems nice.

Uh, well, said Wanda. They're all crackheads.

They are? said the PR.

Sure, said Wanda. I'm one, too.

You're a crackhead, said the PR.

Just a little bit, said Wanda.

Listen to the Music of the Night

The night was full of sounds. These included: the whoosh of traffic from Highway 41; sirens; the metal-on-metal sound of freight trains coupling and uncoupling; hammering sounds as several Study Area residents made nighttime improvements to their dwellings; a bullfrog in the junk pile next to the PR's tent.

Through the night, heedless of the human convention of staying quiet while others tried to sleep, the Study Area residents emitted shouts, invective, imprecations, jokes, requests for clarification, and non sequiturs, including:

(1)

AFRICAN-AMERICAN WOMAN:
[facetious, affectionate] You niggah bee-yotch!

AFRICAN-AMERICAN MAN:
[in affectionate response] You bee-yotch!

(2)

FEMALE VOICE, UNCERTAIN ETHNICITY:
Hey, motherfucker!

MALE VOICE, UNCERTAIN ETHNICITY: Shut up!

FEMALE VOICE: You shut up!

(3)

IN A NEARBY TENT: [A loud fart.]

WOMAN: [affectionately] Stop it!

The woman and a man laugh together.

MAN: [imitating a popular TV commercial] Can you hear me now?

(4)

MALE VOICE: [angrily, into cell phone] I don't like that! I don't know you! I don't like that!

(5)

MALE VOICE: [calling out desperately] Mikey! Mikey! Do you know what time it is?

It occurred to the PR that he was not the only person in the Study Area anxious for the night to end.

Some Data Regarding the PR's Mental State, Night One

The wind picked up, twisting and pulling the PR's tent, exactly mimicking the effect of a strong man trying to wrest the tent from the ground prior to entering the tent to cut off the tent-dweller's finger, in order to steal his wedding ring.

In his sleep, the PR dreamed he was a beautiful blond woman, like Sharon Stone in *Basic Instinct*, who possessed considerable confidence in her powers of seduction. The PR was naked, in a hot tub, surrounded by male inquisitors. The PR posed and preened in the hot tub, refusing to answer the questions. This approach, it seemed, had worked before. This part of the dream was seen from the point of view of the PR: He could feel his feminine power, sense the mounting frustration of his inquisitors. Then the dream cut to an external point of view: a shot of the PR, female, naked, wet, being carried away on a stretcher, mouth bandaged and bleeding, vagina bandaged and bleeding, mouth and vagina having been irreparably damaged by brutal phallic intrusion.

The PR woke in an agitated state. The meaning of the dream was clear: a combination of naïveté and condescension could prove catastrophic.

The PR slept fitfully until just before dawn, when Wanda, dragging a plastic garbage can past the tent, inquired whether he was still alive. He replied that he was. Didn't know if you survived, Wanda said, then went off shouting, Morning! Morning! Morning! at the top of her lungs, to all corners of the camp, in what struck the PR as a kind of protective/preemptive birdcall.

Early-Morning Observations

A sparrow was observed to light on the roof of Ernesto's house. Just outside the PR's tent was a mound of feces, which the PR assumed to be dog feces, although the size of the mound did not rule out a human source and furthermore did not seem commensurate with the size of the only dog thus far observed in the immediate area, i.e., Ernesto's tiny dachshund, Chiquito. Near the feces was a pair of rusty pruning shears, which the PR secured and placed inside the tent for security purposes.

During Day One, the PR had heard frequent mentions of an area west of the Study Area, across the freight yard, which included several facilities catering to the homeless, in addition to another, smaller, tent community called the Hill.

The PR resolved to spend the morning exploring this area.

Site Visit: The Hill

The Hill was a long row of tents running parallel to G Street under the freeway overpass. The PR entered through the gate on East California Avenue. A chained, barking pit-bull mix was observed. Two African-American men in their late twenties approached. The taller of the men inquired as to what the PR needed. He had weed, the man said, he had rock. The PR here affected the Study Area habit of prevarication. He had no money, he said, making his voice weary, he was totally wiped out. Feeling the conspicuous absence of a reasonable explanation for his presence, the PR asked if it would be possible for him to put up his tent. The tall man responded warmly that it would. Everyone was welcome. He then produced a complicated wad of electronic devices, including a large pink cell phone that appeared to be from some earlier era of cell phones. The PR reminded the man that he was wiped out. The man accepted this graciously and then, desperate to sell something, played what he evidently felt to be some sort of trump card.

Got a white girl in there, he said in an undertone, indicating a tent in the weeds. White girl with red hair.

That she was a white girl seemed to be one selling point. That she had red hair seemed to be another. The PR demurred. It was tempting, but he was still wiped out. He continued up the Hill. He could sense the men behind him, discussing his inexplicable presence.

Then, at the top of the Hill, he saw something extraordinary, a tent unique among all tents observed in the Study Area. The owner had built, as a platform for his tent, an impressive treated-lumber deck. The deck was beautiful. It evoked suburbia. It drew the eye, its series of straight, clean lines conveying an almost military precision. If the Hill had been a medieval community (and it might well have been, with all the wood smoke and squalor), the resident of this highest tent would have been its king, surpassing all others in his mastery of the physical realm.

No one appeared to be home.

A Moral Inquiry

Retreating down G Street, the PR considered the white girl with red hair. Was she being held against her will? Likely she was a junkie, in some sort of long-term relationship with the tall man, who served as her pimp. Who had she been before she was the white girl with red hair? The PR reminded himself that the white girl with red hair had been a whore in that tent long before he arrived and would be a whore in that tent long after he left. All of these people had been living thus before he arrived and would continue living thus long after he went home. Anything he could do for them would only comprise a small push in a positive direction before the tremendous momentum of their negative tendencies reasserted itself. The PR was put in mind of a single shot from a gun being fired into a massive orbiting planet.

Still, what would happen if he decided to abandon the Study and commit all of his resources to the sole purpose of extracting the white girl with red hair from that tent and getting her into whatever treatment program was required? Wasn't it possible—wasn't it, in fact, likely, given his resources—that he could effect a positive change in the life of the white girl with red hair? And if so, wasn't it, at some level, a moral requirement that he do so? That is: by continuing down G Street, the white girl with the red hair becoming less real with his every step, was he not essentially consenting to her continued presence back there in the tent, waiting to be sold, by the tall man, to anyone who happened by? Wasn't he, in a sense, not only allowing that to happen but assuring that it would happen?

Yes.

Yes, he was.

The Pov

North of the Hill was a facility central to the life of all Study Area residents: Poverello House ("the Pov"). Free meals were available here, no questions asked. Laundry could be done, showers taken, medical assistance obtained. At times the existence of the Pov seemed like a kind of miracle of clear-sighted, unconditional generosity. At other times, it seemed like a gigantic enabling machine: the free food supplied by the Pov seemed to be the main reason for the existence of the Study Area.

Entered from Santa Clara Street, the Pov presented as the campus of a small community college: black wrought-iron fence, Spanish-style buildings, trees, recessed courtyards, milling people. A man with long white hair passed by in an electric wheelchair. The PR asked if the line across the courtyard was the line for breakfast. No, the man explained, that was the line for showers. That line there, the longer line—that was the line for breakfast.

How did this breakfast deal work? the PR asked. Did you need a ticket, or did you—

The man's face brightened.

No, you just go in there and eat, he said.

Many Are His Battles

The handsome bearded young man looked like a German U-boat captain in a movie except for a long string of snot that ran from his nose, through his mustache, down to his chin. The snot string looked fixed and immovable, as if poured from plastic. The young man stated that he was dying of internal injuries; the general and his men had beaten him up just outside the gate of the Pov. Heather was also dying. Heather was his girlfriend. She was from England. If Heather's parents back in England found out about all of this—about Heather dying, the low manner in which she was living—they would die, too. He seemed baffled and humiliated to have come to this pass. He had not always been so low. He had served in the French Foreign Legion, had spent time in Algeria, in the Sudan.

The PR and the young man entered the dining room. The young man mentioned that while in the Sudan, he had once won a whole war by himself. He indicated a group of men at a table.

That's four of my men, he said sadly. That one there? He was my sergeant.

The alleged former sergeant was an ancient Mexican-American man merrily chewing.

I think your best friend's got a Ph.D. after his name, a sunburned man in a black bandanna said to the snot-bearded young man.

I started out with twenty-three thousand men, the young man said, looking at the table of four with affection. And them's all that's left.

Better make that one less, the man in the bandanna said. 'Cause you're fucking brain-dead.

Breakfast consisted of apple oatmeal, a muffin, an apple, and chocolate milk. The PR sat with the man in the bandanna. The young man with the snot in his beard sat elsewhere. He was never joined by Heather, or any woman, leading the PR to conclude that Heather existed only in the bearded young man's mind, a notion later confirmed by Valerie, who said she knew this guy, he'd been dating this one Mexican chick for a while, but then she'd left him, probably because he was so fucking nuts.

A Partial Camp Death Roll, in the Collective Voice

Oh, lots of people die in here.

The Ho man died. Gladys died. Ferdinand over here died. A guy by the name of Tupac got ran over by a train right here. Richard died, the guy they called the Birdman. He got hit by a train, just back in January, January 31. Because the Mission denied him to stay overnight, he got a blanket from a friend and stayed behind one of the train cars, and lo and behold, they were switching at night, and he was asleep, and evidently they just popped him like a strawberry basically. Really a super guy. But mentally challenged. He would shoot birds, thinking they were there. Very strange fellow. Not with an actual gun, no. Just with his fingers.

There was Edson. He was alcoholic, a good man, but mind you, his son was a professional baseball player. He could have lived differently, but he chose to be out here drinking. There was a lady got hit on the freeway couple months ago. She was crossing the 99, wasn't paying attention. We've had overdoses, stabbings. One homeless guy got burned in his blankets. Some juveniles poured gas on him. We had two people shot here in the past three months. One of them, I was sitting right here when I heard five sharp pops from under the bridge. Then here came this little gal, racing by, shrieking, I told you I'd do it! I told you I'd do it! And she disappeared from Tent City and was never seen again, and the guy she shot in the face died.

People come here to die. There's a guy dying here right now. Name of Rusty. Got bone cancer. They offered him an experimental treatment, but he don't want to be no guinea pig, and I don't blame him.

Just a lot of pain out here.

We got a woman, Pamela—you seen her? Nice-looking lady. Looks like a teacher. Always holds one arm up over her head, like she's snapping pictures. Used to be a married woman, out in the world, with a kid and a house and a husband. Then, one day, the husband executes the kid with a gunshot to the head, then shoots himself in the head, too. Just leaves Pamela alive. Then she comes out here, gets raped. You'll see her walking around, acting all crazy. But she's not that crazy. She'll talk to you. If she knows you. And if she wants to talk to you.

And sickness, don't even get me started. You get ticks out here, you get bedbugs. Look at my leg. At least I ain't got crabs, because I haven't fucked in so long.

Ha ha.

The Look of Love

The PR accompanied Valerie to the recycle center, to gain insight into the basic economy of the Study Area.

Stuck in behind the various pipes and wires of the big recycling-center scale were a number of small stuffed figures of the type won at carnivals, including SpongeBob SquarePants and Stewie from *Family Guy*, stained oily black from months of being crammed grotesquely behind the various wires and pipes, twisted into grotesque postures, as if longing to escape.

Valerie: Usually there's a big old white woman that's over here doing this shit.

Two gentlemen approached the scale, pushing a shopping cart each.

Valerie: Quack-Quack! What's up?

One of the gentlemen, presumably Quack-Quack, responded: Quack-Quack!, as if this were a tradition between him and Valerie. Per Valerie, these men were a gay couple. Per Valerie, it was surprising that Quack-Quack was still with this same guy, Quack-Quack not being known for lengthy relationships.

The aforementioned big old white woman appeared and began operating the scale.

VALERIE: How's your grandbaby?
WOMAN: He's fine, adorable. You know.
VALERIE: My husband's coming home from jail in two weeks.
WOMAN: I know you're gonna be busy in two weeks.
VALERIE: Oh, hell yeah. I'm gonna be sore, too.
WOMAN: [laughing] Shame on you!

As she stood at the payout counter, the look on Valerie's face remained that of a schoolgirl with a crush. Her earnings for the transaction totaled $4.20.

Why Valerie's Husband Is in Jail

Valerie's husband, Pablo, was in jail for beating up that punk Rusty. Rusty looked just like a guy named Rusty would look, Valerie said: a cross between Danny Bonaduce and that Mad Magazine dude. He'd been drunk on vodka and took her cigarettes. She wasn't putting up with that shit and grabbed them back. Then Rusty punched her in the face. Yeah, with his fist. When Pablo found out, he beat the shit out of Rusty. Nearly killed him. Somebody ran and got the security guard. The security guard called the police.

Valerie produced Pablo's driver's license. Pablo was a handsome, sturdy Mexican-American with shoulder-length hair that gave him the appearance of a buff confrontational Jesus.

When Pablo got out, Valerie said, Rusty was gonna be dead.

Wasn't Rusty the guy with bone cancer? the PR said.

Yup, Valerie said.

Two Who Got Away

Ernesto invited the PR to attend a Fresno Grizzlies baseball game. The way the homeless of Fresno attended a baseball game was to stand at a fence in right-center field, through which was afforded an unimpeded view of the game.

About the third inning, Ernesto and the PR were joined by a colorful couple, Lyle and Brenda. Lyle wore a 1950s-fedora-style hat, the kind former hippies began wearing ironically in the early 1970s as a way of underscoring how little they had in common with, for example, Frank Sinatra. Brenda, who at all times stayed close by Lyle's side, presented as a fussy toothless woman bright with affection for all things.

The following conversation ensued, under the occasional roar of the crowd.

ERNESTO: So you out of the streets for good.
LYLE: We're out of the streets for gooooooood.
BRENDA: We even have a pet rat named Zooey. After the J. D. Salinger novel *Franny and Zooey*.

Brenda had a drunken slur that seemed at first like a parody of a drunken slur but then never went away.

LYLE: Can't have a dog, can't have a cat, but the guy said: You can have a rat. So we went and bought this rat, the biggest, meanest motherfucker . . .

There followed a discussion about a liquor store that, lamentably, didn't open for another hour. Lyle said you had to be careful in that neighborhood, because you'd hear (Lyle lapsed into an imitation of a clichéd African-American voice): Gotta dollah? Gotta quarter?

That's amazing, Lyle continued. Panhandlers panhandling panhandlers. I trip out on that, I'm sorry.

Lyle and Brenda had formerly lived on a loading dock. Ernesto had once lived on this dock. But Lyle and Brenda now had an apartment. At the Peacock. Near Tulare and F. Above that former fish store. Those nice brick apartments.

BRENDA: Well, you know what's nice?
LYLE: To have a carpet.
BRENDA: And a microwave. And you plug it in and it works.
LYLE: And a toilet.
BRENDA: A shower.
LYLE: We used to be at the Komodo.

BRENDA: Are you boys at the Komodo?

ERNESTO: We're at the camp. The H Street camp.

LYLE: Well, that's better than the Komodo. Fuck the Komodo.

PR: What's the Komodo?

LYLE: The Komodo's right across from Central Valley Fish. They charge four hundred dollars for a room the size of your ass. It's bullshit. You gotta share the same toilet, there ain't no kitchen. On a good day there's a microwave and a watercooler.

BRENDA: Oh, we have a nice pet rat. Zooey is so wonderful. You boys can have dinner with us.

LYLE: We're having salmon tonight. That rat's gonna tear into that. He eats everything we do. He's a good little critter. He nibbles a little, but he don't bite hard.

BRENDA: He kisses me.

LYLE: He don't draw blood.

BRENDA: He kisses me. He puts his tongue in my mouth. Lyle said he never saw a rat do that. Doesn't he kiss me? He puts his feet like this on either side of my mouth, and he puts his tongue in my mouth. He kisses the hell out of me.

LYLE: You know why we got a rat? Because the guy that owns the place—Larry—he was forced to eat them as a youngster.

BRENDA: He's from China. He is four feet tall.

LYLE: He's from China.

BRENDA: He will not let us have a cat.

LYLE: His parents fed him rats. So we gotta hide the rat . . .

BRENDA: No, they fed him cat.

LYLE: We gotta hide the rat, because Larry smiles at the rat, like: hey, dinner!

BRENDA: And I go: Lawrence! I call him Lawrence. He hates it.

LYLE: Don't mind us, we're crazy. Come on, honey. Let's go around the front, hit those two barrels, get some recyclables for tomorrow.

BRENDA: Oy vey.

LYLE: You guys be cool!

BRENDA: I grew up with a lot of Jewish.

LYLE: Then we'll get us another bottle of vodka and get fucked up.

Brenda and Lyle walked off into the night, seemingly awash in happiness. Although they appeared to be, as Ernesto claimed they were, alcoholics, and were, by their own admission, on their way to panhandle and dig through trash cans until it was time to return home and kiss the rat on the mouth before sitting down to dinner with the rat, still, a significant difference was observed between Lyle/Brenda and the people living at the Study Area, namely a wacky, buoyant quality the onlooker felt as hope. Had Lyle and Brenda always possessed this quality? Because Ernesto seemed subtly irritated by this quality, the PR was inclined to think it was a new quality, related to the fact that they now had a home, which had empowered them and taken the edge off their shame.

A Message from an Old Friend

The first three nights of the Study, the PR woke in the night with a hard-on unique in that it felt completely devoid of sexuality. It was more like a fear hard-on. Its function seemed to be to wake the PR up so he could reevaluate his safety. Why are you sleeping? the PR's penis seemed to be saying. Shouldn't you be awake and watchful? His arms and legs would be freezing, but his cock would be hot and ready to flee. Was he horny? Did he want to masturbate? Ha ha. In here? No. He'd go back to sleep, but his penis would stay awake, complaining, at full attention, about the danger in which it had been placed so late in its life, having served so honorably for so long.

About Day Four, the fear hard-ons ceased. The PR believed this to be related to a general evolving comfort with his surroundings.

Midstudy Data Summary

The crack dealing continued apace, day and night. During the course of the Study, the PR was offered crack, weed, and prescription muscle relaxers, as well as comic books and sunflower seeds "of all different flavors."

Sometimes the Study Area seemed like a tumor that had burst on the side of capitalism. Other times it seemed like something ancient and sensible: people building dwellings, then improving them. These houses seemed like an intelligent revolt against what modern culture had declared a house, i.e., an elaborate box built by professional builders of such boxes, part of a mutual-enrichment scheme between city and builder. But were these not houses? Were there not rugs in there and chairs and treasured little stupid items? Did the residents not look forward to returning there at the end of a long day?

At times the Study Area residents seemed bumbling, sweet, hapless, and victimized. Other times they seemed vicious, aggressive, and vituperative, unable to say a kind word about one another—self-defeating, excuse-making machines, spoiled rotten by free food.

Sometimes it seemed unimaginable that such poverty could exist in America and that the residents accepted it so passively. Why didn't the place explode? Other times—when, for example, the PR had been out driving around the pleasant neighborhoods of Fresno—the Study Area seemed like a tiny blip on the radar, the necessary detritus of an insanely affluent country. The presence of three hundred losers in a city of winners seemed not like a crisis, but rather a reasonable embodiment of Christ's admonition that the poor would always be with us.

(FIGURE 2)
THE CRUEL DOTTED LINE

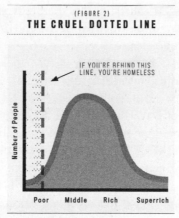

The Cruel Dotted Line

Figure 2 illustrates the distribution of wealth in an idealized capitalist culture. At the far right are the super rich; we note that there are not very many. In the middle, in greater abundance, are those of average wealth. To the far left are the poor. Now, let the dotted vertical line represent the level at which one becomes so poor as to become homeless.

The goal of any citizen in a capitalist society is to avoid blundering left of the dotted line. The goal of the society at large should be to minimize the negative consequences for those individuals who do happen to blunder into that region, i.e., show mercy. The true measure of a culture might be said to lie in its answer to the question: how severely are those who blunder to the left of the line punished?

The Study Area presented a unique and vexing case: with all basic needs (food, shelter, laundry, etc.) met, did all suffering vanish? Based on the observations made during the Study, it did not. The well-fed homeless of Fresno, it was observed, suffered considerably.

They suffered with feeling inadequate and left behind. They spent considerable time and energy telling and retelling the story of their lives, as if looking for the place where things had gone astray. They were lonely and seemed to long for the better things in life: ease, property, companionship. Perhaps not surprisingly, this longing sometimes manifested as anger; also impatience, derision, a tendency to gossip ungenerously. In this the Study Area was similar to any other human community, but with the endemic poverty serving as a kind of process accelerator.

Site Visit: Return to the Hill

On the afternoon of Day Three, the PR sat drinking with Jesse O., the man who had built the regal porch on the Hill. The treated porch lumber was redolent of affluence. The beer was cold. Across G Street, an ancient black woman sat on the curb in the midday heat, head between her knees. Fifty feet away, an ancient black man sat in the same posture. If only they could meet and comfort one another, the PR thought. But both appeared unconscious. A pickup flew past, ruffling their garments.

Jesse and the PR discussed many things in an increasingly friendly, telegraphic, and blurry manner. After the painful breakup of his marriage, Jesse had left Los Angeles, headed north. Passing through Fresno, he became part of a hundred-car pileup in the fog and nearly lost a leg. The hospital dropped him off in front of the Rescue Mission without even a wheelchair. He lived in the Mission briefly but didn't like it—didn't like the rules, the way they shoved religion down your throat, the general lack of dignity—so he came out here and built this deck and put up this tent and was now just waiting for the insurance settlement so he could get the hell out of here.

Once, Jesse had gone to a psychic. The psychic asked Jesse what he most desired in the world. Jesse said: to be anointed from the Horn of David. The psychic predicted this would come to pass. The PR felt he should know what the Horn of David was. But all that came to mind was a coat of many colors. One day a preacher was blessing Jesse, and Jesse saw that the container from which the blessing oil was being drawn was made in the exact likeness of the actual Horn of David. Thus the prophecy was fulfilled.

The PR's forty-ounce Bud Ice was nearly gone.

Yahoo, the PR thought. Now we're getting somewhere.

Back in Los Angeles, Jesse made $300 a pop for personalized homemade greeting cards which would include drawings of, for example, animals or race cars, as well as a personalized poem he would inscribe in calligraphy, such as the following example, composed in honor of the birth of a friend's first son, which the PR drunkenly copied into the project notebook:

we have a son
just a baby, our baby
the image of both you and i
so pure, so innocent so
fascinating is life's beginning.
by the grace of god and the virtue of heredity
and the goodness of nurture
set out to become the product of his unique experiences.
ever still, if meeting you was all i had ever accomplished in life,
my past would be one pleasant memory.
and i thank god for your birth. and i love you. thank you.
signed: jesse o.

Jesse stated that the mother of the baby (to whom the lines "Ever still, if meeting you was all I had ever accomplished in life, my / Past would be one pleasant memory" had been slyly directed) had accused him, Jesse, of trying to use the poem, for which she was paying, to hit up on her. Jesse confessed that this indeed had been his intent. But there was nothing wrong with trying, right?

People around here looked up to Jesse, he knew that. He was known as El Sabudería (which he translated from street lingo as "Mr. Wisdom"), tried to keep the peace up here—not by force, but by listening to people, hearing them out—but it was hard. People were crazy, people were angry, people were on crack. The sadness made it a volatile place.

Where was he, the PR, living at? Jesse asked.

Over in the tent city, the PR said.

Yeah, but where exactly? Jesse said.

The PR described the location of his tent.

Jesse was mortified. There was dealing going on there all the time. The PR wasn't safe. They were going down there right now, get him moved, over by the white people, to the north end of Taco Flats, with some friends of his who'd look out for the PR.

A Step Down

The PR, Jesse, Ernesto, and a couple of white guys were hustling across the Study Area, carrying the PR's tent between them like a wounded guy on a stretcher.

Mobile home! the PR shouted.

Some Mexicans in a doorway laughed at the PR, not with him. The PR could feel the dead weight of his stuff inside the tent, sliding downhill to the center sag.

The group stopped in front of a compound at the southwest corner of the Study Area and hefted the tent over the gate with a strange urgency, as if the need to work toward some common cause, long dormant from chronic unemployment, had suddenly come alive.

The matron of the compound appeared, a kindly woman with a touch of a Mexican accent. Where would the PR like his tent to go?

She suggested a spot. The tent was dropped. Someone, outraged, pointed out that, oriented that way, the PR wouldn't even be able to get in. The tent was lifted, rotated, dropped again.

Jesse embraced the PR. He, Jesse, could at least sleep now. This was one of Rusty's compounds. He'd be safe here. Rusty was good people.

Rusty? the PR thought. The same Rusty who'd punched Valerie in the face, whose ass had been kicked by Pablo, who was supposedly dying of bone cancer?

Once Jesse left, the PR asked the Matron why Jesse felt his old location was dangerous.

Well, she said, the dangerous thing was, maybe in the night you hear, you know, a damsel in distress, or something like that? And you think: I should go help her. Only, in here, there ain't no damsels. Everybody be drunk, be partying, you hear something, someone getting hit or slapped, you go to help and wind up getting stabbed yourself or whatever . . .

The PR liked Jesse. But Jesse had sort of bitched him around, hadn't he? He hadn't wanted to move, but Jesse had made him. He was now in a relationship with Rusty, living under Rusty's protection. Rusty, who had punched Valerie, grandmother of seven and a half, in the face. What if Rusty tried to bitch him around? Would he be expected to fight Rusty? This was a world of badly directed energy, primitive idiotic vows, pointless, vicious fights. The disposition of a cup or license plate, the nonpayment of a two-dollar debt, might come to violence if the people involved got shitfaced enough. It was too much. He needed a break. Where was Ernesto? Did Ernesto want to go to the ball game? Tonight they'd get real seats, like real people, leave this moronic place behind.

Let's go, said Ernesto.

At the Ball Game

Near the dugout, a group of Asian-American teenagers were flirting with the players. Ernesto and the PR sat looking with longing and consternation at the demonstrative slender Asian girls in their tight jeans and lingerie tops and spiked heels. It occurred to the PR that in these girls, affluence manifested as confidence: a sort of hubris, an overflow of capability and life force and sexuality that felt, in this context, almost bullying.

Ernesto was sad about the PR's new location, sad and worried, mournful even. It was much more dangerous than the old place, especially if Rusty and his friends got to drinking. The PR asked if there was crack in his new neighborhood. Ernesto said there was crack everywhere. Ernesto had done crack himself once, he admitted, a long time ago, back in Vietnam.

Crack? the PR said. In Vietnam?

The PR had always thought of crack as a newish drug.

Yes, they'd come across the plant in the wild and smoked it right there in the jungle, Ernesto said. That had been a crazy time. Before their first battle, their officers had even injected them with steroids to make them less scared.

At the front gate, Ernesto turned suddenly self-conscious about his appearance.

Maybe, he suggested, you could say I'm your friend who just got off work and didn't have time to change clothes.

The PR had tender feelings for Ernesto, who was courteous and intelligent and always seemed happy to see the PR. And yet Valerie had claimed Ernesto was a miserable punk, a liar. Albert agreed: Ernesto was a bitch, because when Ernesto's wife, Jodi, got beat up, Ernesto just cowered behind her.

They took their excellent box seats and had a couple of beers. The Fresno mascot appeared, a yellow-orange bear with stained fur, standing on a chair back to perform a groin thrust in some college kid's face. Ernesto recalled that he had gone to grade school with Barbara Bush.

Barbara Bush? the PR said. That doesn't quite . . .

Laura Bush, Ernesto corrected himself.

You went to school with Laura Bush? the PR asked.

It was at DeZavala Elementary, in Midland, Texas, Ernesto said. When he first saw her, he'd believed her to be a Mexican girl. She looks a little bit Mexican, he explained. He had a crush on her. He remembered they used to have to stand in a big field before school, for attendance. He would look over, find her. It always made him happy to see her.

Then Ernesto grew up, moved to Amarillo, got drafted, was sent to Vietnam. His girlfriend loyally waited for him.

I came home, he said, asked her to marry me. She say okay, sounds good, man. We got married. It was good in Amarillo. But then we lost our first kid. And I got into trouble with drinking. This was way back in '85. In '89, that was when I lost my wife. In a car accident. You know the way it is, the road going to the mall? That's the way. That's where it happened. Interstate 40. So I said okay. That was really hard. And I took my little daughter to my mom and I say: You know what? I'll be back. I told her: I'll be back. But I never came back. I never saw my daughter again after that. After my wife died, I just lost everything.

After the death of their infant son, his wife had gone a little crazy, he said. She used to go out to the graveyard and try to dig the baby up. Then she died herself. His current wife, Jodi, is always saying that the reason he refuses to own a car is his first wife's death in that car crash. And it's true, Ernesto says. Her death was the end of him.

The PR excused himself, went to the bathroom, stood at the urinal, fighting tears.

Jesus, he thought. Jesus Christ. Would Valerie and Albert still consider Ernesto a bitch and a punk if they knew about his dead son and his wife digging up their dead baby, and that same wife shortly dead herself, and their daughter abandoned all these years? Hell, maybe they would. Mercy was, it seemed, in short supply in the Study Area, and Valerie and Albert had stories of their own.

Last night, Fresno had lost big. Tonight, Fresno was ahead. If Fresno won, Ernesto stated, there would be fireworks. You could see the fireworks from the camp. But tonight, sitting inside here, they would really be able to see them. That is, if Fresno won.

Fresno continued to lead until the top of the eighth, then fell apart: a Tacoma single, a walk, a double, and then Fresno was down by three in the bottom of the ninth, and the saddened crowd acutely felt the impossibility of hitting a pitched ball even once, and were then confirmed in their pessimism by three straight Grizzly outs, and the game was over.

No fireworks, the PR said.

No fireworks, said Ernesto, in a not unhappy tone that seemed to indicate he'd never really expected them anyway.

Revelation: A Brief Flash-Forward

A few days later, inspired by Ernesto's story, the PR sneaked away from camp and Googled Ernesto's brother in Odessa and gave him a call.

Yes, he had a brother named Ernesto, the guy said, but he hadn't seen him in fifteen years. Last they knew, he was living in Fresno. If this man really was Ernesto, the brother would love to talk to him. The PR then told the man everything he knew about Ernesto. Their family was from Guatemala, the brother confirmed. He himself, Ernesto's alleged brother, was, yes, a preacher in Odessa, whose middle name was, in fact, Rudolpho. But something was off. Ernesto had never been to Vietnam. Ernesto had never been in the military at all. Ernesto had said he was sixty-five? He was nowhere near sixty-five. Ernesto had a son who died as a baby, yes. But he never had a daughter. Absolutely not. Their mother was still alive, and if a daughter had been left with her, they would have, uh, noticed. So something was off.

Something's off all right, the PR thought. Everyone in this place is a liar, even sweet, broken Ernesto.

Enough Is Enough

After the game, Ernesto and the PR walked back to the camp. It was quiet because, Ernesto said, everyone was flat busted. It would get lively and dangerous when people who got money from the government got their money from the government.

Inside the PR's tent, it looked like a tornado had hit. He hadn't been back inside since the transport. He wished desperately to be back in his old spot. Good old Valerie, good old Wanda. But now attention had been called to his presence. Jesse, as he'd led the tent movement, had made it clear to everyone listening that the PR was not homeless but here for an important purpose. He was doing a

Study. Jesse had called over one of the guys from the Watchtower, told him that, though it might look like the PR was a narc, the PR was not a narc, just a guy doing a Study. The Watchtower guy said he had no problem with a guy doing a Study, as long as the Study didn't mention drugs.

Everything seemed to have changed in some unhappy way.

The PR woke to the sound of a woman being fucked or hit, he couldn't tell which. Her cries were rhythmic and laden with sorrow. Woman, he thought, you really are the nigger of the world. Unless that is a pleasure sound. And even then, you still are. Because look where you are, and who you're getting that pleasure from, and at what cost.

Enough was enough. He had a wife, he had kids. He had to get out of here before something bad happened. He was lying about who he was as much as anybody else in here, and it now seemed clear that the uncovering of this lie must lead to resentment, and resentment, in turn, to some retributive cost.

Time to go.

First he'd have to give away all his stuff: his sleeping bag and pad, his little light, the tent itself. Wanda had been asking for the tent. Valerie had advised him against giving the tent to that little crackhead Wanda. He'd also considered giving it to Suzanna, a lost soul just out of jail, stranded here in Fresno with no tent of her own, also a crackhead, but a crackhead more adrift than Wanda, who, though a crackhead, was also well connected and fat and slothful, always begging and playing the angles. Per Wanda, Suzanna had sold her jail-issued train ticket for crack; why give a brand-new tent to someone like that? By rights, Valerie should get the tent. Valerie was his pal. Valerie was no crackhead. Valerie was a grandmother of seven and a half. Then again, Valerie already had like five tents. Why did she need another one? Arguing in Wanda's favor was the fact that she had been hit by a train and could barely walk and was awfully genial and forgiving for someone so down on her luck.

Jesus, he couldn't wait to get out of here.

The camp dogs were going nuts, stirred up by someone strolling the camp and whistling a repetitive seven-note figure. The dogs in here were like the people, the PR reflected: They liked to bark unhappily at shit for no reason. The barks and yips gave way to the sound of vicious outright fighting. No one intervened. The dogs were left on their own, to rend, tear, and kill one another.

As the PR started to doze off, a sound came from the freight yard, a beautiful echo-chamber freight-whistle effect that sounded like this: Whhhhhyy did it? Whhy why why did it? Whhhhhy?

The whistle made a long show. It was a gorgeous lovely sound to be half-awake to.

Then the whistle left off and there came the most complex exotic birdsong he'd ever heard, a sound made more beautiful by its occurrence in such a godforsaken place, as if the bird did not discriminate but made beauty wherever it went, just because it could, a song that then resolved itself into what it actually was: the yelp of a dog in pain—kicked, maybe, or wounded in a fight, or just tied too long to a fence by its absent, wasted master.

The Cratchit Confusion

At times, as indicated above, the PR found certain residents of the Study Area irritating, even maddening. At one particularly low point, when very tired, not himself at all, the PR, who in real life prided himself on his kindheartedness, even wrote, in the project notebook: "Exterminate the brutes." For several days afterward, he felt bad about this while, at the same time, continuing to feel exasperated with the Study Area residents. Then the PR realized the error of his thinking, an error he thereafter thought of as The Cratchit Confusion.

Bob Cratchit, the hero of Charles Dickens's novel *A Christmas Carol*, is poor yet virtuous. He is honest, forthright, hardworking, clean, and articulate. He loves his family and is forgiving of those who oppress him. He is, in other words, easy to sympathize with. In the real world, however, the unfortunate may not be so likable. They may be stupid, dishonest, lazy, or mean. They may obfuscate, they may attack those weaker than themselves, they may claim their poverty is the fault of an unfair world, they may invent lives for themselves in which they are heroic sages, ahead of the curve. These negative qualities, in fact, may be the root cause of their misfortune.

But to love the unfortunate, it is not necessary to feel fond of them or tenderness toward them. Momentary irritations are inevitable, the PR came to feel; they are also irrelevant. All we must do is what we would do if we could see the unfortunate purely. Our minds can be kind when our hearts cannot. In time, he predicted, his irritation would recede and all that would remain would be feelings of sadness and protectiveness toward the Study Area residents, who, after all, had not killed or abused him but had let him walk among them with impunity, and had even been kind to him, if not always to one another.

Good Country People

A white pickup comes into the Study Area. Three couples from a local church hop out in ranchwear—starched jeans, button-down shirts—and start distributing toiletry kits and sack lunches.

Sir, one of the women says to the PR, would you like lunch?

The PR says he's just had lunch, but thanks very much.

No, thank you, she says. Thank you for your honesty.

The PR isn't used to being thanked for his honesty. This is like being thanked for brushing his teeth. He likes these people. They are doing it just right: they are friendly but not too friendly; they don't seem to be getting off on what they are doing; the lunch isn't shit; the little toiletry kits are actually useful.

Meanwhile, Wanda is sprawled in the burning direct sunlight in front of her tent, looking frazzled and cooked, like someone who, as part of a torture regimen, has been staked out in the desert without food or water. She's been getting high on crack since early this morning, on twenty dollars given to her by a reporter she described as "a Howdy Doody–looking dude."

Hey! she shouts to the PR, can you bring me a lunch? I'm hungry!

The PR approaches the woman who complimented his honesty and, to preserve her good opinion of him, goes to great lengths to explain that the lunch he's requesting is not for him, but for his friend, over there. He is going to such great lengths to explain it all that he soon becomes aware that he is sounding insane. The more she looks askance at him, the harder he tries to convince her that he is just like her, the more the pity in her face drifts toward panic.

Finally, the PR cuts his losses by doing a difficult thing: he shuts up, takes the lunch, and turns away, letting whatever she's thinking about his life and his sanity stand uncorrected.

The Kidnapped Tent

On the last day of the study, the PR went around the Study Area giving away his things. He gave his reading light to Valerie, so she could play dominoes after dark; his leftover water to the Matron; his sleeping bag to the couple known as Big Mama and Sweet Daddy. He had decided to give his tent to Wanda. He had, after all, promised it to her. The thought of Wanda realizing she'd been lied to once again was just too sad.

Hey! someone shouted. I got your tent!

A red-haired man was standing in the entrance to a compound, hands on his hips. Wait a minute. Was this Rusty? He was just as Valerie had described him: a cross between Alfred E. Neumann and Danny Bonaduce.

Rusty stepped over aggressively.

You been staying there in my place all this time, Rusty said in an angry whine. You didn't come to see me, didn't offer to pay me nothing. All my friends that are living over there in my compound pay me a little something, ten bucks a month or something. So it's not fair. You can have your tent back for five dollars.

Behind Rusty, in the compound, was the PR's tent, upside down, being guarded by a leashed pit bull.

The PR was flustered. Rusty was basically extorting him. Rusty had kidnapped his tent? His poor loyal tent lay there like a bug on its back, a humiliated hostage. This was too much. But what was he supposed to do, fight Rusty? Kick the ass of a guy three inches shorter than him who was dying of bone cancer? Or, conversely, get his ass kicked by a guy three inches shorter than him who was dying of bone cancer?

His impulse was to pull out his wallet and just pay the five bucks.

But if he pulled out his wallet and Rusty saw all the money in there, Rusty might increase the ransom, or grab the wallet.

Buying himself a little time, the PR claimed his money was in his wallet, which was back in the van.

Where's the van? Rusty demanded.

Over at the Mission, the PR said.

Max! Rusty barked. Go with him.

A strange apparition appeared: a teenage boy who seemed to be on a drug that raised the body temperature to unbearable levels and made a boy sweat and look hangdog and prematurely elderly. The kid's head sweat was giving him a wildly unlikely forelock of hair.

The PR started off for the Mission. What to do? He could refuse to pay, leave the tent there. But then Rusty would have Wanda's tent. He could call the cops. What? Call the cops on a dying homeless guy over five bucks? That would be pretty low. If you're going to slum incognito, he thought, it's hardly fair to call in the big guns when something doesn't go your way.

Still, shit, was he really going to capitulate to that little asshole Rusty? Rusty had punched Valerie in the face. Jesse hadn't said anything about needing to pay Rusty. And he hadn't even needed Rusty's protection in the first place! He could have just stayed where he was and saved the five—

Ah, fuck it, the PR thought. It's five dollars.

Five dollars to a dying guy, so he, the PR, could bequeath his tent to Wanda, a poor little crackhead who'd been hit by a train.

He felt himself forcibly pulling himself away from a sort of Homeless-Logic Vortex.

He took out his wallet, got out a five, handed it to Max. Max went through the front gate of the compound and dumped the tent over the fence.

The PR dragged the tent wearily across the camp. It was pretty light with nothing inside. Wanda wasn't around. Suzanna, the lost soul from L.A., sat on the mattress stuffed inside Wanda's tent, staring blankly, her Afro front-trending and oddly asymmetrical. He was leaving Wanda this tent, he told her. She, Suzanna, was to get Wanda's old tent, this tent she was now sitting inside. Did she understand? Would she tell Wanda?

Suzanna nodded gravely.

Boy, he hoped Suzanna wouldn't sell the tent for crack. He hoped Suzanna wouldn't mislead Wanda and keep the nicer tent for herself. He hoped Wanda wouldn't sell the tent for crack. He hoped . . .

There was so much to worry about, and yet he knew that a few days from now, he wouldn't be worried about any of it.

We Sat and Talked / About Things on Our Minds

An hour or so after the extortion, the PR saw Rusty sitting at a picnic bench outside the Pov and attempted to eradicate his mild shame at having been bitched around by Rusty by joining Rusty at the table and asking him some intrusive questions.

Yes, he had bone cancer, Rusty said. He wasn't even supposed to be alive right now. He wasn't supposed to have made it past New Year's. But here he was. He'd watched his parents and all four grandparents die of cancer, in the hospital, and wasn't having any of that. He was going to die right here. He'd served in all four branches of the military and had decent VA benefits. It was supposed to be a really painful death, yes, but he was on a superhigh dose of morphine and had sleeping pills he took every night.

He hadn't told anybody about the cancer, not his sister, not his kids, not his ex-wife. He didn't want to be a burden or ask anyone for anything.

Was he scared of dying? the PR asked.

Yeah, yeah, Rusty said. The thing is, you have to make your peace with yourself. You have to ask yourself, have I been a good person?

Rusty has a nice way about him, the PR thought. And of course, even someone who'd punched a woman in the face and so forth could find a way to fit that into a larger narrative in which he was a good person.

He was satisfied, Rusty said. He'd been all over the world, done everything he wanted to do in life. He'd skydived, had three great kids: twin teenage sons and another son in veterinary college on a full scholarship.

Everyone, the PR reflected, made a sort of sense when you gave them time to explain themselves. Rusty made sense to Rusty. Rusty was just a guy. The PR imagined Rusty dying in his tent, nauseous, no one to care for him, waiting for the end. Soon, Valerie's husband, Pablo, would be home from jail, gunning for Rusty, and might beat the shit out of him again, after which Rusty would have to crawl back to his tent and continue dying, until such time as he was shitting and pissing himself in what would probably be, by then, the heat of the coming Fresno summer.

The PR asked about Rusty's famous fight with Pablo.

Rusty warmed to this topic. The way that went down was, Pablo had attacked him with a board. But what Pablo didn't know was that back in the service, Rusty had received special hand-to-hand training. He'd taught martial arts in El Salvador, when he was down there in the '80s, as part of a secret CIA mission. So poor Pablo wore himself out swinging that board, but the board never even touched Rusty. Pretty soon, Pablo got exhausted. Then, luckily for Pablo, the cops showed up. Rusty had said it loud and clear, for everyone to hear: he didn't want to press charges. But sadly for Pablo, stupid Pablo was out on parole. So off to jail he went.

Not long afterward, five paisas attacked Rusty, trying to avenge Pablo. Using the same techniques, he fought them off single-handedly in an epic battle that spanned the tent city, from one end to the other. Finally, the paisas got so frustrated, scared, and exhausted, they just gave up and ran away.

Once, in El Salvador, Rusty said, they'd come into this village. Nobody would give them any information. Everyone was too scared of the rebels. In that village, he'd befriended a seven-year-old girl, real sweet kid.

A few weeks later, when they returned to that village, he brought the kid a bunny.

A bunny, the PR said.

A rabbit, Rusty said. Like for a pet.

But the rebels had already been there. They'd torched the village. The horrible things they did to that little girl, Rusty said. He got hold of all kinds of shit he wasn't supposed to have, weapons and whatnot. But luckily, his gunnery sergeant had talked him down.

They, uh, mutilated her? the PR said.

Skinned her, Rusty said. Everything but her face.

The PR realized he had reached an exquisite level of perfect Study Area immersion: he honestly didn't know if Rusty was lying or not. And he didn't care. It didn't matter. What mattered was the display. It was beautiful to hear Rusty, this dying man, this vanishing soul, say the crazy things he was saying, whether they were true or not.

Soon Rusty would be gone. Soon the camp would be gone. The City of Fresno had initiated a radical and seemingly enlightened plan to place every person in the Study Area in an apartment and assign him or her a case worker who would help that person with whatever he or she needed—get them into rehab, identify unclaimed government benefits to which they were entitled, help them find jobs—and the city had just approved half a million dollars for this program.

It was all just gorgeous smoke: Rusty, the camp, the Study, the PR, the world itself.

So you're just going to die out here in your tent? the PR asked.

Yep, Rusty said. I'm hoping to just wake up dead someday.

In parting, the PR expressed his wish that everything in Rusty's future would go well.

As good as it can go anyway, Rusty said.

KURT VONNEGUT

■

The Nice Little People

FROM *Zoetrope: All-Story*

IT WAS A HOT, DRY, GLARING JULY DAY that made Lowell Swift feel as though every germ and sin in him were being baked out forever. He was riding home on a bus from his job as a linoleum salesman in a department store. The day marked the end of his seventh year of marriage to Madelaine, who had the car, and who, in fact, owned it. He carried red roses in a long, green box under his arm.

The bus was crowded, but no women were standing, so Lowell's conscience was unencumbered. He sat back in his seat and crackled his knuckles absently and thought pleasant things about his wife.

He was a tall, straight man, with a thin, sandy mustache and a longing to be a British colonel. At a distance, it appeared that his longing had been answered in every respect save for a uniform. He seemed distinguished and purposeful. But his eyes were those of a wistful panhandler, lost, baffled, inordinately agreeable. He was intelligent and healthy, but decent to a point that crippled him as a master of his home or an accumulator of wealth.

Madelaine had once characterized him as standing on the edge of the mainstream of life, smiling and saying, "Pardon me," "After you," and "No, thank you."

Madelaine was a real estate saleswoman and made far more money than Lowell did. Sometimes she joked with him about it. He could only smile amiably and say that he had never, at any rate, made any enemies, and that, after all, God had made him, even as he had made Madelaine—presumably with some good end in mind.

Madelaine was a beautiful woman, and Lowell had never loved

anyone else. He would have been lost without her. Some days, as he rode home on the bus, he felt dull and ineffectual, tired, and afraid Madelaine would leave him—and he couldn't blame her for wanting to.

This day, however, wasn't one of them. He felt marvelous. It was, in addition to his wedding anniversary, a day spiced with mystery. The mystery was in no way ominous, as far as Lowell could see, but it was puzzling enough to make him feel as though he were involved in a small adventure. It would give him and Madelaine a few minutes of titillating speculation. While he'd been waiting for the bus, someone had thrown a paper knife to him.

It had come, he thought, from a passing car or from one of the offices in the building across the street. He hadn't seen it until it clattered to the sidewalk by the pointed black toes of his shoes. He'd glanced around quickly without seeing who'd thrown it, then picked it up gingerly and found that it was warm and remarkably light. It was bluish-silver in color, oval in cross section, and very modern in design. It was a single piece of metal, seemingly hollow, sharply pointed at one end and blunt at the other, with only a small, pearl-like stone at its midpoint to mark off the hilt from the blade.

Lowell had instantly identified it as a paper knife because he had often noticed something like it in a cutlery window he passed every day on his way to and from the bus stop downtown. He'd made an effort to locate the knife's owner by holding it over his head and looking from car to car and from office window to office window, but no one had looked back at him as though to claim it. So he had put it in his pocket.

Lowell looked out of the bus window and saw that the bus was going down the quiet, elm-shaded boulevard on which he and Madelaine lived. The mansions on either side, though now divided into expensive apartments,' were still mansions outside, magnificent. Without Madelaine's income, it would have been impossible for them to live in such a place.

The next stop was his, where the colonnaded, white colonial stood. Madelaine would be watching the bus approach, looking down from the third-story apartment that had once been a ballroom. As excited as any high school boy in love, he pulled the signal cord and looked up for her face in the glossy green ivy that grew around the gable. She wasn't there, and he supposed happily that she was mixing anniversary cocktails.

Lowell: said the note on the hall mirror, *Am taking a prospect for the Finletter property to supper. Cross your fingers. —Madelaine.*

Smiling wistfully, Lowell laid his roses on the table, and crossed his fingers.

The apartment was very still, and disorderly. Madelaine had left in a hurry. He picked up the afternoon paper, which was spread over the floor along with a paste pot and scrapbook, and read tatters that Madelaine had left whole, items that had nothing to do with real estate.

There was a quick hiss in his pocket, like the sound of a perfunctory kiss or the opening of a can of vacuum-packed coffee.

Lowell thrust his hand into his pocket and brought forth the paper knife. The little stone at its midpoint had come out of its setting, leaving a round hole.

Lowell laid the knife on the couch cushion beside him and searched his pocket for the missing bauble. When he found it he was disappointed to discover that it wasn't a pearl at all, but a hollow hemisphere of what he supposed to be plastic.

When he returned his attention to the knife, he was swept with a wave of revulsion. A black insect a quarter of an inch long was worming out through the hole. Then came another and another—until there were six, huddled together in a pit in the cushion, a pit made a moment before by Lowell's elbow. The insects' movements were sluggish and clumsy, as though they were shaken and dazed. Now they seemed to fall asleep in their shallow refuge.

Lowell took a magazine from the coffee table, rolled it up, and prepared to smash the nasty little beasts before they could lay their eggs and infest Madelaine's apartment.

It was then he saw that the insects were three men and three women, perfectly proportioned, and clad in glistening black tights.

On the telephone table in the front hall, Madelaine had taped a list of phone numbers: the numbers of her office, Bud Stafford—her boss, her lawyer, her broker, her doctor, her dentist, her hairdresser, the police, the fire department, and the department store at which Lowell worked.

Lowell was running his finger down the list for the tenth time, looking for the number of the proper person to tell about the arrival on Earth of six little people a quarter of an inch high.

He wished Madelaine would come home.

Tentatively, he dialed the number of the police.

"Seventh precin't. Sergeant Cahoon speakin'."

The voice was coarse, and Lowell was appalled by the image of Cahoon that appeared in his mind: gross and clumsy, slab-footed, with room for fifty little people in each yawning chamber of his service revolver.

Lowell returned the telephone to its cradle without saying a word to Cahoon. Cahoon was not the man.

Everything about the world suddenly seemed preposterously huge and brutal to Lowell. He lugged out the massive telephone book and opened it to the "United States Government." *Agriculture Department . . . Justice Department . . . Treasury Department*—everything had the sound of crashing giants. Lowell closed the book helplessly.

He wondered when Madelaine was coming home.

He glanced nervously at the couch and saw that the little people, who had been motionless for half an hour, were beginning to stir, to explore the slick, plum-colored terrain and flora of tufts in the cushion. They were soon brought up short by the walls of a glass bell jar Lowell had taken from Madelaine's antique clock on the mantelpiece and lowered over them.

"Brave, brave little devils," Lowell said to himself, wonderingly. He congratulated himself on his calm, his reasonableness with respect to the little people. He hadn't panicked, hadn't killed them or called for help. He doubted that many people would have had the imagination to admit that the little people really were explorers from another world, and that the seeming knife was really a spaceship.

"Guess you picked the right man to come and see," he murmured to them from a distance, "but darned if I know what to do with you. If word got out about you, it'd be murder." He could imagine the panic and the mobs outside the apartment.

As Lowell approached the little people for another look, crossing the carpet silently, there came a ticking from the bell jar, as one of the men circled inside it again and again, tapping with some sort of tool, seeking an opening. The others were engrossed with a bit of tobacco one had pulled out from under a tuft.

Lowell lifted the jar. "Hello, there," he said gently.

The little people shrieked, making sounds like the high notes of a music box, and scrambled toward the cleft where the cushion met the back of the couch.

"No, no, no, no," said Lowell. "Don't be afraid, little people." He held out a fingertip to stop one of the women. To his horror, a spark snapped from his finger, striking her down in a little heap the size of a morning-glory seed.

The others had tumbled out of sight behind the cushion.

"Dear God, what have I done, what have I done?" Lowell said heartbrokenly.

He ran to get a magnifying glass from Madelaine's desk, and then peered through it at the tiny, still body. "Dear, dear, oh, dear," he whispered.

He was more upset than ever when he saw how beautiful the woman was. She bore a slight resemblance to a girl he had known before he met Madelaine.

Her eyelids trembled and opened. "Thank heaven," he said. She looked up at him with terror..

"Well, now," Lowell said briskly, "that's more like it. I'm your friend. I don't want to hurt you. Lord knows I don't." He smiled and rubbed his hands together. "We'll have a welcome to Earth banquet. What would you like? What do you little people eat, eh? I'll find something."

He hurried to the kitchen, where dirty dishes and silverware cluttered the countertops. He chuckled to himself as he loaded a tray with bottles and jars and cans that now seemed enormous to him, literal mountains of food.

Whistling a festive air, Lowell brought the tray into the living room and set it on the coffee table. The little woman was no longer on the cushion.

"Now, where have you gone, eh?" Lowell said gaily. "I know, I know where to find you when everything's ready. Oh ho! A banquet fit for kings and queens, no less."

Using his fingertip, he made a circle of dabs around the center of a saucer, leaving mounds of peanut butter, mayonnaise, oleomargarine, minced ham, cream cheese, catsup, liver pâté, grape jam, and moistened sugar. Inside this circle he put separate drops of milk, beer, water, and orange juice.

He lifted up the cushion. "Come and get it, or I'll throw it on the ground," he said. "Now, where did you get to? I'll find you, I'll find you." In the corner of the couch where the cushion had been lay a quarter and a dime, a paper match, and a cigar band—a band from the sort of cigars Madelaine's boss smoked.

"There you are," said Lowell. Several tiny pairs of feet projected from the pile of debris.

Lowell picked up the coins, leaving the six little people huddled and trembling. He laid his hand before them, palm up. "Come on, now, climb aboard. I have a surprise for you."

They didn't move, and Lowell was obliged to shoo them into his palm with a pencil point. He lifted them through the air, dumped them on the saucer's rim like so many caraway seeds.

"I give you," he said, "the largest smorgasbord in history." The dabs were all taller than the dinner guests.

After several minutes, the little people got courage enough to begin exploring again. Soon, the air around the saucer was filled with piping cries of delight as delicious bonanza after bonanza was discovered.

Lowell looked happily through the magnifying glass as faces were lifted to him with lip-smacking, ogling gratitude.

"Try the beer. Have you tried the beer?" said Lowell. Now, when he spoke, the little people didn't shriek but listened attentively, trying to understand.

Lowell pointed to the amber drop, and all six dutifully sampled it, trying to look appreciative but failing to hide their distaste.

"Acquired taste," said Lowell. "You'll learn. You'll—"

The sentence died, unfinished. Outside a car had pulled up, and floating through the summer evening was Madelaine's voice.

When he returned from the window, after watching Madelaine kiss her boss, the little people were kneeling and facing Lowell, chanting something that came to him sweet and faint.

"Hey," said Lowell, beaming, "what's this, anyway? It was nothing—nothing at all. Really. Look here, I'm just an ordinary guy. I'm common as dirt here on Earth. Don't get the idea I'm—" He laughed at the absurdity of the notion.

The chant went on, ardent, supplicating, adoring.

"Look," said Lowell, hearing Madelaine coming up the stairs, "you've got to hide until I get squared away in my mind what to do about you."

He looked around quickly and saw the knife, the spaceship. He laid it by the saucer and prodded them with the pencil again. "Come on—back in here for a little while."

They disappeared into the hole, and Lowell pressed the pearly hatch cover back into place just as Madelaine came in.

"Hello," she said cheerfully. She saw the saucer. "Been entertaining?"

"In a small way," said Lowell. "Have you?"

"It looks like you've been having mice in."

"I get lonely, like anybody else," he said.

She reddened. "I'm sorry about the anniversary, Lowell."

"Perfectly all right."

"I didn't remember until on the way home, just a few minutes ago, and then it hit me like a ton of bricks."

"The important thing is," Lowell said pleasantly, "did you close the deal?"

"Yes—yes, I did." She was restless, and had difficulty smiling when she found the roses on the hall table. "How nice."

"I thought so."

"Is that a new knife you have?"

"This? Yes—picked it up on the way home."

"Did we need it?"

"I took a fancy to it. Mind?"

"No—not at all." She looked at it uneasily. "You saw us, didn't you?"

"Who? What?"

"You saw me kissing Bud outside just now."

"Yes. But I don't imagine you're ruined."

"He asked me to marry him, Lowell."

"Oh? And you said—"

"I said I would."

"I had no idea it was that simple."

"I love him, Lowell. I want to marry him. Do you have to drum on your palm with that knife?"

"Sorry. Didn't realize I was."

"Well?" she said meekly, after a long silence.

"I think almost everything that needs to be said has been said."

"Lowell, I'm dreadfully sorry—"

"Sorry for me? Nonsense! Whole new worlds have opened up for me." He walked over to her slowly, put his arm around her. "But it will take some getting used to, Madelaine. Kiss? Farewell kiss, Madelaine?"

"Lowell, please—" She turned her head aside and tried to push him away gently.

He hugged her harder.

"Lowell—no. Let's stop it, Lowell. Lowell, you're hurting me. Please!" She struck him on the chest and twisted away. "I can't stand it!" she cried bitterly.

The spaceship in Lowell's hand hummed and grew hot. It trembled and shot from his hand, under its own power, straight at Madelaine's heart.

Lowell didn't have to look up the number for the police. Madelaine had taped it to the telephone table.

"Seventh precin't. Sergeant Cahoon speakin'."

"Sergeant," said Lowell. "I want to report an accident—a death."

"Homicide?" said Cahoon.

"I don't know what you'd call it. It takes some explaining."

When the police arrived, Lowell told his story calmly, from the finding of the spaceship to the end.

"In a way, it was my fault," he said. "The little people thought I was God."

AMY WALDMAN

■

Freedom

FROM *Boston Review*

RICHARD BENSON CRANED TO SEE the approaching faces, but he couldn't get a bead on them beyond a blur of dark hair. The sun was blasting his eyes, and the waves were tossing the dinghies like a stomach trying to expel a bad meal. By the time the inflatable convoy motored onto land, the men were green from the brief journey, gill-sick, and a few were sunburned, too. Benson congratulated himself for ordering a lifetime supply of SPF 70.

The guards helped the men from the dinghies and removed their plastic cuffs. Their garb surprised Benson: he knew they wouldn't be in orange jumpsuits—those were so 2002—but he hadn't expected the khaki pants, light blue shirts, and loafers, all vintage L.L. Bean, before him. The men looked like professionals, like Benson himself, out for a weekend stroll. Only their discarded wraparound sunglasses, lurking like crabs on the sand, suggested otherwise. Black-out goggles: the camp commandant must have insisted on them for the trip.

The men stood on the rocky beach like chess pieces waiting to be moved. A few shuffled a bit, then braced for the guards to yell. Soon enough one did.

"Go on!" bellowed a burly buzz-cut. "You can do anything you want, goddamnit. Go, go! You're free!"

"We can't yell at them anymore," Benson told him. "They're no longer prisoners. Besides, they still need their orientation." He had it all planned: the tour of the island, the name games, the trust exercises. They had to learn to trust again—they might as well start with each other.

The word "orientation" spread an oily smirk across the guard's face. "Trust me, yelling's the best thing we can do for them," he said. "They haven't shit in six years without someone telling them to and then watching them do it. You expect them to just waltz"—he pronounced it "walls"—"off and decide if they want to grill steaks or go to a movie? Free will's a muscle, dude. And theirs is as weak as your biceps."

As Benson gave thanks this guard wouldn't be staying, two of the men began running back and forth along the beach, screaming, whooping, flapping their arms. They veered toward Benson, canine snarls issuing from their throats. He stepped back in fear and yet felt a small thrill: they grasped his power.

The guards stepped in front of him and cocked their M-16s.

"We want to go home," he heard in accented English. "We want to go home."

"You are home," Benson called out over the hedge of olive-green backs.

CLASSIFIED
TO: THE DEPARTMENT
FROM: RICHARD BENSON
RE: FREEDOM

They've arrived.

The youngest was twenty-one; he had passed almost a third of his life in The Prison. The oldest was sixty-one; he had turned gray there. Once they had been Yemenis, Uighurs, Uzbeks, Algerians, Tunisians; sheepherders, doctors, mullahs, and cooks; educated and illiterates; men and boys; but those distinctions had been so thoroughly ironed out at The Prison that the men themselves no longer remembered.

There were eighty-two of them. All told they had clocked some five hundred years in captivity, waged and survived a half-dozen hunger strikes, sat through hundreds of combatant status review tribunals, endured thousands of hours of isolation. The more these numbers grew, the more the men shrank, and as a result, although Benson was only five-foot-six, he towered over them.

He was thirty-two, unmarried, with five years in the Foreign Service. He spoke some Arabic after a posting in Egypt, and this, along with a capacity for endearing himself to his superiors, was perhaps his chief qualification for his new role. But he was wary at first. He'd never heard of a country called Freedom.

"That's because it's brand new," explained Janice Milkowski. She'd been assigned to brief him at The Department.

She walked him through Freedom's history, which didn't take long. Six years after being declared the "worst of the worst," the most dangerous terrorists on the globe, so evil they had to be imprisoned on an island beyond the reach of American law, the men had been found to be, well, not so bad. They were free to leave The Prison, but they had nowhere to go. Every country on Earth—the ones where they were born or migrated to, the one that imprisoned them—refused to accept them, barring a few that promised to torture them.

The men's plight became a public relations problem so severe it reached even the president's ears. "Find a solution," he told his Cabinet secretaries, that surly edge in his voice. "I don't care what it is. Just find it."

As the story went—every country needs its founding myths—the president's interest inspired unprecedented interdepartmental cooperation. The Committee on the Status of The Cleared worked round the clock. It made no progress; even Albania balked at taking more detainees, despite large pledges of aid. "We need to start a new country—it's the only way," Milkowski said late one night, so tired she could barely keep her eyes open. Years later she would say that Freedom had been a joke.

For a young foreign-service officer, there couldn't be a lowlier post than a country so fresh from the womb. But looked at it from the angle Benson chose, he was a viceroy—master of the antipodes, lord of this human Galapagos. That first glimpse of his men, Freedom both their new status and new nation-state, fostered an almost paternal desire to make a home for them.

The Department had contracted a private firm to scour the globe for a site for Freedom. They found it in the South Pacific. The Solomon Islands, just hit by a tsunami, needed the money, and America needed the real estate. Fatutaka was the easternmost island, and the most remote; for the Solomons, it would be like losing a toenail. It was .625 square miles, which still allowed room for growth. The landscape was rocky—an extinct volcano—but it would do. The tiny island would swallow an outsized problem and, everyone hoped, not choke on it.

The same contractors who created Baghdad's Green Zone and Kabul's behemoth embassy built Freedom. Sparing America's taxpayers no expense, they broke rocks and imported tons of soil, sand and concrete. They planted trees and laid roads, although the only cars would be golf carts. They built a gym and a restaurant, a medical clinic, a community center with a library, a post office, and a mosque. When they finished, eighty-two small homes, 1,222 square feet apiece, awaited their occupants. A suburban subdivision of cul-de-sacs: barring the sea view, it could have been the Inland Empire. Benson's house—also 1,222 square feet; no grand viceregal residence for him, that would be un-American—was set in a different "neighborhood," a gated community really, that had been built for The Department's personnel and the "security managers," as the guards were called. Freedom was a friendly country, but at the outset it was thought prudent to treat it like an enemy one.

From the files, Benson learned that some of the ex-detainees had grown up without electricity, clean water, or toilets. He guessed many of them had never had a room of their own, other than their prison cells. To be given a whole house with the most modern infrastructure—it was like winning the lottery. The men were set for life, which was not just an expression. The condition for a ticket from The Prison to Freedom was that they never try to leave. They would be exiled from their own countries, from every country, until their deaths.

The Department hired an employment placement firm specializing in tough cases to provide exit counselors. They flew to The Prison carrying eighty-two questionnaires, translated, as needed, into Arabic, Urdu, Uighur.

"You may soon be granted your freedom," the first page read.

* * *

The United States of America is a generous country, and will assist you with planning for the future. You can re-launch your career, or perhaps get the fresh start you've dreamed of!

• Please check which of the following areas best describes your previous line of work:

—Security
—Transportation
—Media
—Agriculture
—Law
—Hospitality
—Medical
—Construction
—Other

• Please describe your work history prior to 2001.

• Please list any skills you have.

• Please list five occupations that sound appealing to you. (Examples: nutrition counselor, landscape architect, social worker.)

• Your new home will have the following occupational needs. Do any of them sound appealing? Please let us know!

—post office (LITERACY REQUIRED)
—clothing procurer (familiarity with the costumes of the Muslim world an advantage)
—grocery store manager
—librarian (LITERACY REQUIRED)
—HEALTH CLUB manager
—cook (not short-order, not fine cuisine—level of Olive Garden)
—waiter (see above)
—police officer
—doctor or nurse

The questionnaires came back torn to pieces.

The orientation did not go as planned. At roll call, the men didn't respond to their names, and Abdullah, a gaunt young man with onyx eyes and decent English, came forward to explain. At The Prison they had been given Internment Serial Numbers. They wanted to keep them. He would answer only to Abdullah237.

This minor recalcitrance barely registered with Benson, who was otherwise occupied. The Department had hired a public relations firm to spread the word about Freedom's virtues, and after creating Freedom's slogan — "As good as America" — it arranged for hundreds of international news crews to visit the island. Benson gave 811 interviews. He made sure the ex-detainees, whose privacy he wanted to protect, gave none.

It was some time, then, before he got around to observing his charges, before he understood that the freed man is qualitatively different from the free man. Freedom's residents rarely stirred before noon. They demanded every flavor of ice cream, every kind of bread — or else forgot to eat. A few of them didn't talk at all, except to themselves. The only initiative they displayed was to request plywood and steel mesh for home improvements. Some rarely bathed, developing a stink so profound Benson couldn't stand within six feet of them. He took to coughing — "can't shake this virus," he would say — into an Old Spice-scented handkerchief.

CLASSIFIED
TO: THE DEPARTMENT
FROM: RICHARD BENSON
RE: FREEDOM

Think island mood would benefit from psychiatric counselors or, barring that, medication.

Only the Uighurs were industrious. They set up a furniture workshop, fashioned exquisite joints. Knowing how eager The Department was to promote free markets, Benson proposed exporting the Uighur's products, believing the same type of customer who bought coffee harvested by pygmies or necklaces hand-fashioned by Romanian street children would covet chairs made by ex-detainees. But The Department deemed the security concerns too great — who knew what messages could be embedded in a table leg? Milkowski pronounced the enterprise too reminiscent of prisoners making license plates.

The Uighurs were unfazed, as if accustomed to denial. To Benson's surprise they continued building the same objects again and again, trying each time to improve on the last. As the houses filled up, furniture sets began to appear around the island. Benson, on a stroll, would come across a table for ten; empty armoires; rows of bare bed frames, as in a hospital ward awaiting patients. It gave him the creeps.

The other men, for the most part, spent their time spinning sand through their fingers or bobbing, like corks popped to irrelevance, in the blue lagoons.

Abdullah237 had once been a waiter—in London, which explained his good English—and on Freedom he became one again. A waiter: the job title became literal in the customer-free hours at the Salaam Café. Each morning Abdullah237 would take the chairs down from the tabletops and set each table with napkin, fork, knife, and spoon. He would place a water glass at each spot and fill each glass. Then he would sit and read, or chat with the cook, also an ex-detainee. The only customers were Benson and his security coterie. They quickly worked their way through the menu—the chewy pizza, the over-boiled pasta, the hamburgers that never came cooked the way they asked—as the fans turned desultorily overhead. The hours stretched like lengthening shadows, and at closing time, which crept a little earlier each day, Abdullah237 would empty the water glasses, wipe the silverware down, set the chairs atop the tables, sweep the floor, and pretend to count his tips. Benson asked him one day why no one came. Abdullah237 shrugged. They had been forced to eat so many meals alone at The Prison they'd gotten used to it.

Benson tried to keep Abdullah237 talking. He told himself he was cultivating intelligence—not an informant or informer per se, just someone who would provide information—but the truth was he was eager for friendship. Abdullah237 struck him as bookish, intelligent—the light in those dark eyes, the refinement in those long fingers—but at every conversational foray Abdullah237 clammed up like Benson was an interrogator.

Benson began to obsess over the country's poor morale, even

though he knew The Department didn't care if Freedom was a happy place as long as it looked like one. The Prison's dark lore he had seen as a bodily cavity where he had no business being, but now he decided the past needed a colonoscopy. Using encounter groups, one-on-one "entry" interviews, memoir-writing classes, a "wiki-history" of The Prison, he tried to get the men to disgorge their experiences. Nothing worked. Their memories were locked away, hoarded, and so, to the man trying to pry them loose, golden. He dug into the files from The Prison, and in the cool of his living room, paced off the dimensions of a cage seven feet by eight. It was small.

The post office had mailboxes for each Freedom resident and slots for outgoing mail. All it lacked was honesty: the men's outgoing letters went through the slots and into the waiting hands of the security managers, who sent them off to The Department for translation.

Before coming to Freedom, Benson had been trained in how to escape a minefield, although this challenge seemed peripheral at best to his station. Still, he had played along, learning how to inch forward on his hands and knees and very gently insert a pen into the soil, circumnavigating any spot where it struck something hard. It occurred to him, as he practiced on a small dirt patch, that if you managed to avoid the hard object, you would never know whether it was a mine or a rock. Screening the letters for danger felt the same way, right down to the pen with which he underlined words, unable to tell if they were inert or explosive. When Abdullah237 said he was bored, was that a signal to launch a rescue? When Salman765 wrote about craving his wife's stuffed peppers did that have some more nefarious meaning (or, as Benson thought more likely, a sexual one)? Had Waheed004 embedded—enjambed—a clue to Freedom's location in his poem, which began:

The sun shines 365 days a year
But it is always winter here

They tried every code-cracking technique. The sentences promised knowledge and delivered mystery. Where did literal speech end and metaphor begin? Every phrase seemed to contain the potential for double, or triple, meanings; all language took on the complexity of wartime maneuvers. The letters, The Department ruled, could not be sent.

But Benson believed the men needed communication or the illusion of it. So, late at night he took on the personages of mothers and brothers, wives and children, and wrote replies. Because the residents of Freedom would never return to the external world, it didn't matter what happened there. Benson eliminated all pain and suffering, all loss and cruelty, from the responses. Salman765's mother, whose health her son so fearfully inquired after, made a full recovery. Hamid, Jamal202's little brother, was accepted to university, praise be to God! Praise be to God: Benson wrote that phrase a lot.

The letters were translated, forged in the handwriting of the Freedomites' relatives, and given to the men. All this epistolary ebullience, un-redacted, made them suspicious, but they had no way to challenge the version of events on the page, no channel through which to fact-check. To Benson, this was a benevolent subterfuge, an improvement on anti-depressants: rather than trying to regulate the human reaction to difficult events, he had rewritten the events.

Benson suggested that they play games for prizes like towels and toothpaste. It would pass the time, of which there was so much to be passed. Explaining bingo's rules, he imagined the community center echoing with the joyous chorus of called numbers. But the men announced a boycott of The Liberty Games. This time their spokesman was Yusuf55, a hollow-cheeked Yemeni cleric who addressed Benson only in Arabic. Even without money, the games were gambling, Yusuf55 insisted, and thus un-Islamic. Benson argued, without success, that any game with toilet paper as a prize could not be un-anything.

The boycott worried Benson—the unanimity, the hint that the fundos held sway. A garden of beards had sprouted on the island, and the men had begun to proselytize him. Benson had argued against allowing Christian missionaries to preach to Freedom's eighty-two captive, unsaved souls. He didn't like the discovery that he was the captive soul, in more ways than one. At orientation Benson had taught the men charades, and now they began to play. They mimed sticking feeding tubes down each other's noses and fingers up their anuses, the men roaring with laughter and weeping like babies and rocking like asylum inmates all at the same time. They hurled phantom fecal cocktails in Benson's direction. They limped like they were shackled and reenacted their tribunals, four judges looking stonily past a frantic man collecting papers to prove his innocence. That little tableau always ended with the four judges shaking their heads "no," in unison.

One day Abdullah237 asked if English had a word for a place where everything was perfect, but you still felt miserable. The question unsettled Benson. What if you made it to heaven but felt like hell? Could hellish memories travel with you through the pearly gates, leak into the firmament? These thoughts plagued Benson's nights until something else erupted to disturb them.

The men began blasting music—to Benson it sounded like drowning gypsies—from the edge of his "neighborhood," even after the security managers asked, then ordered, them to turn it down.

"It's a free country," said Abdullah237, betraying Benson's hopes for him. "Our country."

The music came the next night and the next. Every time Benson drifted off, it would start up, as if they were watching him. And each morning before dawn, Yusuf55 began wailing the call to prayer over the megaphone Benson had obtained for bingo.

Four sleepless nights left him a mess. It occurred to him that Freedom had no laws, no regulations, occurred to him as well that order was more easily enforced than happiness. He instituted a sonic buffer zone around all "neighborhoods." Violators would be subject to a mandatory six hours in the community center listening to Verdi at high volume. This was not, strictly speaking, a punishment. Snacks would be provided, and no civilized country could ever call opera torture.

CLASSIFIED

TO: THE DEPARTMENT

FROM: RICHARD BENSON

RE: FREEDOM

Have begun to construct the skeleton of a legal system.

* * *

The men had promised never to try to escape Freedom, but suicide was not forbidden. The first one tied a stack of library books to his back and walked into the sea. The books floated him, then, once soaked, sank him. Suicide by book—Benson had never heard of such a thing. The evidence, sodden and ruined, was brought to him—a real waste of a good encyclopedia set. If he had monitored the library records, he would have smelled something amiss. The man couldn't read English.

CLASSIFIED
TO: THE DEPARTMENT
FROM: RICHARD BENSON
RE: FREEDOM

Have had to create a cemetery. The contractors neglected to. RB

"*Bidoun.*" Without.
"*La makan.*" No place.
"*La bilad.*" No country.
"Halfway—we are halfway to freedom."
"*Al Qae-.*" Cackles, swallows the rest.
"*Al Wayl.*" Misery.
"*Al A'raf.*" The place between Paradise and Hell.
"It's a black site—no, not black . . ."
"Gray. A gray place. *Al Ramadi.*"
"*Khara.* Shit. America shit us out. This island's a turd."
"Forgotten."

This one really rankled Benson. How could they say they were forgotten? The global press corps had visited. Poor people from across the planet were writing The Department to ask if they would get houses with electricity and water if they moved to Freedom. Political dissidents were asking whether they could seek asylum here. Beacon: what was the Arabic word for that? By the time the men approached to say they wanted to rename Freedom, Benson had readied a legal defense. Wiping Freedom from the map by changing its name constituted an attempted escape and thus grounds for return to The Prison.

He had watched their whole discussion via the closed-circuit television system he'd set up after a second suicide attempt, this one by razor. (He'd missed the signs again: the man had a beard down to his breastbone; what did he need with a razor?) Displeased at this "mutinous self-mutilation," as Benson described it, The Department demanded unspecified "preventive measures" against further suicides. And so Benson, inspired by an episode of *Real World Miami* on his satellite television, chose surveillance. On his instruction, cameras were embedded in trees around the island, concealed in bedroom ceilings. He felt a new closeness to the men. Each night he waited for the Freedomites to curl into their fetal positions before turning in himself. Seeing that they had hemmed themselves in — seven feet by eight — with the steel mesh and plywood, he grasped how, after years of confinement, the open space, open sky, open sea, and open time of their new home must have terrified them. The less they did the more he watched: nothing matched a man sitting on his bed and staring into space.

The closed-circuit system, designed for the men's protection, had ancillary benefits for Benson. At night, he discovered, Yusuf55 was running an Islamist indoctrination course with a radical bent, undoing Benson's own daytime instruction in moderate Islam. Benson promptly decreed the Qur'an so valued on Freedom that for the sacred book's own protection, all copies would be locked away, just as America's Constitution was. The confiscation happened before the men could react. In the community center the Qur'ans were displayed behind glass like babies in a nursery and rendered harmless, opened only to the benign suras Benson used for his class. They had lost the ability to turn the page. Many of the men knew the Qur'an by heart, but Benson's reeducation campaign made them mistrust their own memories.

CLASSIFIED
TO: THE DEPARTMENT
FROM: RICHARD BENSON
RE: FREEDOM

Islamist indoctrination underway. Have devised means to monitor. Am inclined to let it play out as test of extremist recruitment in a free society.

The Islamists won.

Knowing that democracy-promotion remained in vogue at The Department and that a success, however small, wouldn't hurt his career, Benson had decided to make Freedom a democracy. Perhaps, he thought, giving the men some control over their destiny might ease their sense of being condemned by fate. But destiny was a devil: the hard-liners came away with a majority on the governing council, whose powers were as yet unspecified.

Still, he had a council to write home about—"the world's smallest Muslim democracy"—even if its decisions were necessarily subject to his veto, which he used, with regret, on the winning entry in the competition to design Freedom's flag. Jamal202 was a talented artist, but a snake, coiled in the shape of a crescent, behind barbed wire? This would not play well on the world stage, or, more pertinent to Benson, the Washington one. Like dogs hemmed in by an invisible electronic fence, the men had to learn their limits.

CLASSIFIED
TO: THE DEPARTMENT
FROM: RICHARD BENSON
RE: FREEDOM

Preventive measures in place, but tensions remain high; I believe they are sexual. The detainees have been without women for seven years. They need wives.

Benson's message provoked consternation at The Department. The U.S. government could not procure concubines for Freedomites. But it also couldn't afford to lose the island's entire population to self-inflicted attrition. The men were not "temporary" detainees, as they had been at The Prison, but permanent residents of Freedom. The government could hardly mandate that they live as bachelors, celibates, forever.

But then someone—Janice Milkowski, always the clever one—pointed out that maybe Benson had omitted a word by accident. Maybe he meant to say, "They need *their* wives." This the government could do, indeed should have done. Family reunification. They could send the wives and children to the island. This decision was dispatched to Benson, who—despite concerns about having his forgery operation exposed—dispatched it to the men.

When Abdullah237 came the next day to say the men didn't want their families joining them, Benson sputtered in shock. They had pined for their wives—their children!—for more than six years. Wasn't he desperate to be with his son, who had been just two when his father went to The Prison? The extremists must have forced him into this.

Abdullah237's black eyes glistened. No one had forced him into anything, he said. He didn't want his son breathing Freedom's air.

CLASSIFIED
TO: THE DEPARTMENT
FROM: RICHARD BENSON
RE: FREEDOM

The men have rejected family reunification. Appears to be a case of manipulative self-deprivation. Please advise.

The Department couldn't force the men's families on them, but it could dangle an alternative. It was decided, after constructing a rationalization connecting connubiality and mental hygiene, to find the unmarried men wives. Benson offered this option to the married ones, too: second wives, or third, for those who already had two at home. This they accepted, seeming to have no problem with strangers breathing Freedom's air.

A new questionnaire was drawn up. This time all eighty were filled out and returned:

> Please list some of the qualities you seek in a wife: (Examples: good cook, intelligent, tall, good dancer, religious.) We aim to please but there are no guarantees that we can match your preferences!

- PREFERRED AGE? (MUST BE 18 OR OVER)
- ANY ABSOLUTE NOs? (FACIAL HAIR, BODY MASS INDEX OVER 25, PREVIOUS MARRIAGES)

The Department hired a marriage-by-mail broker who placed discreet ads in newspapers around the world, seeking women interested in marriage abroad. Inquiries from Moldova, as well as Romania and Albania, flooded in, although some of the women withdrew when they learned more about their husbands. Still, it was surprising how many women would forsake homeland, family, and history for a place they had never seen and could never leave.

The broker sent dossiers on the women to the island. As warned, they did not match the men's preferences: facial hair abounded, for instance, although no one had requested it. Benson, feeling both squeamish and efficient, decided to organize a lottery-cum-bazaar for the men to choose. He spread the photos and bios on the tables in the community center. The men drew numbers, and the highest lots got first dibs. As the trading waged, the center hummed with the happy activity he'd envisioned bingo bringing.

They came wafting from the sky like snowflakes. The men stared up with their mouths open, as if to catch them. The plan had been to bring the women by helicopter from Guadalcanal, but a budding cyclone thwarted their landing. The women were lowered in giant slings, with security managers on the ground easing their final descent. Trina, Katarina, Amina, Ayesha, and more floated into new lives from which floating would be the only way out. Out of respect the closed-circuit system was turned off for the weekend.

The first pregnancy provoked all the excitement—and surprise—that greets rare pandas conceiving in a zoo. Somehow The Department hadn't anticipated that coupling men and women would produce offspring. The babies were cute, cuddly, their names less so. The first child born was named Osama, and he was not the last. There were Jihads, Zawahiris, too, not a Richard among them. Qutb. Who names a child Qutb? Benson's only revenge was to announce that these toddling mockeries would learn at a school named for himself.

And so his farewell to Freedom was held in the auditorium of the Richard Benson Academy. The Department, counting Freedom a success, was promoting him, but for the first time in his life, he wasn't anxious to get ahead. To go from a place where you made the rules, invented the protocols, back to a world where you followed them—it was like being sent to a kind of prison.

He was posted to Cyprus, Sri Lanka, Great Britain. From time to time he dreamt that he stood before a panel of four Freedomites who made outlandish accusations based entirely on circumstantial evidence. His protests of innocence went unheard, as if he were speaking in thought bubbles. He would wake in a sweat, shocked not to find himself shackled.

His friends at The Department copied him on the correspondence from his replacements on Freedom. Death and disease, divorces and remarriages, children's report cards, a teenage pregnancy, fights, seven more suicides, a murder—with time and distance Freedom became as good as America after all. Fourteen years after his departure came a message with an extra note: "RB: This one may interest you."

Over the years Freedom's children had made repeated requests to leave the island and always been refused. But now the security managers had gotten wind that they were building boats and preparing to launch them. The Department was in a state. Could it prevent their escape? The lawyers pronounced the attempted egress legal. The conditions attached to the fathers' freedom did not apply to their children.

"Go, go!" the guard had yelled on Freedom's first day. A generation later, they were going. They weren't interested in shrinking their horizons, as their fathers had. Like teenagers anywhere, they wanted to blow them out.

Benson used every chit he had to get unscheduled leave and permission to join the surveillance flight. Through the plane window he saw clouds hunched in a corner of the sky. Did these kids know anything about navigating? The nearest island was more than thirty-five miles away, its people unlikely to let them land.

The pilot circled the island twice, looking for activity near the water's edge. At last their quarry emerged: six dozen teenagers tugging four huge boats.

The parents followed them, and through his binoculars Benson picked out not just his old friends—Abdullah237, Yusuf55—but the new gray in their hair. The young people and their fathers pushed the boats into the sea, the teenagers clambering aboard, the fathers wading in to their knees. When the boats began to float, the adults returned to shore and waved as if seeing off a cruise. The teenagers rowed hard, looking like minnows against the whale of the sea. Specks.

The plane followed and descended for a clearer view. The teenagers looked up and shook their fists. A few gave the finger. Then they turned away as if they no longer could be bothered.

CONTRIBUTORS' NOTES

Sherman Alexie is the author of numerous books of poetry, three short story collections, and four novels, including *The Absolutely True Diary of a Part-Time Indian*, for which he won the National Book Award. Alexie wrote and directed the film *The Business of Fancydancing*. He also wrote the award-winning screenplay for *Smoke Signals*. He lives in Seattle.

Haider Al-Kabi was born in Basra, Iraq in 1954. He is the author of a book of poems called *Bombardment*.

Rachel Aviv has written about religion, education, medicine, and mental illness for *Harper's*, the *New York Times Magazine*, the *Nation*, and the *Believer*.

Sophie Blackall is a Brooklyn-based Australian illustrator of children's books, magazine articles, animated TV ads, album covers, and the occasional friend's tattoo. She has worked with the singer Mika on several collaborations, including *The Drawing Game*, a back and forth, cross-Atlantic, cross-cultural version of the surrealist game "Exquisite Corpse." A book of her missed connections paintings, *You Probably Won't Read This*, is being published by Workman next year.

Nora Bonner divides her time between the U.S. and Thailand, where she lived and worked for two years at a political polling center in Bangkok. She's currently completing an MFA at Florida State University.

Lilli Carré was born in 1983 in Los Angeles, and currently lives in Chicago. Her animated films have screened in festivals around the world, and her books of comics are *Tales of Woodsman Pete, The Lagoon,* and *Nine Ways to Disappear.* She also contributes to the *Believer.*

Stephen Colbert is the host and executive producer of *The Colbert Report.* A graduate of the famed Second City improv troupe, Colbert co-created and starred in *Strangers with Candy.* He was a regular contributor to *The Daily Show with John Stewart* and the author of *I AM AMERICA (And So Can You!).* Among the many animals named after him are Stephen Jr., a bald eagle at the San Francisco Zoo, and Stelephant Colbert, an elephant seal tagged off the coast of California.

Joey Comeau is the author of, among other things, *Lockpick Pornography* and *One Bloody Thing After Another.* He also creates the comic *A Softer World* with photographer Emily Horne. He lives in Toronto.

Rana Dasgupta was born in Canterbury in 1971. His first book, *Tokyo Canceled,* a cycle of thirteen stories, was published in 2005 by Fourth Estate and Grove Atlantic, and was shortlisted for the 2005 John Llewellyn Rhys Prize. His novel, *Solo,* published in 2009 in the UK and this fall in the United States, won the Commonwealth Writers' Prize. Dasgupta lives in Delhi.

Salam Dawai was born in Baghdad in 1970. He is the author of *That Bitter Rain,* a book of poems published in 1998.

Tamas Dobozy has published two books of stories, *When X Equals Marylou,* and *Last Notes.* He has also published in *Fiction, Agni, One Story, Alaska Quarterly Review,* and other places. He makes money by toiling as a professor in the Department of English and Film Studies at Wilfrid Laurier University, and lives with his wife and four kids in Kitchener, Ontario.

Nathan Englander is the author of two books of fiction. He translated "What, of this Goldfish, Would You Wish?" for his friend Etgar. He is the author of a story collection (*For the Relief of Unbearable Urges*) and a novel (*The Ministry of Special Cases*).

Bryan Furuness's stories and essays have appeared in *Ninth Letter, Southeast Review, Sycamore Review, Barrelhouse, Hobart,* and elsewhere. He teaches at Butler University, where he also serves as the associate editor for *Booth. On Earth as It Is,* an anthology of prayer narratives he's curating, is due out next year.

Elizabeth Gonzalez earned her Master's in Writing at Johns Hopkins University. She is working on a story collection, *The Speed of Sound,* and a narrative exploration of the Atlantic octopus, *Notes to the Mechanic.* She lives in Lancaster, Pennsylvania.

Andrew Sean Greer is the best-selling author of four works of fiction, including *The Confessions of Max Tivoli* and *The Story of a Marriage.* He lives in San Francisco, at work on his next novel. He drives a 2002 Mini Cooper, manual transmission, but not very fast.

Emmanuel Guibert has written many graphic novels for readers young and old, including the *Sardine in Outer Space* series and the sweeping World War II biographical epic *Alan's War.* Guibert lives in Paris with his wife and daughter.

Born in Tel Aviv in 1967, **Etgar Keret** is one of Israel's bestselling authors. His books have been published in twenty-six languages. In 2007, Keret co-directed his first feature film, *Jellyfish,* which won three prizes in the Cannes film festival, including the prestigious Camera d'Or. The film *$9.99,* based on Keret's short stories and co-written by him, was released in the U.S. in June 2009.

Sabah Khattab was born in Tikrit in 1956. Over the years, he has lost many of his literary manuscripts during journeys in exile across Iran, Afghanistan, Pakistan, and New Zealand. He lives now in Australia.

Didier Lefèvre was a French photojournalist who traveled the world extensively, often reporting from remote or harrowing situations. His work appeared in publications all over the world. He died in 2007.

Mara Faye Lethem's recent translations include works by David Trueba, Albert Sánchez Piñol, Juan Marsé, and Pablo de Santis.

Frédéric Lemercier is a graphic designer. He has worked for many cultural institutions in France.

Barry Lopez is the author of thirteen works of fiction and nonfiction, most recently *Resistance*, a collection of interrelated stories. He received the National Book Award for *Arctic Dreams*, and he writes regularly for *Orion*, the *Georgia Review*, and other periodicals. His work has been widely translated.

Wendy Molyneux contributes writings to various publications, including the *L.A. Weekly*, McSweeneys.net, and MonkeyBicycle.net. She lives in Los Angeles and is currently a writer on the first season of the animated show *Bob's Burgers*, premiering on Fox in January.

Born in 1964, **Sadek Mohammed** holds a doctorate degree in English Literature from Pune University in India. He is an Associate Professor of English at Al-Mustansiriyah University and he also serves as an editor of *Gilgamesh*, an Iraqi arts and culture magazine.

Courtney Moreno has worked the past two years as an emergency medical technician in Los Angeles. She received a Bachelor of Science from UC Berkeley, and her varied professional experience includes dance and performance, teaching, editing, and molecular biology research. She is working on an MFA in creative writing from the University of San Francisco.

Soheil Najm, born in Baghdad in 1956, is a poet and translator. He is the author of *Breaking the Phrase, I Am Your Carpenter Oh Light*, and *No Paradise Outside the Window*. He translated into Arabic *The Gospel According to Jesus Christ* by José Saramago. He's an editor at *Gilgamesh*.

Téa Obreht was born in Belgrade in the former Yugoslavia in 1985, and has lived in the United States since the age of twelve. Her writing has been published in *The New Yorker* and the *Atlantic*, and her novel, *The Tiger's Wife*, is forthcoming from Random House. She is a graduate of the MFA program at Cornell University and she lives in Ithaca.

T. Ott, whose first name is Thomas, was born in 1966. He lives and works in Zurich. Since 1987, he has worked as a freelance comics artist and illustrator, known for his scratchboard works. He has published his comics and illustrations in various anthologies and magazines all around the world. Many of his works first appeared in the Zurich-based international comics anthology *Strapazin*.

Patricio Pron, born in Argentina in 1975, is the author of the story collections *Hombres infames* and *El vuelo magnífico de la noche*, and the novels *Formas de morir, Nadadores muertos, Una puta mierda*, and *El comienzo de la primavera*. He holds a doctorate in literature from Georg-August-Universität in Göttingen.

Khadijah Queen joined the Navy in 1998, at the age of twenty-two. She served on the USS *Cole*. Her poems have appeared in many journals, including *Poemmemoirstory, jubilat*, and *new ohio review*. She has been nominated three times for a Pushcart Prize, and she is the author of *Conduit*, a book of poetry. Queen lives in New Jersey and curates a multicultural, multi-genre reading series, "Courting Risk."

By the time you read this book, **Nazlee Radboy** will be twelve. She lives in Seattle. She says: "I see the world as a big canvas. We the people create 'painting' every day as a picture to create the life before us. I see people as highly distinctive and amazing. I see society as confusing and interesting. I feel misunderstood most of the time. I believe everyone should be treated equal, even those whose occupation is much higher and more important. I don't pray to any god. I would like war in the world to end. I like hip-hop, friends, and stuff."

Evan Ratliff is a freelance journalist whose writing appears in *The New Yorker*, the *New York Times Sunday Magazine*, *Outside*, *Men's Jour-*

nal, New York, and many other publications. A contributing editor for *Wired,* he is the co-author of *Safe: The Race to Protect Ourselves in a Newly Dangerous World.*

David Rohde is a two-time Pulitzer Prize–winning reporter for the *New York Times* who has covered war in the Middle East and the Balkans. He is the author of *Endgame: The Betrayal and Fall of Srebrenica, Europe's Worst Massacre Since World War II* and the co-author of the forthcoming book *A Rope and a Prayer: The Story of a Kidnapping.*

George Saunders, a 2006 MacArthur Fellow, is the author of six books (including the short story collections *CivilWarLand in Bad Decline, Pastoralia,* and *In Persuasion Nation*) and, most recently, the essay collection *The Braindead Megaphone.* He teaches at Syracuse University.

David Sedaris is the author of the forthcoming book *Squirrel Seeks Chipmunk: A Modest Bestiary,* and his six previous titles have been published in twenty-five languages. He is a contributing writer to *The New Yorker* and can often be heard on Public Radio International's *This American Life.* He also edited *Children Playing Before a Statue of Hercules,* a collection of his favorite stories by contemporary authors, that benefited 826 NYC. He lives in London and Paris.

Maurice Sendak, one of the most preeminent and prolific children's book authors and illustrators, received the Caldecott Medal in 1964 for *Where the Wild Things Are.* He also received the Hans Christian Andersen International Medal in 1970 for his body of illustration work (he was the first American to be so honored).

Alexis Siegel has worked as a translator for fifteen years. He has adapted more than a dozen graphic novels for various publishers.

Brian Turner earned an MFA from the University of Oregon before serving for seven years in the Army. He was an infantry team leader for a year in Iraq with the 3rd Stryker Brigade Combat Team, 2nd Infantry Division. Prior to that, he was deployed to Bosnia-Herzegovina during 1999 and 2000 with the 10th Mountain Division. His poetry appears widely. He has received a U.S.A. Hillcrest Fellowship in Literature, an NEA Literature Fellowship in Poetry, the Amy Lowell Traveling Fellowship, and a fellowship from the Lannan Foundation. He teaches at Sierra Nevada College, and he is the author of two books of poems: *Here, Bullet* and *Phantom Noise*.

Kurt Vonnegut was born in Indianapolis in 1922. He wrote works blending satire, dark humor, and science fiction, such as *Slaughterhouse-Five, Cat's Cradle*, and *Breakfast of Champions*. He died in New York City in 2007. Vonnegut said, "Here we are, trapped in the amber of the moment. There is no why." He also said, "Be careful what you pretend to be because you are what you pretend to be."

Amy Waldman's first novel will be published by Farrar, Straus and Giroux in 2011. She has worked as a journalist for the *Atlantic* and the *New York Times*, where she was co-chief of the South Asia bureau from 2002 to 2005. She lives in New York.

Abdul-Zahra Zeki was born in Baghdad in 1955, and he is the author of three books of poetry: *The Hand Is Discovering, The Book of Paradise*, and *The Book of the Magician*.

THE *BEST AMERICAN*
NONREQUIRED READING
COMMITTEE

THIS YEAR AGAIN, the student committee in San Francisco was joined from afar by a group of intrepid Michigan high schoolers. Based at 826 Michigan (in Ann Arbor) and under the guidance of Jared Hawkley, this contingent of the *Best American Nonrequired Reading* committee—like the students in San Francisco—dug up articles and stories, read them, argued over their merits and flaws, and helped with the massive task of assembling this book.

 Travon Anderson attended Mission High School in San Francisco, and after this book was finished, he graduated. By the time you read this, he will be a freshman at Miami State University. Travon is an outgoing guy and he likes to read. He prefers people who are good at being themselves and who are uncomfortable being someone else.

Molly Bolten went to Castilleja School in Palo Alto during her *Best American* tenure. She is now a freshman at Princeton University. Her nervous habits include biting her nails and picking up new instruments, such as piano, guitar, drums, and ukulele, in that order. She likes music, ramen, movies, Billy Collins, Nick Shiles, children's cereals, painting, and the West Coast. She hates mayonnaise and wants to see the northern lights. She has recently admitted that Annie's macaroni and cheese is better than Kraft.

Sophie Buchmueller is a junior this fall at Pioneer High School in Ann Arbor, Michigan. She enjoys traveling, and lived in France, Australia, and California before moving to Michigan. She loves playing lacrosse and Ping-Pong, as well as sharing mangoes with her dog, Bluenn. She has absolutely no idea what she wants to be when she grows up.

Julia Butz is beginning her senior year at Greenhills School in Ann Arbor. She is thrilled to have been part of this project for a second year, and she always looks forward to Monday nights at the robot shop. She loves going on "adventures" with her brothers and sister and spending time with her friends. Her favorite places include her host family's house in Delhi, Clearwater Camp for Girls in Wisconsin, and Flying Point Beach in Watermill, New York.

While working on *Best American Nonrequired Reading*, **Gina Cargas** went to Lowell High School in San Francisco. She is now a freshman at Cornell University, and a firm supporter of crumpets, Oscar Wilde, and Bananagrams. She wishes people still wore hats on a daily basis, and she likes most things, except mustard and romantic comedies.

Bianca Catalan was born and raised in San Francisco and, while working on this book, attended San Francisco University High School. She is now a freshman at St. Mary's College. Her father is Salvadoran and her mother is Choctaw and Mexican- American. They had four daughters and one boy, the youngest. Bianca is the middle child. She participates in many writing classes and workshops. She hopes to one day become a children's author.

Adam Colás is probably studying films as a freshman at the School of Visual Arts in New York City
as you read this. He's probably busily cutting away
at some grand new film project at this very moment.
He's probably making history with his cinematic
genius. Or maybe he couldn't afford tuition and is currently taking a
year off. (He attended Huron High School in Ann Arbor while working on this anthology.)

 Gabe Connor is a neo-anarchist, has every seven inch
ever made, rides only a David Byrne–approved bike,
publishes zines, is a strict vegan, and lived once for a
little while in Brooklyn. Gabe pretends to be in a folk-
tronic band called Sasquatch Taxidermy that releases
music exclusively on homemade DIY demo tapes. His most profound struggle is correctly pronouncing the last name of the writer
Michael Chabon. Gabe has counted at least thirteen ways in which
you could do so (alliteration included). He lives in San Francisco,
attends Gateway High School, and is currently a sophomore.

Joseph Cotsirilos lost his innocence at eleven when
he killed a puffer fish (see his biographical note in
Best American Nonrequired Reading 2009). Joseph
graduated from Berkeley High School. If you are
reading this in the fall of 2010, then he is just beginning his freshman year at Bard College. He likes to write comics, so
be careful around him, or he might just write a story about you. You
wouldn't want that, would you?

 Molly Doyle is from San Francisco and she graduated from George Washington High School. She is
now a freshman at UC Santa Cruz. Molly loves the
smell of tape and loves to eat the inside of French
bread. She also likes chocolate. In her spare time,
Molly enjoys reading, sleeping, and making slide shows. She's memorized the entire intro to the *Fellowship of the Ring* movie. Whenever
she tries to draw herself, it comes out distorted.

Carlina Duan is from Ann Arbor, where she is currently a senior at Pioneer High School. She appreciates word play, traveling around the globe, and homemade dinners with family. She currently aspires to be either a journalist or a teacher of literature. She is very grateful for all things in life that have led her to laughter.

 Will "The Hammer" Gray attended Crystal Springs High School while working on this book. He's from San Mateo and he is now a freshman at Carleton College. He enjoys playing frisbee, watching movies, and hanging out with cats. He does not like stories in which cats get hurt. Will's people hail from the old country of Norway, where they were prune-juice-drinking gunslingers.

Michelle Grifka is a junior at Community High School in Ann Arbor. She is currently attempting to make herself into a real renaissance woman by participating in as many things as she can. Someday, she will be a very rich septuple threat—singing, acting, dancing, writing, drawing, baking, and doctoring.

 During her time as a *Best American* editor, **Anita Lee** attended Lowell High School in San Francisco. She is now a freshman at Amherst College. Anita has an extensive collection of ceramic mugs. From a young age, she has been a big fan of Shel Silverstein and his poems about animals. She's a big fan of animals—in general. She looks forward to studying abroad in Costa Rica or India, where she will hopefully find more mugs for her collection.

Dorrian "Lyric" Lewis attended Mission High School while helping edit this collection. She is now a freshman at City College in San Francisco studying music. She is a cancer survivor, but still keeps a smile on her face. She sings and writes poetry, and she performs it at schools and other local events. Dorrian loves to laugh.

Alma Lizardo lives in Oakland. As of this fall, she's a senior at Oakland Unity High School. She has one brother and one sister, and she is younger than both of them. Her goal is to become a professional photographer and then to study animation. She hopes to work for Pixar.

By the time you read this book, **Charlotte "Charley" Locke** will be a freshman at Yale University, studying languages, dead or alive. She's from Berkeley and attended Berkeley High School. She enjoys hypothetical scenarios and swings. She's not discerning about desserts, but is a self-proclaimed apple expert, highly recommending a crisp Pink Lady or the classically tart Granny Smith.

 Stephanie Mannheim lives in New York City, where she attends Barnard College. While helping edit this anthology, she attended Pioneer High School in Ann Arbor. She's also a cartoonist who puts out two minicomics: "Nate the Nonconformist" and "Roxie." She recently had work shown at the Altered Esthetics gallery in Minneapolis. You can usually find Stephanie plucking out songs on some crummy guitar, going gallery hopping with her friends, or eating really awful cafeteria food.

As of this fall, **Liova Marcelos** is a junior at Gallileo High School in San Francisco. Currently, says Marcelos, he's "on that boss status and loving life . . . OMG!" Liova likes nonfiction and non-boring writing. During meetings, he likes to be the guy sipping the twenty-ounce soda in the back, quietly forming severe opinions.

 JuJu Miao is a sophomore this fall at Huron High School in Ann Arbor. She is from Beijing, China. She enjoys reading just about anything that isn't a biography or a textbook, but she especially loves reading Japanese manga comics. She is dying to publish her own series one day. JuJu's favorite pastime is doodling in her massive sketchbook while listening to her iPod and singing loudly to whatever song is playing. She also hopes to travel around the world someday in the near future (preferably not in eighty days).

Tenaya Nasser-Frederick grew up in San Francisco. As of this fall, he is a senior in high school, but he doesn't attend an actual high school—he studies independently. He also studies Hindustani music and is a Swedish-massage enthusiast.

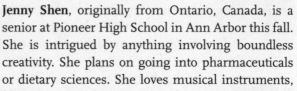

Jenny Shen, originally from Ontario, Canada, is a senior at Pioneer High School in Ann Arbor this fall. She is intrigued by anything involving boundless creativity. She plans on going into pharmaceuticals or dietary sciences. She loves musical instruments, slam poetry, bubble tea, improving, and most of all, writing.

Rachel Shevrin is also from Ann Arbor, and she, too, is a senior this fall at Pioneer High School. She pre- fers pancakes to waffles, but will happily eat both, in case you were wondering. While working on this book, she's made many new friends, which happens

to be one of her favorite pastimes. Miss Shevrin also enjoys the sun- shine, blowing bubbles, and reading.

This fall, **Nick Shiles** is a senior at Sacred Heart Cathedral Prep (for ninjas). He is a native San Fran- ciscan. In his spare time, which there isn't much of, he enjoys writing, reading, riding bikes, and wear- ing Wayfarer sunglasses. His likes include any kind of physical activity, sleeping, listening to music, Molly Bolten, and showering. His dislikes include mayonnaise, avocados, math, any Los Angeles sports team, and people who are grumpy or mean for no reason.

Carlos Reyes Tambis is fifteen and attends the San Francisco School of the Arts. He was born in Atlixco, Puebla, Mexico. He came to the United States when he was three, and at the age of four he was adopted by his wonderful father, John. The one goal he has in his head right now is to graduate from high school and go to college and hopefully be successful in life.

Virginia Urzua graduated from Oakland Unity High School. She was voted most likely to appear in America's Most Wanted. Her birthday is December 28th: Day of the Innocents. Her penmanship changes based on her mood, but usually it's italicized. She hopes to buy a Waterman fountain pen with purple ink to write her notes during the classes she is taking at UC Berkeley right now.

Chloe Villegas is a senior at International High School in San Francisco. She is still writing short fiction and wearing animal-themed hats. Fans of Chloe's hat-wearing ways include Maurice Sendak, Zach Weiner, and Pretty Much Everyone Besides Her Parents. She is grateful for the support.

As of late 2010, **Marley Walker** is a senior at the San Francisco School of the Arts. Marley has been a life-long vegetarian, but gave up eating marshmallows on November 29, 2009 at 9:18 p.m. We will see how long this lasts.

Elise Wander is a junior this fall at Community High School in Ann Arbor, her hometown. She is a writer, an artist, and sometimes a lawyer. In her spare time, she plays the piano and talks to people. She plans to study the liberal arts and the sciences in college, when she gets there. Her favorite thing about summer is the birdsong.

Ellen Watkins is a freshman at UCLA. While working on this book, she attended George Washington High School in San Francisco. She likes fall squash. She looks forward to retirement.

Karen Yu enjoys reading mysterious and adventurous fiction, including romance and manga. She is from San Francisco, and she is a senior this fall at Galileo High School. She decided to join the *Best American Nonrequired Reading* committee because she was curious. "Being in this group," she says, "has allowed me to read and analyze many different types of writing. Reading takes a lot of time, but it is just so enjoyable!"

Paolo Yumol is currently a junior at Lick-Wilmerding High School in San Francisco. He writes very self-consciously, and recently wrote a quick story involving the actor Tony Shalhoub. He fears the story may haunt him for a long time. He plays guitar, but spends more time pining over potential bandmates. He is simultaneously caressed and disturbed by the emergence of David Schwimmer's face wafting up listlessly from the annals of his mind.

Special thanks to assistant (to the) managing editor **Jared Hawkley**, and to editorial assistants **Elizabeth Deatrick**, **Hannah Edber**, **Jenny Howard**, **Ben Shattuck**, **Jessie Roy**, and **Michael Zelenko**. Thanks also to the following organizations and citizens: 826 Valencia, 826 Michigan, Houghton Mifflin Harcourt, Nicole Angeloro, Mark Robinson, Brian McMullen, Eli Horowitz, Andrew Leland, Jessica Schwartz, Jordan Bass, Juliet Litman, Andi Mudd, Mimi Lok, Chris Ying, Michelle Quint, Greg Larson, Laura Howard, Ninive Caligari, Leigh Lehman, Erin Archuleta, Ryan Lewis, Mariama Lockington, Lauren Hall, Cherylle Taylor, Margaret McCarthy, María Inés Montes, Miranda Tsang, Vickie Vértiz, Justin Carder, Marisa Gedney, Emilie Coulson, Andrea Beauchamp, Jeff Parker, Jim Ottaviani, Gina Gagliano, Amy Sumerton, Stephanie Long, Amanda Uhle, Lauren LoPrete,

Chris Reade, Shannon David, Christian and Liz at Vault of Midnight, Ian Huebert, Sadek Mohammed, P.J. Woodside, E.G. Kaufman, Rebecca Worby, Dawg Conceived, Whitney Pow, Jude Roy, Colin Smith, Paul Keelan, Joseph "Sunra" Copeland, Elissa Bassist, Krista Halverson, Jennifer Lavonier, Gina Gagliano, Nicole Aragi, Christopher Benz, Dan Veach and the *Atlanta Review*, Cristina Concepcion, Marshall Hayes, The Hopwood Room at the University of Michigan, Ibarra Brothers, Babylon Burning, and Golden Gate Copy Service.

NOTABLE
NONREQUIRED READING
OF 2009

SALAR ABDOH
  Sad Bully with a Big Badge, *The Drawbridge*
BERNARDO ATXAGA
  The Mystery of the Four Birds, *The Threepenny Review*
RAMONA AUSUBEL
  Saver, *pax americana*
NEGAR AZIMI
  Arabic as a Second Language, *Bidoun*

MAZIAR BAHARI
  118 Days, 12 Hours, 54 Minutes, *Newsweek*
NICHOLSON BAKER
  A New Page, *The New Yorker*
CHRISTIAN BAUMAN
  Our Father, *Identity Theory*
GABRIELLE BELL
  Helpless, *Cecil and Jordan in New York*
AIMEE BENDER
  Faces, *The Paris Review*
WENDELL BERRY
  Andy Catlett: Early Education, *The Threepenny Review*
AMY BLOOM
  Compassion and Mercy, *Granta*

ADIN BOOKBINDER
Meteorology, *One Story*
RYAN BOUDINOT
I Used to Be a Plastic Bottle!, *We Are the Friction*
T. CORAGHESSAN BOYLE
All the Wrecks I've Crawled Out of, *Narrative Magazine*
THOMAS BURKE
The Long-Form Burrito Champion of The World, *Tin House*

AKHIM YUSEFF CABEY
Boy Squared, *The Sun*
CHRISTOPHER COOK
Banned in Britain, *Columbia Journalism Review*
MATTHEW COOPER
Henderson, *Hayden's Ferry Review*
FRANCES YA-CHU COWHIG
Monkeys of the Sea, *Glimmer Train*

STEPHANIE DICKINSON
The Village of Butterflies, *Green Mountains Review*
LUKE DITTRICH
Four Days on the Border, *Esquire*
ANTHONY DOERR
The River Nemunas, *Tin House*

JENNIFER EGAN
Safari, *The New Yorker*
STEPHEN ELLIOTT
Where the Bus Was Going, *MAKE*
THEO ELLSWORTH
Sleeper Car

LUCY FERRISS
Writing the Body, *The Southern Review*
GARY FINCKE
Smart Boy, *Crazyhorse*

TIM JOHNSTON
Dirt Men, *New Letters*

MAIRA KALMAN
May It Please the Court, *New York Times* blog
SUSUMU KATSUMATA
Red Snow
DIMITER KENAROV
The Mask of Sanity, *The Virginia Quarterly Review*
STEPHEN KING
Morality, *Esquire*

PAUL LA FARGE
A Scanner Darkly, *The Believer*
ERIC GABRIEL LEHMAN
Salt, *Raritan*
ANNA LENZER
Fiji Water: Spin the Bottle, *Mother Jones*
JONATHAN LETHEM
Crazy Friend, www.jonathanlethem.com
CARON A. LEVIS
Permission Slip, *Fence*
AIMEE LEVITT
Death Watch, *Riverfront Times*

ADAM MANSBACH
The Audacity of Post-Racism, *The Speech*
EVA MARER
Pleasure, *Open City*
NINA MCCONIGLEY
Curating Your Life, *American Short Fiction*
ELIZABETH MCCRACKEN
The Lost and Found Department of Greater Boston, *Zoetrope: All-Story*
VESTAL MCINTYRE
Late in Life, *Open City*

EMILY QUINLAN
  Bloody Shadow, *Green Mountains Review*

SCOTT RAAB
  John Demjanjuk: The Last Nazi, *Esquire*
PAUL RAWLINS
  Dreamsicle, *Epoch*
SHANN RAY
  How We Fall, *Montana Quarterly*
EVAN REIIILL
  Landon Sheinblatt, *American Short Fiction*
PAUL REYES
  Opportunity Knocks, *The Virginia Quarterly Review*

GEORGE SAUNDERS
  Al Roosten, *The New Yorker*
INGRID SATELMAJER
  How to Be a Disciple, *Cutbank*
SHEILA SCHWARTZ
  Finding Peace, *One Story*
SETH
  George Sprott
GARY SHTEYNGART
  Montana's Luxury Winter Lodge, *Travel + Leisure*
TRICIA SPRINGSTUBB
  In the Dark, *The Iowa Review*
SAŠA STANIŠIĆ
  My Yellow Tastes Sweet, *The Drawbridge*
NEIL SWIDEY
  Trapped, *Boston Globe*

ED TAYLOR
  Grendel, *Southwest Review*
JUSTIN TAYLOR
  In My Heart I Am Already Gone, *Canteen*

ABOUT 826 NATIONAL

Proceeds from this book benefit youth literacy.

A LARGE PERCENTAGE of the cover price of this book goes to 826 National, a network of tutoring, writing, and publishing centers for youth in eight cities around the country.

Since the birth of 826 National in 2002, our goal has been to assist students ages six through eighteen with their writing skills while helping teachers get their classes passionate about writing. We do this with a vast team of volunteers who donate their time so we can give as much one-on-one attention as possible to the students whose writing needs it. Our mission is based on the understanding that great leaps in learning can happen with one-on-one attention, and that strong writing skills are fundamental to future success.

Through volunteer support, each of the eight 826 chapters—in San Francisco, New York, Los Angeles, Ann Arbor, Chicago, Seattle, Boston, and Washington, DC—provides after-school tutoring, class field trips, writing workshops, and in-school programs, all free of charge, for students, classes, and schools. 826 centers are especially committed to supporting teachers, offering services and resources for English language learners, and publishing student work. Each of the 826 chapters works to produce professional-quality publications written entirely by young people, to forge relationships with teachers in order to create innovative workshops and lesson plans, to inspire students to write and appreciate the written word, and to rally thousands of enthusiastic volunteers to make it all happen. By offering all of our programming for free, we aim to serve families who cannot afford to pay for the level of personalized instruction their children receive through 826 chapters.

The demand for 826 National's services is tremendous. Last year we worked with more than 4,200 volunteers and over 22,000 students across the nation, hosting 459 field trips, completing 223 major in-school projects, offering 346 evening and weekend workshops, welcoming over 200 students per day for after-school tutoring, and producing over 800 student publications. At many of our centers, our field trips are fully booked almost a year in advance, teacher requests for in-school tutor support continue to rise, and the majority of our evening and weekend workshops have waitlists.

826 National volunteers are local community residents, professional writers, teachers, artists, college students, parents, bankers, lawyers, and retirees from a wide range of professions. These passionate individuals can be found at all of our centers after school, sitting side-by-side with our students, providing one-on-one attention. They can be found running our field trips, or helping an entire classroom of local students learn how to write a story, or assisting student writers during one of our Young Authors' Book Projects.

All day and in a variety of ways, our volunteers are actively connecting with youth from the communities we serve.

To learn more or get involved, please visit:

826 National: www.826national.org
826 in San Francisco: www.826valencia.org
826 in New York: www.826nyc.org
826 in Los Angeles: www.826la.org
826 in Chicago: www.826chi.org
826 in Ann Arbor: www.826michigan.org
826 in Seattle: www.826seattle.org
826 in Boston: www.826boston.org
826 in Washington, DC: www.826dc.org

826 VALENCIA

Named for its location in the heart of San Francisco's Mission District, 826 Valencia opened on April 8, 2002, and consists of a writing lab, a street-front, student-friendly retail pirate store that partially funds its programs, and satellite classrooms in two local middle schools. 826 Valencia has developed programs that reach students at every possible opportunity—in school, after school, in the evenings, or on the weekends. Since its doors opened, over fifteen hundred volunteers—including published authors, magazine founders, SAT course instructors, documentary filmmakers, and other professionals—have donated their time to work with thousands of students. These volunteers allow the center to offer all of its services for free.

826NYC

826NYC's writing center opened its doors in September 2004. Since then its programs have offered over one thousand students opportunities to improve their writing and to work side by side with hundreds of community volunteers. 826NYC has also built a satellite tutoring center, created in partnership with the Brooklyn Public Library, which has introduced library programs to an entirely new community of students. The center publishes a handful of books of student writing each year.

826LA

826LA benefits greatly from the wealth of cultural and artistic resources in the Los Angeles area. The center regularly presents a free workshop at the Armand Hammer Museum in which esteemed artists, writers, and performers teach their craft. 826LA has collaborated with the J. Paul Getty Museum to create Community Photoworks, a months-long program that taught seventh-graders the basics of photographic composition and analysis, sent them into Los Angeles with cameras, and then helped them polish artist statements. Since opening, 826LA has provided thousands of hours of free one-on-one writing instruction, held summer camps for English language learners, given students sportswriting training in the Lakers' press room, and published love poems written from the perspectives of leopards.

826 CHICAGO

826 Chicago opened its writing lab and after-school tutoring center in the West Town community of Chicago, in the Wicker Park neighborhood. The setting is both culturally lively and teeming with schools: within one mile, there are fifteen public schools serving more than sixteen thousand students. The center opened in October 2005 and now has over five hundred volunteers. Its programs, like at all the 826 chapters, are designed to be both challenging and enjoyable. Ultimately, the goal is to strengthen each student's power to express ideas effectively, creatively, confidently, and in his or her individual voice.

826MICHIGAN

826michigan opened its doors on June 1, 2005, on South State Street in Ann Arbor. In October of 2007 the operation moved downtown, to a new and improved location on Liberty Street. This move enabled the opening of Liberty Street Robot Supply & Repair in May 2008. The shop carries everything the robot owner might need, from positronic brains to grasping appendages to solar cells. 826michigan is the only 826 not named after a city because it serves students all over southeastern Michigan, hosting in-school residencies in Ypsilanti schools and providing workshops for students in Detroit, and Lincoln and Willow Run school districts. The center also has a packed workshop schedule on site every semester, with offerings on making pop-up books, writing sonnets, creating screenplays, producing infomercials, and more.

826 SEATTLE

826 Seattle began offering after-school tutoring in October 2005, followed shortly by evening and weekend writing workshops and, in December 2005, the first field trip to 826 Seattle by a public school class (Ms. Dunker's fifth graders from Greenwood Elementary). The center is in Greenwood, one of the most diverse neighborhoods in the city, and many space travelers stop by the Greenwood Space Travel Supply Company at 826 Seattle on their way back from the Space Needle. Revenue from the store, as from all 826 storefronts—along with the generous outpouring from community members—helps to support the writing programs.

826 BOSTON

826 Boston kicked off its programming in the spring of 2007 by inviting authors Junot Díaz, Steve Almond, Holly Black, and Kelly Link to lead writing workshops at the English High School. The visiting writers challenged students to modernize fairy tales, invent their ideal school, and tell their own stories. Afterward, a handful of dedicated volunteers followed up with weekly visits to help students develop their writing craft. These days, the center has thrown open its doors in Roxbury's Egleston Square—a culturally diverse community south of downtown that stretches into Jamaica Plain, Roxbury, and Dorchester. 826 Boston neighbors more than twenty Boston schools, a dance studio, and the Boston Neighborhood Network (a public-access television station).

826DC

By the time you read this book, 826 National's newest chapter, 826DC, will have opened its doors in the city's Columbia Heights neighborhood. Like all the 826s, 826DC will provide after-school tutoring, field trips, after-school workshops, in-school tutoring,

help for English language learners, and assistance with the publication of student work. It'll also be offering free admission to the Museum of Unnatural History, the center's unique storefront. Already hard at work, 826DC volunteers have been tutoring throughout this past year in the neighborhood's many local schools. They recently helped the students of two nearby high schools publish *Get Used to the Seats: A Survival Guide for Freshmen*, a book of advice for incoming high schoolers.